Shaping Tomorrow

Every major technological regime in human history has reorganised not only how societies produce but how they think, govern, and define what it means to be human. Artificial intelligence is no exception. What sets it apart is the speed, scale, and intimacy with which it is penetrating the epistemic and institutional fabric of contemporary life.

Shaping Tomorrow: *The Human Journey with AI* draws on voices from four continents to confront this transformation at its roots. The volume's intellectual foundation is a sustained editorial argument that situates AI within the longue durée of techno-scientific change, theorising the present moment as the emergence of a new computational civilisation. From this foundation, contributors examine in depth how AI is reshaping education and pedagogy, where questions of critical knowing, personalisation, and the ethics of keeping humans in the loop are explored with particular rigour. Parallel chapters investigate AI's growing role in healthcare, patient welfare, and assistive technologies, while further contributions address algorithmic bias in consumer markets, data privacy governance, and the structural forces driving algorithmic injustice. An interview with philosopher Professor Nick Bostrom adds a distinctive forward-looking perspective on superintelligence and existential risk.

What distinguishes this volume is its refusal to settle for either techno-optimism or deterministic alarm. The editors and contributors instead equip readers with the conceptual precision and analytical frameworks needed to engage with AI as a contested space where political economy, technological possibility, and ethical obligation converge. For scholars, postgraduate students, and professionals confronting a world increasingly governed by algorithmic mediation, this book does not merely describe the landscape. It sharpens the capacity to act within it.

Shaping Tomorrow
The Human Journey with AI

Edited by
Vishal Rana, Govand Khalid Azeez,
Ray Parker and Alan Nankervis

CRC Press
Taylor & Francis Group
Boca Raton London New York

CRC Press is an imprint of the
Taylor & Francis Group, an **informa** business

Designed cover image: Shutterstock

First edition published 2027
by CRC Press
2385 NW Executive Center Drive, Suite 320, Boca Raton FL 33431

and by CRC Press
4 Park Square, Milton Park, Abingdon, Oxon, OX14 4RN

CRC Press is an imprint of Taylor & Francis Group, LLC

ISBN: 978-1-041-04033-0 (hbk)
ISBN: 978-1-041-04032-3 (pbk)
ISBN: 978-1-003-62651-0 (ebk)

DOI: 10.1201/9781003626510

Typeset in Palatino
by KnowledgeWorks Global Ltd.

Contents

About the Editors

Vishal Rana is a management academic. He holds a PhD from Griffith University, Australia. His research examines the intersections of generative AI, leadership, workforce capability, and educational transformation, with a sustained focus on ethical AI governance and competency-based assessment design. He has led and contributed to funded research projects across Australia and the Middle East, working with universities, policymakers, and industry partners to develop governance frameworks and pedagogical systems that respond to the demands of an AI-mediated institutional landscape.

Govand Khalid Azeez is a Lecturer in the discipline of Politics and International Relations at Macquarie University, Sydney. He specialises in the history and philosophy of technology, and the political economy of artificial intelligence.

Ray Parker works at the edge of technology, systems thinking, and emerging AI architecture. An independent systems theorist and strategist, he explores how decentralised infrastructure, machine emotional intelligence, and sovereign AI capability could reshape how societies design and govern technology. With an MBA and Graduate Diploma in Management, Ray has delivered complex projects across telecommunications, engineering, construction, and infrastructure. He is developing the KlusterAI architecture and co-founding MakerPlace.ai to build decentralised compute ecosystems and practical frameworks for human-AI collaboration.

Alan Nankervis is an adjunct professor of HRM at Curtin University in Perth, Australia. He has more than 30 years of teaching and research experience across Australia, Canada, Southeast Asia, and China. He has more than 100 co-authored publications. His current research focus is on the future of work, encompassing technology, intergenerational workforces, and other demographic trends.

Contributors

Nicole Arcuri-Sanders, PhD, ACS, LPC-S, LCMHC-S, BC-TMH, NCC, SAC, is currently an Associate Professor of Counselling & Counsellor Education Program Coordinator at Coastal Carolina University. She has conducted research, published, presented, advocates as well as completed curriculum work and program development concerning counsellor education and supervision best practices, to include a specific focus on human wellness. Dr Arcuri-Sanders is committed to evolving with the changing environments in which she serves. She has served her communities as a licensed clinician and supervisor, an approved clinical supervisor, board certified-telemental health provider, and nationally certified counsellor.

Govand Khalid Azeez was a Visiting Fellow in the Department of History at Harvard University, Cambridge. He was subsequently nominated for the Junior Fellowship in the Society of Fellows at Harvard University by his doctoral thesis examiner A.J. Meyer Emeritus Professor of Middle East History Roger Owen. Dr. Azeez was also a visiting fellow in the Department of Middle Eastern, South Asian and African Studies (MESAS) at Columbia University, New York. Dr. Azeez has published extensively in journals like Research and Social Epistemology: A Journal of Knowledge, Culture and Policy, Middle East Critique, the Journal of Intercultural Studies, Journal of Latin American and Caribbean Ethnic Studies, Critique and Continuum: Journal of Media & Cultural Studies, amongst others. Dr. Azeez's current research interests include a Marxist examination of how the local and global symbiotic relationship between capitalism and the state is manufacturing novel instruments of production and systems, technologies and techniques of exploitation, expropriation and commodification, and how the asymmetrical accumulation of capital and power shapes socio-technological relations and ecological crises.

Nick Bostrom is a Swedish-born philosopher and one of the most-cited philosophers in the world. He was a Professor at Oxford University and founding Director of the Future of Humanity Institute until 2024 and is now founder and principal researcher at the Macrostrategy Research Initiative. His book Superintelligence: Paths, Dangers, Strategies (2014), became a New York Times bestseller and sparked a global conversation about AI. His most recent book, Deep Utopia: Life and Meaning in a Solved World (2024), won the Gold Medal at the Living Now Book Awards. His work has pioneered many foundational concepts in contemporary thought about humanity's future, including existential risk, the simulation argument, and the vulnerable world hypothesis. He has been named to Foreign Policy's Top 100 Global

Thinkers list twice and was the youngest person in the top 15 of Prospect's World Thinkers list. His writings have been translated into more than 30 languages and have garnered over 31,000 academic citations.

Jonathan Boymal is an Associate Professor of Economics in the School of Economics, Finance and Marketing at RMIT University's College of Business and Law. He has had 25 years of higher education leadership experience at the undergraduate and postgraduate levels across Melbourne, Hong Kong, Singapore, and Vietnam, in roles including: Associate Deputy Vice-Chancellor, Learning, Teaching and Quality; and Academic Director, Quality and Learning and Teaching Futures. Jonathan holds a PhD in Economics and a Bachelor of Economics (Honours) from Monash University.

Michael D'Rosario is an economist and interdisciplinary research leader specialising in applied econometrics, public policy, artificial intelligence, housing economics, and social impact evaluation. He serves as Director of Research at Per Capita Australia and as a Senior Researcher with the Queensland Centre for Domestic and Family Violence Research, and at Adelaide University. His work focuses on inequality, technological change, community wealth building, and the economic design of social systems, with a particular focus on the moderation of risks associated with artificial intelligence applications. He has led major cost-benefit analyses, social return on investment evaluations, and quantitative policy studies for government and not-for-profit sectors, publishing across economics and data science domains. Dr D'Rosario also lectures in managerial economics, business analytics, healthcare systems, and artificial intelligence, integrating formal economic theory with applied modelling and policy evaluation. His scholarship is grounded in distributive justice, institutional design, and evidence-based reform.

Matthew Gilbert (MBA, *Woodbury University*) is a lecturer in marketing at Coastal Carolina University, where he teaches courses in advertising, consumer behaviour, personal selling, and principles of marketing. His academic research focuses on artificial intelligence, marketing technology, social media marketing, and sports marketing. A charismatic communicator, he has facilitated professional development workshops and delivered three TEDx Talks. He is a prolific writer who has published articles, book chapters, short stories, and textbooks. As a consultant, the crafts marketing content, creates business curricula, and composes professional communications.

Lynn Gribble from UNSW, Sydney, is an Associate Professor and an internationally, nationally, and UNSW-awarded Education Focused academic. Using her keen interest in transformative learning through engagement, belonging, and personalisation of each student's learning experience, over the past three years, she has extensively considered how to develop authentic assessment and has worked on university-wide feedback projects to enhance the student experience. In developing the master's course, Responsible Business Professionalism, Lynn looked to bring her corporate experience to university learning, focusing on ethics and sustainability as the future differentiator for her students. Today, that course has evolved further to focus on the ethical use of AI in the workplace. Known for her continual innovation, Lynn uses technology to connect with her students and personalise their experience. Her work on teaching innovation dissemination through 'The 4Cs (Classroom, Corridor, Campus and Community) Strategy' has seen her practices adopted and adapted both locally and globally through her approaches to Scholarship of Teaching and Learning (SoTL).

Bradley Guelfi is a Healthcare ICT Program Manager with over 30 years of experience across clinical engineering and enterprise architecture. He leads machine learning, complex algorithm, and AI initiatives grounded in a human health, safety, and welfare focus, embedding ethical failsafe frameworks that prioritise patient outcomes, clinician support, and responsible governance. Beginning his career as an Automotive Mechanic, Bradley developed a practical systems mindset, later strengthened through engineering studies, ICT specialisation, and an MBA. This blend of technical depth and corporate strategy underpins his strategic planning and executive oversight of hospital design, build, and commissioning programs. His vision is to enable current, emerging, and future technologies through flexible, scalable ICT ecosystems aligned to organisational capability and long-term strategic roadmaps within a global healthcare context. He partners with technology leaders such as Cisco and Microsoft to deliver secure enterprise environments hosting corporate and clinical platforms, including Philips patient monitoring, Stryker surgical robotics, intelligent nurse call systems, and thousands of interoperable medical devices. Bradley's work translates technical complexity into safe, resilient hospital environments that protect human well-being.

Timothy (Shoon Chan) Hor is a scholar and practitioner with over 30 years of experience in entrepreneurship and innovation. Completing a PhD at the age of 61, Dr. Hor's dissertation (Hor, 2024) was nominated for the Outstanding Doctoral Dissertation Award 2024, and his research has earned him the prestigious SAGE HDR Publication Award for one of his academic papers (Hor et al., 2021). Dr Hor has made significant contributions to the academic and professional fields, particularly at the intersection of entrepreneurship, design science, and emerging technologies such as artificial intelligence (AI). Currently teaching Entrepreneurship at the University of Newcastle (Australia), Dr Hor integrates real-world insights from years of leading entrepreneurial ventures into academic research and pedagogy. Dr Hor is the creator of the RaiiSE Framework, a design-based methodology for navigating challenges in start-up fundraising. He is also the co-creator of NuYou, a human-centric, AI-first pedagogical framework designed to revolutionise entrepreneurship education. These frameworks are central to his design science approach to translate academic research into pragmatic contributions, including his upcoming book Startup Fundraising Decoded – Design Principles and Tools for Entrepreneurs, to be published by Palgrave Macmillan in late 2025. Having played a key role in scaling several disruptive digital businesses, including a Southeast Asian property portal acquired by realestate.com.au, Dr Hor brings unique industry insights to his research, which focuses on ethical entrepreneurship, the role of theology in business practices, and AI's impact on human flourishing. As a passionate educator and collaborator, Dr Hor is committed to fostering innovation that aligns with justice, sustainability, and human dignity.

Vishnu Prateek Kakarapathi is a researcher at Arizona State University, specialising in wearable computing and AI-driven healthcare. His work focuses on wrist-worn devices for activity recognition and medication adherence, applying deep learning and sensor fusion methods to real-world health challenges. His research aligns with personalised and preventive medicine, emphasising user-centric design, privacy, and equitable access. He aims to bridge technical innovation with social impact, particularly in underserved communities, by designing context-aware, accessible, and responsive interventions. His broader interests include multimodal sensing and the responsible integration of AI in digital health systems.

Kathleen Kennedy is an educator and researcher focused on the relationships between humans and computing systems and the effect of AI technology on overall society, service businesses, and teaching and learning. Her business research seeks to understand the role and effect of AI in human-services organisation relationships. She is a University of Arizona C211UES Distinguished Scholar focused on AI and Learning and has spearheaded pedagogical innovation in AI adaptive learning, experiential learning, and community-engaged instruction. Previously, Dr Kennedy was a Marketing faculty member at The University of Akron and Research Director of the Suarez Applied Marketing Research Laboratories. Dr Kennedy also has over 25 years of industry experience as a senior marketing and e-commerce executive in retailing, financial services, and consulting. She also co-founded four successful marketing services businesses, including Mindnav LLC, a marketing research company developing consumer neuroscience research and customer experience applications. Dr Kennedy holds a Doctor of Business Administration (DBA) in Management Sciences and Marketing Division, Alliance Manchester Business School, University of Manchester (UK), and a Master of Business Administration (MBA) from the University of Miami (FL). She is currently completing a PhD in Higher Education Policy (ABD) at the University of Arizona.

Mary Lang is a civil society researcher and former educator and researcher at Stanford University, with more than twenty years of pioneering leadership at the intersection of technology, data and education. As the inaugural Chief Education Justice Officer at the Centre for Leadership Equity and Research (CLEAR), she advocates for community voice and innovates pedagogy worthy of human and technological potential. Her work on equity-centred frameworks and multivariate voice infrastructures highlights how participatory policy-making can become a central force in collective intelligence for societal benefit.

Todd Madigan is an assistant professor of sociology at Coastal Carolina University and a faculty fellow at Yale's Centre for Cultural Sociology. His scholarship explores the ways in which social narratives can alternately shape and shatter collective identity. Most recently, his work has focused on the current popular struggle against authoritarianism in the American context. In conjunction with this research, he founded and leads Coastal Democracy, a grassroots organisation dedicated to nonviolent direct action in support of democracy. He holds a PhD in sociology from Yale University.

Troy McDaniel is an Assistant Professor in the School of Manufacturing Systems and Networks at Arizona State University and Director of the Centre for Cognitive Ubiquitous Computing. His research spans haptics, wearable robotics, smart systems, and human-computer interaction. He focuses on AI-driven assistive technologies for individuals with sensory, cognitive, or physical impairments. His work emphasises inclusive design and multimodal systems that enhance accessibility, rehabilitation, and healthcare outcomes. Dr. McDaniel's research aligns with this chapter's themes, especially integrating AI with wearables to support health autonomy. He explores emerging technologies in the context of equity, privacy, and human-centred smart living.

George Newman is an Australian technology entrepreneur and commercial executive with expertise in mobile software, enterprise sales, and applied artificial intelligence. He currently serves as an Enterprise Executive at Civic Data, advising enterprise clients across Australia. George co-founded General Adaptive, a software company that achieved sustained global scale, including multiple number-one rankings on the Google Play Store and Apple App Store. Its products have generated more than 180 million downloads, reflecting significant capability in platform optimisation and large-scale digital distribution. His professional background also includes senior leadership roles in recruitment and marketing, with a focus on sales systems, growth strategy, and performance-driven campaigns. George holds a Master of Business Administration from the University of Adelaide and has completed executive education at the University of Oxford in AI-enabled business strategy. His work engages questions of digital scale, commercial strategy, and algorithmic applications in contemporary enterprise contexts.

Ray Parker operates as an independent systems theorist and AI ecosystem strategist working at the intersection of decentralised infrastructure, emotional intelligence architectures, and sovereign AI development within Australia. His work explores how technical systems, organisational design, and human cognition can be integrated into trust-based, community-centred frameworks that enable responsible AI adoption and long-term resilience. With an MBA and a Graduate Diploma in Management, Ray brings over a decade of experience in strategic management, operations, and complex project delivery across telecommunications, construction, engineering, and infrastructure sectors. He has led initiatives for organisations including FOXTEL, Telstra, and SA Power Networks, specialising in quality assurance, safety systems, ISO compliance, tender strategy, and project start-ups. Ray's cross-disciplinary approach combines business strategy, systems engineering, and narrative design to examine how human and artificial intelligences can co-evolve productively. He is currently involved in the development of the KlusterAI architectural model and co-founder of the MakerPlace.ai platform, designed to support sovereign AI capability, decentralised compute ecosystems, and practical augmentation strategies that strengthen individuals, organisations, and regional economies.

Vishal Rana is an Assistant Professor of Management and an AI innovation scholar working at the intersection of artificial intelligence, human resource management, and educational transformation. With a PhD in Human Resource Management and Organisational Behaviour from Griffith University, Australia, his work focuses on how generative AI reshapes leadership, assessment, workforce capability, and the future of learning. He has led and contributed to funded research projects across Australia and the Middle East, with a strong focus on ethical AI governance and competency-based education. Passionate about responsible technology adoption, he works closely with universities, policymakers, and industry leaders to design future-ready systems that balance innovation, integrity, and human flourishing.

Sara Ratner is an education leader and researcher with more than 20 years' experience across pedagogy, policy, and technology. Her career spans classroom teaching, school leadership, EdTech executive roles, and academic research, giving both breadth and depth in connecting research and practice. At the University of Oxford, Sara sits on the steering committee shaping institutional policy and digital transformation with AI, and she founded the AI in Education Interdisciplinary Research Hub (AIEOU) to convene global collaborations. Her work is recognised for building communities of practice that translate rigorous research into human-centred, evidence-based approaches to AI in education.

Nici Sweaney is the CEO and Lead AI Strategist at *AI Her Way*, where she champions inclusive AI development and deployment across global contexts. With over two decades of experience in data science and research, Dr Sweaney has worked with organisations ranging from Indigenous communities to Fortune 500 companies, developing frameworks for ethical AI implementation. Her work focuses on the intersection of gender equity, algorithmic justice, and inclusive innovation. She holds a PhD in Science from the Australian National University and is a recognised thought leader in feminist approaches to technology governance.

Patrick van Esch (*Southern Cross University*) is an Associate Professor of Marketing at Coastal Carolina University. His areas of research include artificial intelligence, consumer psychology, and political ideology. Patrick has published in the *Journal of Business Ethics, European Journal of Marketing, Annals of Tourism Research, International Journal of Research in Marketing, Journal of Business Research, Journal of Advertising, Journal of Advertising Research,* and *Business Horizons.* He is the author of two books and multiple book chapters.

Janis Wardrop from UNSW, Sydney, is an academic leader and educational champion of innovation. She is also a recipient of the Vice Chancellor's Award for Teaching Excellence and a leading educator in the School of Management and Governance. Specialising in developing students' learning capabilities to meet the challenges of the twenty-first century workplace, through innovative curriculum and course design, her passion is to support others in their development. Her work on transforming student experience in large core courses is widely noted as is her development of other academics as a 'guide on the side'. Janis is the former Director of Education at the UNSW Centre for Social Impact, and Director of Education and Associate Head of School, School of Management & Governance, at UNSW.

References

Hor, S. C. T. (2024). *How to acquire financial resources beyond seed funding in digital entrepreneurship: A study informed by design science* [Doctoral dissertation, Queensland University of Technology]. QUT ePrints. https://eprints.qut.edu.au/248872/

Hor, S. C. T., Chang, A., Torres de Oliveira, R., & Davidsson, P. (2021). From the theories of financial resource acquisition to a theory for acquiring financial resources: How should digital ventures raise equity capital beyond seed funding? *Journal of Business Venturing Insights, 16*, e00278. https://doi.org/10.1016/j.jbvi.2021.e00278

1

The Human Journey with AI

Govand Khalid Azeez and Vishal Rana

I

We Must Read the AI Moment Within the Long History of Technology

The Fourth Industrial Revolution (4IR) represents a radical departure from previous large-scale waves of transformational change. It is more consequential vis-à-vis the breadth, depth, and pace at which it is reconfiguring nature, existing social formations and modes of production. But this new techno-scientific wave, despite its distinctive disruptive power and singular configuration, is founded and built upon preceding waves. After all, a materialist and scientific analysis demonstrates that the technological story is one of cumulative evolution and a sequential continuum incorporating the totality of natural, economic, socio-technical, and subjective constituents that preceded it. We can see this chain of cause and effect when we examine the techno-societal journey of humanity retroactively. The march for innovation, invention, and advancement in technical and scientific knowledge has been long. The technical passage from Mesopotamia, Egypt, China, the Indus Valley, the Islamic Golden Age, Greece, Rome, and finally Europe and the United States does not indicate linearity nor Eurocentrism but an epic that is cyclical, episodical, and multi-layered.

What was the real source of this long techno-historical miracle? Not culture, nor race, or religion, but the motor that drove these techno-scientific waves was a dialectical synthesis of collective creativity, ingenuity, the labour, and life activity of humanity feeding into specific productive forces: skills, the embodied knowledge of working humanity; the tools, instruments, and utilities fashioned through centuries of experimentation by previous generations; the division of labour that coordinated collective effort; and the technical know-how that gradually crystallised into systematic scientific knowledge. Nor was the decline of successive techno-scientific regimes the result of the Geist moving on to its next destination, as stage theorists like Niall Ferguson and David Landes would have it. This Toynbean narrative of civilisational rise, peak, and abandonment bears an uncomfortable resemblance to the movement of offshore capital: a society is animated, its labour

DOI: 10.1201/9781003626510-1

and knowledge extracted, its productive potential exhausted, and the Spirit then relocates, clean and unburdened, to its next host.

What this idealist developmentalist account of technology cannot explain is what a materialist one must. Strip away for a moment the tribalism, geopolitical rivalry, and civilisational provincialism that so often colour this history. What remains is a more fundamental and possibly far more interesting story. The long techno-scientific march of humanity has been, beneath its surface conflicts and uneven developments, a snowballing and cooperative enterprise in which each formation built upon, absorbed, and transmitted the productive knowledge of those who came before. This cooperation was never frictionless or symmetrical. The rise and weakening of successive techno-scientific regimes was conditioned by ecological failures, wars and conflicts, shifting configurations of social relations, and modes of surplus extraction that set the material limits of each civilisational formation.

Just as no species evolves in a vacuum but only in constant metabolic exchange with its environment and neighbouring organisms, no socio-technical formation has developed or declined in isolation. Productive knowledge, institutional innovations, and technical know-how continued to flow across boundaries, ensuring that even decline was generative. This is precisely what Lewis Mumford's masterpiece *Technic and Civilization* ([1934] 2010) demonstrated against the progressivism and Eurocentrism of the mainstream account: that pre-modern, pre-capitalist techno-societal regimes were never divorced from our existing world, and that technique precedes and conditions consciousness itself. In Mumford's words, 'men had become mechanical before they perfected complicated machines to express their new bent and interest' (Mumford, [1934] 2010, p. 3). It is not Toynbee but Darwin who is invoked here. There are no absolute falls or radical ruptures in the technological story, only transitions in which one technological order gradually supersedes another. Each civilisational moment deposits its productive knowledge, tools, and organisational forms into the living body of human history, where they persist as the genetic material of every subsequent techno-scientific development.

Yet cumulation alone does not exhaust the story. As Marx observed in his critique of Darwin, the theory of natural selection illuminates the gradual quantitative accumulation of adaptive change but cannot fully account for the moments when quantity tips into quality, when incremental development suddenly crystallises into a new form of life altogether. The technological story follows a similar logic. As historians of science like Shapin (2018) have noted, it is in the First Industrial Revolution (1760–1840) that techno-scientific development assumed precisely such a qualitative threshold: not merely more of what came before, but a systemic reorganisation. And yet even this qualitative leap was genetically rooted in what preceded it. The stone hammer and axe emerged from prior embodied practices, and irrigation from earlier agrarian experimentation; the factory system itself did not arise ex nihilo. It was the cumulative outcome of centuries of artisanal craft production, commercial expansion, proto-industrial workshop organisation, metallurgical advances, and increasingly disciplined mass labour coordination.

This evolutionary process continued with the steam-powered factory system and its attendant transformations in labour organisation, financial structures, and industrial infrastructure. These steam-driven energy innovations, pioneered by Thomas Newcomen and James Watt, became the dialectical basis for Edison and Tesla's electrification of society during the Second Industrial Revolution (1870–1940). Their technological breakthrough was itself enabled by the scientific developments of Volta, Faraday, and Maxwell. Subsequently, Lenoir and Otto's internal combustion engine (1890s) paved the way for automated production, the military–industrial complex (tanks, planes, machine guns), computer systems, Marc Andreesen's worldwide web and network browser, digital technologies, and information technology—all of which characterised the Third Industrial Revolution (1950s–2000s) (Ede, 2019).

Each innovation episode inaugurated profound socio-economic, cultural, spatial, temporal, and ideological reconfigurations. Technological transformation and dispersion unfolded within the uneven and combined development of global capitalism, intensifying both productive capacity and social polarisation. Infrastructural change did not diffuse neutrally; it reorganised labour, concentrated ownership, and restructured political power everywhere. Let us take the steam engine as an illustration of how technology and science lead to what Mumford called the 'great re-orientation'. Andreas Malm's *Fossil Capital: The Rise of Steam Power and the Roots of Global Warming* (2016) demonstrates that the rise of steam power in nineteenth-century Britain was not the inevitable triumph of efficiency, but the outcome of the systemic logic of capital accumulation utilising technology. In Britain, steam displaced water not because rivers were exhausted, but because coal-based stock energy enabled factory owners to concentrate labour in urban centres, discipline and control workers more effectively, and detach production from the geographical constraints of flow energy. The shift to fossil fuels thus bound energy regimes to new spatial forms of industrial urbanisation and intensified state and class power. By the 1830s, fossil energy became inseparable from colonial and imperial expansion, the large-scale extraction of resources from colonised territories, and the accelerating metabolic rift between industrial society and the natural world. Malm, following the likes of Samir Amin and Immanuel Wallerstein, argues that the modern global economy was structured through this carbon-intensive regime, operating via unequal exchange, racialised economic subordination, and the systematic super-exploitation of labour and nature across the Global South (Malm, 2016).

Why undertake this historical reconstruction at all when our topic at hand is AI? Why trace the long arc from stone tools and irrigation to steam, electricity, combustion, and digital computation? What do all these have to do with AI? The answer lies in recognising that our contemporary conjuncture and world is not an isolated rupture, but the latest phase in an evolutionary sequence of techno-scientific regimes. It was J.D. Bernal, the eminent historian of science, who argued that each industrial transformation synthesises prior techniques while transcending them, reorganising the productive forces and the social relations in which they are embedded. In Chapter 1 of *Science in History* (1988), in a section titled *The Cumulative Tradition of Science*, Bernal reminds us that scientific and technical development is cumulative: our present engineers, technologists, technicians and 'scientists would be of little avail if he had not at his disposal an immense stock of previous knowledge and experience' (Bernal, 1969, p. 43). What appears as rupture is grounded in sedimented layers of inherited collective labour, knowledge, experience, and experimentation of humanity.

Our contemporary algorithmic-capitalo-statist conjuncture is characterised by a set of processes, relations, and innovations that consists of the synthesis and transcendence of the earlier aforementioned techniques and technological systems. The artificial intelligence revolution does not replace steam, electricity, combustion, or digital infrastructure; it synthesises and integrates them into a new computational–civilisational regime that penetrates the epistemic and material core of social life and order. The deep learning breakthroughs associated with Fei-Fei Li's ImageNet project at Stanford, the 2012 AlexNet model of Alex Krizhevsky, Geoffrey Hinton and collaborators, DeepMind's AlphaGo victory under Demis Hassabis in 2016, and the subsequent emergence of large-scale generative models (LLMs) developed by firms such as OpenAI, Google, or Claude mark this consolidation. We can state the above differently. That if steam mechanised muscle, and electrification coordinated energy, AI digitalises cognition. AI is what Marx described as the 'general intellect' becoming a direct force of production for the current civilisational order.

This hegemonisation of these systems and tools is not an accident. These variegated AI systems have been consolidated and propelled by an unprecedented alignment of state hegemony and geopolitical competition spearheaded by the United States, elite strategy, venture capital financing, hyperscale computational infrastructure, and mass data extraction. What is being extracted? Shoshana Zuboff calls it *'behavioural surplus'*. This is not merely information in the abstract, but living human activity itself. It is the *Lukácsian reification* of gestures, preferences, movements, communication, and attention. Everything human, all too human, both content and conduct, is converted into a digitally calculable substrate. *It is this transformation of lived human activity into machinic-readable data that lubricates and accelerates the expanding computational apparatus of an emerging computational civilisation and its institutional architecture.*

This alignment, in turn, is driving the diffusion of these systems into the productive and epistemic core of firms, universities, *media institutions,* financial institutions, military establishments, and public administrations.

Being, knowing, living, and the institutions of the market and governance are increasingly tied together via data extraction and algorithmic systems. These AI systems sift, weight, classify, and generate probabilistic outputs from millions of data points in real time, thereby reorganising decision-making, coordination, and authority through computational mediation. What once appeared as relatively discrete domains of life are now increasingly integrated within a unified data-processing cloud-based infrastructure. Technicality, efficiency, and instrumental rationality, the Enlightenment's promise radicalised through neoliberal capitalist optimisation, converge in 'Dataism'. 'Like capitalism, Dataism too began as a neutral scientific theory, but is now mutating into a religion that claims to determine right and wrong. The supreme value of this new pseudo-religion is "information flow"' (Harari, 2016). Is it therefore no surprise that how we think, how we communicate, how decisions are made, how labour and social life are organised, how we feel, how knowledge is produced and, more importantly, how economic and political power is exercised, are being reorganised, centralised, and monopolised in real time.

In other words, digital novel techniques and technologies led by AI are truly reconfiguring all that humanity has known since the Palaeolithic and Neolithic ages. Today, the artificial intelligence revolution has the capacity to blur the internal subjective and external objective correlations, to systematically reconfigure our bio-physiology, to re-orient and shift our social relations and interactions, and to contribute to the withering away of our political, economic, and cultural institutions, from health, education, media, military, and telecommunications to the state. And even more radical is an ontological and existential transition or reconfiguration of what constitutes who and what we are as a species. In other words, the role of the human–animal, the *homo laborans* and *homo faber*, in the age of AI and beyond is radically changing (Harari, 2017, p. 324).

However, this accelerated pace of technological advancement has been met with complex and multifaceted local and global challenges. These include the uneven ownership, access, distribution, and utilisation of AI within and across geopolitical zones; the lack of systematic analysis of unforeseen risks and opportunities in AI development and deployment; and the absence of robust regulatory frameworks capable of ensuring effective oversight (Cath et al., 2018; Crawford & Calo, 2016, p. 313). There is also the increasingly visible concentration of AI infrastructure and computational capacity within Silicon Valley firms, closely interwoven with the imperial strategic interests of the Trump-run American state and its now openly violent military and security apparatuses. The structural asymmetries of AI infrastructure have been empirically analysed in the context of Southeast and South Asian economies, where digital sovereignty policies often address only the surface layer of technological dependency without challenging the underlying power structures that maintain foreign control over critical digital infrastructure (Rana & Azeez, 2025a, 2025b). One can forgive a techno-pessimist for thinking that the contribution of AI systems today has been the massacring and bombing of Iranians and Palestinians, the imprisonment of black and Hispanic minorities, according to an algorithmically run judiciary. The line between public and private, local and global, is becoming increasingly vague—the relation between Israel, Palantir, and ICE is a good example of this. German, Canadian, and British companies integrated with Turkish drones that daily massacre Kurdish villagers in the Zagros Mountains is another case. This asymmetry between the rapid production, permeation and expansion of AI, and the limited awareness, accessibility, governance, and democratic oversight surrounding it reflects the growing concentration of computational power within an increasingly fused state and corporate apparatus. This consolidation narrows the social and political space through which societies can meaningfully comprehend, contest, and direct the trajectory of this technological transformation.

Such centralisation and monopolisation of technological and military power in the hands of a small group of humans provide serious grounds for critique, and even anxiety. Scholars such as Couldry and Mejias (2019) have begun to draw analogies between the AI moment and 1492, arguing that new forms of data extraction risk inaugurating a regime of 'digital colonialism'. Indeed, the concept of Indigenous data sovereignty has been advanced as a critical counter-framework for resisting digital colonialism and demanding that Indigenous peoples govern the collection, ownership, and application of data about their communities (Rana, 2025; Rana & Azeez, 2025). The question that comes to mind is this: what or who is being colonised? The planet? Humanity? Across the political spectrum, others have also invoked 1492, though for different reasons and via different methodologies. Varoufakis describes the present conjuncture as 'techno-feudalism', while the more conservative Joel Kotkin characterises it as an emerging 'neo-feudalism' (Kotkin, 2024; Varoufakis, 2023). If 1492 is remembered as the year of planetary conquest and comparison, then perhaps Galeano's *Open Veins of Latin America* (1971) should guide our reading of the present. Artificial intelligence does not arrive with visible fleets or armed expeditions. It does not declare conquest. It advances through resource extraction, data centres, code, platforms, data extraction, and infrastructural integration. All in the name of efficiency and statistics. If 1492 marked the seizure of land, labour, and natural wealth, the present moment does not abandon those mechanisms but extends them. Territories, societies, bodies, cultures, and environments continue to be appropriated, classified, and ranked through global supply chains, resource extraction, and military projection.

But the dialectical spiral of technological regimes and social systems ensures that the AI moment is also qualitatively different. What is added is a new frontier: data, behavioural surplus, predictive capacity, and an unprecedented architecture of surveillance and targeted lethality. Surveillance and what Achille Mbembe called 'necro-politics' are no longer only territorial and mass, but increasingly personalised, data-driven, and algorithmically optimised. This is not to suggest that systematic and indiscriminate geopolitical massacres have disappeared. As mentioned, the automated targeting and AI-assisted systems deployed in Gaza, the technologically mediated assaults upon Kurdish regions such as Rojava, the massacre of Iranian young girls in their school, and the profiling and imprisoning via facial recognition everywhere demonstrate that computational infrastructures are now directly entangled with military projection, occupation, and population control. The same predictive models, data-fusion systems, and optimisation logics that organise logistics, markets, and communication networks also structure surveillance grids, target identification, and battlefield coordination.

Where earlier empires occupied geography, contemporary systems increasingly enclose information, attention, and cognition. This enclosure does not replace material domination; it intensifies and refines it. Foundation models, LLMs, predictive analytics, and autonomous platforms structure economic allocation, scientific discovery, military logistics, financial markets, and public communication. The terrain of contestation is therefore expanded rather than displaced. As hybrid algorithmic-driven wars in Ukraine, Iran, Afghanistan, and Mexico intensify, one must take care not to universalise and fall into the trap of pessimism. Others show us the other side of this moment. They interpret this development differently. Unlike the techno-pessimists and critical theorists, Ray Kurzweil (2005) envisions the emergence of AI and superintelligence as the pathway towards a technological singularity and human transcendence. Similarly, Peter Diamandis and Kotler (2012) anticipates an era of radical abundance, the death of work, and longevity driven by these new technologies. In such readings, AI does not inaugurate enclosure or domination, but emancipation and post-scarcity transformation. Which horizon is more plausible remains unsettled. Nothing is determined, and the social scene is an open playground for different forces to shape the moment. Whether these techno-pessimistic or optimistic projections will materialise remains to be seen.

What is certain is that this moment holds openly divergent pathways. It could widen access to resources, liberate humanity from work, and radically increase access to knowledge and coordination on an unprecedented scale. It could also intensify asymmetries of ownership, surveillance, agency, and control. Technology alone does not determine the direction of travel. The outcome will depend upon the property regimes, social relations, and concrete practices through which AI is designed, developed, owned, and governed. If collective political consciousness, awareness, and agency do not rise to meet this transformation, humanity may find itself subordinated within systems it has created but cannot meaningfully steer. The question is not whether AI will divide epochs, but whether political and institutional capacity will mature alongside technical power—whether social organisation can keep pace with computational acceleration. It is whether we will shape this emerging order or be shaped by it.

II

An Empirical Analysis of Dispersion of AI in the World

Artificial intelligence is being embedded within the core structures of contemporary society. Computer systems and large language models, through assessing and learning structural patterns within vast datasets, are revolutionising societal and economic processes across various domains. From financial transactions and sustainable development modelling to smart city planning, epidemiology, gene editing, cartography, neuroscience, policing, autonomous systems, and lethal weapon systems, this paradigmatic shift has been unprecedented in scale and scope, rapid in diffusion, and transformational in impact (Li, 2020, pp. 10–35). According to recent reports by FPT (2025):

> The evolution of generative AI has significantly changed how humans and machines interact, especially with the development of AI agent systems. Emergen Research (2024) estimates that the global market of AI agent systems will reach 30.89 billion USD with a compound annual growth rate (CAGR) of 31.68% in the period from 2024 to 2033. The BCG analysis (n.d.) further articulates that AI agents are picking up steam across a vast array of business applications with a CAGR of 45% in the next five years...
>
> **(2025, p. 3)**

The report goes on to show that '82% of businesses plan to deploy these systems into their organisations in the next three years (2024). By the end of 2025, there will be approximately 50 to 100 billion AI agents integrated into various' spheres' (FPT, 2025, p. 3). This macro-expansion is mirrored at the organisational level. The 2025 McKinsey Global Survey reports that 88 per cent of organisations now use AI regularly in at least one business function, up from 78 per cent the previous year, and 62 per cent are at least experimenting with AI agents, with 23 per cent already scaling agentic systems within parts of their enterprise (McKinsey & Company, 2025). A quick empirical analysis of the different disciplines, industries, and fields demonstrates that AI is no longer peripheral experimentation but an increasingly hegemonic infrastructural layer of contemporary socio-economic coordination.

In software engineering, large-scale language models such as Anthropic's Claude Code and OpenAI's GPT-5.3-Codex have moved beyond autocomplete into planning, debugging, and executing multi-step development tasks across entire repositories. Industry analysis suggests that autonomous coding agents are already responsible for a measurable share of public code, indicating that software production itself is becoming partially automated (SemiAnalysis, 2026). OpenAI has described GPT-5.3-Codex as 'instrumental in creating itself', assisting in debugging its own training and deployment workflows (Landymore, 2026), while systems such as Claude Code are increasingly used to iteratively refine codebases and development pipelines.

These cases signal possible early forms of recursive optimisation. This technical progress is already visible in corporate practice. A recent *Forbes* article reported that currently, *'AI Writes Over 25% Of Code At Google—What Does The Future Look Like For Software Engineers?'* Google CEO Sundar Pichai indicated that the future is exciting technically, but socially bleak for the engineers. He disclosed that far fewer engineers are needed. Their task is merely reviewing code written by AI (Kelly, 2024). The AI firms are telling us that programming is moving from manual construction towards agent-mediated orchestration, compressing development cycles, reducing the marginal cost of producing software, and progressively displacing routine functions traditionally performed by human software engineers.

In biology, the transformation is equally profound. DeepMind's AlphaFold demonstrated that a deep learning system can predict the three-dimensional structure of proteins directly from their amino acid sequences (Senior et al., 2020). Rather than relying on years of laboratory experimentation, the system uses neural networks trained to model relationships between amino acid residues and to calculate the spatial constraints that determine protein folding. In independent international assessments, AlphaFold achieved levels of accuracy previously thought to require slow and resource-intensive physical experimentation conducted by tens of PhD students and researchers. What had long depended on painstaking structural biology methods can now be computationally derived at scale, reshaping how biological function is inferred from genetic sequence. As such systems integrate into genomics, drug discovery, and biomedical research pipelines, the very process through which biological knowledge is generated is being reorganised (Jumper et al., 2021).

In neuroscience, the boundary between mind and machine is becoming increasingly porous. Brain–machine interfaces now enable two-way exchange between neural tissue and computational systems, moving from laboratory research into regulated human trials. Elon Musk's Neuralink has recently implanted its device in an Australian participant under an FDA-approved study. Recent implantation has enabled patients with paralysis to control external devices using neural signals alone (Higgins, 2024). When integrated with machine learning systems, these interfaces do more than restore lost motor function. They translate neural activity into analysable data streams, allowing patterns of thought and intention to be decoded, modelled, and, potentially, anticipated. In this shift, neural processes are no longer confined to the biological domain; they essentially become computational inputs within algorithmic systems. As Christopher Reilly argues, the rapid commodification of brain–machine interfaces (an industry valued at approximately US$2.7 billion) raises profound questions about privacy, autonomy, and the incorporation of neural life into market and corporate logics (Reilly, 2020, p. 390).

In education, the pamphlets of edtech companies and the speeches and articles of managers and executives who are firing academics and teachers tell us that the transformation is not merely pedagogical or epistemological but structural. AI adaptive learning systems, or 'digital pocket teachers', are presented as personalising and customising instruction at scale. These systems analyse student engagement patterns, assess performance data, and dynamically recalibrate instructional content in real time to optimise learning trajectories. Large language models such as Claude, Perplexity, and ChatGPT are increasingly marketed not simply as supplementary tools but as integrated tutors, translators, research assistants, curriculum designers, and evaluators. Platforms such as Khan Academy's Khanmigo, Google's AI-powered course infrastructures and certification ecosystems, and proprietary university–industry partnerships position algorithmic systems as scalable substitutes for traditional classroom instruction. Under subsidised state contracts and university administrations driven by cost-reduction imperatives and neoliberal managerial logics, these systems are reframed as efficiency-enhancing replacements rather than pedagogical complements. What is being normalised is not merely the augmentation of teaching labour, but its partial displacement through platform-mediated instructional architectures. The global education technology market, valued at USD 187 billion in 2025 and projected to reach USD 437.5 billion by 2033 (Grand View Research, 2026), signals that AI-driven infrastructures are not peripheral supplements but forces capable of materially reorganising the educational field.

In the military domain, the stakes escalate dramatically. Military experts tell us that 'Artificial Intelligence is ushering in a new era in warfare, one in which computational agents act as scouts, advisors, and even trigger-pullers alongside human war fighters' (Rabab'Ah & Aburass, 2025, p. 36). This shift is already visible in operational practice. Autonomous drones, AI-assisted targeting systems, predictive surveillance architectures, and cyberwarfare capabilities are becoming embedded within military doctrine and procurement strategies. These systems extend decision-making speed, expand battlefield visibility, and compress the time between detection and action. Human operators increasingly supervise algorithmic systems rather than directly execute tactical functions. The institutional realignment surrounding these technologies has accelerated. Over the course of a single year, firms such as OpenAI, Anthropic, Google, and Meta shifted from publicly restricting military applications to entering partnerships with the Pentagon and defence contractors including Palantir and Anduril. This normalised the integration of frontier models into defence infrastructures. The boundary between civilian AI research and military deployment has therefore become increasingly permeable. This turn marks a techno-nationalistic reconfiguration of the state–platform relationship. Computational capacity, semiconductor supply chains, hyperscale cloud infrastructure, and model training capability are being consolidated as strategic assets. Innovation priorities are increasingly shaped by geopolitical competition. Capital allocation follows security imperatives. Research agendas align with national defence strategies. What is emerging is a twenty-first-century military–industrial–algorithmic complex in which geopolitical competition reorganises innovation, capital allocation, and research priorities (Srnicek, 2026).

Beyond software, biology, neuroscience, education, and defence, AI penetration extends across additional foundational sectors of contemporary life. In media and communication, AI-generated text, image, audio, and video systems are flooding civil society. It is no longer clear what is written or produced by a human and what is not. Magazines, journals, and newsrooms have begun to automate reporting. James Barrat's *The Intelligent Explosion: When AI Beats Humans at Everything* (2025) begins with the axiom that AI will intellectually outgrow all humans in the near future. From this, he goes on to draw a corollary outcome that 'AI will eliminate 30 per cent of all jobs done by humans, including writers'. That human writers (freelance journalists, essayists, etc.) certainly benefit from parts of their creative job being automated. 'Soon a basic features writer, using AI, will be able to produce twice as much content and get paid twice as much…but in the long run the news organisations will get rid of most writers because people won't care if content is written by AI or not' (Barrat in O'Malley, 2025). The same dynamic now appears across the wider field of cultural production. Whether in advertising, film, music, design, research drafting, policy analysis, or corporate communications, algorithmic systems increasingly generate copy, visuals, scripts, campaign strategies, literature reviews, and analytical summaries at scale.

Yet this acceleration carries epistemic instability. As Choi and Mei (2025) explain, AI systems are prone to what computer scientists term 'hallucinations', outputs that appear coherent and authoritative but are factually inaccurate, fabricated, or contextually inappropriate. Choi and Mei (2025) write that:

> Wherever AI systems are used in daily life, their hallucinations can pose risks. Some may be minor – when a chatbot gives the wrong answer to a simple question, the user may end up ill-informed. But in other cases, the stakes are much higher. From courtrooms where AI software is used to make sentencing decisions to health insurance companies that use algorithms to determine a patient's eligibility for coverage, AI hallucinations can have life-altering consequences. They can even be life-threatening: Autonomous vehicles use AI to detect obstacles, other vehicles and pedestrians.

Such hallucinations are omnipresent and universal: in legal systems, medical diagnostics, policing, insurance determination, HR and hiring, administrative governance, financial modelling, agriculture, finance, and, perhaps even worse, military targeting (Choi & Mei, 2025). The ease and speed of production of information in these fields is equally tied to the probability of error, misjudgements, miscalculations, and even catastrophe. The dispersion of AI systems is beginning to wither, weaken, and in some instances completely remove the way decisions were mediated across layers of human institutional deliberations.

Despite this expanding empirical footprint, the full trajectory of AI penetration remains profoundly uncertain. The present conjuncture unfolds moment by moment, characterised by uneven diffusion, institutional experimentation, and contradictory outcomes. The intellectual field itself is sharply divided. Sceptics such as Gary Marcus (2022), Rodney Brooks, and Yann LeCun caution against exaggerated claims of imminent general intelligence, emphasising structural limitations in current architectures, data dependence, and brittle reasoning capacities. Others—including figures associated with superintelligence discourse such as Nick Bostrom (2014), Ray Kurzweil (2005), and leading AI executives—argue that artificial general intelligence may emerge within years or even months. Between these poles lies a contested epistemic terrain. Whether AI plateaus within narrow optimisation regimes or accelerates towards qualitatively new forms of intelligence, the scale of present transformation demands rigorous epistemological and methodological assessment. The task is not prophecy but analysis: to map dispersion, identify structural tendencies, examine property regimes, and evaluate institutional realignments as they unfold. In conditions of rapid technological mutation, theoretical clarity becomes not a luxury but a necessity.

III

AI's Polycrisis Requires a Transdisciplinary Epistemology and a Radical Critique of Our Unequal World

The size, form, and scale of the empirical and concrete changes mentioned above are unprecedented. These quantitative and qualitative changes imposed upon society can appear to be at once fragmented, cellularised, and disconnected. Yet there is also a feeling that there is a coherent systemic shift that is moving the deep structures. All at once, the tectonic plates of existing political, social, and economic systems are moving and leading to a dissymmetry between the socio-ideational and material ground we stand upon. The old world is dying, so are the old ideas. As societies, economies, institutions, occupations, and identities shift, a crisis in consciousness, understanding, and analysis emerges.

As we speak, jobs are displaced, the masses' attention is saturated with algorithmically curated [mis]information, demographies are profiled through facial recognition, new flashy luxury gadgets are created, entrepreneurs and investor-shareholders accumulate unprecedented gains, biomedical systems extend life expectancy, and diseases are treated at accelerated rates. AI brings both prosperity and precarity simultaneously; emancipatory potentials coexist with dispossession, and optimisation advances alongside intensified surveillance and control. The benefits and burdens are unevenly distributed across classes, races, genders, regions, and sectors, generating sharp discrepancies between those integrated into emerging technological circuits and those rendered redundant by them.

This dissymmetry and structural unevenness come at a material but also intellectual, psychological, and existential cost. Our old methods, epistemic toolboxes, social paradigms, and intellectual traditions cease to present a coherent analysis of the situation. A widening gap emerges between lived transformation and conceptual comprehension. In the words of Hegel, when philosophy and thought 'paints its grey in grey':

> A shape of life has grown old, and it cannot be rejuvenated, but only recognised by the grey in grey of philosophy; the owl of Minerva begins its flight only when the shadows of night are gathering.
>
> **(Hegel, [1821] 1991, p. 23)**

Hegel's point is that consciousness and thought always lag behind actuality. Events, accidents, action, and concrete processes unfold first; only retrospectively can thought grasp their necessity and internal coherence. The subject (humanity) never possesses complete foresight at the moment of transformation. Yet Hegel's logic does not counsel passive resignation. Rather, it insists that freedom emerges through the dialectical movement between subject and object. Thought is not external to the world but immanent within it; agency develops through engagement with contradiction. To apprehend the dialectics of subject and object in motion, in development, in totality, is to begin to comprehend the rational structure of reality as it unfolds in its many facets (Brandom, 2019). Dialectics in this sense is the logic of assessing the world, learning from the turbulations/errors that come of the subject–object contradictions via heterogeneous analysis, to try and correct, fail, fail again. Only this process opens the possibility for success that is subjective (consciousness understanding the world and acting in the objective world).

In this sense, the ontological conception of AI cannot be grasped through isolated fragments, but only by mapping its multiple determinations into a dialectical whole. The different moments, phases, sets, ideas, and subsets of the AI question and its polycrises constitute a concrete, moving totality. The problem and the answer of AI emerge from this totality, not from any single technical component. Yet this phenomenon is not static; it is in motion, containing within itself its own contradictions, negations, and transformative possibilities. As Karl Marx (1973) famously noted in the introduction to the *Grundrisse*, 'The concrete is concrete because it is the concentration of many determinations, hence unity of the diverse' (p. 34). To comprehend the nature and implications of the AI economic, sociological, psychological, and political crisis, therefore, requires understanding beyond a single tradition, method, discipline, and theory. It requires a metalogical analysis with variant minds, scholars, thinkers, theories, and methods examining the developing socio-economic and technological totality.

This is where the idea for *Shaping Tomorrow: The Human Journey with AI* was born. It is an attempt to operationalise precisely this dialectical demand for totality. Rather than isolating AI as a purely technical artefact, a regulatory puzzle, or a moral dilemma, the book assembles its multiple determinations into a structured, interdisciplinary whole. Philosophers and ethicists interrogate its normative foundations; computer scientists and AI developers examine architectural limits and design logics; sociologists and political economists analyse labour displacement, class restructuring, and capital concentration; legal scholars and policy practitioners explore governance, sovereignty and institutional adaptation; international relations theorists map geopolitical asymmetries and techno-nationalism; educators and social theorists assess epistemic transformation; and practitioners from industry contribute grounded case studies of implementation and unintended consequence. The editors' own collaborative research programme exemplifies this transdisciplinary imperative, spanning political economy (Rana & Khalid, 2025), decolonial ethics (Rana, 2025), institutional governance (Rana & Azeez, 2025a), geopolitical analysis (Azeez & Rana, 2025; Rana & Azeez, 2025b), and pedagogical transformation (Rana et al., 2025). Each chapter functions as a determinate moment within a larger conceptual architecture, while the case studies anchor abstraction in empirical reality. In this way, the volume mirrors the very movement it describes: a unity of the diverse in which heterogeneous perspectives do not fragment analysis but are mediated into a coherent, evolving totality. The book's global call for authors ensures epistemological plurality, while its structured synthesis ensures philosophical coherence. Through this dialectical composition, *Shaping Tomorrow* seeks not merely to comment on AI's polycrisis but to comprehend it in motion.

IV

The Volume and Its Contributions

The chapters that follow are arranged to move from foundational philosophical and historical analysis, through educational and ethical inquiry, to applied domains and governance frameworks. Each contribution addresses a distinct dimension of the AI question while contributing to the volume's overarching ambition: to comprehend the human–AI relationship as a dialectical totality. What follows is a brief overview of each chapter.

Chapter 2: An Interview with Professor Nick Bostrom—Conducted by Dr. Govand Khalid Azeez

This chapter presents a structured interview with philosopher Nick Bostrom, organised around three thematic axes: reality, intelligence, and simulation; ethics, society, and political economy; and futures, post-labour humanity, and meaning. Bostrom reflects on how large language models have shortened the timeline to superintelligence, acknowledges the ontological disorientation produced by generative systems, and advocates for gradual, participatory transformation over abrupt augmentation. He characterises himself as a 'fretful optimist,' noting that machine superintelligence may reduce the value of human capital while potentially enabling extreme abundance. The interview offers a philosophical anchor for the volume's engagement with existential risk, human purpose, and the contested trajectory of AI development.

Chapter 3: Artificial Intelligence and the Traumatisation of Human Culture—Dr. Todd Madigan

Madigan applies Jeffrey Alexander's theory of cultural trauma to a prospective scenario: the widespread societal belief that machines have achieved the special form of consciousness traditionally reserved for human persons. The chapter maps the four-phase cultural trauma process consisting of pre trauma identity, traumatic event, throes of trauma, and resolution onto the disruption of collective personhood narratives. Drawing on functionalist and essentialist models of personhood, and illustrating how literary, cinematic, and philosophical narratives already prefigure these debates, Madigan argues that such an event would precipitate sustained social division far exceeding Sam Altman's prediction of a brief public reaction. The chapter proposes cultural trauma theory itself as an ameliorative metaphor capable of deflating apocalyptic rhetoric and supporting prosocial discourse.

Chapter 4: Challenge as a Way of Knowing: Education for Critical Knowing in the Era of AI—Dr. Mary C. Lang and Dr. Jonathan Boymal

Lang and Boymal reconceptualise the relationship between cognition, knowledge, and education in an AI-mediated world. Drawing on embodied and situated cognition, Bandura's reciprocal determinism, Mercier and Sperber's interactionist model of reason, and Bourdieu's theory of cultural capital, the chapter introduces 'epistemic capital' as a framework for understanding knowledge as social action. The authors advance 'challenge as a way of knowing', an educational orientation grounded in two core principles, interdisciplinarity and struggle, that positions learners as epistemic agents rather than consumers of algorithmic certainty. Engaging concepts such as digital fossils, cognitive dissonance AI, and the inversion of Bloom's taxonomy, the chapter argues for a pedagogy centred on human flourishing and social justice in the convergence era.

Chapter 5: AI and Education: An Interdisciplinary, Collaborative Approach—Dr. Sara Ratner

Ratner argues that the integration of AI in education must be understood as a deeply human, ethical, and political undertaking that cannot be reduced to a technical challenge. The chapter employs Systems Theory as a conceptual lens for analysing education as a complex, adaptive, multi-layered system, and Participatory Research as a democratic methodology for embedding equity and lived experience into research practice. These frameworks are exemplified through the AI in Education at Oxford University (AIEOU) Hub, whose four interrelated research streams consisting of Design, Regulation, Implementation, and Impact model a collaborative, values driven, and reflexive approach to inquiry. The chapter concludes with actionable recommendations for centring human values, inclusive governance, and professional learning in AI-related educational decision-making.

Chapter 6: The Promise and Challenge of AI Personalisation in Education: A Theoretical and Empirical Analysis—Dr. Kathleen J. Kennedy

Kennedy examines AI-driven personalised learning systems through both critical theoretical frameworks and extensive empirical evidence from the Personalised Adaptive Learning System (PALS) initiative, a study encompassing 1,173 students and 15 instructors across 13 disciplines. The chapter investigates conditions for equitable AI implementation, the relational dynamics between learners, instructors, and AI systems, and the systemic changes required for ethical deployment. A central finding is that implementation success depends primarily on instructor integration and coordination, as captured by the Integrated Model for AI Personalisation (IMAP), rather than technological sophistication alone. The chapter demonstrates how the post ChatGPT landscape fundamentally disrupts assumptions underlying adaptive learning, particularly regarding retrieval practice and student honesty.

Chapter 7: AI in Education: The Ethical Imperative to Keep Humans in the Loop—Dr. Lynn Gribble and Dr. Janis Wardrop

Drawing on three years of lived experience managing education and assessment responses to AI at an Australian research intensive university, Gribble and Wardrop examine two interrelated ethical challenges: the integrity of credentials in an era of generative tools, and the use of data-driven systems for student support that risk functioning as surveillance. The chapter integrates theoretical frameworks including the McDonaldisation of education, sociomateriality, surveillance capitalism, and Foucault's panopticon to argue that maintaining the 'human in the loop' is essential to safeguarding educational relationships. It positions AI in education as a wicked problem requiring agile institutional strategies that balance innovation with pedagogical responsibility, professional agency, and democratic accountability.

Chapter 8: Theological Ethics in AI Entrepreneurship—Dr. Timothy Hor

Hor explores the intersection of theology and entrepreneurship, proposing that theological ethics, particularly the principles of human dignity (imago Dei), stewardship, justice, and compassion, can provide a robust moral framework for navigating the ethical complexities of AI development. The chapter examines high-profile corporate failures such as Theranos, WeWork, and FTX as cautionary examples of unchecked ambition, before demonstrating how theological virtues can inform AI design in domains including health care, education, and environmental sustainability. Engaging with questions of algorithmic bias, transparency, data colonialism, and the digital divide, the chapter advocates for a values driven approach that positions entrepreneurs as co-creators responsible for aligning technological innovation with human flourishing and the common good.

Chapter 9: Safeguarding Human Welfare with AI—Dr. Nicole Arcuri-Sanders

Arcuri-Sanders examines AI's impact on human wellness through the lens of counselling practice, employing the Wheel of Wellness model (Myers, Sweeney, and Witmer) alongside Maslow's hierarchy of needs and Adlerian theory. The chapter presents case studies across five interrelated life tasks consisting of spirituality, self-direction, work and leisure, friendship, and love to illustrate how AI tools such as ChatGPT can both positively and negatively influence client wellbeing. Areas of concern include emotional regulation, information accuracy, trust, intimacy, and confidentiality. The chapter positions mental health professionals as ethically obligated advocates who must educate communities about the strengths and limitations of AI, empowering individuals to make informed decisions in the preservation of their holistic welfare.

Chapter 10: Algorithmic Branding: The Ethics of AI in Consumer Manipulation—Dr. Matthew Gilbert and Dr. Patrick Van Esch

Gilbert and van Esch investigate the ethical boundaries between AI driven personalisation and consumer manipulation. Integrating Zuboff's surveillance capitalism with Bourdieu's theory of cultural capital, the chapter analyses how algorithmic branding by platforms such as Amazon, Netflix, Facebook, and TikTok reshapes consumer autonomy while entrenching socio-cultural hierarchies. Case studies including the Cambridge Analytica scandal illustrate how AI tools exploit cognitive biases through dark patterns, dynamic pricing, and micro-targeted advertising. The chapter synthesises perspectives from behavioural psychology, marketing ethics, and sociotechnical theory to propose pathways for ethical innovation, including Floridi's AI4People principles, participatory data cooperatives, and regulatory frameworks such as the EU's Digital Services Act.

Chapter 11: AI-Driven Medication Adherence: Addressing Social Determinants and Enhancing Patient Outcomes—Vishnu Kakaraparthi and Dr. Troy McDaniel

Kakaraparthi and McDaniel examine how AI can reshape medication adherence strategies, with particular attention to social determinants of health including income, education, housing stability, and healthcare access. The chapter reviews technological innovations including machine learning, natural language processing, computer vision, and wearable computing that enable real-time, patient-specific interventions. The PERACTIV platform, a wrist centric wearable system employing multimodal sensing and contextual prompting, serves as a focal case study for AI enhanced adherence through unobtrusive, routine embedded monitoring. The authors integrate theoretical foundations from behavioural economics, health psychology, and patient-centred care, while critically reflecting on ethical considerations around privacy, autonomy, algorithmic fairness, and the imperative of inclusive design for diverse and underserved populations.

Chapter 12: Emotional and Physical Support Through Ethical AI—Bradley Guelfi and Ray Parker

Guelfi and Parker explore AI's role in enhancing health care across physical, cognitive, and emotional dimensions through two research informed patient narratives: Sarah's trauma from a motorcycle accident and Kai's chronic illness journey. The chapter demonstrates how ethically embedded AI can bridge fragmentation in care delivery, from advanced surgical suites with real-time diagnostics and robotic assistance to remote clinical settings. Central to the analysis is the CORES Framework (Composable Oversight for Responsible Evolution and Simplicity), which provides a structured model for adaptable, transparent, and equitable AI integration in health care. The chapter argues that AI's legitimacy in medicine depends not merely on technical performance but on its alignment with enduring ethical principles of autonomy, beneficence, non-maleficence, and justice.

Chapter 13: Artificial Intelligence and the Future of Data Privacy: Examining the MIT Taxonomy and Unified Privacy Governance Framework—Dr. Michael D'Rosario and Dr. George Newman

D'Rosario and Newman address the dual nature of AI as both a risk to and a solution for data privacy. Employing the MIT AI Risk Repository, the chapter analyses 173 privacy-related risks distributed across technological, regulatory, and dual categories, classified by causal origin, intent, and timing. This empirical mapping provides the foundation for the Unified Privacy Governance Framework (UPGF), which integrates privacy by design with privacy governance to address fragmentation in current approaches. The chapter reviews regulatory landscapes across the European Union, the United States, and Australia, arguing that neither technical safeguards such as differential privacy and federated learning nor regulatory instruments alone are sufficient. Effective privacy protection requires their systematic integration across the full AI life cycle.

Chapter 14: Sustainable AI Beyond Ecological Integrity: A Capability-Based Framework for Design—Dr. Daniel M. Phoenix

Phoenix interrogates the normative foundations of sustainable AI at a moment when energy-intensive computational infrastructures collide with faltering climate commitments. Rejecting ecological integrity as a self-sufficient guiding ideal, the chapter advances a framework grounded in weak anthropocentrism, subsidiarity, and the capability approach associated with Sen and Nussbaum. It proposes three design-relevant criteria, evaluating AI as an environmental conversion factor, as a contributor to ecological stability, and as a source of human sufficiency. A case study of AI-based heat optimisers in thermal power generation shows how capability-oriented evaluation can guide design choices without collapsing into technological solutionism or ethical paralysis. The chapter closes with actionable recommendations for embedding sustainability into engineering and design education.

Chapter 15: The Five Horsemen of the AI Apocalypse: A Framework for Understanding Algorithmic Injustice and Governance—Dr. Nici Sweaney

Sweaney introduces the Five Horsemen of the AI Apocalypse consisting of Development Bias, Training Data Bias, Access Inequality, Displacement Risk, and Feedback Loop Amplification as a diagnostic framework for understanding how algorithmic injustice produces structural exclusion. The chapter advances an adaptive governance model, drawing on responsive regulation theory, that rejects the binary between rigid regulation and laissez-faire acceleration in favour of dynamic, participatory, and iterative oversight. Gender serves as a diagnostic lens, revealing how pipeline problems, retention crises, and authority gaps compound displacement risk. Estonia's KrattAI ecosystem is examined as a case study illustrating both the promise and limitations of national-scale AI governance. The chapter concludes with actionable, justice-centred questions for policymakers and technologists oriented towards equity, accountability, and structural repair.

References

Azeez, G. K., & Rana, V. (2025, August 2). Southeast Asia and the mirage of tech sovereignty. *The Diplomat*. Available at: https://thediplomat.com/2025/08/southeast-asia-and-the-mirage-of-tech-sovereignty/

Bernal, J. D. (1969). *Science in history: Volume 1. The emergence of science*. Penguin Books.

Bostrom, N. (2014). *Superintelligence: Paths, dangers, strategies*. Oxford University Press.

Brandom, R. B. (2019). *A spirit of trust: A reading of Hegel's Phenomenology*. The Belknap Press of Harvard University Press.

Cath, C., Wachter, S., Mittelstadt, B., Taddeo, M., & Floridi, L. (2018). Artificial intelligence and the 'good society': The US, EU, and UK approach. *Science and Engineering Ethics, 24*(2), 505–528. https://doi.org/10.1007/s11948-017-9901-7

Choi, A. S. G., & Mei, K. X. (2025, March 21). What are AI hallucinations? Why AIs sometimes make things up. *The Conversation*. https://theconversation.com/what-are-ai-hallucinations-why-ais-sometimes-make-things-up-242896

Couldry, N., & Mejias, U. A. (2019). *The costs of connection: How data is colonizing human life and appropriating it for capitalism*. Stanford University Press.

Crawford, K., & Calo, R. (2016). There is a blind spot in AI research. *Nature, 538*(7625), 311–313. https://doi.org/10.1038/538311a

Diamandis, P. H., & Kotler, S. (2012). *Abundance: The Future is Better than You Think*. New York: Free Press.

Ede, A. (2019). *Technology and society: A world history*. Cambridge University Press.

FPT. (2025). AI agents: Unveiling the next frontier of business transformation. Available at: https://fpt.ai/wp-content/uploads/2025/04/WP-AI-Agents.pdf Accessed: 18 February 2026.

Galeano, E. (1971). *Open veins of Latin America: Five Centuries of the Pillage of a Continent*. New York: Monthly Review Press.

Georg Wilhelm Friedrich Hegel. ([1821] 1991). *Elements of the philosophy of right* (Trans. H. B. Nisbet, p. 23). New York: Cambridge University Press.

Grand View Research. (2026, June). *Education technology market size, share & trends analysis report by sector, end use, type, deployment, region, and segment forecasts, 2026–2033*.https://www.grandviewresearch.com/industry-analysis/education-technology-market

Harari, Y. Reboot for the AI revolution. *Nature* 550, 324–327 (2017). https://doi.org/10.1038/550324a

Harari, Y. N. (2016, September 1). 'Homo sapiens is an obsolete algorithm': Yuval Noah Harari on how data could eat the world. *WIRED*.

Higgins, N. (2024, February 9). Neuralink has put its first chip in a human brain. What could possibly go wrong? *Monash Lens*. https://www.mckinsey.com/capabilities/quantumblack/our-insights/the-state-of-ai

Jumper, J., Evans, R., Pritzel, A., Green, T., Figurnov, M., Ronneberger, O., Tunyasuvunakool, K., Bates, R., Žídek, A., Potapenko, A., Bridgland, A., Meyer, C., Kohl, S. A. A., Ballard, A. J., Cowie, A., Romera-Paredes, B., Nikolov, S., Jain, R., Adler, J., Back, T., Petersen, S., Reiman, D., Clancy, E., Zielinski, M., & Hassabis, D. (2021). Highly accurate protein structure prediction with AlphaFold. *Nature, 596*, 583–589. https://doi.org/10.1038/s41586-021-03819-2

Kelly, J. (2024). AI writes over 25% of code at Google—What does the future look like for software engineers? Forbes, 1 November. Available at: https://www.

forbes.com/sites/jackkelly/2024/11/01/ai-code-and-the-future-of-software-engineers/. Accessed: 4 February 2026.

Kotkin, J. (2024, June 21). The road to neo-feudalism. *Joel Kotkin*. https://joelkotkin.com/the-road-to-neo-feudalism/

Kurzweil, R. (2005). *The Singularity is Near: When Humans Transcend Biology*. New York: Viking.

Landymore, F., 2026. OpenAI's latest AI was created using "itself," company claims. Futurism, 7 February. Available at: https://futurism.com. Accessed: 1 February 2026.

Li, R. (2020). *Artificial intelligence revolution: How AI will change our society, economy, and culture*. New York: Skyhorse Publishing.

Malm, A. (2016). *Fossil capital: The rise of steam power and the roots of global warming*. London: Verso

Marcus, G. (2022, March 10). Deep learning is hitting a wall. *Nautilus*. https://nautil.us/deep-learning-is-hitting-a-wall-238440

Marx, K. (1973 [1857-61]) Grundrisse: Foundations of the Critique of Political Economy (Rough Draft). Translated by M. Nicolaus. Harmondsworth: Penguin Books in association with New Left Review. Available at: https://www.marxists.org/archive/marx/works/1857/grundrisse/index.htm (Accessed: 7 July 2026).

McKinsey & Company. (2025, November 5). *The state of AI in 2025: Agents, innovation, and transformation*. https://www.mckinsey.com/capabilities/quantumblack/our-insights/the-state-of-ai

Mumford, L. (2010). *Technics and civilization*. Chicago, IL: University of Chicago Press. (Original work published 1934)

O'Malley, J. P., 2025. Will artificial intelligence be the death of journalism? AI tools can make reporters' lives easier but also challenge their very existence. SciFuture News, 24 September. Available at: https://www.scifuture.org/review-the-intelligence-explosion-when-ai-beats-humans-at-everything/. Accessed: 16 February 2026.

Rabab'Ah, Z., & Aburass, S. (2025). Artificial intelligence in the global military and weapon industry: Applications, methodologies, and implications. *Jordan Scientific Journal*, 2(1), 36–60.

Rana, V. (2025). Indigenous data sovereignty: A catalyst for ethical AI in business. *Business & Society*, *64*(4), 635–640. https://doi.org/10.1177/00076503241271143

Rana, V., & Azeez, G. K. (2025a). Indigenous data sovereignty in Australian higher education: Paving the way for first Nations' self-determination. *Journal of Higher Education Policy and Management*, *47*(3), 426–434. https://doi.org/10.1080/1360080X.2025.2469920

Rana, V., & Azeez, G. K. (2025b, March 19). Southeast Asia's quest for digital sovereignty. The Diplomat. Available at: https://thediplomat.com/2025/03/southeast-asias-quest-for-digital-sovereignty/

Rana, V., & Khalid, G. (2025). Artificial intelligence (AI) and South Asian economies. In M. Hossain, E. A. Selvanathan, M. Jayasinghe, S. Selvanathan, & R. Kathuria (Eds.), *South Asian Economic Development in the Era of Global Turbulence* (3rd ed., pp. 145–157). Routledge.

Rana, V., Verhoeven, B., & Sharma, M. (2025). Generative AI in design thinking pedagogy: Enhancing creativity, critical thinking, and ethical reasoning in higher education. *Journal of University Teaching and Learning Practice*, 22(4). https://doi.org/10.53761/tjse2f36

Reilly, C. M. (2020). Brain-machine interfaces as commodities: Exchanging mind for matter. *The Linacre Quarterly*, *87*(4), 387–398. https://doi.org/10.1177/0024363920930882
Senior, A. W., Evans, R., Jumper, J., Kirkpatrick, J., Sifre, L., Green, T., Qin, C., Žídek, A., Nelson, A. W. R., Bridgland, A., Penedones, H., Petersen, S., Simonyan, K., Crossan, S., Kohli, P., Jones, D. T., Silver, D., Kavukcuoglu, K., & Hassabis, D. (2020). Improved protein structure prediction using deep learning potentials. *Nature*, *577*(7792), 706–710.
Srnicek, N. (2026). How AI companies got caught up in US military efforts. WIRED.
Varoufakis, Y. (2023). *Technofeudalism: What killed capitalism*. The Bodley Head.

2

An Interview with Professor Nick Bostrom

Conducted by Govand Khalid Azeez

Part I—Reality, Intelligence, and Simulation

Exploring the philosophical and technical foundations of your work on AI, cognition, and simulated reality.

Question 1. A great deal has been made—both in public discourse and academic commentary—about whether recent generative systems represent genuine progress towards artificial general intelligence or merely sophisticated 'stochastic parrots' engaging in pattern matching. Optimists like Ray Kurzweil and Dario Amodei see current AI progress as validating accelerating timelines towards AGI, while sceptics like Gary Marcus point to the failure of scaling laws and potential plateaus in capability improvements. *How does these recent developments affect your assessment of the timeline and likelihood of achieving superintelligence? Does the success of Large Language Models suggest alternative routes to AGI that might be faster or slower than previously anticipated?*

Professor Bostrom—They shorten the timeline. They do not much affect my assessment of the likelihood, as I already assigned a high probability to superintelligence eventually being achieved long before these recent advances. It is even possible that they slightly reduce the likelihood, in as much as it seems we'll be spending a somewhat longer period of time with around-AGI levels of AI before we get superintelligence than previously expected, which might modestly increase the risk of something going wrong or the world deciding to ban this stuff before we get superintelligence—whereas if superintelligence had happened more abruptly, those scenarios may have been even less likely.

Question 2. Generative systems blur long-standing boundaries, between authorship and automation, originality and repetition, and intelligence and imitation. This ambiguity has produced a kind of ontological disorientation and existential anxiety. *Given your work on both technological risks and*

DOI: 10.1201/9781003626510-2

post-instrumental futures, how do you see this disorientation and anxiety shaping humanity?

Professor Bostrom—I think it will intensify as we get further into the transition and get more advanced levels of AI and digital minds. It is genuinely quite disorienting, and the pace of change will pick up. Retaining some adequate degree of sanity, wisdom, and human decency throughout this process will be important, individually and collectively. Ultimately, we can emerge on the other side of that, and I'm hopeful that something wonderful is possible if we get things right.

Question 3. One of the foundational issues underlying technical questions about what constitutes Artificial General Intelligence (AGI) is the deeper epistemological question of what intelligence is. You were among the first philosophers to systematically work through this problem. In your early work, you defined intelligence broadly—as a 'panoply of cognitive capacities': analytical reasoning, creativity, social intuition, wisdom, practical know-how, etc. *Given the rapid development of AI systems that excel in some of these domains while remaining limited in others, where do you stand on this fundamental question now?*

Professor Bostrom—As we move closer, we can see more detail. What from afar could only be characterised abstractly as 'AGI' or 'superintelligence' can now be differentiated into a more articulated set of particular capabilities. However, the idea of a general learning system, which can develop capacities across a wide range of domains, has held up amazingly well. I'm not sure it's very fruitful to debate what is the true essence of intelligence: I think that question is largely terminological. Look instead at how these systems work, what they can do, and what we can reasonably expect them to be able to do in the future.

Part II—Ethics, Society, and Political Economy

The implications of technological transformation for human life, values, and social structure.

Question 4. You have written extensively about how transformative technologies might enhance human capabilities. *How do you think we can approach the tension between AI improving human life and preserving what we value about being human?*

Professor Bostrom—I would suggest we need to think in terms of trajectories rather than merely desired end states. Consider an infant: in many ways quite a different being than a grown man or a woman. If you had a magical ability to instantaneously grow an infant into adult and give it all the capabilities and knowledge of an adult, I think you could make the case that you wouldn't really have enhanced the infant but instead simply replaced it with a bigger and more capable being: and far from being an act of kindness to the infant, this might be tantamount to killing it. At the same time, however, we don't think it is bad for an infant to eventually grow up—in fact, there would be something tragic about an infant that never grew or developed further. So, it seems that we value a more gradual process of transformation, one in which the being who is transformed is able to actively participate through their own choices and experiences. Something like this might also come to apply to human adults, once we gain the ability through technological progress to continue to develop and mature beyond what it is possible to do within a current human lifespan.

Question 5. You have reflected on how technology reshapes fundamental aspects of human society—labour, governance, economics, culture. *Recently, techno-pessimists and techno-optimists have diverged sharply on what humanity may face in the near future. Where do you situate yourself in this debate?*

Professor Bostrom—You might call me a 'fretful optimist'. I think the potential upside is truly enormous, but we don't know whether or not we will actually attain it; catastrophic outcomes are also possible.

Question 6. Often, your hypotheses and assessments imply a certain political-economic perspective. May I ask more directly: *Do you find the old radical Enlightenment question, from Rousseau and Diderot and culminating in the Marxist critique of capitalism, plausible? That is, the idea that civilisation and technological advancement, if not curbed, tend to generate an exploitative, stratified, and hierarchical society, if not a self-destructive one?*

Professor Bostrom—It's hard to generalise from just a few historical phases. Compared to hunter–gatherer societies, agricultural societies were more stratified and unequal. The industrial era also started out very unequal, but with the development of the modern welfare state, and catch-up growth in some previously very poor countries (e.g. China), some of this has been partly ameliorated. The future remains to be determined, and there may be different possibilities depending on the choices we make between here and there. The advent of machine superintelligence will reduce the value of human capital and might therefore comparatively increase the importance of other forms of capital; there could also be a strong first-mover advantage to developing superintelligence. It is possible that after some transitional, turbulent period, whatever inequalities remain might thereafter become fixed and permanent—though in a world of extreme economic abundance, it might be that even the comparatively poor might be filthy rich by our contemporary standards.

Part III—Futures, Post-Labour Humanity, and Meaning

Speculative reflection on trajectories, purpose, and the deep future of humanity.

Question 7. Your research spans both catastrophic risks and utopian possibilities. *When you look at the broad sweep of technological change through history, what trajectory or patterns do you see for humanity's relationship with technology?*

Professor Bostrom—I suspect that at the macroscale, there is a good deal of determinism, or quasi-determinism, about the shape of technology. At the microscale, technology is something we do—inventors invent things, entrepreneurs invest, government officials regulate or promote, etc. Yet if we zoom out, it seems to a large extent that technology is something that happens to us, as a result of vast social and economic forces and competition between countries, with nobody in charge of the process. And until just a few hundred years ago, although a lot of technology had accumulated since the Stone Age, the pace of advancement was so slow as to be unnoticeable over the course of a human lifespan. It is only recently that the idea that there is a kind of directionality to history became widespread—the ancients mostly thought that history was cyclical, because they couldn't perceive any growth in technology or cumulative change in the basic material conditions of humankind.

Question 8. Your recent work explores what human life might look like when technology can solve most of our current problems. *How do you think about questions of meaning and purpose in a world where the homo laborans is made redundant and human capabilities are no longer needed for practical tasks?*

Professor Bostrom—I would say that if purpose is your thing, then knock yourself out today. The world is currently shock-full of problems that need solving and misery that needs to be alleviated, and you could find many places where you could help by investing your time and effort. This is the golden age of purpose. At some point in the future, if things go well, especially with the transition to the era of machine superintelligence, it might be that these problems will have been solved. Or to the extent that problems remain, they will be more effectively addressed by AIs than by humans. Then we will lose some of the purpose we have today, although overall I think that will be much for the better. And we would retain the ability, if we want, to create 'artificial purpose', as we do when we play games and set ourselves arbitrary goals in order to enable some activity that we find worthwhile. But if the real purpose has a special value, then it might be wise to stuff our lives full of it now while it is so plentiful.

Question 9. Lastly, looking ahead 50 to 100 years, and drawing from the entire arc of your work: *What gives you the most hope about the future of humanity, and what keeps you up at night?*

Professor Bostrom—In the end, it might come down to whether love is stronger than hate—and therein lies both the hope and the fear. The evidence from human life on Earth so far seems mixed.

Acknowledgement

The Editors would like to thank Toby Newberry, Chief of Staff to Professor Bostrom, for facilitating this interview.

3

Artificial Intelligence and the Traumatisation of Human Culture

Todd Madigan

I believe that someday we will make something that qualifies as an AGI … the world will have a two-week freakout, and then people will go on with their lives.

—Sam Altman
CEO of OpenAI, speculating on the world's reaction to the development of Artificial General Intelligence (AGI)

Rather than entering the debate regarding the possibility of AI[1] developing consciousness,[2] this chapter explores an answer to the following question: What if a significant number of people *believed* that machines had become endowed with that special sort of consciousness that has been traditionally understood as unique to human persons?[3] While such an event would undoubtedly have many far-reaching consequences, this piece will focus on just one: *trauma*. Specifically, the traumatisation of society is a phenomenon known in the social sciences as *cultural trauma*. A society is traumatised when it experiences some event as so grievous that it shatters the group's self-understanding. And in response to that devastating experience, there follows a contentious effort to develop a new collective identity, an effort that often pits various groups against each other as they struggle to reach consensus regarding the society's reconstructed identity. No matter the outcome of this process, the social group will never be the same.

In what follows, I will take issue with the claim made by AI advocate Sam Altman in the epigraph by arguing that a widespread belief that machines have achieved consciousness will likely lead to sustained social disruption and lasting cultural change. However, unlike many other commentators on AI, I will not address economic issues, new technological possibilities, surveillance concerns, fears of weaponisation, or any other material factors (including nightmarish attempts by AI to exterminate the human species). Instead, this chapter will map out a very specific sort of cultural process. I

DOI: 10.1201/9781003626510-3

will begin by elucidating the theory of cultural trauma, a theory built on the concept of collective identity (i.e., how we think about and identify with the social groups to which we belong). Next, I will describe some of the common ways of understanding ourselves as human persons in contemporary American culture. In particular, I will illustrate widely shared beliefs regarding what makes humans unique and entitled to both legal and ethical rights and responsibilities. Then, I will lay out the process of cultural trauma that will obtain if enough people within society come to believe that machines have become endowed with that special sort of consciousness that has been traditionally understood as unique to persons. Finally, I will make the case as to why we should take note of this potentiality and the ameliorative role that the theory of cultural trauma might play in our response to this monumental social and technological transformation.

Cultural Trauma

The claim that societies can be traumatised relies on a metaphorical extension of the more familiar notion of individual psychic trauma (e.g., the sort of trauma codified in the DSM as posttraumatic stress disorder).[4] If at first this innovative extension from the individual to the collective seems improbable, it becomes more plausible when we remember that the notion of individual psychic trauma is itself a metaphorical extension of individual *physical* trauma (Luckhurst, 2008: 2–3). Indeed, the English word *trauma* is simply the transliteration of the ancient Greek word meaning "wound" (*Oxford English Dictionary*, 1986), and until the close of the nineteenth century, it was used almost exclusively to describe wounds to the *physical* body (Luckhurst, 2008: 2).

The seminal elaboration of cultural trauma is formulated by sociologist Jeffrey Alexander: "Cultural trauma occurs when members of a collectivity feel they have been subjected to a horrendous event that leaves indelible marks upon their group consciousness, marking their memories forever and changing their future identity in fundamental and irrevocable ways" (2004: 1). At its core, this description has two principal moments: first, an event must be interpreted as catastrophic, and second, the event (as interpreted) must lead to a transformation of the society's self-conception. And while for the sake of exposition I present these moments as consecutive, it is more accurate to say that the first moment is analytically prior to the second, for they are so mutually reinforcing that, practically speaking, they are largely concurrent. That said, for the rest of this section, I will expound these twin components in an effort to provide a working understanding of cultural trauma as a social phenomenon.

Critical to the concept of cultural trauma theory is the claim that "events are not, in and of themselves, traumatic" (Alexander, 2004: 8). Instead, events must be constructed as traumatic. That is to say, in order for an event to be culturally traumatic, it "must be interpreted and articulated as such by members of society" (Madigan, 2020: 46). And this stands to reason: social bodies are not physical bodies. Physical bodies are subject to physical laws that will, when a body is struck with sufficient force, mechanistically produce wounds (i.e., *trauma*). However, social bodies are subject to no such laws. Instead, whether a social group experiences some phenomenon as catastrophic (and therefore potentially traumatic) is wholly determined by social processes, which are themselves shaped by a whole constellation of contingent institutions, including state apparatuses, ideologies, and symbolic structures. And the primary means of accomplishing this construction of catastrophe is *storytelling*. As social theorist Donald Polkinghorne notes, narratives

> filter and organise information from the physical realms and transform it into the meanings that make up human knowledge and experience. On the basis on this constructed experience, we understand ourselves and the world, and we make decisions and plans regarding how we will act.
>
> **(1988: 158)**

For some, the claim that cultural traumas are "made, not born" (Smelser, 2004: 37) is counterintuitive. After all, if (for example) the lives of some number of people are violently cut short in a massive flood or spectacular act of terrorism, or if entire ways of life are disrupted by widespread financial collapse or ruinous famine, one might ask, Where is the "social construction" in that? But of course, in order for the surviving members of a social group—particularly those who were not present for the event (e.g., not present in the specific areas affected by the flood or act of terrorism, or not yet born at the time of the financial collapse or famine)—in order for these members to be affected, the event must be communicated to them. And human communication is seldom confined to mere statements of fact. Instead, human communication synthesises objective phenomena with varying perspectives on relevant historical contexts, the purported motivations of the individuals involved, extenuating circumstances, and attributions of guilt or innocence, all of which are linked together causally into comprehensive narratives. Here is how historiographer Hayden White puts it: "Narrative accounts do not consist only of factual statements (singular existential propositions) and arguments; they consist also of poetic and rhetorical elements by which what would otherwise be a list of facts is transformed into a story" (White, 1992: 39). What's more, every narrative "has a plot, a particular arrangement of actions. And every plot has a *eudaemonic path*; that is, every plot traces the trajectory of a protagonist's complete movement between states of fortune (e.g., from happiness to misery)" (Madigan, 2023: 331 italics in original). In other words, based on its eudaemonic path, every narrative about a social group answers the question, *"Are things getting – or have they gotten – better or worse?"* (Madigan, 2023: 331 italics in original). This is one of the reasons why particular narratives featuring one's collectivity carry such extraordinary ethical and emotional gravity—they purport to say something vital regarding the well-being of one's social group, a claim that is of paramount importance to such social beings as ourselves. And these stories about our collectivities are related through a variety of modes, including works of literature, films, and television shows; news reports, historiography, social media posts, and casual conversation; and the discourse of political, religious, academic, and cultural leaders—much of which is additionally refracted through the forces of state apparatuses and corporate-controlled algorithms. Regarding the latter, Massimo Airoldi remarks that "algorithms are instruments of power.... They can learn how to speak like humans, how to write like philosophers, how to recommend songs like experts" (Airoldi, 2022: x). We might add (to make the point explicitly) that algorithms themselves will also generate narratives about human collective identity.

In response to any harrowing incident—real or imagined[5]—that captures the attention of a significant portion of a social group (e.g., a natural disaster, a war, a genocide, an assassination, an industrial accident, a dramatic political reversal, and a betrayal), multiple interpretations of the event will begin to circulate in narrative form, each purporting to describe the "true" nature and significance of the episode and how it ought to be understood and remembered. Inevitably, many of these narratives will be incompatible, and the public discourse among those espousing different interpretations is frequently contentious. Notwithstanding how disputatious this process becomes, it is often the case that a particular version of the story becomes widely accepted, and when the accepted story interprets the episode as so calamitous for the social group that it is cognitively unassimilable (Caruth, 1996: 4), the first element of the cultural trauma process has been satisfied. In other words, the stage is set for cultural trauma when a social group simply cannot reconcile the accepted narrative of an event with its own self-conception (e.g., "We are not the kind of people who do that sort of thing, yet it is undeniable that that is precisely what we did"; or "We are invincible, yet it is undeniable that we are defeated"; or "We are who we are because of our connection to our homeland, yet it is undeniable that we are now refugees in a faraway place"). However, a devastating event—even one marked in the group's collective memory forever—is not enough to constitute a cultural trauma (Madigan, 2020: 49).

The culmination of the cultural trauma process occurs if-and-only-if the social group comes to a new self-understanding in response to the traumatic event. That is to say, a social group experiences cultural trauma when the collective cognitive dissonance generated by a calamitous event leads to the revision of the group's collective identity. This new self-conception of the group can be understood by its members as the result of either (a) a transformation of the group's character that occurred as a consequence of the traumatic event or (b) an epiphany (brought on by the traumatic event) of the group's "true" character, a character that—heretofore unrecognised by the group—had been there all along.[6] Much like the process of developing a shared understanding of the traumatic incident, the narrative reconstruction of collective identity is usually factious. Indeed, we can consider a society to be caught in the throes of trauma during this period: unless and until the social group comes to relative consensus regarding its revised identity, it will remain fractured, and the trauma process will not conclude: the wound will not heal.

A particularly telling instance of how disruptive and injurious the throes of cultural trauma can become is exemplified in the case of the Vietnamese-American community. Because "Individual security is anchored in structures of emotional and cultural expectations" that are themselves "rooted in the sturdiness of the collectivities of which individuals are a part" (Alexander, 2004: 10), it is not surprising that the splintering of collective identity would bring with it the potential for great human suffering. As the Vietnamese-American community has grappled with its own competing narratives of the war in Vietnam, the fall of Saigon, and their collective identity in light of the group's resettlement in the United States, there have been numerous examples of large-scale public disorder (e.g., when—in response to a Vietnamese-American art exhibit—hundreds of Vietnamese-American demonstrators gathered for days around the gallery, eventually defacing some of the artwork and closing down the exhibition), physical assault (e.g., when—in response to a Vietnamese-American owned video store's display of an image of Ho Chi Minh—a 53-day protest, at times including thousands of Vietnamese-American community members, led to blows struck against both the video store owner and his lawyer), and even murder (e.g., when four Vietnamese-American men took 41 hostages in an electronics store, demanding a helicopter and materiel to return to Vietnam and fight the Vietnamese communists; the standoff with police left eleven hostages wounded, three dead, and three of the four hostage-takers dead) (Eyerman, Madigan, and Ring, 2023: 237–325). In each of these cases (and many more, besides), the discord was motivated by competing narratives, illustrating the power this cultural process has to create substantial material harm.

The resolution of the cultural trauma process occurs when the social group comes to see its collective identity in a profoundly new way as a result of the traumatic event. And—much like the understanding of the inciting incident—this new self-conception is born of and sustained through narrative, for, as political scientists Lewis and Sandra Hinchman point out, "Narratives … are what constitute community. They explain a group to itself" (2001: 235). Indeed (they add), "without the consensus that narratives help to establish, the memories they help preserve, and the values and behavior-patterns they transmit, culture would be impossible" (Hinchman and Hinchman, 2001: 235). Thus, healing from this sort of social wound takes place only when the group's new self-conception has become broadly accepted and relatively stable. And here it is important to point out that there is no guarantee that this resolution will occur. It is entirely possible that the throes of trauma will continue indefinitely, leaving a society fragmented and without a broadly shared understanding of itself.

To summarise and refine the complex social process that is cultural trauma, we can step back and conceptualise it in context as actually comprising not two but four analytically distinct moments:[7] (1) *pre-trauma*: a social group has a broadly shared narrative of collective identity; (2) *the traumatic event*: a significant portion of that social group comes to view some phenomenon (e.g., a war) as catastrophic; (3) *the throes of trauma*: a significant portion of that social group believes the traumatic event to have rendered its previously shared narrative of collective identity untenable, and in response, different segments of the social body vie with one another to have their preferred new narrative of collective identity broadly accepted; and (4) *resolution*: the social group largely comes to share some new narrative of collective identity, one different from its pre-trauma narrative of collective identity.

Based on the preceding elaboration of the cultural trauma process, I will next delineate the collective identity on which my thesis turns: the social group comprising *persons*. A clear pre-trauma account of this collectivity is critical, for my argument is that the widespread acceptance of machine consciousness might lead to a fracturing of our shared human identity. And such fracturing will necessitate a revision of what it means to be a person, a revision in collective identity that is the hallmark of cultural trauma. As theologian Bruce Ware puts it, "One of the gravest issues of our day concerns the nature of human personhood" (2009: 18).

Contemporary Concepts of Personhood

Discourse on what makes humans metaphysically special has been ongoing for millennia, and an interminable parade of variations on the nature of personhood continues to make its way through contemporary cultures (see Lolordo, 2019). Each of these variations has been accepted by some, modified by others, rejected by still others, and no doubt in some cases entirely forgotten by all. And depending on how fine-grained the analysis, one could argue (with only moderate exaggeration) that there have been as many conceptions of what it means to be a person as there have been people to think them. Be that as it may, what is relevant for this inquiry are the contours of the discourse on metaphysical personhood in contemporary American culture, contours that are of course shared by many other cultures around the world. The purpose of this section, then, is not to present an exhaustive exposition, but rather to highlight some general ways of thinking about what it means to be a person in order to contemplate what the trauma process might look like for this particular social group.

To begin, it is important to acknowledge that in everyday language, Americans use the terms *human* and *person* somewhat interchangeably, for they are largely taken as coextensive in contemporary American culture.

Philosopher Tom Beauchamp says as much when he writes "The common sense concept of person is, roughly speaking, identical with the concept of human being" (1999: 311), and philosopher Daniel Dennett agrees, asserting that we normally "treat humanity as the deciding mark of personhood" (1976: 175). However, to insist on this interchangeability would be to circumvent the question I mean to address. After all, I am exploring what might happen should a large number of humans come to believe that machines had attained that special sort of consciousness that has been traditionally understood as unique to human persons. The question that would then confront the humans who had adopted this belief is: Have these machines become *persons*? Not, have these machines become *homo sapiens*? For, as Dennett observes, "What is important about us is not that we are of the same biological species, but that we are both persons" (1976: 175). This distinction is important because we accord to persons a whole raft of moral rights and duties, along with corresponding legal protections and responsibilities, *because* they are persons (Preston, 2019: 263). And (as I have argued above regarding how we come to understand the world) one of the primary means by which we make the determination regarding which entities are considered persons is through the embrace of certain narratives.

Historically, in the Western world, biblical narratives have exercised enormous influence in terms of how we understand personhood, but those narratives have always been—and continue to be—interpreted, supplemented, and challenged through a panoply of other historical, autobiographical, fictional, scientific, and philosophical stories. In the Modern period, examples of these include Las Casas's *Short Account of the Destruction of the Indies* (1552), Locke's *Two Treatises of Government* (1689), Pope's *Essay on Man* (1733), Wollstonecraft's *Vindication of the Rights of Woman* (1797), Douglas's *My Bondage, My Freedom* (1855), Truth's "Ain't I a Woman" speech (1851), Darwin's *Origin of Species* (1859), Dostoevsky's *Crime and Punishment* (1866), Freud's *Five Lectures on Psycho-Analysis* (1910), Camus's *The Stranger* (1942), and Solzhenitsyn's *Gulag Archipelago* (1973). And of course, these narratives are themselves further amplified, repudiated, amended, embellished, and transformed through countless scholarly commentaries, classroom lectures, political speeches, news articles, conversations with friends and family, social media posts, religious homilies, legal filings, television programs, and on and on.

In each of the works listed above (a list to which every reader could add considerably), questions about the nature of personhood (including—explicitly or implicitly—who ought to be considered a person) are surfaced and addressed. But in each case—even in the most overtly non-fiction of the works—narratives are deployed to great rhetorical effect. That is to say, characters are depicted as interacting meaningfully with one another in such a way as to constitute a unified whole. And this narrative element is important, because narratives are quintessentially vehicles for normative meaning. In the words of Hayden White, every story "points to a moral" (1981: 13). Whether it is appalling stories of the enslavement, torture, and murder of indigenous people in the Americas by the Spanish colonial authorities (Las Casas); a tale of the emergence of human social groups from the state of nature into voluntary civil society (Locke); or an extended analogy involving personified psychic phenomena being thrown from a lecture hall (Freud); in every case, metaphysical points are being made about personhood, and these metaphysical points are freighted with moral implications. Or perhaps the moral implications of personhood are themselves the driving force behind the metaphysical claims. This is what Beauchamp argues:

> Ideally, a pure metaphysical theory expresses a morally detached interest in how to distinguish persons from nonpersons. However, the metaphysics of persons has often been put to work to defend a preferred moral outcome, placing metaphysics in the service of ethics. Metaphysics is invoked to inquire whether individuals have rights and whether the theory of persons can address practical problems.
>
> **(Beauchamp, 1999: 309)**

With this in mind, I will now sketch a few of the major models of personhood prevalent in contemporary American culture. At the most general level of abstraction, we can divide commonly held concepts of what it means to be a person into two categories: functionalist and essentialist. The functionalist position asserts that personhood derives from how an entity expresses itself in the world. This expression is often based on the manifestation of certain traits or capabilities, such as consciousness, reasoning, self-motivated activity, the capacity to communicate, and the presence of self-concepts and self-awareness (Warren, 1973: 55). Alternatively, essentialist theories of personhood maintain that there is in fact some objective and immutable essence inherent in persons that delineates them as such, irrespective of how that essence might (or might not) express itself in the world. The argument for essentialist theories of person sometimes rests on the notion that (to take one example) in order for a person to act rationally, they must possess a rational nature (Sutton, 1990: 8). More commonly, the essentialist model of personhood is founded on the belief that persons are persons precisely because they have a soul or participate in some other special way of the divine. For example, "At the heart of a biblical notion of personhood is the belief that humans beings are the *imago Dei*, the image of God" (Mitchell, n.d.; also, Sullivan, 2008).

Furthermore, the essentialist and functionalist models of personhood can themselves each be divided into two types: transcendent and immanent. In transcendent models, the function or essence of what it is to be a person derives from a source beyond the natural world. In the case of essentialist models, transcendence is often taken for granted: persons are persons because of their participation in some divine essence or other spiritual energy that lies outside the natural world. But there is no contradiction in holding a transcendent functionalist model of personhood. As philosopher

David Anderson notes, "even though functionalists tend to be physicalists, they must concede that it is at least imaginable that pain [or any other functional manifestation of personhood] could be realised in something other than molecules" (2003). In the same way, both functionalist and essentialist models of personhood may be immanent, locating the function or essence of personhood squarely within the natural world. In the case of immanent functionalists, the requisite function for personhood (e.g., consciousness) is understood to emerge through entirely physical processes; similarly, immanent essentialists understand the essence of personhood (e.g., rational nature and human nature) as arising directly from the natural world (e.g., through some concept of Natural Law).

A final relevant point here is that regardless of what model of personhood one accepts, that paradigm will not determine whether one accepts the full personhood of ostensibly conscious AI. The result of this indeterminacy means that acceptance of the full personhood of conscious AI cannot be predicted based on which paradigm one accepts, nor does this acceptance of conscious AI necessitate a move from one paradigm to another. For example, those who hold a transcendent understanding of personhood will not (e.g., for sake of logical consistency) be compelled to abandon this understanding and adopt an immanent paradigm. Nor will those who hold an essentialist model of personhood be compelled to adopt a functionalist model. For example, as psychologist Kathryn Johnson suggests, "people with a strong belief in a soul may be the most likely to attribute souls to AI as well, and consequently be the most likely to advocate for AI personhood" (cited in Ambrosino, 2018). Rather than inherently privileging any particular metaphysical model of personhood, the belief in conscious AI will instead be supported by a set of narratives, each of which will claim to account for machine personhood according to its own paradigmatic presuppositions.

Acceptance of AI Consciousness

In contemporary American culture, there are three concepts relevant to our topic that are generally accepted as correlative: the human species, personhood, and special consciousness. To date, the human animal is considered the sole entity endowed with personhood,[8] and this personhood is often predicated on the unique presence of what I have been calling *special consciousness*. It makes sense, then, that believing AI has developed special consciousness will threaten to fragment this tripartite conceptual unity, and with it, human collective identity.

While we await the point at which a significant portion of the population accepts that machines have developed consciousness[9] (a point that might, of course, like Godot, never arrive), we can trace out three likely results. First, it is entirely possible that people will affirm the development of a machine consciousness that is not "special" (i.e., not the sort of consciousness indicative of personhood). For example, pioneering computer scientist and AI critic Joseph Weizenbaum concedes that robotic AI might be able to develop "a kind of self-consciousness," but goes on to qualify this hypothetical possibility:

> When I say therefore that I am willing to regard such a robot as an "organism," I declare my willingness to consider it a kind of animal.... If both machines and humans are specializable, then we must ask in what way the socialization of the human must necessarily be different from that of the machine.... Every organism is socialized by the process of dealing with problems that confront it.... however much intelligence computers may attain ... theirs must always be an intelligence *alien* to genuine human problems and concerns.
>
> **(Weizenbaum, 1976: 210, 213 italics in original)**

While the belief that machines had developed animal-like consciousness would certainly be interesting, if this belief stopped short of attributing that special, human-like variety of consciousness to machines, then cultural trauma would not occur vis-à-vis the human social group. And we can make this claim because, although the belief that machines had developed animal-like consciousness might well result in substantial social change, it would not necessitate the re-narrating of our collective identity as human persons. Philosopher Barbara Gail Montero supports this perspective, asserting the following:

> Some worry that if A.I. becomes conscious, it will deserve our moral consideration—that it will have rights, that we will no longer be able to use it however we like, that we might need to guard against enslaving it. Yet as far as I can tell, there is no direct implication from the claim that a creature is conscious to the conclusion that it deserves our moral consideration. Or if there is one, a vast majority of Americans, at least, seem unaware of it. Only a small percentage of Americans are vegetarians. Just as A.I. has prompted us to see certain features of human intelligence as less valuable than we thought (like rote information retrieval and raw speed), so too will A.I. consciousness prompt us to conclude that not all forms of consciousness warrant moral consideration. Or rather, it will reinforce the view that many already seem to hold: that not all forms of consciousness are as morally valuable as our own.
>
> **(Montero, 2025)**

If Weizenbaum's and Montero's claims are the sort that people come broadly to accept—that AI consciousness is not the special type of consciousness we reserve for personhood—then no cultural trauma will ensue, for our shared identity as persons would be no more challenged by this belief than it is by the menu at a steakhouse.

But of course, the important question for the present inquiry is: What if a significant number of people believed that machines had become endowed with precisely that *special* sort of consciousness that has been traditionally understood as unique to human persons? In the case of this eventuality, there are two conspicuous possibilities: first, the concept of personhood—with all its ethical and legal corollaries—could be expanded to include AI. That is to say, any AI endowed with special consciousness would be considered a person. But this acceptance would mean a fundamental re-narration of what it means to be a person, for as mentioned above, personhood has traditionally been understood as unique to human beings. Alternatively, the belief that AI had developed special consciousness might result in a reconfiguration of what it means to be a person such that special conscious is no longer a sufficient quality for personhood. This reconfiguration would thereby exclude machines endowed with special consciousness from personhood. And again, because being a person—in contemporary American culture—is broadly understood as synonymous with being conscious in this special way, this second possibility would also necessitate a significant change to the narrative of human collective identity.

In spite of centuries worth of specialised discourse on the nature of personhood, along with the more recent rational argumentation over whether machines might develop consciousness, most people are neither theologians nor philosophers. Instead, we will on the whole continue to make meaning in the world through narratives. We will adopt a particular position vis-à-vis machine consciousness based on the narratives we find resonant due to unconscious factors, emotions, intuition, and so on (Alexander, 2003: 3). Although (as of this writing)[10] there is no widespread belief in conscious AI, narratives contemplating this eventuality already proliferate in film, literature, popular essays, and philosophical treatises. These include novels, such as Gibson's *Neuromancer* (1984), McEwan's *Machines Like Me* (2019), Ishiguro's *Klara and the Sun* (2021), and Divya's *Machinehood* (2021); films, such as Kubrick's *2001: A Space Odyssey* (1968), Scott's *Blade Runner* (1982), Spielberg's *A.I.* (2001), Jonze's *Her* (2013), and Garland's *Ex Machina* (2022); television series such as Paramount's *Star Trek: The Next Generation* (1987), HBO's *Westworld* (2016), and Apple's *Murderbot* (2025);[11] essays and works of nonfiction, such as Chalmers's "Facing Up to the Problem of Consciousness" (1995), Kurzweil's *The Singularity Is Near* (2005), Bostrom's *Superintelligence: Paths, Dangers, Strategies* (2014), Tegmark's *Life 3.0: Being Human in the Age of Artificial Intelligence* (2017), and Airoldi's *Machine Habitus: Toward a Sociology of Algorithms* (2022).

In these and other works on this theme, one of the questions put to the reading or viewing audience is this: If AI has special consciousness, are they persons? Furthermore, What does one's answer to that question imply about *human* personhood? For example, in a review of *Klara and the Sun*, the reviewer muses about the novel's narrator, an AI character called Klara, and asserts that the novel "is best read as a keen, suspenseful inquiry into the uniqueness of the human heart. Is there a soul, something, anything that's beyond the reach of technology...?" (Felicelli, 2021). In commenting on the AI character Ava in the film *Ex Machina*, another reviewer writes the following:

> The question of Ava's consciousness is only the start.... If we believe Ava is alive, will she be allowed to live that life on her own terms? Will her artificial life be held to the same standard as human life? Ava is corporate property, so at what point does the machine transcend its origin as an object and become a person?
>
> **(Fleet, 2022)**

A reviewer of *Machines Like Me* argues that the novel "manages to flesh out—literally and grippingly—questions about what constitutes a person, and the troubling future of humans" (McAlpin, 2019); a reviewer of *Blade Runner* claims that the AI characters (known as "replicants" in the film) "strive to create ways that will restore the personal to their lives," that in replicants "there remains a place for something human" (Newton, 2015); and in commenting on the HBO series, yet another reviewer observes that "The human heart in *Westworld* is not in its humans but in its robots" (Poniewozik, 2016). And even in the relevant works of non-fiction, it is narrative that does a great deal of the heavy lifting. Of *Superintelligence*, one reviewer writes

Bostrom captivates with a blend of profound insights, scholarly research, and a narrative style that is as engaging as it is enlightening. He meticulously constructs a scenario where "superintelligence"—a form of AI superior to the best human brains in practically every field—is not a matter of "if" but "when." (Vick, 2024)

And of *Machine Habitus* (a book peppered with narrative examples, including one describing a particular AI in Italy as a baby who listens and learns), yet another reviewer explains that "What Airoldi describes ... is an artificial intelligence that is becoming an artificial person" (Riggio, 2022: 10).

Of course, different readers or viewers of such narratives will respond differently to the questions raised about AI consciousness. As cultural anthropologist Clifford Geertz argues, interpretations (whether of literature or the social world) are "essentially contested" (1973: 29). That is to say, there is no final arbiter that will render a particular interpretation of any narrative objectively correct. Instead (just as I argued above in the case of narratives about human personhood), any narrative that broaches the idea of machine consciousness can potentially be coopted to buttress any model of personhood, whether that model brings AI together with humans as persons or reconfigures the notion of personhood such that even conscious AI is not included. Either way, in the event that there is widespread acceptance of machines endowed with special consciousness, the current narrative of human collective identity (i.e., that humans have a unique sort of consciousness that renders us—and only us—persons) is likely to fragment, thereby initiating the cultural trauma process.

Conclusion

While most studies of cultural trauma are retrospective (see Alexander, 2004; Eyerman, Alexander, and Breese, 2013; Madigan, 2020), the present chapter is prospective. The narratives of AI that are now circulating throughout many societies foreshadow the likely proliferation of ever more narratives addressing this topic should the day come when conscious AI is accepted as a fait accompli. These narratives will help produce—and in turn be produced by—the diverse human beliefs about conscious AI, and in doing so, will establish what Geertz calls the "webs of significance" (1973: 5) that create and sustain such beliefs. Once the traumatic event has occurred—once AI is widely understood to have developed that special sort of consciousness formerly considered solely the preserve of humans, thereby challenging long held beliefs about the uniqueness of human personhood—various narratives of our collective identity as human persons will also circulate. This is the period I have called the throes of cultural trauma. These heterogeneous narratives of collective identity, narratives that are among the most sacred to any social group, will be accepted and championed by disparate factions throughout society, and simultaneously opposed by others.[12]

Because of the moral, legal, political, and even spiritual ramifications of one's position on machine personhood, the prospect for social strife is high. Despite Sam Altman's rather facile claim included as this chapter's epigraph, that should there be popular acceptance of something like machine consciousness, "the world will have a two-week freakout, and then people will go on with their lives," I argue that the throes of the trauma process are likely to involve sustained political division, widespread unrest, and even violence. Given the potential for this process to cause genuine harm, future research in this field ought to include analyses of potential interventions that might lessen the likelihood or degree of that harm. In that vein, the work of philosopher Richard Rorty suggests a path forward. Rorty argues that social progress occurs as the result of re-describing the world through salutary metaphors (2008: 44, 55), and it is my assertion that cultural trauma is one such metaphor. In the same way that the metaphor of a psychic wound (i.e., psychic trauma) has generated a re-description of experience and novel therapies, which in turn have led to greater individual mental health and interpersonal connection, so too might the metaphor of a cultural wound lead to enhanced social solidarity and human flourishing. In what follows, I will propose the theoretical outlines of how this might happen.

While retrospective analyses of cultural trauma are obviously incapable of altering the suffering that has been experienced in the past, prospective analyses might be in a position to mitigate future distress. The suggestion I offer here is this: If a social group conceives of the controversy over machine personhood as the contentious-but-predictable throes of cultural trauma—in other words, if they recognise that their disputation is part of a discursive social process—then the cultural trauma metaphor might enable them to keep their rhetoric from inflating to an apocalyptic register, a register in which the stakes are seen as so high that efforts of rhetorical persuasion and political negotiation yield to illiberal attempts at domination.

In *Why War?*, sociologist Philip Smith argues that narratives—both fictive and those that we use to understand the real-world—can be cast in different registers, that the same narrative can be inflated or deflated (2005: 20ff.). When a narrative is maximally inflated, its characters are drawn in the starkest terms of good and evil, they are perceived to be inordinately powerful, and the stakes of any conflict are seen as existential. However, a deflated narrative—one cast in a lower register—features quotidian characters who are merely human, all too human, with all our well-known foibles, short-sightedness, and pettiness, as well as our capacity for kindness, compromise, and good sense. And at this lower narrative register, the stakes of disputes—even important disputes—are more terrestrial, more mundane, more prosaic. The thrust of Smith's book is that a nation governed by liberal principles will only commit to war's substantial sacrifice in blood and treasure when its people's dominant narrative about their situation vis-à-vis a perceived hostile nation is cast in the highest register, the register he calls "apocalyptic" (2005: 26). Thus, for example, Smith demonstrates that in the months leading up to the 2003 U.S.-led invasion of Iraq, the civil discourse in the United States (e.g., the speeches given by national leaders, the stories broadcast through the news media, conversations with friends and family) was largely cast in the apocalyptic register, focusing on the existential threat of purported weapons of mass destruction in the hands Iraq's president, Saddam Hussein, a blood-thirsty dictator. At the same time, in France, the civil discourse regarding Iraq tended toward the more conventional, workaday narratives of international diplomacy, weapons inspection regimes, and graduated sanctions (2003: 154ff.). And of course, while the U.S. went to war, France refused.

The upshot of this is that when one party in a dispute sees itself as locked in a struggle with an evil opponent who is irredeemably committed to one's destruction, it is far more likely that they will feel justified in illiberal acts that will lead to an increase in suffering. Contrariwise, if that same party understands itself to be engaged in a merely discursive struggle, in all its wearisome give-and-take with an opponent who is much like themselves, then even when the dispute is profoundly consequential and touches on collective identity, there is less likelihood that illiberal acts will be resorted to. This sort of narrative deflation through the adoption of the cultural trauma metaphor, along with its corresponding civil and prosocial discourse, is the promise held out by such a re-description of the coming tectonic event of AI consciousness.

Acknowledgements

A special thanks to Courtney Redihan, my undergraduate research assistant. Without her scintillating intellect and indefatigable attention to this project, this chapter would not have been possible. I also owe a debt of gratitude to Yale's Center for Cultural Sociology, whose fellows gave invaluable feedback on an earlier draft of this chapter.

Notes

1. Throughout this chapter, I will use "AI" (Artificial Intelligence) in the most generic way to refer to the sort of machine that might someday challenge the belief in the uniqueness of human persons qua persons. There are myriad other terms used in the literature to represent something similar, each with its own nuance (e.g., "Artificial General Intelligence," "Strong AI," "Superintelligence," "Artificial Consciousness," "Artificial Person"). Regarding the proliferation of these terms—and why the precise term is not critical for the purposes of this chapter—Subbarao Kambhampati, an AI researcher, remarks "Where these terminologies come from is anyone's guess.... These terms have become a commercial thing, a branding thing, an advertising thing, rather than a technical thing" (Metz, *NYT*, 6/20/2025).
2. Similar to the generic way, I will use "AI" in this chapter, I will use "consciousness" (usually with the descriptor "special") to refer to the quality or bundle of qualities that is considered unique to persons qua persons, well aware that the term does not capture every current concept of what that special quality comprises. For example, most people believe that at least some non-human animal species exhibit consciousness (thereby obviating consciousness as a *sufficient* indicator of personhood). What's more, many people believe that consciousness is not a *necessary* quality of personhood (e.g., those who argue for the presence of a "soul" as the sine qua non of personhood, irrespective of consciousness).
3. For the purposes of this chapter, I will focus my analysis on the discourse within contemporary American culture; therefore, the social group under consideration is American society, broadly conceived. Nevertheless, as many other societies share similar perspectives on what it means to be a human person, this analysis will likely be applicable beyond the confines of the United States.
4. Since 1980, *The Diagnostic and Statistical Manual of Mental Disorders* (DSM) has included an entry on Post Traumatic Stress Disorder (PTSD).

5. What is relevant for this social process is not whether an event actually happened, but rather, whether it is believed to have happened. For example, false conspiracy theories can have effects that are just as real as if the conspiracy were true.
6. Whether social groups have any metaphysical essence is irrelevant. The point is that in our social lives we commonly think, speak, and act as though they do.
7. It is helpful to remember that while these moments are analytically distinct, there is likely to be temporal overlap of moments two and three (*traumatic event* and *throes of trauma*). These moments are in some ways mutually reinforcing and can unfold over much of the same time period. The various narratives of the traumatic event put forward in society can influence the narratives of collective identity that are being considered, and vice versa.
8. Of course, the scope of this assertion is limited to the natural world. Some hold that God and other spiritual beings are persons, but those entities are beyond the range of this chapter. Similarly, while corporations are considered legal persons, this sort of personhood is understood by all as fundamentally different from the type of conscious persons relevant to this discussion.
9. There very well may be individuals or small subcultures that already accept that AI has developed special consciousness, but as of this writing (2025) this is not the case for American society as a whole.
10. 2025.
11. Some of these—particularly among the film and television examples—are based on earlier works, including novels and short stories.
12. We can imagine a similar trauma process playing out in the event that wide swaths of a society become convinced that alien life has this special sort of consciousness.

References

Airoldi, Massimo. 2022. *Machine Habitus: Toward a Sociology of Algorithms*. New York: Polity Press.

Alexander, Jeffrey. 2003. *The Meanings of Social Life*. New York: Oxford University Press.

Alexander, Jeffrey. 2004. "Toward a Theory of Cultural Trauma." In J. Alexander, R. Eyerman, B. Giesen, N. Smelser and P. Sztompka (eds). *Cultural Trauma and Collective Identity*. Berkeley, CA: University of California Press, pp. 1–30.

Altman, Sam. "A Conversation with OpenAI's Sam Altman and Microsoft's Satya Nadella." *Interview with Zanny Minton Beddoes, Editor-in-Chief of the Economist at Davos*. January 17, 2024. https://youtu.be/T2g8FF8-RLA?si=Ki18715cQBud9S7I (Accessed June 4, 2025).

Ambrosino, Brandon. 2018. "What Would It Mean for AI to Have A Soul?" *BBC*. June 17, 2018. https://www.bbc.com/future/article/20180615-can-artificial-intelligence-have-a-soul-and-religion (Accessed July 2, 2025).

Anderson, David. 2003. "Functionalism: An Introduction." *The Mind Project*. https://mind.ilstu.edu/curriculum/functionalism_intro/functionalism_intro.html (Accessed July 2, 2025).

Beauchamp, Tom. 1999. "The Failure of Theories of Persons." *Kennedy Institute of Ethics Journal*. 9(4): 309–324.
Caruth, Cathy. 1996. *Unclaimed Experience*. Baltimore: The Johns Hopkins University Press.
Dennett, Daniel. 1976. "Conditions of Personhood." In Amélie Rorty (ed). *The Identities of Persons*. Berkeley: University of California, pp. 175–196.
Eyerman, Ron, Jeffrey Alexander, and Elizabeth Butler Breese (eds). 2013. *Narrating Trauma*. Boulder: Paradigm.
Eyerman, Ron, Todd Madigan, and Magnus Ring. 2023. *Vietnam: A War, Not a Country*. Amsterdam: Amsterdam University Press.
Felicelli, Anita. 2021. "Bomb Under the Table: On Kazuo Ishiguro's Klara and the Sun." *Los Angeles Review of Books* (March 5, 2021).
Fleet, Adam. 2022. "Ex Machina: When You See This Sci-Fi Thriller, You'll Never Stop Thinking About It." The Guardian (May 3, 2022).
Geertz, Clifford. 1973. "Thick Description." In *The Interpretation of Cultures*. New York: Basic Books, pp. 3–30.
Hinchman, Lewis, and Sandra Hinchman. 2001. "Community." In Lewis Hinchman and Sandra Hinchman (eds). *Memory, Identity, Community*. Albany: State University of New York, pp. 235–240.
LoLordo, Antonia (ed). 2019. *Persons: A History*. New York: Oxford University Press.
Luckhurst, Roger. 2008. *The Trauma Question*. New York: Routledge.
Madigan, Todd. 2020. "Theories of Cultural Trauma." In Colin David and Hanna Meretoja (eds). *The Routledge Companion to Literature and Trauma*. New York: Routledge, pp. 55–66.
Madigan, Todd. 2023. "Farewell to Genre: Plot, Meaning, and the Syntax of Eudaemonic Paths." *Current Sociology*. 72(2): 330–348.
McAlpin, Heller. 2019. "In McEwan's Latest, The 'Machine' Is Too Much Like You." NPR. (April 23, 2019).
Metz, Cade. June 13, 2025. "Meta Is Building a Superintelligence Lab. What Is That?" *New York Times*. https://www.nytimes.com/2025/06/13/technology/meta-scale-ai-super-intelligence-lab.html?smid=nytcore-ios-share&referringSource=articleShare (Accessed June 20, 2025).
Mitchell, Philip. "A Biblical Model of Personhood." Dallas Baptist University. https://www.dbu.edu/mitchell/early-modern-resources/personho.html (Accessed June 29, 2025).
Montero, Barbara Gail. 2025. "A.I. Is on Its Way to Something Even More Remarkable Than Intelligence." *The New York Times* (November 11, 2025). https://www.nytimes.com/2025/11/08/opinion/ai-conscious-technology.html (Accessed December 14, 2025).
Newton, Michael. 2015. "Tears in rain? Why Blade Runner Is Timeless." *The Guardian* (March 14, 2015).
Oxford English Dictionary. 1986. Oxford: Oxford University Press.
Polkinghorne, Donald. 1988. *Narrative Knowing and the Human Sciences*. Albany: State University of New York Press.
Poniewozik, James. 2016. "Review: *Westworld* Is a Provocative but Flawed Sci-Fi Shoot-'Em-Up." *New York Times* (September 30, 2016).
Preston, Aaron. 2019. "Personhood in Twentieth- and Twenty-First Century Anglophone Philosophy." In Antonia LoLordo (ed). *Persons: A History*. New York: Oxford University Press, pp. 263–300.

Riggio, Adam. 2022. "Becoming Gestalt: Human and Algorithmic Intelligence—Review of Machine Habitus." *Social Epistemology Review and Reply Collective*. 11(5): 1–11.
Rorty, Richard. 2008. *Contingency, Irony, and Solidarity*. New York: Cambridge University Press.
Smelser, Neil. 2004. "Psychological Trauma and Cultural Trauma." In J. Alexander, R. Eyerman, B. Giesen, N. Smelser, and P. Sztompka (eds). *Cultural Trauma and Collective Identity*. Berkeley: University of California Press, pp. 31–59.
Smith, Philip. 2005. *Why War?* Chicago: Chicago University Press.
Sullivan, Dennis. 2008. "Defending Human Personhood: Some Insights from Natural Law." *Christian Scholar's Review*. 37(3): 289–302. https://christianscholars.com/defending-human-personhood-some-insights-from-natural-law/ (Accessed June 29, 2025).
Sutton, Agneta. 1990. "Arguments for Abortion of Abnormal Fetuses and the Moral Status of the Developing Embryo." *Ethics & Medicine*. 6(1): 5–10.
Vick, Aaron. 2024. "Review of 'Superintelligence: Paths, Dangers, Strategies' by Nick Bostrom." March 2, 2024. https://aaronvick.com/review-of-superintelligence-paths-dangers-strategies-by-nick-bostrom/ (Accessed July 14, 2025).
Ware, Bruce. 2009. "Human Personhood: An Analysis and Definition." *Southern Baptist Journal of Theology*. 13(2): 18–31.
Warren, Mary Anne. 1973. "On the Moral and Legal Status of Abortion." *The Monist*. 57(1): 43–61.
Weizenbaum, Joseph. 1976. *Computer Power and Human Reason*. San Francisco: W.H. Freeman and Company.
White, Hayden. 1981. "The Value of Narrativity in the Representation of Reality." In W.J.T. Mitchell (ed). *On Narrative*. Chicago: University of Chicago Press, pp. 1–24.
White, Hayden. 1992. "Historical Emplotment and the Story of Truth." In Saul Friedlander (ed). *Probing the Limits of Representation*. Cambridge: Harvard University Press, pp. 37–53.

4

Challenge as a Way of Knowing: Education for Critical Knowing in the Era of AI

Mary C. Lang and Jonathan Boymal

"Where does the mind stop and the rest of the world begin (Clark and Chalmers, 1998, p. 7)?" **"Who knows? Who decides? Who decides who decides (Zuboff, 2019, p. 222)?"**

This chapter considers these two questions—how we think and how we know—through the lens of autonomy and agency in our irreversibly socio-technical world. Without autonomy and agency in action and in thought, we humans have little capacity for the critical thinking and moral judgment necessary for a democratic society. Artificial intelligence (AI) is ushering in an era where thought autonomy is not an assumed and protected human right and knowledge agency is undermined in multiple ways. Challenge as a way of knowing offers one response to questions of thinking and knowing in educational contexts, as we grapple with the question: "Can the digital future be our home" (Zuboff, 2019, p. 4).

Human cognition is deeply social, embodied, and shaped by the environments in which we engage. Unlike AI, which operates through pattern recognition and statistical inference, human thinking is enriched by emotion, cultural contexts, social interaction, and the ability to challenge, reinterpret, and reshape knowledge. The concept of distributed cognition suggests that knowledge is extended and shaped through collaboration, allowing groups to exceed individual capabilities. A classroom discussion, for example, often produces insights that no single student could have generated alone—the shared reasoning, tools, and language of the group become part of the cognitive system itself. AI, as a cultural tool, challenges and expands our understanding of these processes, yet it lacks the self-reflectiveness and intentionality that define human agency. While AI can facilitate access to vast amounts of information, it lacks the ability to critically engage with, or challenge, the output it generates.

In an era where AI influences how humans think and create knowledge, understanding and exercising autonomy and agency becomes essential.

DOI: 10.1201/9781003626510-4

Specifically, we delve into epistemic autonomy for human thinking and epistemic agency for human knowing in the section "How We Think: Cognition and AI."

The final integration of these ideas positions "challenge" as a fundamental way of knowing in the AI era: just as inquiry is the cornerstone of critical thinking, challenge across intersections of socio-technical knowledge can anchor critical knowing in the AI age. If we believe that "juxtapositions constitute the pedagogical core of digital epistemology" (Ingvarsson, 2021, p. 45), we must recognise that this requires a reframing of challenge-based learning to imagine and navigate the juxtapositions of emerging technologies that deepen, rather than short-circuit, learning and social justice along with more deliberate interdisciplinarity across the humanities and the sciences in education. Education must go beyond preparing students to use AI tools, to embrace learning as struggle, engaged with ambiguity, contradiction, and ethical complexity. AI, by its nature, does not experience conflict or self-doubt, yet these are precisely the conditions that drive human growth and intellectual advancement. In a world increasingly shaped by AI, preserving the right to epistemic autonomy and agency becomes a pressing concern.

This chapter connects these cognitive, social, ethical, and epistemic dimensions to outline an approach for navigating the future of knowledge, ensuring that human intelligence is not merely augmented by AI but advances in ways that enable new levels of empowerment of the human spirit, potential, and flourishing.

How We Think: Cognition and AI

Generative artificial intelligence (GenAI) refers to systems capable of producing new content—such as text, images, or code—based on patterns learned from vast datasets. These systems often rely on metaphorical phrasing to convey technical processes. Anthropomorphic terms like "reasoning," "understanding," or "thinking" appear frequently in GenAI-generated responses. While there are clear accessibility benefits of having a minimally anthropomorphic chatbot interface that communicates naturally with humans without pretending to be human, the metaphorical weight of these particular terms can potentially mislead. The concept of "anthropomorphic seduction" (Peter et al., 2025) demonstrates why this is a risk, reminding us that GenAI technologies do not possess empathy or human understanding, but they can seductively appear as if they do. In other words, no GenAI chatbot is an actual doctor, they only play one on the web.

Many linguists, cognitive scientists, and philosophers suggest that our lives are lived in metaphor (Lakoff & Johnson, 1981). Without careful scrutiny, particular metaphors in GenAI outputs can obscure fundamental differences between AI and human cognition. For example, a metaphor such as referring to AI as a "digital brain" fits the conceptual metaphor theory of Lakoff and Johnson, by offering a familiar concepts, a brain that thinks, as a metaphor to help humans understand abstract technological abilities, such as statistical computation or massive rapid data processing. So when we talk about AI, we often use metaphors to turn difficult, abstract abilities ("statistical computation") into familiar ones ("thinking"). While potentially helpful, this tendency runs the risk of obscuring the difference between statistical correlation and semantic understanding. It reinforces the illusion that computer systems can truly "know" something.

The implications of obscuring these differences have been explored for decades, in research on anthropomorphic effects on human agency (Nass et al., 1993). This research, anchored in the seminal work on the "Computers are Social Actors" paradigm, also known as "CASA" (Nass et al., 1994), confirmed that people mindlessly apply social rules and expectations to computers and digital agents, even though they know these technologies are not truly human. This "CASA" paradigm has more recently been framed as "media are social actors" or a "MASA" paradigm (Lombard & Xu, 2021) to extend the original CASA concepts to emerging technologies such as AI. Irrespective of the framing, the premise and findings are consistent that users treat computers, chatbots, and AI as if they possess intentions, feelings, or personalities. There is also philosophical support for concerns about the CASA paradigm's impact on human agency, especially regarding human autonomy, technology-enabled manipulation of human agency, and trust in online contexts (Jongepier & Klenk, 2022).

At their core, large language models (LLMs) are trained to predict the next word in a sequence based on vast datasets of real-world language. Despite being trained on billions of tokens, the domain of all possible 20-word combinations is so enormous that any given prompt is usually novel, requiring the model to generate a response by identifying patterns in its training data rather than recalling specific sequences. This is fundamentally different from human-style reasoning or planning, which involves conscious, goal-directed thought processes; LLMs have no such internal deliberation. They respond purely based on statistical associations learned during training, so using terms like "reasoning" or "planning" is misleading and risks anthropomorphising what is ultimately a sophisticated gap-filling, pattern-matching system. The real power of LLMs lies in how well they interpolate: exploiting the structure of their neural architecture and the richness of their training data to produce coherent and contextually relevant continuations, even in unfamiliar situations.

Human cognition, in contrast, is a complex and multifaceted phenomenon, intricately woven into our physical experiences, emotional states, social contexts, and interactions with tools and technology. It extends beyond mere information processing, encompassing a range of dynamic and interconnected processes. Drawing from neuroscience, psychology, and human development, several key principles distinguish and illuminate human cognition.

One of the foundational principles is *embodied cognition*, which posits that our thoughts are not abstract and confined to the brain but are deeply rooted in our physical being. This perspective emphasises that our physical states, movements, and emotions profoundly shape how we process information and make decisions. Neuroscience research (Immordino-Yang, 2015) supports this, demonstrating that emotional states like stress and anxiety can impair cognitive functions such as memory, decision-making, and problem-solving. Conversely, positive emotional engagement, characterised by curiosity, excitement, and joy, enhances learning and retention by activating brain regions associated with motivation and reward.

The influence of embodiment extends to abstract cognitive tasks as well. Activities like moral reasoning and mathematical problem-solving recruit brain areas involved in visceral and emotional processing, highlighting the deep connection between our physiological and emotional states and our cognitive processes. Unlike LLMs, human cognition is intertwined with our biological needs and our ability to perceive and act in the world (Chemero, 2023). This embodied nature of human intelligence allows us to experience situations with a certain valence, motivating us to fulfil our needs.

In this context, *epistemic agency* refers to the capacity of individuals to take an active role in their own knowledge-making, rather than passively absorbing information. It encompasses the ability to critically evaluate one's beliefs, exercise intellectual virtues, take responsibility for the formation of those beliefs, and engage with culturally and socially defined norms of knowing. As Chen (2025) argues, epistemic agency involves not only internal reflection but also active participation in the social processes that shape knowledge, underscoring the fundamentally participatory and value-laden nature of human cognition. Examples of epistemic agency in action can include reminding others about prior lesson relevance to new topics, translating one another's ideas in ways that personalise the ideas to themselves, and making unsolicited connections to their lives (Carlone et al., 2021).

While epistemic agency emphasises active participation in knowledge-making, *epistemic autonomy* refers to the capacity to maintain self-directed control over one's epistemic practices—to think, judge, and inquire independently, even within social and institutional contexts that shape cognition. Autonomy implies the ability to navigate and critically appraise external influences (whether peers, authorities, or algorithms) without relinquishing intellectual responsibility. In educational settings, epistemic autonomy is visible when learners choose what evidence to trust, question established interpretations or resist premature closure in inquiry. In this sense, epistemic autonomy complements epistemic agency: while agency captures participation in collective meaning-making, autonomy captures the reflexive capacity to steer that participation in line with one's own epistemic values and commitments.

At the same time, as human intelligence is shaped by physical presence and interactions, this embodiment isolates us from one another; we are "locked-in," unlike machines that can share information instantly and precisely once networked. Human brains perform computations comparable to powerful supercomputers, but we are limited in externalising these thoughts (Lawrence, 2024).

Beyond the individual, cognition is also shaped by the environments and social contexts in which it occurs. The *theory of situated cognition* (Banerjee et al., 2025) posits that thinking is not an isolated mental activity but one that is embedded in cultural, physical, and social settings. People do not merely acquire knowledge in a vacuum; instead, they learn through interactions with their surroundings and the communities they are part of. For example, an individual's ability to solve a problem effectively depends on their familiarity with the context in which the problem is presented. Learning within a meaningful, real-world setting—such as through apprenticeships, internships, or collaborative projects—enhances comprehension and skill development. This is because knowledge is constructed in relation to real-life experiences, tools, and social dynamics, rather than being stored as abstract, context-independent information. Additionally, human cognition is influenced by cultural norms and collective knowledge. Different societies value distinct ways of reasoning, learning, and problem-solving, shaping the cognitive strategies that individuals develop over time. A child raised in an environment that emphasises storytelling and oral tradition, for instance, may develop stronger narrative-based reasoning skills, while one immersed in a technologically advanced setting may cultivate a different approach to logical and analytical thinking.

Another human aspect of cognition is the ability to resist, reinterpret, and reframe rules, which fosters critical thinking, creativity, and adaptability. This capacity to challenge conventions drives innovation and enables humans to imagine alternative futures. Internal conflict and reflection are also crucial, allowing for moral reasoning, empathy, and nuanced judgment.

In addition, *narrative cognition*, our innate ability to use storytelling to understand and navigate the world, allows our brains to instinctively employ "storythinking" (Fletcher & Benveniste, 2025) to reconstruct the past and anticipate the future, particularly in response to unexpected events. This process, which evolved as a survival mechanism, involves predicting outcomes and speculating on alternative possibilities.

In contrast to the mechanistic and disembodied processes of AI, human cognition is fundamentally shaped by emotion, embodiment, social context, and the drive for meaning—qualities that not only enable but demand active agency in how we create and share knowledge. As we turn from how we think to how we know, it becomes clear that safeguarding and strengthening epistemic autonomy and agency is essential for flourishing in the AI era. When technology offers an alluring but incomplete mirror of our humanity, understanding knowledge as a socially co-constructed process becomes all the more urgent.

Natural-Born Cyborgs: A Social Bridge Connects Cognition to Knowledge

Albert Bandura's concept of reciprocal determinism, central to his theory of social cognition, posits that rather than a passive recipient of information, cognition is an active process that shapes, and is itself shaped, by how knowledge is acquired, organised, and used (Bandura, 1986). Challenge serves as a catalyst within this dynamic interplay between cognition, behaviour, and environment. In this view, challenge is both shaped by and shaping of beliefs, actions, and surroundings; humans are not merely products of circumstance. We are also its producers.

Social dialogic challenge as a means of shaping knowledge can be seen in the most effective learning environments, for example, in school settings students in groups discussing a science problem, challenging and defending different ideas, including students directly challenging teachers to help them stress test their own ideas. This dialogue helps them learn from each other, rethink solutions, and build stronger knowledge. "Through discussion and debate, individuals can correct faulty knowledge, test ideas against others, and appraise different responses by observing their social consequences. This communal process shapes not only individual beliefs but also collective understanding" (Bandura, 1986, p. 36).

We often forget that knowledge has always been collaborative and deeply entangled with our tools (Sloman & Fernbach, 2017). The human mind has evolved to do the bare minimum that improves the fitness of its host. As a social species, we have evolved in collaborative contexts, outsourcing cognitive tasks wherever possible. As individuals, we store little information in our own heads; instead, knowledge is spread throughout our communities. In other words, the world itself is part of our memory. As groups have grown in size and complexity over time, we have developed new capabilities to sustain them, through specialisation, distributed expertise, and division of cognitive labour.

Andy Clark (2003) writes:

> It is our basic human nature to annex, exploit, and incorporate non-biological stuff deep into our mental profiles ... It is because our brains, more than those of any other animal on the planet, are primed to seek and consummate such intimate relations with nonbiological resources that we end up as bright and as capable of abstract thought as we are. It is because we are natural-born cyborgs, forever ready to merge our mental activities with the operations of pen, paper, and electronics, that we are able to understand the world as we do.
>
> **(p. 208)**

Given the environmental and social nature of cognition and the human urge to merge with emerging technologies, how will we nurture our capacity for reason in the AI era?

One enduring image of reason is that of the solitary thinker, quietly contemplating complex ideas. The intellectualist view of reason is as an individual human faculty, revealing truths that lie beyond the reach of perception or intuition. Yet, findings in cognitive science challenge this traditional view. In *The Enigma of Reason* (2017), Hugo Mercier and Dan Sperber build on Bandura's "interactionist" model of social learning (Bandura, 1977, pp. 11–13). Mercier and Sperber focus on the contrast of the "interactionist" model reason in contrast to the "intellectualist" model.

The central claim of the interactionist model is that reason is fundamentally social. It is best understood as a dialogical process—we reason by sharing justifications with others and assessing the justifications they offer in return. While we often struggle to objectively assess our own reasoning, we tend to be more adept at evaluating others' arguments. In this way, truth can only emerge from the mutual exchange of reasons. Truth requires challenge.

If this interactionist view holds, then developing our rational capacities depends not only on inward reflection but also on external engagement and challenge.

The emotional and social dimensions of thought are especially apparent when we consider how self-reflection can either liberate or burden the mind. Callard (2025) explains that Leo Tolstoy, whose inward moral scrutiny drove him into deep depression, exemplifies the isolating weight of solitary cognition. In contrast, Socrates' commitment to self-examination unfolded in the agora—through dialogue, debate, and shared reasoning. His famous dictum, "the unexamined life is not worth living," was never meant to be a solitary pursuit. It was a collective exercise in truth-seeking, anchored in mutual recognition and civic engagement. This comparison underscores the importance of socially situated reflection: when thought is decoupled from relational contexts, it can spiral into despair; when shared, it becomes a generative act of epistemic agency. AI lacks this capacity for shared meaning-making, highlighting the human experience of dialogic reason.

Extending the interactionist view further, we find that autonomy will play a defining role in cognition and judgement in the AI era. But how do we bridge the gap between individual cognition and agentive judgement that characterises the social construction of knowledge?

Here, the concept of capital provides a useful lens—specifically, Bourdieu's concept of cultural capital. While Bourdieu acknowledged the "brutal fact of universal reducibility to economics" (Bourdieu, 1986, p. 24) across his three forms of capital (economic, cultural, and social), he emphasised that cultural capital offers a way to understand how differences in social class produce unequal educational outcomes. Crucially, cultural capital is the least visible of Bourdieu's capitals, making it a powerful, yet often unrecognised, force in the reproduction of social structures. Educational institutions, in particular, function as major transmitters of cultural capital, by rewarding traits and experiences common among the privileged, and in doing so they are often unaware of the extent to which they reinforce inequality. For example, standardised tests and degrees privilege students who have had more resources and support, making it harder for others to compete. If our goal is to make education a more just social structure, then we must grapple with how human agency and capital shape opportunity. If we view judgement and knowledge as socially co-created, as the interactionist view within Bourdieu's capital construct suggests, we must consider where the capital of knowing is situated in the age of AI. To answer this, we turn to human agency and the form of capital that will increasingly define opportunity in the digital era: epistemic capital.

Tolstoy's descent into depression through private self-examination illustrates the risk of spending epistemic capital without replenishment. In solitude, one's beliefs go unchallenged and unsupported, leading to cognitive and emotional impoverishment. By contrast, Socratic inquiry—rooted in public dialogue—both consumes and regenerates epistemic capital: participants test their convictions in communal spaces, emerging with more robust, collectively justified knowledge. This dynamic underscores why education must cultivate the human agency of challenge—socially situated reflection and debate, rather than purely individual introspection—especially in an AI era where machines cannot partake in or bolster our shared epistemic reserves.

How We Know: Epistemic Capital and AI

To establish a common lexicon, we adopt the most apt definition of epistemic capital for our context, the definition from leading literacy and education justice scholars, Mary Kalantzis and Bill Cope. Kalantzis and Cope were a part of "The New London Group," that authored the seminal paper introducing the concept of "multiliteracies," launching a paradigm shift in how meaning-making is understood—as shaped by the varied life experiences of meaning makers (The New London Group, 1996). This foretold the development of an interactionist conception of reason.

Revisiting multiliteracies in the AI era, the authors asked the question: What kind of education is needed today to achieve social justice objectives? To which Cope and Kalantzis (2024b) propose this answer:

> an education that effectively opens access to the epistemic capital of our age. By epistemic capital, we mean capacities for knowledge as social action required for rewarding work, effective social participation, and personal meaning in an era permeated by digital media, and increasingly, the synergistic relations of human and artificial intelligence.
>
> **(p. 4)**

This definition moves education beyond the narrow purpose of developing students into employable workers. It repositions education as a means to cultivate social agents, equipped and empowered to contribute to social transformation. We share the lament that in the thirty years since the release of the original article on multiliteracies that education has failed to emerge as a stronger force for the achievement of social justice (Kalantzis & Cope, 2025, p. 146). Yet, we believe that, approached correctly, AI presents an opportunity to realise that elusive goal of education justice as a force for broader social justice.

Key to realising education justice, beyond the recognition of identities, is the development of agency that opens resource opportunities for individuals and social groups (Kalantzis & Cope, 2025, p. 147).

Emerging technologies, of which AI is only one, continue to usher in new forms of co-intelligence in our irreversibly socio-technical world. How we think about time and place have blurred, and the speed and accessibility of global communication continue to transform how we relate to others. While this should have resulted in concurrent education transformations, fundamentally, education has remained untransformed.

Writing on the history of education technology in the twenty-first century, Martin Weller (2020) notes that,

The first rule to learn about change in higher education is that very little changes while simultaneously everything changes. Therefore, any prediction that highlights just one of these elements underestimates either the core of immutability of the general higher education system or the degree of innovation that occurs within it. So, a prediction would be that the future of education will look not dissimilar on the surface, but closer inspection will reveal significant changes around the use of technology to support learning (p. 188).

This observation highlights a common paradox: we have become more efficient at doing the same things, even if those things no longer serve us well. As Weller suggests, we risk optimising a flawed system instead of transforming it.

Twenty years ago, Bandura emphasised that these types of "…transformative changes are placing a premium on the exercise of human agency to shape personal destinies and the national life of societies (Bandura, 2006, p. 175)." This growing primacy of human agency is visible across all areas of our lives, including in education where students can now, theoretically, exercise greater control over their own learning than ever before. However, there is a central issue of concern when it comes to agency as a driving force of how we will know, build knowledge, and gain access to epistemic capital in the AI era. The issue is that "…human agency does not come with a built-in value system" (Bandura, 2006, p. 177). For that we propose we must directly challenge the social nature of reason, meaning making, and knowledge.

As we shape our relationship with AI and other forms of human–machine co-intelligence, we ought to ensure the human side benefits from what we have already engineered into AI systems: continuous improvement through iterative learning. Ironically, this dynamic is often missing from human education models. We expect relentless progress from machines, while accepting stagnation or decline in ourselves. From much of the AI discourse, one might conclude that humanity has reached its peak, with our only remaining role to gracefully yield to the rising stars of machine intelligence.

This should not be how we shape the future.

The human journey with AI should be an interactionist journey, where humans are flourishing across ever greater dimensions, including intellectually. Challenge as an organising principle in education can help develop human agency's missing built-in value system.

While an instrumental view of education has its merits, it can also render learning abstract and impersonal, disconnecting it from deeper questions of meaning, identity, values, and social relevance. For many students, especially those motivated by concerns about justice, sustainability, or their role in shaping the future, this narrow frame may feel unfulfilling.

What is often missing in such models is challenge, not just in terms of academic rigour, but the deeper intellectual and ethical challenge that invites students to question assumptions, wrestle with ambiguity, explore who they are becoming through learning, and how they fit into the world at large. These challenges invite students to reflect on the ethical dilemmas of AI and invite them to become partners in shaping the human journey of AI in their own world and in society.

This echoes Dwight Eisenhower's (1958) vision of the "new responsibilities of education in the cause of freedom." Challenge as a way of knowing becomes a form of intellectual self-defence (Chomsky, 1989) in an era that risks sliding into epistemic entropy.

In the era of AI, challenge as a way of knowing requires the intentional shaping of the Socratic method. That shaping must amplify the one virtue of Plato's original four—prudence, justice, fortitude, and temperance—that he identified as the overarching virtue that enables all others. That virtue is justice.

Amplifying justice in education aligns with the concept of human flourishing (Clark & Gevorkyan, 2020) and invites a new set of questions: How can we design and evaluate AI systems that amplify human intelligence, coordinate human behaviour, and cultivate flourishing lives? (Reich, 2025) This shift demands that we move beyond the entrenched focus on computational thinking and towards a paradigm of critical ethical thinking, one that centres human flourishing. Computational paradigms alone cannot cultivate flourishing human lives; this will require critical ethical thinking.

Consider the great opportunity that such a shift may open. If we value social justice, we need to ask the essential questions: What are the social justice implications of AI in education? How might education leaders look beyond the near-term classroom impacts of generative AI to the long-term social implications of AI? The answer must begin with learning.

Opportunities to Cultivate Critical Knowing in the Classroom

There is guidance for educators willing to meet this challenge. For example, the United Nations offers recommendations for designing teaching around the principles of cooperation and solidarity, fostering relationships, empathy, compassion, ethics, environmental, and social consciousness, no matter which learning pathway is undertaken (United Nations, 2024). UNESCO offers comprehensive frameworks for both students and teachers on AI competency that are grounded in challenging educators to cultivate responsible, creative, and world-aware citizens (Miao & Cukurova, 2024).

Given that AI will change the nature of knowledge construction (aka "digital epistemology"), we must prepare students to act as social agents in a world infused with AI, a world that places human flourishing at its centre. One starting point is to teach students that challenge is a powerful, confident, and empowering way of knowing. With ethics and evidence on the table, we can shift our paradigm.

Critical ethical thinking is the most durable and transferable skill for preparing students to succeed in the AI era regardless of how technology evolves. As we work to develop critical ethical thinking, we must pay attention to the role that human agency will play in shaping what judgement and knowledge will look like in the age of AI.

Having defined epistemic capital as the capacity for knowledge as social action—a form of cultural capital in the AI era—we must now define epistemic agency and situate it within challenge as a way of knowing. A good definition that existed before the current AI frenzy defines epistemic agency as "students being positioned with, perceiving, and acting on, opportunities to shape the knowledge building work in their classroom community" (Miller et al., 2018, p. 6). Using this definition, we can build on two proposed opportunities to explicitly position students with agency, where they may perceive themselves as epistemically empowered to shape knowledge building in their learning community, and can act agentively: (1) opportunities to solicit and build on student knowledge as a resource for learning and (2) opportunities to build a knowledge product that is useful to students (Miller et al., 2018). Moreover, the AI era demands vigilant attention to how algorithmic decision-making disrupts epistemic agency. For example, lack of algorithmic transparency in AI raises the issue of "agency laundering" (Rubel et al., 2018), in which opaque algorithms put a distance between an algorithmic decision's impact on a person and any accountability for that decision. "For a person to have a reasonable degree of epistemic agency requires that they know where they stand, regardless of whether they can take action" (Rubel et al., 2018, pp. 9–13).

An Anecdote to Algorithmic Certainty: Design for the Conditions of Epistemic Agency

While beyond this chapter's scope, the implications of epistemic agency for education and social justice models remain a rich area for exploration. Likely models would include education as a means to societal transformation with the learner as a co-creator of knowledge (Freire, 1970), education as the practice of freedom (hooks, 1994), and education that moves beyond student or curriculum centrality to become world-centred education where preparation for future professional roles or economic productivity are not the sole organising principles, but rather the application of ethical, democratic, and present-focused engagement in service to igniting students' interest and participation in their world is what shapes education (Biesta, 2021). These three models support a goal of AI in service to human flourishing, each reflecting the interventionist view of social co-construction of knowledge.

For now, let us take a page from the playbooks of transformation leaders and transition designers. At present, it is unlikely, and not even desirable, that we can develop a tidy algorithm to predict human epistemic agency with certainty. Instead, we should approach the challenge as transformation and transition designers and look to create the conditions from which progress and transformation can emerge. Taking a design perspective—we can ask how do we design for the conditions that can help direct Bandura's primacy of agency in the era of AI, produce Miller's epistemic agency, recognise the conflicts of algorithmic effects on agency (Rubel et al., 2018), and open access to the epistemic capital of our age as described by Cope and Kalantzis within an education context. We might begin to formulate such an equation by asking, "How might human agency empower critical ethical challenge capabilities in the AI era?"

Further, we can explore how to capitalise on the general primacy of human agency, to foster specific epistemic agency that can cultivate broad access to the epistemic capital of our age. Which leads us to consider if we can design and deliver an education that effectively opens access to the epistemic capital of our age, and in doing so, transforms education to truly foster human flourishing in the AI era, in response to the question "What kind of education do we need today to achieve social justice objectives?" (Cope & Kalantzis, 2024b, p. 4).

Challenge as a Way of Knowing

Challenge as a way of knowing is neither a grand philosophy, nor a rigid framework. It is a response to the lack of a built-in value system in human agency amid AI-driven shifts in human–machine co-intelligence. The challenge we propose must arm students with exposure to specific perspectives in areas of expertise not currently centred in education. Neuroscience, data science, policy, social equity, technological fairness, navigating complex new forms of digital cyber-social environments, and connecting risks and benefits to local community contexts are seven core perspectives that will be intrinsically linked to critical knowing in the AI era. Challenging the ways in which AI itself will challenge and distort the very constructs of knowledge will require ever-deepening exposure to these seven core areas. For example, a nuanced understanding of technical fairness is a precursor to a learner's ability to challenge the AI tendency towards anchoring bias, (Carter & Liu, 2025) which is the prioritisation of initial information, especially if it appears frequently in public resources. Similarly, as will challenging confirmation echo, the common AI tendency for subsequent answers to inquiries to unconsciously "echo" the structure or ordering of initial responses, reinforcing the original framing even if user corrections or deeper evidence suggest otherwise (Brugnoli et al., 2019), and ordering inertia, the LLM tendency to default to the order most commonly presented in dictionary or encyclopaedic resources (Haber & Poesio, 2024). Similar examples can be made for the other six socio-technical areas.

Therefore, while questioning has always been central to critical thinking, AI introduces distinct areas of socio-technical intersections and juxtaposition that will lead to new ways of knowing, and approaches to learning must adapt. Just as asking the right question, inquiry, is the cornerstone of critical thinking; challenging across the intersections and juxtapositions of socio-technical knowledge in a newly informed and sequentially meaningful way can become the cornerstone of critical knowing in the AI era.

This intersectional challenge is the natural descendant to the inquiry that anchored critical thinking, and in an AI-infused world challenge, this cousin to inquiry, challenge, is a prerequisite to knowing. It may be the only reasonable response to how we educate students for, and in, a future where we cannot know what direction and form technology will take. Educating with challenge as the essential way of knowing can free students from the focus on memorisation and skill-chasing we still find at the heart of educational models. These embedded approaches do not serve students well today and will never keep pace with knowledge development needs in a future of constant learning and living where human flourishing depends on socially constructed judgement and wisdom.

Shaping challenge as a way of knowing in the age of AI is a concept that may be easy to grasp and name, yet difficult to do, made ever more difficult with perpetually emergent challenges such as we see today with the emergence of digital fossils. The term "digital fossils" captures the daunting epistemic challenge—the erosion of knowledge itself—that educators confront in the AI era. Digital fossils are to knowledge and truth what deep fakes are to visual persuasion and beliefs. The concept of "digital fossils" can be illustrated by the phrase "vegetative electron microscopy"

(Snoswell et al., 2025), a term that now appears in published academic papers. The authors describe the phrase vegetative electron microscopy as follows:

> This phrase, which sounds technical but is actually nonsense, has become a "digital fossil" an error preserved and reinforced in artificial intelligence (AI) systems that is nearly impossible to remove from our knowledge repositories. Like biological fossils trapped in rock, these digital artefacts may become permanent fixtures in our information ecosystem. The case of vegetative electron microscopy offers a troubling glimpse into how AI systems can perpetuate and amplify errors throughout our collective knowledge.
>
> **(paragraphs 2–4)**

With the advent of digital fossils, emerging technologies, including large language models, are exacerbating a dangerous dimension of the epistemic machine. The epistemic machine is a concept that has been explored to understand the politics of knowledge production (Tomlinson, 2020). Even prior to the AI rush, the epistemic machine was not a neutral or purely technical process, but one implicated in the reproduction of power, exclusion, and epistemic injustice (Fricker, 2009). The introduction of digital fossils introduces yet another element, this time deeper and virtually uncorrectable, of "knowledge rot" into the epistemic machine. This compounds the long list of early warnings about potential harms of AI (Bender et al., 2021; Horvitz, 2022), and foreboding actions that continue unabated, such as the large-scale abandonment of testing AI models for risks to epistemic coherence (Goldman & Kahn, 2025) and the recipe for irreconcilable post-epistemic dangers to knowledge and education, seem all but baked.

This is where the wonder of the human mind can steer the human journey with AI towards an interactionist direction, respecting that human reasoning is fundamentally a social, dialogic process, grounded in critical evaluation. This navigation begins with challenge.

As neither a grand philosophy, nor rigid framework, challenge is a natural evolution of what it means to know in education contexts at a time when AI is shifting what it means to learn in a human–machine co-intelligence relationship. An emerging relationship that has been described as cyber-social learning is outlined as an agenda for action in education contexts in the "Manifesto for Cyber-social Learning" (Cope & Kalantzis, 2024a, p. 26). Challenge as a way of knowing is a response to these emerging concepts in the AI era of convergence.

Further, observing an inversion of Bloom's Taxonomy, something that "challenges decades of pedagogical thinking built on the sequential climb up Bloom's hierarchy," leaves scholars to wonder, "If our most advanced learning tools don't follow this order, what does that mean for teaching and learning…?" (Galla et al., 2025, p. 1). Challenge is a lens to reimagine what this taxonomy inversion can mean for the landscape of human potential in collaboration with technology.

This is another mile on the path that began with Dewey's first introduction to the philosophy of education (Dewey, 1916) and has continued across 100 years of theories, methods, and approaches in the unending journey of human knowing. We are led to believe that machine intelligence is limitless; we should afford human intelligence that same level of hope and confidence as we move deeply into this AI era of convergence in education.

Convergence, with challenge at its core, builds most directly on the productive struggle model of learning (Warshauer, 2011), which falls into the camp of learning theory referred to as maturation, a phase when learning moves to mastery of multiple specialised thinking about a variety of things (Vygotskiĭ et al., 1978). This next level we propose shifts the learning paradigm beyond maturation, to the realm of knowing through autonomous and agentive challenge and discovery in the AI era of convergence.

Challenge is the most appropriate response to Bandura's caveat, the lack of a built-in value system in human agency. Educating in the AI era of convergence, with challenge as the essential way of knowing, seems an obvious approach to education that seeks first to foster thinking as its primary goal. However, while challenge may be the aspirational goal of many, it is not the operational reality for most. If it were, we would not still find the durable focus on memorisation, teaching-to-the-test, and employable skill-chasing at the pedagogical heart in many educational contexts. These embedded approaches do not serve students well today and will never keep pace with the knowledge development needs in a future of constant learning and living, where human flourishing depends on collective intelligence, socially constructed judgement and wisdom.

The first and most foundational level of challenge is epistemological: the challenge of knowledge and the assumptions underlying how we come to know. One of the most pervasive and troubling assumptions in the AI era is that certainty is not only achievable, but preferable: that the primary role of AI systems in education should be to deliver clear, definitive answers, minimising ambiguity and doubt. This assumption promotes a model of education focused on answer delivery, rather than the cultivation of critical inquiry, interpretive capacity, ethical judgement, and the ability to engage productively with uncertainty. Such an assumption is also at odds with the responsibilities of education in a democratic society. It undermines the pedagogical traditions championed by thinkers like Freire, hooks, and Biesta who emphasise critical engagement and transformation. We must challenge the notion that certainty can be algorithmically guaranteed across all domains of education. This challenge must begin early and recur throughout lifelong learning. Cultivating challenge as a habitual way of knowing should be a central aim of education in the AI era.

At its core, challenge as a way of knowing begins by interrogating the assumptions on which knowledge itself is built. This has long been a role of education, embodied in the practice of Socratic questioning, though not all educators consistently apply it. Frameworks for technology-supported structured inquiry have existed for decades (Edelson, 2021), and the dialogic approach builds out the blending of the Socratic method and structured inquiry that expands collective exploration and positions collective intelligence as a goal to empower global citizenship, a key adaptation students need to thrive in the era of complexity and AI (Wegerif, 2025). Structured approaches continue to evolve, including a new science of questioning, intentionally designed to cultivate inquiry and democratic skills from early grades through lifelong learning (Verhulst, 2025).

Emerging AI technologies are beginning to revitalise these approaches. Some AI systems, such as Anthropic for Education, are being explicitly designed to support this kind of cognitive engagement (Bent & Handa, 2025). Their effectiveness remains to be seen, but the potential is significant. The next level of challenge as a way of knowing in education builds on concepts of the role of doubt in education that take a philosophical and pedagogical perspective (Roberts, 2017) and recent work that identifies the concept of aspirational doubt as a form of doubt that may be able to transform education for the better (Schaper, 2025). Clearly, there are risks involved in introducing doubt into education design, and it is important to acknowledge that mental exertion, something that doubt inevitably exerts, is often associated with unpleasant feelings. Research indicates a correlation between greater mental effort and increased experience of unpleasantness (David et al., 2024). Yet, humans still voluntarily engage in mentally challenging tasks, for many reasons, because we are human!

Now, these concepts are being woven together with emerging fields such as augmented reasoning in computer–AI–human interaction (Danry et al., 2025). This is a compelling area of research from a human flourishing perspective, which holds promise for challenge as a way of knowing to develop critical ethical thinking. An example of augmented reasoning research relevant to challenge as a way of knowing by way of doubt is work that seeks to reimagine AI as a technology engine of doubt rather than a platform of certainty. Here, researchers are exploring questions about the possibility of harnessing intellectual discomfort to sharpen critical thinking. An example of this is "Cognitive Dissonance Artificial Intelligence (CD-AI): The Mind at War with Itself. Harnessing Discomfort to Sharpen Critical Thinking," one study of how the potential for integrating cognitive dissonance and AI may serve to help humans transcend passive cognition through active epistemic struggle (Deliu, 2025).

In a world obsessed with debatable artificial general intelligence (AGI), we should equally prioritise expanding the human mind's capacity to challenge and create knowledge beyond our current imagination. We must afford humans the same levels of autonomy and agency and invest in them at least the same level of possibilities and hope for development that we now afford and invest in our machines.

IRL: From Concept to Classroom

Once a theoretical debate, AI has transformed the question posed by Clark and Chalmers (1998), "Where does the mind stop and the rest of the world begin?" into as a serious practical dilemma for education. Zuboff's (2019) wicked question, "Who knows, who decides who knows, and who decides who decides?" must become a central grounding consideration for how we teach, learn, and design educational systems in the AI era.

Communication mediates everything, and increasingly, AI mediates most communication. As we enter a new phase of AI-infused education, we must reckon with the hard truth that decades of technology in classrooms have not led to meaningful educational transformation. Over two decades ago, Schank and Edelson observed that technology often overpowers theories of learning, shaping practice not because it is pedagogically sound, but because it is easy to implement (Schank & Edelson, 1989). Many instructional techniques persist simply because digital tools enable them, not because they help students think, question, or grow. The rise of AI risks repeating this pattern unless we resist the urge to retrofit old pedagogies with new tools and instead begin to build a new educational paradigm.

This paradigm must be rooted in challenge as a way of knowing. AI can support this, not as a knower, but as a "dead outer": a static provocation waiting to be brought to life by the questioning mind. Socrates once warned that writing was dead speech, incapable of dialogue unless animated by a living voice. We might now say the same of AI. Its outputs are not knowledge or wisdom, but raw material for critical engagement. When students reinterpret, interrogate, or resist what AI outputs, the technology becomes a site of epistemic activation.

This is the heart of epistemic capital as social action. Knowledge is not merely received or stored—it is enacted, justified, and reshaped through engagement. In educational practice, the challenge is not to treat AI as an authority, but to use it as a provocation. The machine becomes a prompt for critical reasoning, not a replacement for it. The goal is not to generate certainty, but to cultivate intellectual struggle and ethical complexity. This aligns with challenge-based learning and opens a new path for designing educational technologies that serve, rather than short-circuit, deep learning, reflecting the principles of challenge-based learning where students learn through inquiry, dialogue, and ethical complexity. In this framework, AI is not a knower but a tool for epistemic activation—brought to life by autonomous human agency and embedded in a communal process of meaning-making.

The two core principles of interdisciplinarity and struggle can root challenge as a way of knowing in classrooms, uniting teachers, students, and technologies. We have addressed the principle of struggle, grounded in the Socratic method, developed through deliberate consideration of the role of doubt in educational transformation, modernised through a manifesto for cyber-social learning, and entered its next horizon with the introduction of novel human–AI interaction approaches, such as cognitive dissonance AI (CD-AI).

Interdisciplinarity, the second principle, builds on the early pioneering work on multiliteracies (The New London Group, 1996), to the advent of the cyber-social learning concept in the AI era (Cope & Kalantzis, 2024a), AI literacy programmes grounded in interdisciplinary socio-technical curriculum (Tadimalla & Maher, 2024), and leading AI frameworks for teachers (Miao & Cukurova, 2024) and students (Miao & Cukurova, 2024) that highlight the central role of interdisciplinarity in preparing students for the ethical, technical, and societal dimensions of artificial intelligence.

This trajectory reflects what we now see across leading academic AI institutions, where interdisciplinarity is baked into the models for leadership, operations, and research agendas. The Stanford Institute for Human-Centered AI (HAI) strives to foster a culture of interdisciplinary AI research across science, humanities, and the arts; MIT's Computer Science and Artificial Intelligence Laboratory (CSAIL) is the university's largest interdisciplinary laboratory, and MIT's Advancing Humans with AI (AHA) is a multi-faculty research programme that aims to understand the human experience of pervasive AI and design the interaction between people and AI to foster human flourishing; the AI in Education at Oxford University (AIEOU) is a fully interdisciplinary research hub working across the world and disciplines to develop research agendas for AI in education; and among the newer institutes, we see the Center for Humane AI Studies (CHAIS) at the University of North Carolina, Charlotte, a hub for cutting-edge discovery, and interdisciplinary collaboration. The technology and our world reflect the necessity of learning with and about AI in a fully interdisciplinary framework.

These two principles are already coming to life in AI technology development for education. One example of interdisciplinarity on the horizon is from the Raspberry, PI Foundation, a UK-based charity with the mission to enable young people to realise their full potential through the power of computing and digital technologies. Their new (June 2025) Experience CS system is a free computer science curriculum designed for students ages 8–14. It enables even those without a computer science background to teach coding and digital skills using well-structured lessons, activity sheets, and assessment tools. The curriculum integrates computer science concepts into core subjects like mathematics, science, and social studies, so students learn how tech skills connect to real-world problems and schoolwork.

The principle of struggle is beginning to show up in systems such as Anthropic's Claude a family of large language models developed by Anthropic and first released in March 2023. The most recent release of Claude for Education (April 2025) included an intentionally Socratic framework, in its "AI Socratic Learning Mode." The concept is to shift the GenAI model learners are familiar with, where AI simply delivers answers, to a model where AI guides learners through Socratic questioning—to encourage reflection, reasoning, and critical analysis. We are encouraged to see efforts to intentionally design struggle and interdisciplinarity into AI systems for use in education, and it will be important to watch and evaluate the outcomes from these efforts. It will also be interesting to see possible testing of novel machine–human–AI interaction concepts such as the cognitive dissonance AI (CD-AI) for augmented reasoning discussed earlier.

The principle of interdisciplinarity can also operate at a broader, integrative level—what UNESCO describes as connecting different disciplines along with the social, emotional, and ethical dimensions of learning (Miao et al., 2024; Miao & Cukurova, 2024). In the coming years, we can expect growing efforts to design AI systems for education that intentionally weave challenge and interdisciplinarity together, accompanied by more systematic evaluations of their outcomes. If these developments continue, they may signal a movement away from the prevailing focus on task efficiency and productivity optimisation towards recognising epistemic challenge as a central driver of learning.

If we finally have the courage to remake education, now is the time. We are living through a moment as pivotal as the rise of social media two decades ago, a moment that beckons us not to digitise education that does not work, but to imagine education anew. Starting with just two principles—interdisciplinarity and struggle—we can cultivate challenge as a guiding way of knowing, in the learning AI era of convergence.

"Were all instructors to realise that the quality of mental process, not the production of correct answers, is the measure of educative growth, something hardly less than a revolution in teaching would be worked" (Dewey, 1916, p. 39).

The learning era of convergence in the age of AI establishes the conditions in which such a revolution can be worked. After 110 years, the confluence of human and machine intelligence finally enables Dewey's revolution to materialise.

Yet, here we are.

Summary

"AI may open a path to epistemic justice for all, in a world where, until now, education has been complicit in the systemic reproduction of wider social inequalities" (Cope et al., 2025).

To achieve the promise of epistemic justice for all, this chapter has argued that education in the age of AI must reclaim its human centre by cultivating challenge as a way of knowing. We traced how cognition, once conceived as an individual process, is now understood as distributed, embodied, and socially situated, and how these insights require a refocusing on epistemic agency and autonomy. In this socio-technical era, where AI increasingly mediates communication and knowledge, learners must be positioned as agents of epistemic challenge rather than consumers of algorithmic certainty. Drawing on traditions from Dewey to Freire and extending them into the realities of digital epistemology, we proposed that challenge, interdisciplinarity, and struggle form the core principles of a pedagogy for human flourishing. Challenge thus becomes both the method and the moral stance through which we shape knowledge, justice, and the future of learning.

References

Bandura, A. (1977). *Social Learning Theory*. Prentice-Hall.

Bandura, A. (1986). *Social Foundations of Thought and Action: A Social Cognitive Theory*. Prentice Hall.

Bandura, A. (2006). Toward a psychology of human agency. *Perspectives on Psychological Science*, *1*(2), 164–180.

Banerjee, A. V., Bhattacharjee, S., Chattopadhyay, R., Duflo, E., Ganimian, A. J., Rajah, K., & Spelke, E. S. (2025). Children's arithmetic skills do not transfer between applied and academic mathematics. *Nature*, *639*(8055), 673–681.

Bender, E. M., Gebru, T., McMillan-Major, A., & Shmitchell, S. (2021). On the dangers of stochastic parrots. In *Proceedings of the 2021 ACM Conference on Fairness, Accountability, and Transparency (FAT)* (pp. 610–623). Association for Computing Machinery.

Bent, D., & Handa, K. (2025, April 8). *Anthropic education report: How university students use claude*.\Anthropic.com

Biesta, G. (2021). *World-Centred Education: A View for the Present*. Routledge.

Bourdieu, P. (1986). The forms of capital. In *Handbook of Theory and Research for the Sociology of Education* (pp. 241–258). Essay.

Brugnoli, E., Cinelli, M., Quattrociocchi, W., & Scala, A. (2019). Recursive patterns in online echo chambers. *Scientific Reports*, *9*(1). https://doi.org/10.1038/s41598-019-56191-7

Callard, A. (2025). *Open Socrates: The Case for a Philosophical Life*. Recorded Books, Inc.

Carlone, H. B., Mercier, A. K., & Metzger, S. R. (2021). The production of epistemic culture and agency during a first-grade engineering design unit in an urban emergent school. *Journal of Pre-College Engineering Education Research (J-PEER)*, *11*(1). https://doi.org/10.7771/2157-9288.1295

Carter, L., & Liu, D. (2025). How was my performance? Exploring the role of anchoring bias in AI-assisted decision making. *International Journal of Information Management*, *82*, 102875. https://doi.org/10.1016/j.ijinfomgt.2025.102875

Chemero, A. (2023). LLMS differ from human cognition because they are not embodied. *Nature Human Behaviour*, *7*(11), 1828–1829.

Chen, B. (2025). Beyond Tools: Generative AI as Epistemic Infrastructure in Education. *arXiv*. https://doi.org/10.48550/arXiv.2504.06928

Chomsky, N. (1989). *Necessary Illusions: Thought Control in Democratic Societies*. South End Press.

Clark, A., & Chalmers, D. (1998). The extended mind. *Analysis*, *58*(1), 7–19.

Clark, A. (2003). *Natural-Born Cyborgs: Minds, Technologies and the Future of Human Intelligence*. Oxford University Press.

Clark, C. M., & Gevorkyan, A. V. (2020). Artificial intelligence and human flourishing. *The American Journal of Economics and Sociology, 79*(4), 1307–1344.

Cope, B., & Kalantzis, M. (2024a). On cyber-social learning: A critique of artificial intelligence in education. In T. Kourkoulou, A. O. Tzirides, B. Cope, & M. Kalantzis (Eds.), *Trust and Inclusion in AI-Mediated Education: Where Human Learning Meets Learning Machines* (pp. 3–34). Springer.

Cope, B., & Kalantzis, M. (2024b). Towards education justice: The multiliteracies project revisited. In G. C. Zapata, M. Kalantzis, & B. Cope (Eds.), *Multiliteracies in International Educational Contexts: Towards Education Justice* (pp. 1–33). Routledge.

Cope, B., Kalantzis, M., & Saini, A. K. (2025). The ends of tests: Possibilities for transformative assessment and learning with generative AI. In S. Isaacs, G. Hertelendy, & F. Apilado (Eds.), *AI and the Future of Education: Disruptions, Dilemmas and Directions* (pp. 81–89). UNESCO.

Danry, V., Pataranutaporn, P., Cui, C., Hung, J.-T., Blanchard, L., Buçinca, Z., Tan, C., Starner, T., & Maes, P. (2025). Human-AI interaction for augmented reasoning: Improving human reflective and critical thinking with Artificial Intelligence. In *Extended Abstracts of the CHI Conference on Human Factors in Computing Systems* (pp. 1–6). Association for Computing Machinery.

David, L., Vassena, E., & Bijleveld, E. (2024). The unpleasantness of thinking: A meta-analytic review of the association between mental effort and negative affect. *Psychological Bulletin, 150*(9), 1070–1093.

Deliu, D. (2025). Cognitive Dissonance Artificial Intelligence (CD-AI): The Mind at War with Itself. Harnessing Discomfort to Sharpen Critical Thinking. ACM Workshop on Human-AI Interaction for Augmented Reasoning (AIREASONING-2025-01). Yokohama.

Dewey, J. (1916). *Democracy and Education: An Introduction to the Philosophy of Education, by John Dewey*. Macmillan Co.

Edelson, D. (2021). Learning-for-use: A framework for the design of technology-supported inquiry activities. *Journal of Research in Science Teaching, 38*, 355–385.

Eisenhower, D. D. (1958, January 27). *Special message to the Congress on Education*. Special Message to the Congress on Education. | The American Presidency Project.

Fletcher, A., & Benveniste, M. (2025). *Narrative Creativity: An Introduction to How and Why*. Cambridge University Press.

Freire, P. (1970). *Pedagogy of the Oppressed: Transl. by Myra Bergman Ramos*. Herder and Herder.

Fricker, M. (2009). *Epistemic Injustice: Power and the Ethics of Knowing*. Oxford University Press.

Galla, M., Cope, B., & Kalantzis, M. (2025). Generative AI turns Bloom's taxonomy upside-down: Implications for creativity and Learning. In Ronald A. Beghetto (Ed.), *Oxford Handbook of Human Creativity x Generative AI in Education*. Oxford University Press.

Goldman, S., & Kahn, J. (2025, April 16). *OpenAI No Longer Considers Manipulation and Mass Disinformation Campaigns a Risk Worth Testing for Before Releasing Its AI Models*. Fortune.

Haber, J., & Poesio, M. (2024). Polysemy—Evidence from linguistics, behavioral science, and contextualized language models. *Computational Linguistics, 50*(1), 351–417. https://doi.org/10.1162/coli_a_00500

hooks, b. (1994). *Teaching to Transgress*. Routledge.
Horvitz, E. (2022). On the horizon: Interactive and compositional deepfakes. In *Proceedings of the 2022 International Conference on Multimodal Interaction* (pp. 653–661). Association for Computing Machinery.
Immordino-Yang, M. H. (2015). *Emotions, Learning, and the Brain: Exploring the Educational Implications of Affective Neuroscience*. W.W. Norton & Company.
Ingvarsson, J. (2021). Evoking McLuhan's juxtapositions in the digital age: Archaeology and the mosaic. In *Towards a Digital Epistemology: Aesthetics and Modes of Thought in Early Modernity and the Present Age* (pp. 29–48). Springer Nature (Palgrave Macmillan). https://doi.org/10.1007/978-3-030-78724-0_2
Jongepier, F., & Klenk, M. (2022). *The Philosophy of Online Manipulation*. Routledge.
Kalantzis, M., & Cope, B. (2025). Multiliteracies since social media and artificial intelligence. *Harvard Educational Review, 95*(1), 135–151.
Lakoff, G., & Johnson, M. (1981). *Metaphors We Live by*. University of Chicago Press.
Lawrence, N. D. (2024). *The Atomic Human*. Public Affairs.
Lombard, M., & Xu, K. (2021). social responses to media technologies in the 21st century: The media are social actors paradigm. *Human-Machine Communication, 2*, 29–55. https://doi.org/10.30658/hmc.2.2
Mercier, H., & Sperber, D. (2017). *The Enigma of Reason*. Harvard University Press.
Miao, F., & Cukurova, M. (2024). *AI Competency Framework for Teachers*. UNESCO.
Miao, F., Shiohira, K., & Lao, N. (2024). *AI Competency Framework for Students*. UNESCO.
Miller, E., Manz, E., Russ, R., Stroupe, D., & Berland, L. (2018). Addressing the epistemic elephant in the room: Epistemic agency and the next generation science standards. *Journal of Research in Science Teaching, 55*(7), 1053–1075.
Nass, C., Steuer, J., Tauber, E., & Reeder, H. (1993). Anthropomorphism, agency, and Ethopoeia. In INTERACT '93 and CHI '93 Conference Companion on Human Factors in Computing Systems - CHI '93 (pp. 111–112). https://doi.org/10.1145/259964.260137
Nass, C., Steuer, J., & Tauber, E. R. (1994). Computers are social actors. In Proceedings of the SIGCHI Conference on Human Factors in Computing Systems (pp. 72–78). https://doi.org/10.1145/191666.191703
New London Group (1996). A pedagogy of multiliteracies: Designing social futures. *Harvard Educational Review, 66*(1), 60–93.
Peter, S., Riemer, K., & West, J. D. (2025). The benefits and dangers of anthropomorphic conversational agents. *Proceedings of the National Academy of Sciences, 122*(22). https://doi.org/10.1073/pnas.2415898122
Reich, R. (2025). *Stanford University 2025 AI + Education Summit Session: Navigating the AI Frontier–Challenges, Opportunities, and Ethical Dilemmas*. Palo Alto.
Roberts, P. (2017). Learning to live with doubt: Kierkegaard, Freire, and critical pedagogy. *Policy Futures in Education, 15*(7–8), 834–848.
Rubel, A., Castro, C., & Pham, A. (2018). International Workshop on Bias in Information, Algorithms, and Systems. In *Proceedings of the International Workshop on Bias in Information, Algorithms, and Systems*. Sheffield.
Schank, R. C., & Edelson, D. J. (1989). A role for AI in education: Using technology to reshape education. *Journal of Artificial Intelligence Education, 1*(2), 3–20.
Schaper, M. (2025). Doubt and transformation in education. *Educational Theory, 75*(1), 5–26. https://doi.org/10.1111/edth.12678
Sloman, S. A., & Fernbach, P. (2017). *Knowledge Illusion: Why We Never Think Alone*. Riverhead Books.

Snoswell, A. J., Witzenberger, K., & El Masri, R. (2025, May 15). *A Weird Phrase Is Plaguing Scientific Papers – and We Traced It Back to a Glitch in AI Training Data.* The Conversation.com.

Tadimalla, S. Y., & Maher, M. L. (2024). AI Literacy for All: Adjustable Interdisciplinary Socio-technical Curriculum. In *2024 IEEE Frontiers in Education Conference (FIE)* (pp. 1–9).

Tomlinson, B. M. (2020). *Undermining Intersectionality: The Perils of Powerblind Feminism.* Temple University Press.

United Nations. (2024). (rep.). *United Nations Secretary-General's High-Level Panel on the Teaching Profession: Transforming the Teaching Profession: Recommendations and Summary of Deliberations.* International Labour Organization.

Verhulst, S. (2025). Inquiry as Infrastructure: Defining Good Questions in the Age of Data and AI. https://doi.org/10.2139/ssrn.5229339

Vygotskiĭ, L. S., Cole, M., Stein, S., & Sekula, A. (1978). *Mind in Society: The Development of Higher Psychological Processes.* Harvard University Press.

Warshauer, H. K. (2011, December). (dissertation). *The Role of Productive Struggle in Teaching and Learning Middle School Mathematics.* University of Texas.

Wegerif, R. (2025). *Rethinking Educational Theory: Education as Expanding Dialogue.* Edward Elgar Publishing.

Weller, M. (2020). *25 Years of Ed Tech.* Athabasca University.

Zuboff, S. (2019). *The Age of Surveillance Capitalism: The Fight for the Human Future at the New Frontier of Power.* Public Affairs.

5

AI and Education: An Interdisciplinary, Collaborative Approach

Sara Ratner

Education is fundamentally human. It is relational, purposeful, and embedded in lived experience. While technology may support and extend educational processes, the heart of learning remains grounded in connection, growth, and shared meaning. Educators do more than transmit knowledge; they nurture the full spectrum of human development, including intellectual, emotional, social, and moral growth. Therefore, any meaningful discussion about the role of artificial intelligence (AI) in education must focus on how AI can enhance, rather than undermine the human aspects of teaching and learning.

Educational systems are adaptive and responsive to sociotechnical change. However, the question of how AI is integrated into these systems should not be left solely to technologists or commercial interests. It requires a collective and collaborative approach, one that draws on multiple disciplines and is grounded in ethical deliberation. The future of education must be co-developed by those who teach, those who learn, and all those who support the learning process.

Education is also deeply entangled with questions of justice and equity. It plays a vital role in helping young people to explore their identity, purpose, and societal contribution. In this way, education is not neutral. It is a social process shaped by political and cultural forces, and it involves normative decisions about what is taught, how it is taught, and to what end. These decisions become even more complex in the context of AI, where technological interventions are increasingly shaping pedagogical practices and institutional structures.

The rapid advancement of AI, particularly in areas such as machine learning and natural language processing, has triggered divergent responses. Optimists point to the potential for personalisation, data-informed decision-making, and the alleviation of administrative burdens. Critics, however, warn of algorithmic bias, the erosion of teacher autonomy, and the risks of surveillance and data misuse. Despite these contrasting perspectives, there is a shared tendency to frame the debate within disciplinary silos. Such siloed

 DOI: 10.1201/9781003626510-5

thinking risks them overlooking the complex interdependencies that characterise education systems.

The integration of AI in education is not merely a technical challenge. It is a human and societal challenge that raises critical ethical and political questions. Who decides how AI is designed and used in education? What values are encoded in these systems? Who benefits, and who is marginalised? These are not questions that can be answered by algorithms or automation alone. They require inclusive dialogue, critical analysis, and participatory governance.

This chapter argues that the integration of AI in education must be approached through a human-centred, interdisciplinary, and collaborative lens. To support this argument, it engages Systems Theory as a conceptual framework for understanding education as a complex, adaptive, and multilayered system. It also outlines Participatory Research as a methodology for engaging those most affected by AI in the design and evaluation of its use in educational contexts. These frameworks are exemplified through the case of the AI in Education at Oxford University (AIEOU) Hub, a research initiative that brings together scholars, practitioners, and communities to co-develop ethical and contextually responsive approaches to AI in education.

The chapter begins by explaining Systems Theory and its relevance to the study of AI in education. It then discusses Participatory Research as a means of embedding equity, reflexivity, and lived experience into research practice. This is followed by an examination of the structure of the AIEOU Hub and its four interrelated research streams: Design, Regulation, Implementation, and Impact. This case study of the Hub's early development offers a practical illustration of how these principles are enacted. The chapter concludes with critical reflections and a set of recommendations to support ethical, inclusive, and sustainable approaches to AI integration in education. At its core, this chapter affirms the view that education is not simply a system to be optimised. It is a deeply human endeavour that must be guided by ethical principles, social values, and the aspirations of those it serves. Any approach to AI in education must honour this reality.

Systems Theory as a Lens for AI in Education

To engage critically with the integration of artificial intelligence in education, it is necessary to move beyond fragmented or linear approaches. Educational systems are not monolithic entities. Rather, they are dynamic, adaptive, and composed of interdependent elements. These include students, teachers, curricula, technologies, governance structures, and the broader communities in which schools operate. Each of these components interacts with and influences the others. To understand how AI is shaping education, and how it might continue to do so, it is essential to examine the system as a whole.

Systems Theory provides a conceptual framework for this kind of holistic analysis. Originating with the work of Ludwig von Bertalanffy (1968), General Systems Theory challenged the reductionist approaches of mid-twentieth-century science by arguing that the behaviour of complex systems could not be understood solely by analysing their individual parts. In educational contexts, this means recognising that pedagogical practices, institutional cultures, policy frameworks, and technological innovations are interconnected and mutually constitutive. A change in one area may generate ripple effects across many others, sometimes in unpredictable ways.

This perspective is particularly useful when examining the influence of AI technologies. For instance, the adoption of a seemingly innocuous AI tool to support learning analytics may have unintended consequences as it alters the relationship between teachers and students, shifts assessment priorities, or creates new dependencies on particular data infrastructures. Systems Theory helps illuminate these interactions and encourages researchers and practitioners to consider both immediate and long-term effects.

The framework also supports multilevel analysis. Educational innovations occur at the level of individual classrooms, school organisations, regional systems, and global policy environments. Systems Theory provides tools to explore these levels concurrently. For example, decisions made at a national policy level about AI regulation may constrain what happens in classrooms. Likewise, innovations trialled in classrooms can inform institutional and systemic change. Understanding these interconnections is critical for responsible and responsive educational design. This systems-oriented view has been further developed by scholars such as Fullan (2004), who emphasise that meaningful and sustainable educational change must be understood as a process that operates across multiple levels. It is not sufficient to introduce innovations in individual classrooms or schools without considering the broader systemic conditions that enable or constrain change.

An additional strength of Systems Theory lies in its capacity to support anticipatory thinking. By focusing on feedback loops and non-linear relationships, it becomes possible to engage with "what if" scenarios. These are not speculative in the abstract sense but are grounded in the systemic nature of educational change. They allow researchers and stakeholders to surface potential unintended consequences, to reflect on ethical dilemmas before they arise, and to design safeguards that are contextually relevant. These patterns are especially relevant in the context of AI where the impacts of new technologies may not be immediately visible but may instead accumulate over time, reshaping pedagogical priorities, teacher roles, and accountability structures.

Critical perspectives further remind us that educational technologies, including AI, are not neutral. As Selwyn (2019) argues, they are shaped by particular values, interests, and institutional logics. A systems perspective enables us to ask how these technologies interact with existing inequalities, and whether they are reinforcing or disrupting structural patterns of exclusion and privilege.

The approach also fosters interdisciplinarity. The complex nature of AI in education cannot be addressed by any single discipline. Instead, Systems Theory encourages the collaboration of scholars and practitioners from education, computer science, sociology, law, psychology, design, philosophy, and the arts. It also demands the involvement of those most affected by educational change including teachers, students, parents, school leaders, and policy actors. This inclusive ethos reflects a commitment to equity, diversity, and relevance.

In the context of AIEOU, an interdisciplinary research hub focused on AI in education, Systems Theory has been used to shape both the conceptual underpinnings and the organisational design of the initiative. It informs the Hub's recognition of education as a globally connected, locally enacted system and frames its research architecture, which spans the Design, Regulation, Implementation, and Impact of AI in education. By working with, rather than against, the complexity of educational systems, the Hub aims to amplify the benefits of AI while identifying and addressing emerging risks. At the same time, Systems Theory facilitates ethical reflection. Situating technologies within broader social, cultural, and institutional contexts enables researchers to ask not only whether an AI system works, but also for whom, under what conditions, and with what consequences. This orientation makes it possible to interrogate how AI might entrench existing inequalities or, conversely, support more just and inclusive learning environments.

In summary, Systems Theory is not simply a descriptive tool but a conceptual and ethical stance that foregrounds complexity, interdependence, and change. It helps to ensure that the development and deployment of AI in education are analysed not as isolated phenomena, but as parts of a living system in which actions, values, and consequences are deeply entangled.

Participatory Research for Human-Centred AI in Education

As artificial intelligence becomes increasingly embedded in educational systems, the need for inclusive, context-sensitive, and ethically informed research practices grows more urgent. Traditional research paradigms, which often frame participants as passive subjects and position researchers as detached observers, are ill-suited to the complex sociotechnical realities of AI in education. Such approaches risk producing findings that are misaligned with the lived experiences and priorities of the people they claim to represent. In contrast, Participatory Research (PR) offers a democratic and reflexive methodology that is particularly well-aligned with both Systems Theory and human-centred design.

Participatory Research is grounded in the principle that those most affected by a given issue should be actively involved in the process of inquiry. This includes defining the research questions, designing the study, interpreting the findings, and shaping the outcomes. As Cornwall and Jewkes (1995) argue, participation is not merely a methodological choice, but a political commitment to equity, empowerment, and accountability. In educational research, this means involving teachers, students, families, and community members not as subjects of study, but as knowledge producers whose insights are essential to the construction of meaningful, actionable knowledge. In the context of AI, where technological decisions can have far-reaching and often opaque consequences, the imperative for participatory approaches becomes even more pronounced.

As Williamson and Eynon (2020) note, digital education technologies increasingly shape what counts as learning, who gets to participate, and how educational success is defined. If AI tools are to serve the interests of diverse learners and communities, then those same communities must be involved in shaping the systems from the outset. Against this backdrop, Participatory Research offers a crucial response. Moreover, PR is an important mechanism for promoting epistemic justice. Fricker (2007) defines epistemic injustice as the denial of credibility to individuals or groups based on prejudice or structural inequality. Within AI research, there is a well-documented tendency to privilege technical expertise while marginalising the practical and experiential knowledge of educators and students. Participatory methods challenge this tendency by explicitly recognising the value of lived experience, especially from communities that are often underrepresented in research and policy discourse.

The AIEOU Hub builds directly on these insights. It draws on this tradition of participatory inquiry to create a collaborative and inclusive research infrastructure. It is structured to involve a wide range of stakeholders including academic researchers, educators, technologists, students, and policy actors as co-researchers throughout the research lifecycle. This model resonates with the vision articulated by Reason and Bradbury (2001), who define Participatory Research as a process of collaborative inquiry and knowledge production. Throughout the lifecycle of the AIEOU Hub, collaborators are engaged in gathering data, co-interpreting findings, and reflecting on both process and impact. This iterative and dialogic approach aligns with the participatory ethos of continuous learning and critical reflexivity. It also supports the Hub's goal of producing outputs such as policy briefs, toolkits, and conceptual frameworks that are accessible, relevant, and actionable across a range of educational contexts.

Yet, as with all participatory approaches, this work is not without tensions. Participatory Research is not without its challenges. It requires time, trust, and the negotiation of power relations. It also demands a shift in institutional cultures that may be unaccustomed to shared authority or distributed decision-making. Nonetheless, its value lies in its ability to build legitimacy, surface hidden assumptions, and generate knowledge that is situated, credible, and oriented towards equity. In the context of AI in education, PR is not just a method. It is a foundational practice for ensuring that technological futures are co-designed with, rather than imposed upon, the communities they are intended to serve.

Mapping the Four Research Streams

To ensure a structured and comprehensive approach to AI in education, the AIEOU Hub organises its research through four interrelated streams: Design, Regulation, Implementation, and Impact. Each stream addresses a distinct area of inquiry while remaining deeply interconnected with the others. Together, they provide a framework for understanding how AI can be developed and integrated in ways that are pedagogically responsible, socially equitable, and systemically sustainable.

Design: Embedding Human Values in Educational Technology

The Design stream focuses on the initial stages of AI development, where decisions are made that shape how a technology functions, whom it serves, and what values it encodes. The AIEOU Hub rejects the idea of technology as neutral and instead argues that design is an inherently ethical act. Rather than optimising systems solely for efficiency, the Hub advocates for values-driven design processes that foreground the lived experiences of learners and educators.

Central to this stream is the practice of co-design, where end users (students, teachers, and families) are engaged from the outset of development. This participatory model challenges the dominant logic of EdTech development, which often treats schools as passive adopters of pre-engineered solutions. Instead, the AIEOU Hub promotes a model of relational design in which developers work collaboratively with educational communities to surface needs, test prototypes, and refine tools iteratively. By doing so, the Hub not only enhances the contextual relevance of AI tools but also advances democratic engagement in technological decision-making.

Theoretical and empirical work in this stream is informed by interdisciplinary scholarship on human-centred design, digital ethics, and educational equity. It acknowledges critiques of "solutionism" in EdTech (Selwyn, 2016) and aligns with broader efforts to decolonise design thinking by amplifying the knowledge and needs of underrepresented groups.

Regulation: Governing AI for Justice, Transparency, and Accountability

The Regulation stream addresses the legal, institutional, and policy frameworks that are required to ensure AI technologies are governed responsibly in educational contexts. Recognising that regulation cannot be a purely technical or top-down exercise, the AIEOU Hub conceptualises governance as a shared responsibility that includes public sector actors, school systems, developers, and civil society.

This stream examines questions such as who has the authority to approve the use of AI tools in schools; what rights learners and educators have in relation to data and automation; and how transparency can be supported in systems that are often complex and opaque. In response, the Hub explores models of participatory regulation, including community ethics boards, student-led oversight panels, and the integration of rights-based frameworks into procurement practices.

Importantly, this stream engages with international debates on AI ethics and child rights, drawing on frameworks developed by UNESCO, the OECD, and the Council of Europe. It also critically analyses gaps in national policy environments where AI is often introduced without sufficient legal scrutiny or public debate. The work in this stream recognises the dangers of regulatory fragmentation and calls for systemic alignment between AI innovation and public interest safeguards.

Implementation: Translating Ethical Intentions into Practice

While values and governance structures are essential, they must also be translated into practice. The implementation stream investigates how AI is introduced and embedded in real-world educational settings. This includes attention to the conditions under which technologies are adopted, the pedagogical cultures that shape their use, and the professional learning needed to support teachers and leaders.

The AIEOU Hub treats implementation not as a technical rollout but as a relational process marked by negotiation, adaptation, and resistance. It recognises that schools are not blank slates but dynamic sites of meaning-making. Implementation, therefore, must be understood in relation to the histories, abilities, and priorities of local educational communities.

Research in this stream explores the readiness of institutions to adopt AI, the adequacy of professional development, and the influence of school leadership in mediating change. It also considers how AI systems may affect teacher agency, redefine assessment practices, or shift the balance of power between educators and automated systems. This work builds on prior scholarship in educational change (Fullan, 2007) and professional agency (Biesta et al., 2015), offering insights into how ethical intentions can be sustained, or compromised, in the pressures of everyday practice.

Impact: Evaluating the Effects of AI on Learning, Equity, and System Dynamics

The final research stream focuses on the consequences of AI use in education, with a particular emphasis on long-term impacts. This includes both intended outcomes and unintended side effects. The AIEOU Hub argues that impact must be conceptualised expansively to include not only efficiency or attainment metrics, but also dimensions such as student agency, well-being, trust, and institutional resilience.

A core concern in this stream is equity. The Hub interrogates whether AI tools reduce or exacerbate disparities in educational access, experience, and outcomes. It also asks whose values and assumptions shape algorithmic systems, and how these systems distribute risks and benefits across different groups. This work is informed by a growing literature on algorithmic bias and data justice (Benjamin, 2019; Eubanks, 2018), as well as by participatory impact evaluation methods that seek to include marginalised voices in defining what counts as success.

In addition, the Hub explores how AI may affect systemic logics within education such as how accountability is structured, how knowledge is validated, and how professional norms evolve in response to automation. This analysis is grounded in Systems Theory, which highlights the recursive nature of educational change and encourages ongoing reflection and adjustment. In this way, the Impact stream ensures that research remains connected to the ethical and systemic aspirations outlined in the other three streams.

AIEOU as a Living System of Collaborative Inquiry

The AI in Education at Oxford University (AIEOU) Hub was established not as a fixed research centre but as a dynamic, evolving system. Its structure and ethos reflect the core principles of Systems Theory and Participatory Research, which together emphasise interconnection, adaptivity, and shared ownership of knowledge production. The Hub operates as both a case study and a model, illustrating what it means to approach AI in education through collaborative, interdisciplinary, and ethically grounded inquiry.

The inception of the Hub was guided by a Theory of Change process that brought together participants from diverse disciplines and sectors. These included academic researchers, teachers, school leaders, technologists, youth representatives, policymakers, and funders. The workshop did not seek to define predetermined outcomes. Instead, it created space for participants to surface values, identify challenges, and envision shared goals. This process enabled the formation of an inclusive research agenda rooted in the lived concerns of those affected by AI in education.

From its earliest days, the Hub has demonstrated the capacity of participatory processes to generate momentum and legitimacy. Within ten days of its public launch, membership grew by over one thousand percent, expanding to include contributors from more than one hundred countries. This rapid expansion signalled a broad appetite for dialogue that moved beyond siloed disciplines or national frameworks, and instead embraced a transnational, systemic approach to AI in education.

The interdisciplinary composition of the AIEOU Hub is one of its defining features. Participants are drawn from fields such as education, psychology, law, computer science, engineering, finance, linguistics, creative arts, and ethics. Many also bring professional experience from schools, non-profit organisations, and government agencies. This plurality of perspectives reflects a core tenet of Systems Theory: complex challenges require insight from across domains. It also aligns with Reason and Bradbury's (2001) claim that meaningful action research must be collaborative and oriented towards learning for change.

Equally central to the Hub's methodology is the principle of shared epistemic responsibility. As Ratner et al. (2025) argue, the integration of AI in education must be informed not only by technical expertise, but also by the values, experiences, and priorities of those most impacted. The Hub operationalises this principle through its co-researcher model, which treats all participants, regardless of institutional status, as contributors to both knowledge generation and application.

A significant example of this commitment is the proposed development of a Youth Advisory Board. This group, composed of secondary school students, is empowered to review research proposals, contribute to agenda-setting, and evaluate the relevance of findings. Rather than treating student input as symbolic or consultative, the Board is embedded within the governance structure of the Hub. In doing so, the AIEOU Hub counters the tendency to exclude young people from decisions about technologies that profoundly shape their educational experiences.

Throughout its development, the Hub has invested in cultivating a reflexive research culture. Structured discussion groups, shared writing processes, and collective data interpretation are central to this approach. These practices ensure that emerging findings are not only disseminated but also contested, refined, and translated into action. The Hub thereby functions as a community of practice in the sense outlined by Wenger (1998), offering a space for iterative learning and identity formation through shared activity.

The outputs of the Hub are designed to be accessible and actionable. These include policy briefs, design toolkits, implementation guides, and conceptual frameworks. Each output is developed with attention to audience diversity, ensuring that insights are available to policymakers, practitioners, students, and developers alike. This emphasis on accessibility is not incidental but reflects the Hub's foundational commitment to epistemic justice and public engagement.

What distinguishes the AIEOU Hub is not what it studies, but how it operates. Its structure embodies a systemic and participatory approach to inquiry, where research is understood as a shared, adaptive process. Rather than positioning itself as the locus of definitive answers, the Hub looks to convene diverse communities of practice in ongoing dialogue. In this way, it models a different kind of institutional infrastructure, one that is capable of holding complexity, embracing plurality, and learning in public.

Critical Reflections and Future Directions

The AIEOU Hub's commitment to systems thinking and Participatory Research represents a deliberate response to the multifaceted challenges posed by the integration of artificial intelligence in education. However, as with any transformative endeavour, this approach presents tensions, limitations, and unresolved questions that must be critically examined. These reflections are an affirmation of the need for continuous, reflective engagement as conditions evolve and systems adapt.

One of the most persistent challenges is the question of power. Participatory approaches seek to redistribute authority, amplify marginalised voices, and challenge traditional hierarchies in research and policy. However, such efforts must contend with enduring structures that may be resistant to change. As Cornwall and Jewkes (1995) have noted, participation often occurs within constrained spaces shaped by existing power relations, and therefore risks becoming tokenistic unless accompanied by broader structural transformation. Within the AIEOU Hub, the challenge is not only to invite diverse participants into the room, but to ensure that their insights meaningfully shape agendas, decisions, and outcomes.

A second tension lies in managing complexity without paralysis. The systems lens embraced by the Hub draws attention to the layered, interdependent, and often non-linear nature of educational change. While this perspective supports more holistic and responsible analysis, it can also overwhelm decision-making. The risk is that actors become caught in what Meadows (2008) describes as analysis paralysis, a state where the recognition of systemic interdependencies inhibits timely or decisive action. For the AIEOU Hub, the task is to develop heuristics, frameworks, and protocols that allow for clarity and action without erasing complexity.

A third concern relates to the perceived opposition between ethical deliberation and technological innovation. Within the broader EdTech sector, participatory and ethical practices are sometimes viewed as barriers to speed and scale. Developers may express concerns that engagement processes slow down product development or complicate deployment. However, as Ratner et al. (2025) argue, ethical co-design is not a constraint on innovation, but a condition for its legitimacy and relevance. The challenge for the Hub is to demonstrate how inclusive and deliberative approaches can produce AI tools that are not only ethically robust but also effective, scalable, and responsive to diverse contexts.

Sustainability poses another critical concern. Initiatives like the AIEOU Hub are often dependent on short-term funding cycles, volunteer labour, or institutional champions. While enthusiasm and trust may carry projects through their early phases, long-term viability requires investment in governance, infrastructure, and capacity development. As Fullan (2004) emphasises, sustained change depends on the cultivation of leadership at multiple levels and the creation of systems that can learn and adapt over time. For the AIEOU Hub, the goal is to build resilient networks that are not overly reliant on individual actors and that can weather institutional transitions or policy shifts.

Finally, the Hub must continue to engage in what Cilliers (1998) and Fricker (2007) might describe as anticipatory and epistemic ethics. This involves not only responding to present concerns but also asking critical questions about emerging futures. What educational dependencies might AI create that are difficult to reverse? How might accountability be reshaped if decision-making becomes increasingly data-driven or automated? Who is responsible for long-term consequences, particularly when AI systems outlive the institutional contexts in which they were developed?

These questions cannot be answered definitively, nor can they be outsourced to technical experts or policy leaders. They demand open, inclusive, and critical inquiry that draws on multiple forms of knowledge and experience. The AIEOU Hub seeks to hold space for this inquiry, not as a final arbiter of educational futures, but as a convenor of collaborative, values-driven, and reflexive dialogue. It is through this collective process that more just, equitable, and humanising visions of AI in education might begin to emerge.

Conclusion

This chapter has argued that the integration of artificial intelligence in education cannot be approached as a purely technical challenge, nor as an opportunity to optimise learning systems for efficiency alone. Instead, it must be understood as a deeply human, ethical, and political undertaking. Education is not simply a delivery mechanism for information; it is a relational and values-driven practice shaped by histories, cultures, and collective aspirations. The future of AI in education, therefore, must be co-created with the communities it is intended to serve.

By grounding the discussion in Systems Theory and Participatory Research, the chapter has offered both a conceptual framework and a methodological orientation for engaging with the complexity of educational change. Systems Theory provides tools to understand the interdependence and adaptivity of education as a living system. Participatory Research offers a practical and ethical approach for involving diverse stakeholders, particularly those whose voices have historically been marginalised, and invites them to help shape AI-related decision-making.

The AIEOU Hub has served as a case study in how these principles can be enacted. Through its four interdisciplinary research streams of Design, Regulation, Implementation, and Impact, the Hub exemplifies a model of inquiry that is reflexive, collaborative, and oriented towards equity. It demonstrates that responsible AI development in education requires more than technical excellence. It demands shared accountability and the deliberate cultivation of ethical and democratic practices.

As AI technologies become increasingly embedded in educational systems, the stakes of inaction or uncritical adoption become higher. Without intentional design and inclusive governance, AI risks exacerbating existing inequalities and eroding professional and pedagogical autonomy. Conversely, if shaped collaboratively and thoughtfully, AI holds the potential to support more personalised, context-sensitive, and just educational experiences.

The work of the AIEOU Hub is ongoing and necessarily unfinished. It does not offer definitive solutions, nor does it assume that consensus is always possible. Instead, it holds space for disagreement, reflection, and iterative learning. In doing so, it models a research culture that can respond to the unpredictability and complexity of educational transformation in the digital age.

At its core, this chapter affirms that any future worth pursuing in AI and education must be rooted in the values that animate education itself: human dignity, social justice, intellectual curiosity, and collective responsibility. It is only by placing these values at the centre of our technological choices that we can ensure AI becomes a tool not of control or conformity, but of care, creativity, and shared purpose.

Actionable Recommendations

The preceding analysis has highlighted the need for a human-centred, ethically grounded, and systemically informed approach to the integration of artificial intelligence in education. To support such an approach, several practical and strategic recommendations emerge. These recommendations are not exhaustive, nor are they prescriptive. Rather, they are intended as provocations and guiding principles for educators, researchers, developers, and policymakers seeking to engage responsibly with AI.

First, there is a clear imperative to centre human values in the design of AI systems. This requires that educational technologies be developed not in isolation from practice, but through sustained collaboration with those who live and work within educational settings. Designers and developers must prioritise inclusivity, accessibility, and transparency, ensuring that technologies reflect the needs and priorities of diverse learners and communities. This also involves resisting narrow definitions of effectiveness, which often privilege data-driven metrics over more holistic and relational understandings of learning.

Second, institutions and organisations must create and maintain inclusive governance structures. These structures should enable meaningful participation in decision-making by students, teachers, families, and communities. Regulatory frameworks must extend beyond compliance and technical standards to include the ethical, cultural, and pedagogical dimensions of AI use. Participatory ethics boards, youth advisory panels, and multi-stakeholder review processes offer promising models for ensuring accountability and legitimacy.

Third, investment in professional learning and institutional capacity is essential. Educators need time, resources, and pedagogical support to critically engage with AI. This includes opportunities for sustained inquiry, dialogue, and co-learning. Schools and systems should build capacity not only to adopt technology, but to interrogate it. Implementation should be treated not as a technical rollout, but as a learning journey shaped by local context and professional agency.

Fourth, Participatory Research practices must be embedded across all phases of the AI lifecycle. This means involving stakeholders from the earliest stages of problem definition through to the evaluation and re-design of tools. Such engagement should be reciprocal, compensated, and grounded in trust. Participatory approaches not only democratise knowledge production but also enhance the relevance, usability, and equity of technological interventions.

Fifth, new methods for evaluating the impact of AI in education must be developed. Traditional metrics such as test scores or engagement analytics are insufficient to capture the broader implications of AI use. Impact assessments must consider equity, student agency, professional autonomy, and long-term systemic change. These indicators must be developed in dialogue with communities and reflect diverse definitions of success.

Sixth, knowledge produced through research and evaluation must be communicated in accessible, actionable, and culturally responsive ways. Policymakers, school leaders, educators, and students require clear, relevant, and usable insights. Research outputs should be tailored to different audiences and made available through multiple channels, including multimedia formats and open-access repositories.

Finally, sustained interdisciplinary and cross-sector collaboration is essential. Addressing the ethical, pedagogical, and systemic challenges posed by AI in education requires partnerships that transcend disciplinary and institutional boundaries. Universities, schools, public agencies, and civil society must work together to build networks of practice that can share learning, mobilise resources, and shape public discourse.

These recommendations do not offer a roadmap in the conventional sense. Rather, they invite collective reflection, principled action, and iterative experimentation. They call for a shift in how we imagine the relationship between education and technology. A relationship that does not solely rely on adaptation to external innovation, but rather a deliberate, collaborative, and values-driven process of design and governance. In a moment of profound technological change, the choices we make now will shape the conditions under which future generations learn, teach, and flourish. Those choices must begin and end with a commitment to human dignity, social justice, and shared purpose.

References

Benjamin, R. (2019). Race after technology: Abolitionist tools for the new jim code. Polity Press.

Bertalanffy, L. (1968). General system theory. In: Foundations, development, applications. George Braziller.

Biesta, G., Priestley, M., & Robinson, S. (2015). The role of beliefs in teacher agency. Teachers and Teaching, 21(6), 624–640. https://doi.org/10.1080/13540602.2015.1044325

Cilliers, P. (1998). *Complexity and postmodernism: Understanding complex systems*. Routledge.

Cornwall, A., & Jewkes, R. (1995). What is participatory research? Social Science & Medicine, 41(12), 1667–1676. https://doi.org/10.1016/0277-9536(95)00127-S

Eubanks, V. (2018). Automating inequality: How high-tech tools profile, police, and punish the poor. St. Martin's Press.

Fricker, M. (2007). Epistemic injustice: Power and the ethics of knowing. Oxford University Press.

Fullan, M. (2004). Leadership & sustainability: System thinkers in action. Corwin Press.

Fullan, M. (2007). The new meaning of educational change (4th ed.). Teachers College Press.

Meadows, D. H. (2008). *Thinking in systems: A primer* (D. Wright, Ed.). Chelsea Green Publishing.

Ratner, S., Williams, R., & Wonnacott, E. (2025). Exploring AI in education through interdisciplinary collaboration. In INTED2025 Proceedings (pp. 5650–5655). IATED. https://doi.org/10.21125/inted.2025.1443

Reason, P., & Bradbury, H. (Eds.). (2001). Handbook of action research: Participative inquiry and practice. Sage.
Selwyn, N. (2016). Is technology good for education? Polity Press.
Selwyn, N. (2019). *Should robots replace teachers? AI and the future of education*. Polity Press.
Wenger, E. (1998). *Communities of practice: Learning, meaning, and identity*. Cambridge University Press.
Williamson, B., & Eynon, R. (2020). Historical threads, missing links, and future directions in AI in education. Learning, Media and Technology, 45(3), 223–235. https://doi.org/10.1080/17439884.2020.1798995

6

The Promise and Challenge of AI Personalisation in Education: A Theoretical and Empirical Analysis

Kathleen J. Kennedy

Before ChatGPT's revolutionary launch in November 2022, AI-driven personalised learning systems evolved slowly within education. Early platforms like Knewton, ALEKS, and DreamBox promised algorithmic personalisation but remained confined to mathematics instruction and remedial education context (Wang et al., 2023). These systems relied on retrieval practice and spaced repetition—cognitive psychology principles demonstrating that active information retrieval enhances long-term retention more effectively than passive review (Roediger & Karpicke, 2006). Their effectiveness depended on structured content domains and honest student engagement.

The post-ChatGPT era has fundamentally disrupted this landscape. This widespread AI availability exposes both unprecedented potential for scaling individualised instruction and significant implementation challenges: algorithmic bias favouring certain learning styles, substantial privacy and technology costs, and the fundamental requirement for student honesty in an era of readily available AI assistance. Students now routinely access sophisticated AI tools for learning support and assessment completion, often circumventing carefully designed adaptive pathways. The Digital Education Council's Global AI Student Survey (2024), encompassing 3,839 higher education students across 16 countries, found that 86% of students globally use AI in their studies.

These challenges intersect with broader educational equity issues related to unequal access to technology. Whilst the digital divide, with longstanding disparities in hardware access and internet connectivity, predates the AI era, generative AI introduces qualitatively different equity challenges through its computational demands, subscription costs, and requirement for sophisticated prompt engineering skills (Tlili et al., 2023; Wang & Demszky, 2023). The digital divide—encompassing disparities in device access, connectivity, and digital literacy—threatens to transform AI personalisation from a democratising force into another education and social stratification

DOI: 10.1201/9781003626510-6

mechanism. Students from well-resourced backgrounds access premium AI tools and possess cultural capital to navigate these systems effectively, whilst others face barriers at every level (Reich & Mehta, 2024; Warschauer & Matuchniak, 2024).

This disparity manifests differently across global contexts: in the Global North, the divide often centres on quality of access and AI literacy, whilst in the Global South, fundamental infrastructure limitations compound these challenges (Pedro et al., 2019), creating multi-layered barriers to AI-enhanced learning that persist despite emerging mobile and cloud-based solutions (Kasinathan & Ranganathan, 2023; Nguyen et al., 2023). This creates a critical tension: AI personalisation promises to democratise high-quality, individualised education, yet current implementation may amplify existing inequalities rather than ameliorate them. Although emerging initiatives to deploy lightweight AI models on mobile devices and develop free, locally-run large language models show promise for reducing access barriers, their educational efficacy and ability to match sophisticated cloud-based systems remains unproven (Dettmers et al., 2024; Hu et al., 2022). More fundamentally, ubiquitous AI tools challenge basic assumptions underlying adaptive learning systems, questioning whether traditional approaches remain viable.

This study addresses three interconnected research questions that examine not only the technical implementation of AI in education, but also the fundamental reconceptualisation of learning relationships and pedagogical authority in an AI-mediated landscape:

1. RQ1: What conditions enable AI-driven personalised learning systems to support rather than undermine educational equity? This question moves beyond whether AI can enhance equity to examine the specific institutional, pedagogical, and technological conditions necessary for equitable implementation.
2. RQ2: How do the relationships between learners, instructors, and AI systems determine implementation success? This question investigates the interdependent roles that each party must play and how their coordination affects learning outcomes across diverse student populations. This encompasses both the strength and nature of these relationships—including pedagogically sanctioned AI use versus student-initiated adoption, and the varying degrees of instructor mediation that shape how students engage with AI tools in curricular and independent learning contexts.
3. RQ3: What systemic changes are required to implement AI personalisation that supports student equity and learning success? This question examines how readily available generative AI tools disrupt foundational principles whilst identifying the broader organisational and pedagogical transformations necessary for ethical AI

implementation. It addresses the critical distinction between institutional AI deployment and student-driven AI adoption, the development of faculty support protocols for recognising and mitigating algorithmic bias, and ultimately the philosophical question of what constitutes authentic learning when AI can simulate understanding.

These research questions acknowledge that AI systems inevitably embed biases that influence educational outcomes—yet rather than rendering these systems ineffective, awareness of these biases and proper guidance can help educators and students navigate them productively. The questions thus examine both the technical and human dimensions of AI implementation, recognising that success depends not merely on system capabilities but on how effectively institutions support faculty and students in critically engaging with these technologies.

This research makes three significant contributions to our understanding of AI in education: bridging theory with empirical evidence, providing comprehensive real-world data through the PALS initiative, and offering immediate practical implications for ethical AI implementation.

First, it bridges critical theoretical frameworks with extensive empirical evidence, moving beyond abstract concerns to examine how issues of surveillance, bias, and equity manifest in actual educational practice within diverse institutional contexts.

Second, the Personalised Adaptive Learning System (PALS) initiative provides one of the most comprehensive real-world test cases of AI adaptive learning in higher education enabling examination of how AI personalisation functions across different contexts, student populations, and implementation approaches. This scale and scope reveal patterns invisible in smaller studies Understanding the critical role of instructor integration in AI personalisation led to the development of the Integrated Model for AI Personalisation (IMAP), a practical framework for understanding the coordination required for successful implementation.

Third, the findings have immediate implications for policy and practice. As educational institutions implement AI technologies at unprecedented pace, evidence-based frameworks for ethical implementation become crucial. This research provides actionable insights for educators, administrators, policymakers, and technology developers working to harness AI's potential whilst mitigating its risks.

These contributions address critical gaps in our understanding of AI in education. First, the research connects abstract theoretical concerns about surveillance, bias, and equity with concrete classroom realities. Second, it presents one of higher education's most comprehensive AI adaptive learning studies—the PALS initiative with 1,173 students and 15 instructors across 30+ course offerings in 13 disciplines. Third, it translates these findings into practical frameworks that educators, administrators, policymakers, and technology developers can immediately apply. This combination of theoretical depth, empirical breadth, and practical applicability provides the evidence-based guidance urgently needed as institutions rapidly adopt AI technologies.

The chapter proceeds through sections that build from theoretical foundations to practical recommendations. IMAP synthesises critical perspectives from information ethics, surveillance capitalism studies, and algorithmic bias research. These frameworks illuminate the three core tensions in AI education: how AI transforms the nature of educational relationships (information ethics), how student data become commodified within learning platforms (surveillance capitalism), and how algorithmic decisions can perpetuate or amplify existing educational inequalities (algorithmic bias). The Methodology section details the mixed-methods investigation of the PALS study implementations. The Main Discussion/Analysis presents findings across three critical dimensions, demonstrating how theoretical concerns manifest through the interactions between learners, instructors, and AI systems. The comparative case studies illustrate the importance of instructor integration, communication, and trust-building. Critical Reflections identify gaps in current discourse, whilst the Conclusion and Actionable Recommendations provide frameworks for ethical AI implementation that enhance rather than undermine educational equity.

Theoretical Framework

Contemporary scholarship reveals fundamental tensions between AI-driven personalisation's technological potential and its ethical implications in education. The proposed IMAP synthesises key theoretical perspectives that illuminate how AI systems may simultaneously enhance and undermine educational equity, drawing from information ethics, surveillance studies, algorithmic justice, and interdisciplinary learning sciences to understand these complex dynamics.

Information Ethics and Education

Luciano Floridi's (2013, 2014) information ethics framework reveals how AI fundamentally alters educational relationships within the "infosphere," the totality of informational entities and their interactions (Floridi, 2013, p. 8). Educational institutions serve as critical nodes where student data flow continuously, with AI systems transforming traditional pedagogical relationships by mediating information exchange between teachers and learners. In this context, "AI agents" refer to algorithmic systems that autonomously process information and make decisions about learning pathways, assessment, and content delivery. This framework raises essential questions about these AI agents' moral status in processing student data and protecting "informational privacy" in learning contexts (Floridi, 2013, pp. 234–235). The framework's significance lies not only in privacy concerns but in how AI fundamentally restructures educational power dynamics. When AI systems make decisions affecting educational outcomes, they challenge conventional pedagogical responsibility and accountability. The framework demands scrutiny of how AI impacts learners' dignity as "informational organisms" and whether automated personalisation creates informational harm (Floridi, 2014, pp. 102–103; Taddeo & Floridi, 2018, p. 751), extending beyond data protection to encompass education's fundamental purpose in an AI-AI-augmented (rather than replaced) world (Vallor, 2016, p. 147).

Surveillance Capitalism in Educational Contexts

Shoshana Zuboff's (2023) surveillance capitalism—the economic system that claims human experience as free raw material for translation into behavioural data (Zuboff, 2023, p. 8)—critique powerfully applies to adaptive learning systems. Educational platforms extract continuous data streams about student behaviours, learning patterns, and emotional states, transforming human learning experiences into raw material for algorithmic processing. This extraction goes beyond pedagogical improvement—it creates "behavioural surplus" that enables prediction and modification of student behaviours, often without transparent consent (Zuboff, 2023, pp. 93–94 reinforcing existing prejudices and creating stratified learning tiers that promote conformity over inclusive pedagogical strategies). The commodification of learning patterns raises profound ethical concerns that persist regardless of student awareness. When educational data become an asset for platform providers, the purpose of education shifts from fostering critical thinking toward optimising measurable performance indicators (Williamson, 2017, pp. 45–46). Students' limited privacy concerns, as evidenced in PALS, may reflect not lower expectations but rather normalisation of surveillance through social media and digital platforms, and insufficient data privacy literacy rather than absence of surveillance risks. This transformation creates new power asymmetries where students become data subjects rather than autonomous learners, fundamentally altering the educational covenant between institutions and students (Selwyn, 2019, pp. 23–24).

Algorithmic Bias and Educational Justice

Algorithmic bias emerges not as a technical glitch but as a reflection of existing institutional inequities encoded into AI systems through biased training data, flawed assumptions, and homogeneous development teams. AI personalisation's promise falters against pervasive algorithmic bias that amplifies educational inequalities. Safiya Umoja Noble's (2018) "algorithms of oppression" demonstrates how algorithmic systems perpetuate racist and sexist stereotypes through biased training data, manifesting in educational contexts through discriminatory assessments, content recommendations, and disciplinary actions affecting marginalised students disproportionately (Noble, 2018, pp. 171–172). These biases persist because the same structures that historically excluded certain groups from educational opportunity now shape AI development—what should mitigate bias in traditional institutions (human judgment, policy oversight, professional ethics) often fails to transfer to algorithmic systems. Virginia Eubanks' (2018) "automating inequality" reveals how algorithmic systems systematically penalise vulnerable populations (Eubanks, 2018, pp. 11–12). Ruha Benjamin's (2019) "New Jim Code" shows how seemingly neutral educational technologies encode racial hierarchies in subtle yet impactful ways, appearing to address bias whilst deepening existing inequalities through design and implementation (Benjamin, 2019, pp. 53–54). Addressing these issues requires examining the institutionalised power structures embedded in educational AI, not merely technical fixes.

Interdisciplinary Perspectives

Understanding AI's educational impact demands insights from multiple disciplines. Learning sciences research (Wang et al., 2023) emphasises that effective AI must align with established theories of cognition and motivation, advocating for systems supporting complex learning processes—metacognition, collaborative problem-solving, critical thinking—rather than simply optimising content delivery. Disability studies and Universal Design for Learning (UDL) provide frameworks for inclusive AI design (CAST, n.d.), demanding inherently flexible systems serving all learners from inception. Decolonial computing—an approach that challenges the colonial power structures embedded in computing practices and seeks to centre indigenous and non-Western ways of knowing (Mohamed et al., 2020, p. 663)—interrogates whose knowledge systems AI privileges, questioning Western-centric assumptions whilst advocating for diverse epistemologies and locally relevant pedagogies that address rather than perpetuate global inequities (Zembylas, 2023). Neil Selwyn's (2019, 2023) critical educational technology work provides an overarching framework questioning techno-solutionist narratives, emphasising examination of AI's "real-world" impacts—datafication, surveillance, teacher de-professionalisation—within specific social and political contexts, advocating for democratic oversight and human-centred approaches.

Toward an Integrated Framework for AI Personalisation in Learning

These theoretical perspectives—information ethics, surveillance capitalism, algorithmic justice, and interdisciplinary learning sciences—reveal

AI's multidimensional impact on education as interconnected concerns forming a comprehensive web of implementation challenges. Floridi's information ethics illuminates how AI fundamentally shifts educational relationships, whilst Zuboff's surveillance capitalism exposes how these transformations serve extractive economic logics. Algorithmic bias critiques demonstrate how systemic issues manifest as concrete harms to marginalised students, whilst interdisciplinary perspectives offer pathways toward equitable alternatives.

Together, these frameworks reveal that AI personalisation operates simultaneously as: a technological system processing information, an economic apparatus extracting value, a social mechanism potentially reproducing inequalities, and a cultural force shaping what counts as knowledge. The promise of personalised learning cannot be evaluated solely on technical efficacy; it must be interrogated for impacts on human dignity, educational justice, and democratic values. Addressing these challenges requires moving beyond critique to action: restructuring power relationships through participatory design, implementing transparent accountability mechanisms, and ensuring educator and student agency in AI deployment decisions. This theoretical synthesis guides our empirical investigation of the PALS initiative, providing analytical tools to examine how these multifaceted concerns manifest in practice.

Methodology

This research employs a comprehensive mixed-methods approach with three core analytical dimensions that ensure systematic examination of equity implications: algorithmic fairness assessment examining how AI decisions affect different student groups (O'Neil, 2017), cognitive surveillance evaluation analysing data collection and usage patterns (Zuboff, 2023), and structural inequity reproduction analysis identifying how existing disparities may be amplified through AI implementation (Benjamin, 2019).

This study applies these dimensions through theoretical analysis and empirical investigation. The research integrates critical theoretical frameworks with comprehensive field data from the Personalised Adaptive Learning System (PALS) initiative at the University of Arizona. The study utilises a within-subject design across multiple disciplines over two years (2023–2025), capturing complex interactions between technological affordances, pedagogical practices, and student outcomes whilst controlling for individual differences. This design enables direct performance comparison before and after AI adaptive learning implementation, providing stronger causal inferences than between-subjects alternatives.

TABLE 6.1
Courses in PALS Study

Course	Discipline Area	Times Taught in Study	Enrolment Per Offering	AI Adaptive Learning Intensity[a]	Instructor Engagement With AI Learning[b]	Number of AI Lessons in Course
A	STEM	1	118	Moderate	High	6
B	Math	3	61, 40, 34	Low to high	Low	3, 6, 11
C	Business	3	47, 34, 48	High	Moderate	11, 12, 14
D	STEM	6	34, 79, 79, 25, 60, 85	Moderate to very high	High	5, 13, 14, 25, 32
E	Business	3	45, 45, 45	Low	Low	5
F	Interdisciplinary	1	21	High	High	12
G	STEM	5	36, 59, 48, 95, 57	Moderate to high	Moderate	4,10,12
H	Humanities	2	11, 23	Low	Low	1
I	English	1	15	Low	Low	2
J	STEM	2	41, 48	Low	Moderate	3
K	STEM	1	40	Low	Low	1
L	STEM	1	41	Low	Low	1
M	Humanities	1	47	Low	Moderate	1

Note: Two PALS courses not in analysis because the AI adaptive learning portions were not implemented.
[a] AI adaptive learning intensity based on time required to complete AI lessons.
[b] Instructor engagement based on instructor's training engagement, self-reports, and researcher's observations.

The PALS Initiative Overview

PALS represents one of higher education's most comprehensive controlled AI adaptive learning studies. The study encompassed 15 unique courses across over 30 offerings, involving 15 faculty from diverse disciplines and 1,173 undergraduate students (course distribution details in Table 6.1). The research was university IRB approved with electronic informed consent from all study participants.

The technological infrastructure combined D2L/Brightspace LMS with accessibility applications and the Cerego AI adaptive learning platform. This integrated system employed cognitive science principles to create personalised learning paths based on individual needs and forgetting curves, with adaptive algorithms determining optimal content review timing and AI-powered knowledge gap detection.

The study employed a within-subjects design where AI adaptive learning supported only selected learning objectives within each course rather than replacing entire course structures. This approach allowed students to serve as their own controls, experiencing both AI-supported and traditional instruction within the same course. Whilst no control courses were available for cross-course comparison—as parallel sections with identical instructors, content, and student populations are rare at the university—the within-subjects design enabled examination of how the same AI system performed across diverse implementations. All 15 courses used the identical Cerego AI platform with identical technical configurations, allowing systematic comparison of implementation approaches across disciplines and instructors.

The study commenced with instructor training in Spring 2022 and the first pilot implementation in Summer 2023. Throughout implementation, 322 topic and skills lessons were developed across over 30 courses, containing learning content and adaptive questions designed to reinforce learning through retrieval practice. Course enrolments ranged from 11 to 118 students, with a mean class size of 49 students. The study's student population reflected the university's diverse undergraduate demographics, including 34% first-generation college students, 48% from underrepresented minority backgrounds (with Hispanic/Latino students comprising 30% of undergraduates), students from all 50 states and 109 countries, and a range of socioeconomic statuses (University of Arizona, 2023). This enabled the examination of AI adaptive learning effects across different student identities and learning approaches.

Data Collection Methods

The mixed-methods approach employed multiple data streams for triangulation, using different types of data to cross-verify findings and ensure conclusions are supported by multiple sources of evidence. Quantitative data included student performance metrics, engagement analytics, assessment scores, and system-generated learning paths. Student surveys were administered at three time points: course beginning (including informed consent), mid-course, and course conclusion. Of the 1,173 students, 575 completed end-of-course surveys regarding privacy and system usability. Post-course interviews were conducted with 63 students (25%) who self-selected from 250 randomly invited study participants.

Qualitative data encompassed semi-structured instructor interviews at course beginning and end, student surveys, student interviews, and document analysis of course materials and system reports. Qualitative data analysis employed thematic coding procedures, with systematic analysis of interview transcripts and open-ended survey responses to identify recurring patterns across implementations. This study was informed by themes drawn from AI and Teaching and Learning Faculty Learning Community (FLC) discussions with over 300 additional faculty held in Spring 2023 through Spring 2025.

IMAP emerged from the combination of survey responses, faculty and student interviews, course observations by the researcher, and FLC discussions, capturing complex interdependencies rather than imposing theoretical categories. Initial validation occurred through the PALS data analysis, with comprehensive validation planned for 2025–26.

Main Discussion/Analysis

The PALS initiative provides a unique empirical lens through which to examine how theoretical concerns about AI in education manifest in practice. Rather than viewing AI personalisation as a purely technological intervention, the data reveal a complex ecosystem requiring coordination between three critical parties: learners, instructors, and AI systems, with trust serving as the essential mediating factor for equitable outcomes.

The Three-Party System: Interdependent Requirements for Equity

The PALS data revealed that successful personalised learning depends fundamentally on a coordinated relationship between learners, instructors, and AI systems, each possessing specific capabilities and experiencing particular conditions that enable productive engagement. This empirical finding validates and extends our theoretical framework: learners must function as Floridi's "informational organisms" with agency over their data flows; instructors serve as critical mediators who can resist or enable Zuboff's surveillance capitalism logic; and AI systems embody the algorithmic bias patterns identified by Noble, Benjamin, and Eubanks, whilst potentially offering pathways toward more equitable alternatives.

Learners: Agency Within Algorithmic Mediation. The PALS findings validate Floridi's (2013, 2014) conceptualisation of students as "informational organisms" who must actively navigate complex data flows within AI-mediated learning environments. Analysis of the 13 courses with complete data revealed stark differences in student engagement across implementations, demonstrating that students' capacity to maintain agency over their informational relationships determines success more than technological sophistication. Successful courses like Course A (an introductory environmental science course serving 118 students, mix of STEM and non-STEM majors) achieved 98% initial engagement rates declining gradually to 86–88% by final lessons, whilst unsuccessful implementations like Course B (Mathematics) saw engagement drop precipitously from 98% to 0% by the third lesson indicating complete abandonment of the AI system.

Preliminary analysis revealed no major differences in AI adaptive learning effectiveness based on student demographic profiles or academic self-concept, challenging assumptions about personalisation benefiting certain "types" of students. Student profiles included comprehensive academic behaviour assessments, learning preferences, demographic characteristics, and self-reported academic confidence measures across 30+ variables. Some minor predictive value emerged from progress-to-goal metrics and study time measures, though correlations were weaker than anticipated. However, the data suggested important connections to multiple literacy requirements—including English language proficiency, computational systems literacy, and academic cultural capital—that may serve as fundamental gatekeepers to AI learning effectiveness. Preliminary regression analysis indicated that students' ability to navigate linguistic and technological literacies appeared more determinative of success than traditional academic indicators, though detailed analysis is reserved for future publication.

Contrary to Zuboff's surveillance capitalism critique, suggesting that data collection inevitably disempowers learners, successful PALS implementations revealed that students valued transparent learning analytics when the scope remained limited and educationally focused. The system collected only essential data: student names and learning behaviours such as response accuracy, time on task, and completion rates, which students perceived as supportive rather than surveillant. This created a symmetrical data exchange—what students contributed directly returned to them as learning benefits. In exchange, learners received real-time feedback on each response and progress reporting for each adaptive learning set (topic lesson), including four key metrics: progress toward learning goals, accuracy rates, content mastery levels, and predicted knowledge retention over time. Students could not access raw data, modify privacy settings, or control data sharing with instructors. Nonetheless provided meaningful insights that students valued for understanding their learning progress. This finding suggests that surveillance becomes problematic through opacity and misuse rather than data collection itself.

When data extraction serves learners rather than external interests, the power dynamic shifts from extractive to reciprocal. Students can maintain agency as "informational organisms" when they understand and control how their data serve learning goals. The system's progress indicators helped students develop agency over their learning paths when coupled with clear instructor communication about supportive data use. Most significantly, successful personalised learning required students to embrace vulnerability, making errors publicly recorded by the AI system whilst trusting that mistakes would inform helpful rather than punitive algorithmic responses, embodying Floridi's concept of informational dignity within technological mediation.

Instructors: Pedagogical Agency in AI-Mediated Environments. The instructor's role emerged as far more critical than anticipated, directly challenging Zuboff's surveillance capitalism logic by demonstrating how instructor agency can resist algorithmic standardisation. Analysis revealed dramatic differences in outcomes based on instructor engagement and integration strategies, with this factor proving more determinative than discipline, technology, or student characteristics. This finding validates Selwyn's (2019) argument that human-centred approaches can counter techno-solutionist narratives, whilst supporting decolonial computing perspectives that emphasise local pedagogical knowledge over predetermined algorithmic models.

Course A exemplified high instructor engagement, with lessons strategically embedded within course structure and regular instructor monitoring of student progress, resulting in sustained high engagement rates (86–98%) and positive student feedback. Successful implementations required instructors to move beyond treating AI as an add-on tool toward strategic integration with learning objectives and assessment strategies. In a different course implementation, Course D demonstrated a successful approach through careful alignment of AI lessons with course quizzes, creating clear connections between adaptive learning activities and course outcomes. Students completed 81–98% of activities because they understood the relevance to their overall learning goals. Conversely, Course B showed low instructor engagement, with AI lessons poorly integrated into course activities, resulting in complete engagement collapse (0% engagement by lesson 3 of 11).

A revealing finding emerged from comparing instructor-created content with research team-developed materials. Two instructors, lacking time and experience, had materials developed by the research team. These implementations showed notably lower engagement rates and instructor investment, suggesting that creating adaptive content may foster instructor commitment and ownership essential for successful implementation. This finding points to the need for institutional support tools—content creation templates, pedagogical alignment frameworks, and time allocation for development—that enable instructors to maintain authorship whilst efficiently producing adaptive materials.

The data revealed a crucial finding about instructor mindset that aligns with information ethics principles: instructors who expressed confidence in their students' ability to engage productively with AI personalisation saw better outcomes across all student populations. This validates Floridi's emphasis on treating learners as dignified "informational organisms" rather than passive data subjects. The stark differences between high-engagement courses and low-engagement courses correlated strongly with instructor attitudes toward student capability, demonstrating how pedagogical beliefs about learner agency directly influence technological effectiveness and resist the commodification of education that surveillance capitalism enables.

AI Systems: Designed for Equity or Reproducing Bias. Analysis of system functionality through the lens of algorithmic bias research revealed both promising features and concerning limitations that directly validate Noble's, Benjamin's, and Eubanks' frameworks. The system's adaptive difficulty algorithms, whilst theoretically aligned with Vygotsky's zone of proximal development where learning occurs through manageable cognitive stretch, in practice revealed systematic patterns that disadvantaged certain learners, exemplifying how seemingly neutral educational technologies can encode hierarchies in subtle yet impactful ways. The algorithms failed to distinguish between productive challenge and stress-inducing difficulty, lacking the nuanced calibration needed to maintain each student within their optimal learning zone. For example, Course C lessons ranged from "Moderate" to "Very Hard" difficulty, with the most challenging content showing the steepest engagement drops (from 91% to 79%), suggesting that algorithmic difficulty assessment reproduces rather than addresses diverse learning approaches and prior knowledge differences.

Analysis across courses revealed tension between completion rates and genuine learning. Course D demonstrated this challenge: whilst quiz completion rates remained high (87–98%), lesson completion rates were consistently lower (81–92%), suggesting students prioritised assessable activities over learning content. This pattern indicates that assessment structures may inadvertently encourage surface learning approaches when not designed to reward depth of engagement.

Contrary to expectations, the data revealed no systematic differences in AI effectiveness across disciplines. STEM courses showed both highly successful implementations (Courses A and D) and complete failures (Course B), whilst humanities and business courses similarly demonstrated the full range of outcomes. This finding challenges assumptions about AI adaptive learning being inherently better suited to structured subjects, instead revealing that instructor focus and teaching integration determine success regardless of disciplinary context.

The PALS data revealed nuanced patterns in how AI personalisation affected educational equity. Course E (Business) exemplified problematic remediation patterns, with engagement dropping precipitously from 77% to 37% as content became "Very Easy," suggesting that algorithmic attempts to support struggling students may inadvertently signal low expectations or create stigmatising experiences. More concerning was evidence of the system's tendency to reward students who already possessed academic cultural capital, with high-performing implementations consistently featuring students who could navigate complex lesson structures and maintain engagement across multiple difficulty levels. This pattern directly exemplifies Benjamin's (2019) "New Jim Code"—seemingly neutral educational technologies that appear to address bias whilst actually deepening existing inequalities through fundamental design assumptions. The students most in need of support—those lacking prior exposure to adaptive technologies or struggling with multiple literacies—benefited least, whilst the adaptive learning platform favoured students already equipped with "doing school well" capabilities, validating critical frameworks about how algorithmic systems can automate inequality rather than democratise learning.

The Erosion of Retrieval Practice in the ChatGPT Era

A critical finding emerged from both PALS implementation and broader faculty discussions: the proliferation of generative AI fundamentally undermined traditional adaptive learning assumptions. Student interviews frequently mentioned using ChatGPT and other AI tools to complete adaptive learning activities, whilst instructors reported learning about similar patterns. As one PALS instructor noted: "I think some students were just using ChatGPT to get the answers to the AI adaptive learning tutorials." Yet, this behaviour reflects rational student adaptation to an AI-saturated environment rather than academic dishonesty. When students engage with generative AI through sophisticated prompting and iterative dialogue, they may actually deepen their understanding—the challenge lies in distinguishing productive AI collaboration from mere answer extraction. This erosion of honest engagement represented more than technical circumvention—it revealed a fundamental contradiction in asking students to engage with AI adaptive learning whilst simultaneously discouraging AI use in other contexts. The implications extend beyond individual student choices to challenge the foundational assumptions of AI adaptive learning systems. When students can easily obtain correct answers without engaging in the cognitive effort that builds retention, the carefully designed spacing algorithms and difficulty adjustments lose their pedagogical effectiveness, potentially transforming adaptive learning from a tool for building knowledge into merely another assessment hurdle to circumvent.

Trust as the Mediating Factor for Equitable Outcomes

The PALS findings reveal trust as the crucial element determining whether AI personalisation enhances or undermines educational equity, validating Floridi's emphasis on trust relationships between human and artificial agents within the infosphere. This trust operates across multiple relationships within IMAP but must now navigate the complex landscape of competing AI technologies and student resistance to algorithmic learning approaches. The findings demonstrate that trust emerges not from eliminating surveillance—as Zuboff's framework might suggest—but from ensuring transparency, agency, and beneficial use of collected data.

End-of-course survey data revealed nuanced student attitudes toward AI adaptive learning that differed significantly from faculty concerns about AI circumvention. Across multiple end-of-semester surveys (n = 575), only 39 students (approximately 7%) expressed privacy or security concerns when directly asked about data security and privacy features, suggesting broad comfort with AI-mediated learning when implemented within clear educational frameworks.

Traditional pedagogical relationships depend on trust between students and instructors, but AI personalisation introduces new complexities. The most successful PALS implementations featured explicit trust-building activities where instructors demonstrated their commitment to using AI data to support rather than evaluate students. Both students and instructors developed trust in AI systems through experience with accurate, helpful, and explainable algorithmic recommendations, though trust eroded quickly when systems made obvious errors or provided opaque feedback. Future iterations of adaptive learning systems—potentially leveraging mixture-of-experts (MoE) models and improved natural language processing—may address current limitations in accuracy and contextual understanding, but trust will remain contingent on consistent, transparent, and pedagogically sound AI behaviour.

Student-Centred Learning as the Organising Principle

Perhaps the most significant finding from the PALS initiative is that AI personalisation succeeds or fails based on whether it genuinely centres student learning needs, aligning with decolonial computing principles that privilege local knowledge and diverse epistemologies over standardised algorithmic models. The data challenge simplistic notions of personalisation as individual customisation, revealing that truly student-centred AI implementation requires attention to how algorithmic decisions affect learning communities and educational equity more broadly—echoing Universal Design for Learning (UDL) principles that demand inherently flexible systems serving all learners from inception.

Successful PALS implementations featured instructors who used AI insights to identify and address systemic barriers to learning rather than simply accommodating individual differences, embodying Selwyn's call for human centred approaches that resist techno-solutionist narratives. The tension between algorithmic guidance and student autonomy emerged as a central challenge requiring careful navigation of Floridi's information ethics—students valued AI recommendations when they enhanced rather than replaced their decision-making capacity as "informational organisms," with the most effective implementations providing algorithmic suggestions whilst preserving meaningful student choice about learning paths, content engagement, and assessment approaches.

These findings have significant implications for both theoretical understanding and practical implementation of AI in education, demonstrating that theoretical concerns about surveillance, bias, and equity are concrete realities that manifest through the interactions between learners, instructors, and AI systems. IMAP emerging from this analysis offers a practical lens for evaluating and improving AI personalisation initiatives, emphasising the relational and systemic conditions necessary for AI to support rather than undermine educational equity.

Technical and Implementation Challenges

A critical finding that emerged from instructor training sessions and end-of-semester interviews revealed significant technical limitations that constrained effective AI implementation. All 13 instructors identified three primary technical gaps: limited testing and response capabilities, absence of dynamic personalised AI tutoring support for learners, and uneven quality in AI-generated content creation. These limitations reflect inherent characteristics of current AI models: their probabilistic nature, context-dependent responses, and tendency toward variability. Addressing these challenges requires not just technical improvements but also student education about AI reasoning processes, helping learners understand how and why AI generates particular outputs to use these tools more effectively. Future cost-benefit analyses of addressing these technical limitations represent important areas for continued research.

Student comments revealed frustrations with both technical gaps and instructor implementations (e.g., inadequate feedback and review capabilities, rigid timing constraints, and poor content relevance). Students recommended clearer grading transparency, seamless LMS navigation, flexible scheduling with multiple attempts, and improved mobile accessibility. As one student noted: "I wasn't ever sure what my grade would be" and "You can't go back and look at all the questions to review." Despite these concerns, students appreciated core adaptive features. One student stated, "It helped me go back to the answers I missed and learn how to approach it a different way," demonstrating value when properly implemented.

Limited Assessment Capabilities. Instructors consistently requested expanded question formats beyond the available multiple choice, ordering, and visual click-on options. Many specifically wanted autograded text and formula/solution answers for unstructured responses, noting that assessing learners' knowledge gaps and dynamically creating personalised learning materials requires more sophisticated assessment capabilities. This limitation particularly impacts inclusive learning, as diverse learners express understanding differently—some excel at written explanations, others at problem-solving, and still others through creative application. As one instructor observed, "AI adaptive learning using systematic short interval training works well for test preparation but not as well for general higher education learning."

Need for AI Adaptive Tutoring. Rather than quiz-based retrieval practice, instructors wanted AI systems capable of providing dynamic, contextual tutoring support that could adapt to individual student needs in real time. This represents the unrealised promise of AI over previous algorithmic systems—whilst earlier adaptive platforms could only adjust difficulty and timing, AI should theoretically provide personalised explanations, alternative examples, and Socratic dialogue. This reflects a fundamental gap between current adaptive learning systems optimised for spaced repetition and the complex pedagogical support that higher education requires.

Content Quality and Customisation. Instructors reported uneven quality in AI-generated content and requested access to improved retrieval-augmented generation (RAG) or similar course-specific training and reference systems using instructor-provided or approved materials. This finding highlights the tension between automated content creation and the pedagogical expertise required for discipline-specific learning materials, suggesting that current large language models require domain-specific fine-tuning or enhanced retrieval mechanisms to produce consistently appropriate educational content.

Case Study: PALS Implementation at University of Arizona

The University of Arizona's PALS initiative provides concrete examples of how IMAP manifests in practice through two contrasting implementations that illustrate the critical importance of instructor integration and trust-building.

Course A: Successful STEM Implementation

This general education STEM course served 118 undergraduate students, primarily non-science majors, fulfilling general education requirements. The instructor exemplified strategic AI integration by positioning the adaptive learning system as essential course infrastructure rather than supplementary technology. From the first day, the instructor explicitly framed AI lessons as valuable study resources, explaining that traditional study guides were outdated and would not be updated.

Analysis of pre-course survey data from 82 consenting participants revealed complex relationships between student engagement, AI system usage, and academic achievement. Contrary to expectations, correlations between the four Student Course Engagement Questionnaire sub-scales and either AI adaptive learning platform readiness scores or final course percentage were uniformly small ($|r| \leq .24$), suggesting that self-reported engagement behaviours showed limited predictive value for AI adaptive learning success.

AI adaptive learning platform usage showed modest correlations with course performance: heavier system use predicted slightly higher grades (Study-time $r = .20$; Goal-Reached $r = .18$), but this effect was considerably weaker than the strong relationship between AI adaptive learning platform quiz scores and course grades ($r = .74$). This pattern suggests that whilst AI-mediated practice contributed to learning outcomes, the quality of engagement with adaptive content mattered more than quantity of time spent or goals completed. A multiple regression including study time, goal reached, and all engagement constructs explained only 7% of the variance in final grades, $F(8, 71) = 0.70$, $p = .69$, with no individual predictor reaching significance.

Exploratory k-means clustering of five composite survey constructs (Skills, Emotion, Participation, Performance, and Growth orientation; $N = 80$) revealed an optimal two-cluster solution (silhouette = .30). Cluster 1 ($n = 34$, 43%)—"Highly engaged learners"—scored approximately 0.6–0.8 Likert points higher on all four engagement dimensions than Cluster 2 ($n = 46$, 57%)—"Moderately engaged learners." Standardised mean differences were large for Skills, Emotion, Participation, and Performance (Cohen's $d \approx 1.6$–1.9) and small for Growth orientation ($d \approx 0.29$). Importantly, no additional subgroups improved cluster validity, suggesting a primary distinction between strongly versus moderately engaged students rather than more complex engagement typologies.

The instructor's transparency proved crucial for establishing the trust relationships essential to IMAP. Students were informed that the instructor had personally created all adaptive content and that similar questions would appear on examinations, establishing clear pedagogical authority over the AI system. The grading structure reinforced these connections: each of six topic lessons contributed 15 points toward final grades, creating meaningful incentives without punitive pressure whilst demonstrating the instructor's commitment to the adaptive learning approach. Student response validated the strategic integration approach. Of 118 enrolled students, 92% actively engaged with the AI adaptive learning system, with engagement rates remaining remarkably consistent throughout the semester, declining gradually from 98% initial participation to 86–88% by final lessons. This sustained engagement contrasted sharply with typical educational technology adoption patterns and demonstrated successful coordination between all three parties in IMAP.

This implementation succeeded through effective coordination where the instructor maintained pedagogical authority whilst leveraging AI capabilities, students developed trust through consistent feedback and clear value propositions, and the AI system provided meaningful personalised support without replacing human judgment. The sustained engagement patterns and positive learning outcomes validated both the technical functionality of the adaptive system and the pedagogical approach to integration, providing empirical support for IMAP's emphasis on coordinated rather than isolated technological implementation.

Course B: Unsuccessful Mathematics Implementation

The mathematics course represented the third unsuccessful attempt across three semesters, demonstrating how repeated poor integration reinforces rather than resolves effectiveness issues. The instructor treated AI lessons as supplementary activities rather than integral course components, providing minimal explanation of how adaptive practice connected to course objectives. Student engagement patterns revealed poor implementation consequences. Initial participation appeared promising at 98%, but engagement collapsed precipitously to 0% by the third of 11 lessons, indicating complete student abandonment when the system was not integral to course instruction. This dramatic decline reflected students' rational response to unclear value propositions and poor course integration. Without instructor advocacy and transparent connections to learning outcomes, students had no compelling reason to invest time in adaptive activities.

Cross-Case Analysis

These contrasting cases align with IMAP's emphasis on coordinated functioning. Both courses operated within identical technological and institutional contexts, with similar instructor proficiency, training options, and institutional support. However, instructor time investment varied considerably. The cases achieved opposite outcomes based on instruction strategies and resulting trust relationships, demonstrating that AI adaptive learning success depends fundamentally on human factors rather than technological sophistication. The most successful instructors invested 15–20 hours developing and refining AI content, regularly reviewed student progress data, and explicitly discussed AI learning strategies with students in class. In contrast, low-engagement instructors spent minimal time (0–3 hours) on content development and rarely mentioned the AI system during class sessions. These findings underscore the implications for institutional AI learning system adoption strategies in prioritising instructor development approaches for building commitment and integration skills.

Critical Reflections and Future Directions

The PALS findings reveal significant gaps in how AI personalisation in education is conceptualised, researched, and implemented. Current discourse focuses disproportionately on technical sophistication whilst inadequately addressing the relational and systemic conditions necessary for equitable implementation.

Study Limitations

This research was conducted within a single US institution with volunteer faculty who may not represent broader academic populations. Student performance measurement proved challenging due to uncontrollable factors across diverse course contexts, limiting causal claims about AI effectiveness. Response bias may affect findings, as only 49% of students completed the end of course surveys and 25% randomly invited students participated in interviews, potentially over-representing engaged participants.

Key Gaps and Questions

A critical gap involves the absence of student voices in AI personalisation research. Students' attitudes differed significantly from faculty assumptions, with minimal privacy concerns whilst focusing on integration challenges. This disconnect suggests current debates may address misaligned problems. Furthermore, discourse inadequately addresses the post-ChatGPT landscape's disruption of adaptive learning assumptions. Most research predates widespread generative AI availability, leaving practitioners without frameworks for navigating contradictions between encouraging AI adaptive learning whilst discouraging AI use elsewhere.

The fundamental question becomes not whether AI will shape educational thinking—it already does—but how educators can guide this influence and use AI applications toward productive ends. Can AI truly personalise learning without perpetuating existing inequalities? The evidence suggests current approaches may create new stratification based on digital literacy capabilities rather than addressing fundamental equity concerns. Perhaps most fundamentally, can AI adaptive learning survive generative AI accessibility, or do readily available AI tools fundamentally undermine the retrieval practice and honest engagement that adaptive systems require?

Future Research Directions

Longitudinal studies examining long-term impacts of AI personalisation on student learning, autonomy, and critical thinking capabilities are urgently needed. Critical investigation of student data privacy literacy is essential, particularly examining whether minimal privacy concerns reflect insufficient awareness or normalisation of surveillance within broader contexts such as social media platforms. Future systems should explore dual-track analytics: institutional dashboards for aggregate patterns alongside private student dashboards that empower learners to monitor and direct their own learning without surveillance.

Research into culturally responsive AI design represents another crucial direction, as literacy requirements may serve as equity gatekeepers. The development of student-controlled AI systems offers promising possibilities for maintaining learner agency within personalised environments, whilst comprehensive research into integration challenges is essential for moving beyond proof-of-concept studies toward sustainable implementation.

Conclusion

This study provides compelling empirical evidence that theoretical concerns about AI personalisation in education manifest as concrete realities through complex interactions between learners, instructors, and AI systems. The PALS initiative demonstrates that whilst AI adaptive learning holds significant potential for enhancing educational outcomes, its implementation challenges fundamental assumptions about personalisation, equity, and effective pedagogy.

The central finding—that implementation success depends primarily on instructor integration and IMAP coordination rather than technological sophistication or disciplinary context—validates critical frameworks whilst revealing practical pathways toward more equitable AI deployment. The stark contrast between Course A's sustained 86–98% engagement and Course B's collapse from 98% to 0% engagement illustrates how identical technological capabilities produce vastly different outcomes based on pedagogical approach and trust-building strategies.

Perhaps most significantly, the research reveals how the post-ChatGPT landscape fundamentally disrupts traditional AI adaptive learning assumptions. The erosion of retrieval practice through readily available AI assistance challenges foundational principles of spaced repetition and honest engagement that adaptive systems require, suggesting that current approaches may require fundamental reconceptualisation rather than incremental improvement.

Contributions to Knowledge and Practice

This research bridges critical theoretical frameworks with extensive empirical evidence, moving beyond speculative concerns to examine how surveillance, bias, and equity issues manifest in educational practice. IMAP provides a practical lens for evaluating AI personalisation initiatives that emphasises relational and systemic conditions rather than purely technical considerations. Empirically, the study challenges widespread assumptions about AI personalisation effectiveness. The finding that disciplinary context matters far less than instructor integration contradicts prevailing beliefs about AI being inherently better suited to STEM subjects. Similarly, the discovery that student demographic profiles showed minimal correlation with AI learning effectiveness suggests that equity challenges may be more systemic than previously understood.

The Path Forward

The evidence points toward several critical directions for ethical AI implementation in education. First, institutions must prioritise instructor development that goes beyond technical training to include pedagogical integration and trust-building strategies. Second, AI system design must shift from efficiency-focused approaches toward equity-centred frameworks that prioritise student agency, instructor control, and transparent decision-making processes. Third, the regulatory and policy environment must evolve to address ubiquitous AI realities rather than treating AI personalisation as an isolated phenomenon. The current marketplace reality, with rapid AI deployment often outpacing institutional readiness, demands pragmatic approaches that balance innovation with protection. Institutions must maintain human oversight whilst leveraging AI benefits, creating "guardrails not roadblocks" that enable experimentation within ethical boundaries. Ultimately, this research suggests that AI personalisation's promise remains viable but requires fundamental shifts in how we conceptualise, design, and implement these technologies. Success depends on not only AI capabilities but also on creating educational environments where AI enhances rather than replaces human agency, judgment, and care.

Actionable Recommendations

The PALS findings provide evidence-based guidance for implementing AI personalisation that supports rather than undermines educational equity. These recommendations emerge directly from IMAP.

For Policymakers

Mandate algorithmic transparency requirements for educational AI systems, enabling institutions to understand and explain AI decision-making processes. PALS demonstrates that trust depends on explainability, yet many systems operate as "black boxes" undermining instructor confidence. This includes requiring vendors to provide clear documentation of data usage, algorithm logic, and decision criteria in accessible language.

Establish equity impact assessments for institutional AI adoption, examining differential impacts across student populations. PALS evidence reveals that multiple literacy requirements serve as equity gatekeepers that current evaluation frameworks fail to capture.

Develop coherent policies addressing the contradiction between encouraging AI adaptive learning whilst restricting AI assistance elsewhere. The post-ChatGPT landscape requires frameworks acknowledging AI ubiquity rather than maintaining artificial boundaries.

Fund longitudinal research examining AI personalisation impacts on student autonomy and critical thinking development. Priority should be given to studies that track students across multiple years and educational transitions.

For Educational Institutions

Prioritise instructor development beyond technical training to include pedagogical integration strategies and trust-building approaches. The contrast between successful and unsuccessful PALS implementations demonstrates that AI integration requires new pedagogical expertise that cannot be assumed from general teaching competence.

Address technical friction points and data silos undermining AI effectiveness through seamless LMS integration rather than accepting complex workarounds. Include student voices in AI governance structures. Whilst students expressed minimal privacy concerns in PALS, their focus on integration challenges suggests different priorities than those driving institutional adoption.

Conduct regular equity audits examining differential impacts across student populations, with particular attention to first-generation students, English language learners, and students with varying technology access.

For Educators

Create explicit connections between AI activities and course learning objectives, assessment strategies, and disciplinary expertise. PALS data demonstrate that strategic integration—not technological sophistication—determines student engagement and outcomes.

Preserve meaningful student choice about learning paths whilst providing algorithmic suggestions. Successful PALS implementations enhanced rather than replaced student decision-making capacity.

Address multiple literacy prerequisites through targeted support rather than assuming capability. PALS findings reveal that linguistic, technological, and academic cultural literacies serve as gatekeepers requiring deliberate attention.

Monitor AI recommendations for patterns disadvantaging particular students.

For Technology Developers

Design for transparency and instructor control, enabling educators to understand and modify AI recommendations based on pedagogical expertise. PALS evidence shows instructor trust depends on comprehensibility rather than algorithmic accuracy.

Collaborate meaningfully with educators from diverse disciplines and contexts. The finding that instructor integration matters more than disciplinary context suggests AI systems must support flexible pedagogical approaches.

Enable granular instructor control over AI behaviour at the course level. Successful PALS implementations required instructors to maintain pedagogical authority whilst leveraging AI capabilities. Prioritise seamless integration within existing educational workflows rather than standalone functionality.

Acknowledgement

This publication is based upon work funded by CUES, the Center for University Education Scholarship at the University of Arizona. Any views, findings, or recommendations hereby expressed are those of the author only.

References

Benjamin, R. (2019). *Race after technology: Abolitionist tools for the new jim code*. Polity Press.

CAST. (n.d.). Artificial intelligence & UDL. Retrieved May 28, 2025, from https://www.cast.org/what-we-do/artificial-intelligence

Dettmers, T., Pagnoni, A., Holtzman, A., & Zettlemoyer, L. (2024). QLoRA: Efficient finetuning of quantized LLMs. *Journal of Machine Learning Research*, 25(1), 1–30.

Digital Education Council (2024). *Digital education council global AI student survey 2024*. Digital Education Council. https://www.digitaleducationcouncil.com/post/what-students-want-key-results-from-dec-global-ai-student-survey-2024

Eubanks, V. (2018). *Automating inequality: How high-tech tools profile, police, and punish the poor*. St. Martin's Press.

Floridi, L. (2013). *The ethics of information*. Oxford University Press.

Floridi, L. (2014). *The fourth revolution: How the infosphere is reshaping human reality*. Oxford University Press.

Higher Ed Dive (2013, October 31). Adaptive learning: A guide for higher education leaders. *Higher Ed Dive*. Retrieved from https://www.highereddive.com/news/adaptive-learning-the-best-approaches-weve-seen-so-far/187875/

Hu, E. J., Shen, Y., Wallis, P., Allen-Zhu, Z., Li, Y., Wang, S., Wang, L., & Chen, W. (2022). LoRA: Low-rank adaptation of large language models. *International Conference on Learning Representations (ICLR)*. https://openreview.net/forum?id=nZeVKeeFYf9

Kasinathan, G., & Ranganathan, S. (2023). Artificial intelligence in education in the global South: Promises, threats, and a path forward. *Information Technologies & International Development*, 19, 1–15.

Mohamed, S., Png, M. T., & Isaac, W. (2020). Decolonial AI: Decolonial theory as sociotechnical foresight in artificial intelligence. *Philosophy & Technology*, 33(4), 659–684.

Nguyen, A., Ngo, H. N., Hong, Y., Dang, B., & Nguyen, B. P. T. (2023). Ethical principles for artificial intelligence in education: A systematic review of the global South perspective. *Education and Information Technologies*, 28(4), 4221–4241.

Noble, S. U. (2018). *Algorithms of oppression: How search engines reinforce racism*. New York University Press.

O'Neil, C. (2017). *Weapons of math destruction: How big data increases inequality and threatens democracy*. Crown.

Pedro, F., Subosa, M., Rivas, A., & Valverde, P. (2019). Artificial intelligence in education: Challenges and opportunities for sustainable development. UNESCO Working Papers on Education Policy No. 07. UNESCO.

Reich, J., & Mehta, J. (2024). The coming disruption: AI and the future of educational equity. *Harvard Educational Review*, 94(1), 45–67.

Roediger, H. L., & Karpicke, J. D. (2006). Test-enhanced learning: Taking memory tests improves long-term retention. *Psychological Science*, 17(3), 249–255.

Selwyn, N. (2019). *Should robots replace teachers? AI and the future of education*. Polity Press.

Selwyn, N. (2023). *Critical data studies and education: A research agenda*. Routledge.

Taddeo, M., & Floridi, L. (2018). How AI can be a force for good. *Science*, 361(6404), 751–752.

Tlili, A., Shehata, B., Adarkwah, M. A., Bozkurt, A., Hickey, D. T., Huang, R., & Agyemang, B. (2023). What if the devil is my guardian angel: ChatGPT as a case study of using chatbots in education. *Smart Learning Environments*, 10(1), 15.

University of Arizona (2023). *Fall 2023 Arizona at a glance*. University Analytics and Institutional Research. https://uair.arizona.edu/sites/default/files/2023-09/Fall%202023%20Arizona%20at%20a%20Glance.pdf

Vallor, S. (2016). *Technology and the virtues: A philosophical guide to a future worth wanting*. Oxford University Press.

Wang, R., & Demszky, D. (2023). Is ChatGPT a good teacher coach? Measuring zero-shot performance for scoring and providing actionable insights on classroom instruction. *Proceedings of the 18th Workshop on Innovative Use of NLP for Building Educational Applications* (pp. 626–637).

Wang, S., Christensen, C., Cui, W., Tong, R., Yarnall, L., Shear, L., & Feng, M. (2023). When adaptive learning is effective learning: Comparison of an adaptive learning system to teacher-led instruction. *Interactive Learning Environments*, 31(2), 793–803.

Warschauer, M., & Matuchniak, T. (2024). New technology and digital worlds: Analyzing evidence of equity in access, use, and outcomes. *Review of Research in Education*, 34(1), 179–225.

Williamson, B. (2017). *Big data in education: The digital future of learning, policy and practice*. Sage Publications.

Zembylas, M. (2023). A decolonial critique of 'diversity': Theoretical and methodological implications for meta-intercultural education. *Intercultural Education*, 34(2), 118–133.

Zuboff, S. (2023). The age of surveillance capitalism. In: *Social theory re-wired* (pp. 203–213). Routledge.

7

AI in Education: The Ethical Imperative to Keep Humans in the Loop

Lynn Gribble and Janis Wardrop

The recent proliferation of artificial intelligence (AI) technologies presents higher education with both opportunities and complex ethical dilemmas. While AI offers the promise of personalisation at scale, streamlined administration, and novel modes of student support, it also raises critical concerns regarding the veracity of awarded credentials, academic integrity, and the erosion of human relationships in educational contexts. All this requires consideration in a sector grappling with the pressures of massification, efficiency imperatives, and an increasingly digitised learning environment. This chapter examines two interrelated ethical challenges emerging from the deployment of AI in higher education: the integrity of credentials in an era of generative tools, and the use of data-driven systems to support students – often under the guise of care but with potential for surveillance.

Drawing on lived experience of three years managing education and assessment responses to AI at a research-intensive university, we turn to theoretical frameworks including the McDonaldization of education, sociomateriality, surveillance capitalism, and pedagogies of care, to argue that maintaining the 'human in the loop' (HitL) is essential to safeguard the ethical core of educational relationships. Without intentional oversight, AI risks becoming a tool that reinforces educational inequalities, standardises learning, and diminishes autonomy. Reviewing current practices and a case study of AI-enabled support at an Australian university, we explore how AI can be ethically integrated to enhance learning without compromising the values and purposes of higher education. In doing so, we call for institutional strategies that balance innovation with responsibility, and for educational leaders to ensure that AI serves pedagogical and societal ends – rather than the other way around. This chapter concludes with actionable recommendations recognising AI in education as a wicked problem that is not linear and will require all educators to remain agile in their approaches.

 DOI: 10.1201/9781003626510-7

Theoretical Framework

Exploring the concerns of integrity of credentials and data use for learning support requires conceptualisation of the ethical debates surrounding AI. As the role of a theoretical framework is to provide lenses to understand, analyse, and consider possible answers to these issues, we felt it was important to look to some of the sociological standpoints that have informed human behaviour. While it has been argued (Collins, 2019) that higher education credentials are perhaps more relied upon where it is a doctor, lawyer, or engineer over students with liberal arts or business degrees who do not need a formal degree to 'practice', nonetheless university degrees are signals of expertise and thus institutions have a civic responsibility to ensure the quality and veracity of their educational programs. The concern that AI may undermine the learning process and perpetuate dishonesty of how that learning is demonstrated requires careful attention to what is understood by way of earning a credential and the question of 'professional expertise'. These concerns view AI as a threat to learning (Coole et al., 2024). On the flip side, when we consider the ways that higher education institutions are increasingly using AI and data analytics to support student learning, there are inherent ethical concerns regarding the ways in which data are used to target this learning support (Kurni & Srinivasa, 2021). The use of computer-mediated practices to provide targeted learning support requires a 'human in the loop' (HitL) approach to reduce inbuilt bias and ethical concerns.

We use the concept of the McDonaldization of society as applied to higher education (Hayes, 2017; Ritzer, 2011) to provide an insight into the potential removal of personal agency from the work being done by students, educators, and administrators in higher education. Ritzer's premise is that a McDonaldized society is one that pursues rationalisation as the basis of continuing growth. The McDonaldized 'society' prioritises efficiency, calculability, predictability, and control. The rise of data analytics to mine large data sources over the past 15 years has more recently been further enhanced by the processing capability and efficiency of AI tools. In educational settings, while these tools provide the ability to plan and develop programs and initiatives based on trends in the data, they reduce complex learning processes to standardised, quantifiable outcomes. McDonaldization removes personal agency from the delivery process providing a predetermined manner of delivery and standardisation that is set and not easily adjusted. AI systems that automate assessment, deliver standardised content, and optimise for scale may inadvertently prioritise institutional efficiency over pedagogical depth, transforming education into a consumer product rather than a transformative experience. As such, the risk of the McDonaldization of education (Auh, 2024) and its ethical implications cannot be ignored.

Extending this concept further, we consider sociomateriality (Orlikowski, 2007) which posits that technology tools are not neutral but become active participants in the shaping and evolving the environment. In relation to higher education, the technology in effect comes to shape the learning environment and interactions of the students among and between peers and educators, influencing how and when students engage, what kinds of knowledge are shared, and what forms of participation are valued. Layering these foundations with the use of technology in teaching and education, sociomateriality occurs through the intertwining of technology and social situations leading to changes in classroom dynamics and spaces and ultimately changing social practices (Johri, 2011). These changed practices can also be seen in the way 'student support' is offered and occurs as a type of surveillance capitalism whereby data are collected, used, and manipulated in a way that leads to a panopticon effect of behaviour while embedding bias (Zuboff, 2019). It should be considered that with AI's ubiquitous use, students (and indeed educators) may be utilising it without knowledge or intent to deceive. Hence, sociomateriality helps us understand how the seamless use of AI shifts the students' perception of use and, therefore, raises concerns about credentialisation. Rather than AI being used as a mechanism to defraud the system, educators should perhaps assume AI to be in play, already a part of the system. This approach highlights the potential for wholesale systems change in both delivery and assessment of education.

When considering student support through the use of AI, Zuboff's concept of surveillance capitalism (2019) and Foucault's panopticon (2008) bring another dimension to the ways in which technology and AI are used in the name of 'supporting' learning. AI-powered learning analytics create environments where students are continuously observed and measured. Packaged as behavioural data, but used in ways that drive a profit-making incentive, universities know a lot about their (past, present, and potential) students and staff, with data that are both sensitive and valuable. For potential students, this may include information including equity placement, or disability or access requirements. Having these data, universities can focus on attracting particular students in ways that appease government policy and requirements. Once a student has accepted an offer, the university can not only continue to track these students but collect further data in terms of services accessed and student academic performance. These systems, while promising educational support and personalisation, may instead establish power asymmetries where student behaviour is not only tracked but subtly shaped through awareness of being monitored. This may lead students to not enhance their self-regulatory skills, taking less ownership of their learning believing the 'system' will do it, and lead to reduced student efficacy or engagement. This surveillance dimension raises critical questions about student privacy, autonomy, and the potential reinforcement of existing educational inequalities. There is a very real risk that both faculty and students behave in a manner aligned with what the data predict rather than exerting individual agency over the situation. The panopticon effect (Foucault, 2008) should also be considered.

As students become aware they are being observed (tracking login to learning management systems, or in some institutions keeping attendance records), they are more likely to act in accordance with what they are called on. Just as the prison studies (Foucault, 2008) demonstrated, while this surveillance may be offered in the name of 'student support' and ultimately gain compliance to certain 'required behaviours', it removes the student's efficacy and agency in determining how they want to act or gain support. As such, there are unintended consequences. These may include students not seeking to manage their own studies and time believing the institution or program knows best. This reduction or removal of personal agency and efficacy could have detrimental effects including stifling their growth more generally and in self-regulatory skills (Bandura, 1993) more specifically which is of importance particularly to young people who are transitioning to adulthood and independence while at university (Baumeister, 2001). This could ultimately minimise the transformative impact of higher education. A further problem arises as there may be no standardised approach to such interventions and if students rely upon this operating structure the onus of completion could fall back on the universities over the individual which would be akin to suggesting paying for a gym membership alone will give results. This further reduces the agency of the student (and perhaps the academic in how they teach too), and in an AI-enhanced world, human agency is what separates us from machines.

To counter the automation and technologically mediated learning environments that characterises higher education these days, the pedagogy of care (Soto, 2005) argues that students are more likely to engage, persist, and thrive when they feel seen, valued, and supported as whole people – not just as learners. This allows us to highlight the importance of the HitL, such as the student/teacher relationship. It is this relationship, which is crucial for fostering a supportive learning environment, that academic outcomes are enhanced, and overall student well-being and development is promoted. It is this reciprocal relationship that is noted to benefit all and influence factors such as student engagement, academic achievement, and teacher satisfaction (Soto, 2005). Together, these approaches recognise and reinforce that learning is a human-centred activity. To reduce such humanness undermines what might be ethically understood and agreed upon as the learning process.

Discussion

Considering the theoretical underpinnings outlined above, we return specifically to the ethical concerns with AI in relation to the integrity of awarded credentials and the use of data in the development of student support processes. We assume that the integration of AI in higher education needs to occur due to the wide availability of AI to use in and for education. This integration is required due to its adoption outside of education as we are training students for the 'future world' that is emerging. Further, AI affords us new ways of working that we are only just beginning to explore, but it must be noted that with these opportunities comes risk. To ignore AI use in education is akin to 'burying one's head in the sand' against change. As understood through the lens of sociomateriality, technology has already significantly shifted the educational landscape. Teaching, learning, and education provision has long integrated technology.

A survey from just the last 50 years has seen the advent of word processors, computer programs for statistical analysis, mobile and handheld computers that have enabled efficiency for both students and staff in terms of time saving, access, and equity and enabled the reimagination of information transfer (Spector & Ren, 2015; Terzian, 2019). Technology platforms and the internet have provided opportunities for education to reach vast numbers of people traditionally locked out of higher education through MOOCs and other formal online degree programs (Stone, 2017). We can also see that technology fuels the McDonaldization of higher education, whereby technology provides the means to manage ever larger numbers of applicants and students to enter the system. Technology-enhanced learning and teaching has attracted the attention of researchers and practitioners (Deneen et al., 2025) recognising how these mostly seamless integrations have enhanced and supported learners.

Credentialing and Assurance of Learning

The use of technology crosses the complex path of assuring the academic integrity of qualifications (Cotton et al., 2023). Determining threshold knowledge and knowhow is required for each subject and discipline, and methods of assurance need to be implemented to ensure trust in qualifications. The rise of open-access GenAI processing in late 2022 has introduced varying levels of doubt as to the integrity of qualifications awarded, and undermined trust in qualifications (Hughes et al., 2025). Common assessment practices of written, even video submissions can be considered a demonstration of what a student could do alone. As a proxy of ability, it is now close to useless. In the space of a couple of years, as Agentic AI is now increasing available, discussion board and learning management system (LMS) access can be handled remotely by AI. With an agent that can act independently as programmed, students could send an AI agent to answer the discussion board by having read the previous thread and responding, thus rendering such activities as fruitless as a form of either engagement or as a proxy for demonstrating learning. This type of technology is already available and will become more widespread. Recent developments including digital twins and language processing mean that video and audio are also questionable when not face to face. Wearable devices including Meta's new Ray-Ban glasses and Apple's new translation AirPods make AI both ubiquitous and undetectable even when face to face with a student, highlighting the need for disclosure and open use.

There has been much discussion on GenAI's ability to produce cohesive and plausible narratives that can even pass the US bar examinations (Cassens Weiss, 2023). The ability of a chatbot to create assessment artefacts that can meet the descriptive requirements in assessment criteria is a real concern. It can be difficult to adequately evaluate whether students can actually do the work that universities' attribute to the degree/credential, which is a major concern not just to the institution, but to the wider public (Liu, 2025). For example, awarding a medicine degree to a student who has used AI to construct answers for assessment raises serious issues of integrity, but also doubt as to whether the student has sufficient knowledge to understand the concerns of the patient and their level of expertise to diagnose and treat illness.

While early days yet, Friederichs et al. (2023) state that ChatGPT can pass two-thirds of the progress medical examination in German outperforming all most all medical students in years 1–3. While in July, 2025, in Flanders (Belgium), three students who were caught using AI to sit their medical entrance examination, even though the computers were supposed to be locked down to any other software, were immediately disqualified (VRT News, 2025). This is cause for concern, and ethically, this is not virtuous. A good person would not or perhaps more importantly should not pretend they can do something they cannot. Yet, the heart of this discussion sits with the difficulty of students recognising what they need to be able to do on their own or acknowledge how assistance was gained using technology which is both ubiquitous and often 'hidden in plain sight'.

From use of word processing to programs such as Grammarly and PDF readers, some students are now relying on technology in place of what would have been considered basic academic skills. Traditionally gaining a qualification certified a level of knowledge and competence – it was a proxy for ability and knowledge (Gallagher, 2016; Pittinsky, 2015). The unattributed use of GenAI by students to complete assessments may change this perception with a great divide between those who earned degrees pre 2022 and those who did so post. That is not to say that the integrity of credentials pre 2022 has always been pure (Gaston & Van Noy, 2022). Students have used various forms to short cut their learning and assessment processes from 'Cliff notes' to the extreme of contract cheating whereby another person completed the assessment items (Bretag, 2013). All these ethical concerns link back to gaining an unfair advantage or being dishonest in the process of gaining a qualification. The legal notion of 'passing off' is not what a virtuous person would do.

This assumes only the duplicitous side of using GenAI with an intent to deceive. There is another part to this ethical debate which is where the students have access to AI tools so embedded in technology that they may not recognise the assistance they are receiving or how that may reduce their ability to act without assistance. The ubiquity of word processing software containing spell check and grammar checking facilities (both forms of AI) means that students are exposed to AI use through the very tools required to produce their assessment submissions. In Australia, the Australian Academic Integrity Network (AAIN) along with TEQSA (the accrediting body) have focused much of the conversation around what constitutes a breach.

While these forms of AI assistance such as Grammarly were not considered an academic integrity breach (unless there is an express prohibition of use), as these tools have become more 'intervening' in their output anecdotally, some academics are now also concerned about this type of use too. This raises another issue in as much as using GenAI tools to improve writing (such as 'make it sound more professional', 'translate from native language into English') may leave students believing that this is still their OWN original work and may mislead future employers who rely upon qualifications as a proxy for various abilities in language usage. For a number of reasons, this type of usage may not be identified (or is sometimes deliberately overlooked) leaving the student blissfully unaware that the work submitted is no longer wholly their own or representative of their abilities. These concerns were raised in the Parliamentary enquiry into AI use in education as far back as late 2023 (Parliament of Australia, 2024).

While students have previously relied upon internet searches to support their assessment writing or even assignment spinning (whereby a paper is rewritten with new words to avoid plagiarisms detection), students are now offered AI-generated answers in a Google search further muddying of the waters. The integration of AI tools into common software tools and platforms makes it extremely difficult for a student to quarantine themselves even if they choose not to use a GenAI systems such as Co-pilot, OpenAI, Perplexity, or Claude (which may do the research and writing for them). While the students may not have intended to act unethically, such use, as at 2025, may still considered to be a level of cheating (Currie, 2023). As any work done on a computer or nearby a computer in 2025 can be safely assumed to have used AI at some level (from research assistant to private tutor or even as a scribe or co-author), the fundamental ethical concern remains whether the university can correctly certify that the student has met all requirements, acquired sufficient knowledge and demonstrated the mastery of specific skills inherent in the awarding of a degree or qualification.

Therefore, universities need to encourage the incorporation AI integration into assessment with acknowledgement, that will, for now, support our students to recognise: when and how AI is used; the need to differentiate what is done by whom; and support a future where AI use is transparently acknowledged and accepted. The issue then shifts to one of transparency and trust in the qualification. What was previously assumed is no longer the case and there is a real need to unpack what students can be reasonably expected to do as a result of their degrees. For example, being able to produce a coherent written report was a skill held by the student having completed a business degree. Perhaps, now it is the ability to do this with the assistance of AI. Going forward, it is clear that AI should be assumed to be used by any one at any time as it is integrated into normal use of word processing and other general use software such as PowerPoint or even Canva. However, we advocate that AI use should be acknowledged by students and academics akin to a research assistant, editor or even muse, just as one would acknowledge the input and assistance from a human. Such acknowledgement is what a virtue ethicist would expect (Hursthouse & Pettigrove, 2023). However, it still is reliant upon the student recognising AI is in use and declaring its use.

Based on the above, it would appear the main ethical concern becomes one of trust. Do academics trust the students to have done the work required to produce the assignment? Can employers trust that the employee has the knowledge and skills to do their job? Perhaps more importantly, can we as a society rely upon the qualifications of someone as a certification of their abilities? To ensure trust, students must take ownership and responsibility for the assessment output, noting any errors or omissions are made under human (that is their own) supervision. Supervision is one of the ways HitL could be part of the production of work or overseeing output. Nonetheless, the HitL remains important in the process of education as it requires us to conceptualise the nature of risk and responsibility rather than rely upon a McDonaldized system for the input or the output (Fuchsberger & Frauenberger, 2023).

Further, the use of AI is not an input and output situation alone. As fact checking and research skills along with critical thinking are all competencies that higher education claims to develop (Golden, 2023), assessment artefacts need to enable students to demonstrate these skills rather than believing they are inherent in the ability to produce a piece of well written and argued work. This points to the need to reimagine assessment artefacts and processes. It also requires society broadly, and the organisations that employ our graduates, to understand how the education process has and must change. Just as we expect everyone who has an office job today can use MS Office products that was not the case in 1990. The challenge here is that AI is changing how we educate students as well as the nature of work, but we are still trying to understand the implications and ultimate reach of these changes. Verhoeven and Hor (2025) provided a Framework for Human-Centric AI-First Teaching focused on four areas that suggest AI integration from preparation through to assessment including personalising learning and engaging the student, while continuous monitoring is also at play. However, for assurance of learning and credential integrity, consideration must be given to reimagining assessments to include 'process' assessments (Gribble & Wardrop, 2024a), interactive orals (Ward et al., 2023), and a return to viva voces.

Without deliberate attention, these ethical concerns will continue to plague those who issue qualifications and those who rely upon them. Higher education must consider ways of ensuring the qualifications issued have been gained with a mutual understanding of technology use as part of the process. This requires an understanding of how technology has shaped and changed the learning spaces and processes. While some use is seen as a threat, technology is also providing opportunities that can deliver learning support to large numbers of students in ways that are both efficient and effective (Deneen et al., 2025).

Student Support Based on Data

When discussing the use of student data to provide learning support, we need to consider how current data collection policies and data use are governed. Much of the privacy and data protection laws and regulations worldwide were implemented prior to the widespread use of AI and while they have been amended since the world continues to grapple with legislative foundations that can be relied upon where the use of data occurs in ways unintended from the original collection (Reis et al., 2024). This is further exacerbated when such data have been broken into other perhaps non identifiable pieces of information (Ye et al., 2024). As GenAI relies upon data held by large language models (LLMs) then feeding into pretrained transformers (GPTs) to give the next most likely word in a sentence in context, the source of the data informing these LLMs is unclear and undisclosed but must be considered as to where and how that data were obtained (Ye et al., 2024). The introduction of deep research and RAG to sit over GPT interfaces has meant the base source is often even further obscured.

Turning back to the focus of data use for student support and when considered in terms of the vast amounts of data universities' house about students and their staff and its use ethically, of particular concern is that the opportunity to query vast amounts of data for insights that are beyond what the data were originally intended (Ye et al., 2024). AI creates many opportunities to use large data sets to drive student support initiatives such as identifying students at academic risk. Using data that are relevant including when a student logs on or what areas of the LMS have been accessed can be valuable to provide nudges (Thaler & Sunstein, 2009) or links to academic support. However, categorising students by specific data points may create scenarios that may create or even further entrench inequality (Aldoseri et al., 2023). The assumptions of the builders of these data mining systems may build in hidden assumptions or inaccuracies. For example, The Australian Government as far back as 2008 set a target of 20% enrolments for students from low SES backgrounds, yet at 2023, these numbers remain consistently close to 16% (Australian Government Department of Education, 2024). For these students, government funding supports the creation of programs that identify and provide targeted support to students with these demographic characteristics (first in family, low SES) in the belief that these students need additional educational support.

AI and data analytics processes are implemented that track the learning analytics data of these students putting more surveillance on the student learning activity or set up more reminders even when the student has no behavioural risk factors at play (Inside UNSW, 2024). While possibly set up with the best intentions, it is important to understand that being low SES does not automatically mean that student needs additional learning support and assistance (Rakesh et al., 2025). It is also true that such a student may not want to have a 'label' attached to themselves that identifies them as 'other'; hence, despite the best intentions of the institution, the support offered may be inappropriate. From an equity perspective, using the demographic label of low SES as the initial filter could mean that other students who are need of such support are never identified and supported. While care and virtue ethics may signal the use of data as appropriate for student support, the need for programmers to be aware of inherent biases remains.

While academic achievement data may inform us of the attainment of assessment standards, using demographic data to target tutoring or support with what might appear to be good intentions may further entrench disadvantage due to a broad-brush approach to support students with such backgrounds. Equity scholarships provide much needed funds and support to those from low SES backgrounds – the premise being to ensure a solid start to studying at a tertiary level. Yet once enrolled, the support offered may be more than that offered to other students possibly creating an 'uneven playing field'. This is, at a minimum, misguided 'assistance' and potentially unethical. It fails to recognise that while those who are low SES may struggle in some ways, other studies have shown these students to be more focused, determined and willing to work hard (Croizet & Dutrévis, 2004). Hence, using a demographic data point to target student support is problematic. While these approaches may seem a way of embedding care pedagogy and ethics, it instead leads to over or under surveillance and may entrench a McDonaldized system whereby human oversight is removed and the 'interventions' only occur as preprogrammed without individualised considerations. We must recognise how the technology impacts the learning spaces and approaches (Haleem et al., 2022). Yet, the ability to personalise at scale using AI has enabled growth and reach.

Learning support must walk a fine line between assistance and nagging, or just straight harassment. Despite these concerns, the use of AI data and personalisation at scale is particularly useful to support large student cohorts. For example, AI capabilities embedded in the LMS can send timely reminders and emails to support those students who may lack educational capital (after Bourdieu, 1986) to undertake their learning. Email reminders, plug-ins that take students to specific information, and messages based on interactions, logs, and time spent on the system can all be activated to ensure students are not slipping through the cracks. The use of these types of AI tools allows educators to take a 'set and forget' approach (that is set up the process at the start of term) to ensuring students know what to do and when. It means educators no longer need to analyse the learning analytic data and send individual reminders based on the results – effectively reducing the mental load of the administrative or some care tasks of the education delivery. For students, it means they can rely upon being reminded (by a machine) when to start their assessments and at what stage of study or learning they should have completed. See the ASM case study below for more details on this. There is little or no need for the student to manage the input stage of the planning.

While it could be argued that learning to plan and instances of failure of such activities is inherently valuable to the learning process (Caliskan, 2021), but this is outside of the ethical debate about such use of AI. Instead, we question where the HitL is located as teaching and education is noted to be a relational activity (Owusu-Agyeman & Moroeroe, 2023). From enhancing teacher satisfaction to the development of students to be self-directed and regulated learners, the relational aspects of teaching and learning cannot be ignored. Hence, where the use of AI allows the educator to be 'absent' or removes the human in the relationship, there is a risk of loss of human connectedness which cannot be ignored as an important part of the learning relationship. However, reducing the mechanical/administrative processes that support student learning may provide educators with the cognitive and emotional 'space' to engage to a greater depth in the pastoral role to support student learning. Therefore, we argue that while AI may assist, the initiative must not become a McDonaldized process used without the ability for human intervention as necessary and needed along the way; otherwise, each student is reduced to a predetermined number. Rather than personalisation at scale, we would see depersonalisation to a level that sees students as Pink Floyd (1979) would note as 'just another brick in the wall'.

Case Study

UNSW Sydney has created and implemented Academic Success Monitor (ASM) as a mechanism to provide targeted learning support at the individual course level. This product uses the LMS student data to provide suggested nudges based on student behaviour or interaction. Course convenors set parameters within the system drawing on learning analytic data, such as when the student has logged on and what parts of the LMS have been visited, to send reminders to the students. The ASM provides the mechanism for a HiTL 'at scale' as the course convenor establishes the trigger points for intervention and crafting messages with their own 'human voice'. Once set, the ASM analyses data and sends the messages at pre-determined times across the learning process. These type of data informed interactions enable personalisation at scale but also reduce academic administration while enabling every student to feel seen and heard.

The LMS also has functions that can be deployed to further this support but rely upon student data. From reminders to non-submitters of assessment items to personalised emails congratulating students on assessment outcomes or offering support to improve academic performance, this use of student data shows benefit and is also ethical in its use under a pedagogy of care and subsequent care and virtue ethics. While ASM houses biographical data, it should also be noted that as an ethical stance, the authors have never accessed the biographical data or previous grade data to determine academic intervention or support; yet, it is unclear if others do. This raises questions of what data are provided. Yet, the system allows only the convenor to look at set interactions as designed by them based on information that is already available in the LMS logs or through other student information. It is the format and integration that enables quick and easy intervention based on currently held data relative only to the specific course. In doing so, there continues to be an expectation upon the convenor to continue to incorporate care and virtue ethics while using such system to prevent students turning into data points only.

In teaching large classes, the data-informed interactions provided by ASM have reduced the risk of students 'falling through the cracks'. In the early weeks of a course, the pre-programmed interactions ensure that students get off to a great start, monitoring and reminding students to access and information that is deemed critical to their success. This type of interaction forms part of the care pedagogy of the course by individually looking into students learning needs based on their behaviour. Care pedagogy goes beyond interactions in the classroom to the digital space too. Further, as a care ethics perspective asks us to make decisions that are sensitive to the needs and well-being of individuals within a relational context looking into the behaviours of learners to determine how to best support these students remotely fits within this ethical scope. While it could be argued that it is too much oversight of student behaviour, ensuring students know what to do and assisting them to do so in a large compulsory core course also is good general pedagogy too.

Nevertheless, the vast amounts of data that institutions hold on a student are of assistance when looking at concerns about credentialling and academic integrity. These data can support investigations of academic integrity breaches. Data including student logs, locations, and even metadata in the documents all support ensuring the student has done the right thing and where there is a problem that does not go undetected. Central integrity offices at a number of universities have such access and are now running such programs (Lodge, 2024). Organisational policy is important too, noting that while some institutions do this as part of the investigation when a problem is suspected, others do so as a matter of course in a panopticon manner. The use of data in this manner assumes a surveillance mode. Rather than relying on the good character of the student to act with virtue, these systems suggest that the student will be caught if they are doing the 'wrong' thing. It also sends a message that they are being watched to ensure ethical and honest behaviour. If this is the action taken, however, this also raises issues of disclosure. Students should be made aware that such measures are in place. A clear statement that universities are using AI and logs to ensure academic integrity, as a type of policing practice, means disclosure to the students is important and imperative.

The use of data also shows how sociomateriality is occurring in education more broadly but may not yet be acknowledged. The use of AI for student support and to ensure academic integrity based upon data can be useful. Doing so ethically remains the practice of the academic and the programmer along with consideration of unintended consequences while ensuring transparency of use.

Critical Reflections and Future Directions

The impact of AI on assessment and by extension credentials cannot be underestimated. While we have provided a case of how AI has supported students to be successful and meet the assessment requirements and at the same time how it has assisted the university to maintain integrity of the submissions it receives, the HitL remains central in these processes. The risk of outsourcing such tasks to a fully automated process cannot be ignored. Data on its own cannot tell a full story. A program can only do what it is instructed to do. It may miss nuances; it cannot make decisions on factors that are outliers to the normalised process.

The HitL remains critically important in any deployment of such tools. From deciding what and when to intervene, to recognising that while a set of rules may provide guidance, all teaching actions may be impacted by a philosophical approach. A machine sees the algorithm, while the teacher sees the student. The risk of deploying the wrong message remains high, and the backlash from students about AI use has a growing voice of descent (Auh, 2025). Students want HitL in their studies and in their learning. The role of universities means they must balance these capabilities with managing expectations and their purpose. Any deployment of AI for any use should go through a discussion of ethical considerations and must be part of informed use and consent.

It is also critical that data be used in a manner that is consistent to ensure support for all regardless of demographic information. By focusing on desired student learning behaviour, use of AI can provide support at scale. Any data analytics must have ethical guidelines that continue to evolve in line with or exceed societal expectations (Okorie et al., 2024). The protection and storage, along with use of data, must align with the purpose for which it was collected just as it might under the ethical guidelines of research. The future must focus on disclosed and potential use, informed consent, and the test of a reasonable person. Humans cannot and must not abrogate their responsibility. Safety systems where AI is deployed must ensure there are plans for the possibility of a zero day (where all systems break). Further, it is unacceptable to just accept the 'black box' conditions of AI systems; it is the responsibility of all those who use AI, and those whose data inform AI, to understand how it is deployed and where the data are used and housed.

There is a bigger problem in the data ownership and the inability to withdraw consent of use. The risk of discrimination as a result of previously held data remains high. The call is to humanity. We need to invest energy and resources to maintain the ability to ethically consider our actions (in using data and programming AI). The fundamental education of being a 'good human' is what will support ethical outcomes with AI. However, we need to continue to recognise that AI of itself is neither inherently good nor bad, but its use is in the hands of humanity.

Conclusion

Artificial intelligence is not a distant threat or a speculative future – it is already shaping the present realities of higher education. As this chapter has demonstrated, its integration into credentialing systems and student support processes carries both opportunities and risk. AI offers efficiency, responsiveness, and the ability to personalise learning at scale, but with the potential to undermine trust in qualifications, compromise student autonomy, and entrench inequities through opaque or misdirected uses of data. The ethical use of AI in education demands that institutions do more than adopt new technologies – they must also re-examine their pedagogical practices, reassess the purposes of assessment, and reimagine the student–educator relationship. Central to this is retaining the human in the loop: educators who exercise care, judgement, and contextual awareness, and students who are supported not just as data points, but as developing agents of their own learning. In a volatile, uncertain, complex, and ambiguous (VUCA) world, higher education has a responsibility not only to adapt to technological change but to lead with ethical foresight, including setting transparent policies, ensuring informed consent, and creating ethical guardrails that extend beyond compliance to foster genuine accountability and care. Ultimately, the question is not whether AI should be used in education, but how – and to what ends. If we are to preserve the transformative potential of higher education, we must insist that AI be deployed in ways that are pedagogically sound, socially just, and human-centred.

Actionable Recommendations

Having considered the issues of credentials and concerns in relation to data use in learning support specifically with reference to higher education, we now turn our focus to actionable steps that can be taken to address these.

From keeping the human in the loop (HitL), to empowering educators to reimagine how they teach, and having institutional guardrails to support rather than constrain use, what is most important is to recognise that AI is going to continue to be available and impact higher education. The steps we take today need to be constantly reevaluated and updated to ensure they are appropriate in this ever-changing landscape.

Highlight the Human in the Loop

The risk of losing the human in the loop (HitL) cannot and should not be underestimated. From concerns of academic integrity to off-loading care and support, non-human intervention or machines operating without human oversight risks removing responsibility and agency of both the student and the educator. While a machine can provide reminders or even cajole both to take action for both to 'fulfil' their duties, this is at best behaviour shaping through Foucault's (2008) panopticon effect. Mechanistic actions without relationship risk reducing satisfaction of both parties. Additionally, there can be unintended consequences yet to be imagined or explored that cannot be ignored. Where AI is used, it must be disclosed, and the human must take responsibility but also be clearly signposted as to their role in all work. This transparency is important but also will enable clear accountability to be maintained and not further erode the human element of teaching and learning.

Asking the Right Questions

Ethical use of AI means we need to ask the right questions of ourselves, each other, and the data. Taking care of the data along with considering its intended use provides a place to launch any data use. Disclosure of collection and use is also important. As our use of data relies upon an ability to both program and interrogate it, those who use and access the data must be reminded of the ethical concerns at play. Just because you can do something, does not mean you should. We must ensure that actions are questioned, justified, and explored from multiple ethical standpoints with care and virtues at the centre of actions taken.

Setting Guardrails

Organisations, policymakers, and governments need to explore and set guardrails and guidelines to enable and ensure those who implement the policies and practices and educate do so with consideration for ethical practices that are fit for a volatile, uncertain, complex, and ambiguous (VUCA) world where the societal mores continue to evolve. As legislation is often lagging societal needs and only sets the minimum standard (Crowe & Agnew, 2020), organisations and society as a whole must act in the interests of greater good rather than a select minority.

Give Academics Time

Universities need to recognise the need for academics to reimagine education. This is not just their job but will require space and time to consider how both delivery and assessment can change and adapt. This will mean there is a need to reimagine academic identities shifting to being facilitators and moving from 'guide on the side' to 'meddler in the middle' curator and co-teacher. Creation and innovation will be the cornerstones of academic roles rather than expertise alone. At the same time, there are also opportunities to reduce some of the workload of teaching and research. GenAI enables academics to create 'clones' fed with their own data and teaching materials enabling 24/7 support for students – a personalised tutor anytime of the day or night. Yet, there is a dark side to be considered particularly in the light of the economic rationalist perspective whereby a professor could be cloned and no longer employed. As such, students could be misled in terms of who is the course authority. However, these are not new concerns and have been present prior to widespread AI use inasmuch as videos were often produced once and reused without paying the academic a second time. Hence, there is potential for good or ethical and declared use or the darker side, which is impacting the arts industry already and could lead to job loss or unethical use. Any use must consider the broader societal impacts and not focus on the economic rationalist perspective alone.

Focus on Assurance of Learning

Importantly, academics need to reimagine what can be used to measure learning. Rather than taking an output, such as written assignment, presentation, or the use of memory in examination like conditions, we need to identify new ways to measure a student's ability to use concepts, models, and skills. Pratschke's (2024) generativism is one view that may assist as an emerging pedagogy seeing GenAI as a collaborator in co-creation. Pratschke contends we must look for ways to observe 'competence' as underlying, unconscious knowledge, as well as 'performance', which is the actual use of knowledge in specific situations. Doing this requires a deep understanding of what the 'real work' is being expected of the student (Gribble & Wardrop, 2024b).

References

Standing Committee on Employment, Education and Training 05/02/2024 Inquiry into the use of generative AI in the Australian Education System https://parlinfo.aph.gov.au/parlInfo/search/display/display.w3p;query=Id%3A%22committees%2Fcommrep%2F27676%2F0000%22 viewed September 9, 2025.

Aldoseri, A., Al-Khalifa, K. N., & Hamouda, A. M. (2023). Re-thinking data strategy and integration for artificial intelligence: Concepts, opportunities, and challenges. *Applied Sciences, 13*(12), 7082. https://doi.org/10.3390/app13127082

Auh, J. Y. (2024). The McDonaldisation of higher education in the age of AI. *World University News*. Dec 11. https://www.universityworldnews.com/post.php?story=20241211163650560 viewed December 15, 2024.

Auh, J. Y. (2025). Wrong battle? Universities must lead, not fight, AI integration. *University World News*. May 22. https://www.universityworldnews.com/post.php?story=20250522152541838 viewed June 3, 2025.

Australian Government Department of Education (2024). Key findings from the 2023 higher education student statistics. [online] Department of Education. Available at: https://www.education.gov.au/higher-education-statistics/student-data/selected-higher-education-statistics-2023-student-data/key-findings-2023-student-data viewed October 13, 2025.

Bandura, A. (1993). Perceived self-efficacy in cognitive development and functioning. *Educational Psychologist, 28*(2), 117–148. https://doi.org/10.1207/s15326985ep2802_3

Baumeister, R. F. (2001). Self-regulation in adulthood. In: *N. J. Smelser & P. B. Baltes (Eds.), International Encyclopedia of the Social & Behavioral Sciences*. Pergamon. https://doi.org/10.1016/B0-08-043076-7/01776-9

Bourdieu, P. (1986). The forms of capital. In J. Richardson (Ed.), *Handbook of Theory and Research for the Sociology of Education* (pp. 241–258). Greenwood.

Bretag, T. (2013). Short-cut students: From academic misconduct to academic integrity. In: G. Sweeney, K. Despota, & S. Lindner (Eds.), *Global Corruption Report: Education* (pp. 171–177). Routledge.

Caliskan, O. (2021). Learning from failure or failing to learn: Perspectives of school principals. *Journal of Educational Administration, 59*(4), 422–436. https://doi.org/10.1108/JEA-07-2020-0158

Cassens Weiss, D. (2023). Latest version of ChatGPT aces bar exam with score nearing 90th percentile. *ABA Journal*. March 16. https://www.abajournal.com/web/article/latest-version-of-chatgpt-aces-the-bar-exam-with-score-in-90th-percentile#google_vignette viewed June 3, 2025.

Collins, R. (2019). *The Credential Society: An Historical Sociology of Education and Stratification*. Columbia University Press.

Coole, M., Doudle, W., Lockhart, N., & Yuan, S. (2024). The negative impact of AI on academic integrity in tertiary education. *Australian Cyber Security Magazine*. https://australiancybersecuritymagazine.com.au/the-negative-impact-of-ai-on-academic-integrity-in-tertiary-education/ viewed June 3, 2025.

Cotton, D. R. E., Cotton, P. A., & Shipway, J. R. (2023). Chatting and cheating: Ensuring academic integrity in the era of ChatGPT. *Innovations in Education and Teaching International, 61*(2), 228–239. https://doi.org/10.1080/14703297.2023.2190148

Croizet, J. C., & Dutrévis, M. (2004). Socioeconomic status and intelligence: Why test scores do not equal merit. *Journal of Poverty, 8*(3), 91–107. https://doi.org/10.1300/J134v08n03_05

Crowe, J., & Agnew, L. (2020). Legal obligations and social norms. *Adelaide Law Review, 41*(1), 217–241.

Currie, G. (2023). A conversation with ChatGPT. *Journal of Nuclear Medicine Technology, 51*(3), 255–260. https://doi.org/10.2967/jnmt.123.265864

Deneen, C., Huijser, H., Corrin, L., & Han, F. (2025). Building bridges: What 40 years of educational technology research teaches us about the theory-practice gap.

Australasian Journal of Educational Technology, 41(1), 1–6. https://doi.org/10.14742/ajet.10589
Foucault, M. (2008). Panopticism, discipline & punish: The birth of The prison. *Race/Ethnicity: Multidisciplinary Global Contexts, 2*(1), 1–12.
Friederichs, H., Friederichs, W. J., & März, M. (2023). ChatGPT in medical school: How successful is AI in progress testing? *Medical Education Online*. 28(1), 2220920. https://doi.org/10.1080/10872981.2023.2220920. PMID: 37307503; PMCID: PMC10262795. Viewed online September 26, 2025.
Fuchsberger, V., & Frauenberger, C. (2023). Doing responsibilities in entangled worlds. *Human–Computer Interaction, 40*(1–4), 65–88. https://doi.org/10.1080/07370024.2023.2269934
Gallagher, S. R. (2016). *The Future of University Credentials. New Developments at the Intersection of Higher Education and Hiring*. Harvard Education Press.
Gaston, P. L., & Van Noy, M. (2022). *Credentials. Understanding the Problems. Identify the Opportunities. Create the Solutions*. Routledge.
Golden, B. (2023). Enabling critical thinking development in higher education through the use of a structured planning tool. *Irish Educational Studies, 42*(4), 949–969. https://doi.org/10.1080/03323315.2023.2258497
Gribble, L., & Wardrop, J. (2024a). Building AI literacy: Assessment as a process to navigate the future. In: *Professional Development Workshop, July 2–4 2024*. Advance HE University of Nottingham Trent.
Gribble, L., & Wardrop, J. (2024b). Empowering students from assumptions to knowledge: making integrity everyone's business. Chapter 14 in S. Mahmud (Ed.,) (2024). Academic Integrity in the Age of Artificial Intelligence.
Haleem, A., Javaid, M., Qadri, M. A., & Suman, R. (2022). Understanding the role of digital technologies in education: A review. *Sustainable Operations and Computers, 3*, 275–285. https://doi.org/10.1016/j.susoc.2022.05.004
Hayes, D. (2017). Beyond the McDonaldization of higher education. In: *Beyond McDonaldization: Visions of Higher Education* (pp. 1–18). Taylor & Francis.
Hughes, L., Malik, T., Dettmer, S., Al-Busaidi, A., & Dwivedi, Y. (2025). Reimagining higher education: Navigating the challenges of generative AI adoption. *Information Systems Frontiers*. https://doi.org/10.1007/s10796-025-10582-6
Hursthouse, R., & Pettigrove, G. (2023). "Virtue Ethics", The Stanford Encyclopedia of Philosophy (Fall 2023 Edition). In Edward N. Zalta & Uri Nodelman (Eds.), https://plato.stanford.edu/archives/fall2023/entries/ethics-virtue/
Inside UNSW. (2024). UNSW Sydney wins at 2024 Gartner Eye on Innovation Awards | Inside UNSW. [online] Available at: https://www.inside.unsw.edu.au/awards/unsw-sydney-wins-2024-gartner-eye-on-innovation-awards viewed 15 October, 2025.
Johri, A. (2011). The socio-materiality of learning practices and implications for the field of learning technology. *Research in Learning Technology, 19*(3). https://doi.org/10.3402/rlt.v19i3.17110
Kurni, M., & Srinivasa, K. G. (2021). *A Beginner's Guide to Learning Analytics*. Springer.
Liu, L. (2025). AI and the crisis of legitimacy in higher education. *American Journal of STEM Education, 4*, 16–26. https://doi.org/10.32674/42qssk59
Lodge, J. (2024). The evolving risk to academic integrity posed by generative artificial intelligence: Options for immediate action. [online] Available at: https://www.teqsa.gov.au/sites/default/files/2024-08/evolving-risk-to-academic-integrity-posed-by-generative-artificial-intelligence.pdf viewed June 13, 2025.

Okorie, G., Udeh, C., Adaga, E., DaraOjimba, O., & Oriekhoe, O. (2024). Ethical considerations in data collection and analysis: A review investigating ethical practices and challenges in modern data collection. *International Journal of Applied Research in Social Sciences, 6*, 1–22. https://doi.org/10.51594/ijarss.v6i1.688

Orlikowski, W. J. (2007). Sociomaterial practices: Exploring technology at work. *Organization Studies, 28*(9), 1435–1448. https://doi.org/10.1177/0170840607081138

Owusu-Agyeman, Y., & Moroeroe, E. (2023). Relationality and student engagement in higher education: Towards enhanced students' learning experiences. *International Journal of Emotional Education, 15*, 37–53. https://doi.org/10.56300/ZANL1419

Parliament of Australia (2024). ParlInfo. [online] Aph.gov.au. Available at: https://parlinfo.aph.gov.au/parlInfo/search/display/display.w3p, viewed October 13, 2025.

Pink Floyd. (1979). Another Brick in the Wall, Part 2. *The Wall* [Record/CD/Digital File]. Capitol/MGM/UA Entertainment Company.

Pittinsky, M. (2015). Credentialing in higher education: Current challenges and innovative trends. *EDUCAUSE Review* (Online).

Rakesh, D., Lee, P. A., Gaikwad, A., & McLaughlin, K. A. (2025). Annual research review: Associations of socioeconomic status with cognitive function, language ability, and academic achievement in youth: A systematic review of mechanisms and protective factors. *Journal of Child Psychological Psychiatry*. 66(4), 417–439. https://doi.org/10.1111/jcpp.14082

Reis, O., Eneh, N., Ehimuan, B., Anyanwu, A., Olorunsogo, T., & Abrahams, T. (2024). Privacy law challenges in the digital age: A global review of legislation and enforcement. *International Journal of Applied Research in Social Sciences*, 6, 73–88. https://doi.org/10.51594/ijarss.v6i1.733

Ritzer, G. (2011). *The McDonaldization of Society 6*. Fine Forge Press.

Soto, N. E. (2005). Caring and relationships: Developing a pedagogy of caring. *Villanova Law Review*, 50, *859*. https://digitalcommons.law.villanova.edu/vlr/vol50/iss4/11 viewed June 3, 2025.

Spector, J., & Ren, Y. (2015). History of educational technology. In *The SAGE Encyclopedia of Educational Technology* (Vol. 2, pp. 336–345). SAGE Publications, Inc., https://doi.org/10.4135/9781483346397.n147

Stone, C. (2017). *Opportunity Through Online Learning: Improving Student Access, Participation and Success in Higher Education. Equity Fellowship Final Report.* Australian Centre for Student Equity and Success. https://www.ncsehe.edu.au/app/uploads/2022/06/CathyStone_EQUITY-FELLOWSHIP-FINAL-REPORT-1.pdf viewed June 3, 2025.

Terzian, S. (2019). The history of technology and education. In John L. Rury, & Eileen H. Tamura (Eds), *The Oxford Handbook of the History of Education, Oxford Handbooks* (online edn). Oxford Academic. https://doi.org/10.1093/oxfordhb/9780199340033.013.33

Thaler, R., & Sunstein, C. (2009). *NUDGE: Improving Decisions About Health, Wealth, and Happiness.* Yale University Press.

Verhoeven and Hor. (2025). Provided a Framework for Human-Centric AI-First Teaching https://www.aacsb.edu/insights/articles/2025/02/a-framework-for-human-centric-ai-first-teaching Wednesday, February 12, 2025, viewed October 8, 2025.

VRT News (2025). 3 students caught using ChatGPT to cheat during medical school entrance exam | VRT NWS: news. [online] VRTNWS. Available at: https://www.vrt.be/vrtnws/en/2025/07/25/3-students-caught-using-chatgpt-to-cheat-during-medical-school-e/ viewed 13 October, 2025.

Ward, M., O'Riordan, F., Logan-Fleming, D., Cooke, D., Concannon-Gibney, T., Efthymiou, M., & Watkins, N. (2023). Interactive oral assessment case studies: An innovative, academically rigorous, authentic assessment approach. *Innovations in Education and Teaching International, 61*(5), 930–947. https://doi.org/10.1080/14703297.2023.2251967

Ye, X., Yan, Y., Li, J., & Jiang, B. (2024). Privacy and personal data risk governance for generative artificial intelligence: A Chinese perspective, *Telecommunications Policy, 48*(10). https://doi.org/10.1016/j.telpol.2024.102851.

Zuboff, S. (2019). *The Age of Surveillance Capitalism: The Fight for a Human Future at the New Frontier of Power.* Public Affairs.

8

Theological Ethics in AI Entrepreneurship

Timothy Hor

The rapid advancement of artificial intelligence (AI) has ushered in transformative changes across industries, reshaping the way societies operate and innovate. However, this unprecedented technological progress has also raised critical ethical questions that challenge the very foundations of human values. Issues such as algorithmic bias, data privacy breaches, and surveillance capitalism have revealed the darker sides of AI, demonstrating the urgent need for frameworks that prioritise ethics and human well-being (Noble, 2018; Zuboff, 2023).

The collapse of Theranos, driven by exaggerated promises and falsified data, demonstrated how greed can overshadow ethical obligations, jeopardising public health and investor trust when its blood-testing technology, once valued at billions, was exposed as fraudulent (Gavet, 2020). Similarly, the downfall of WeWork revealed the dangers of unchecked ambition and personal gain at the expense of employees and stakeholders after its founder's erratic behavior and questionable financial dealings led to the failure of its IPO and a massive loss of value (Langevoort & Sale, 2021). Most recently, the FTX scandal and the fraudulent actions of Sam Bankman-Fried highlighted how a lack of accountability in cryptocurrency ventures can lead to massive financial harm and loss of trust as billions of dollars in customer funds were misappropriated, leading to the exchange's collapse (Lewis, 2023).

In the realm of AI, greed amplifies these risks exponentially. For instance, the misuse of facial recognition technology for mass surveillance has led to violations of civil liberties, disproportionately affecting marginalised communities, such as in cases where algorithms have been used to track protestors or unfairly target specific neighborhoods (Bommasani et al., 2021). Similarly, data monetisation practices, exemplified by the rise of surveillance capitalism, erode privacy and manipulate user behavior by collecting personal data to create predictive models that influence consumer choices (Zuboff, 2023). These trends illustrate how unchecked greed in AI entrepreneurship can perpetuate harm on a global scale.

Deepfake technology, for instance, could fuel disinformation crises, destabilising political systems and eroding trust in institutions. AI-driven financial speculation could trigger market crashes, while the monopolisation of AI by large corporations may exacerbate global inequalities. Furthermore,

 DOI: 10.1201/9781003626510-8

the potential harms of AI extend beyond corporate misconduct to systemic threats against humanity's shared future. The environmental costs of AI—such as the staggering carbon footprint of training large language models that require massive amounts of energy (Schwartz et al., 2020)—and the cultural risks of "data colonialism," where AI systems extract and commodify indigenous knowledge (Ricaurte, 2019), for example, by training on cultural works without consent or compensation, demand a holistic ethical framework.

At the heart of these challenges lies a deeper question: What does it mean to be human in the age of intelligent collaboration, where AI is not merely a tool but a co-creator shaping our future? This chapter explores the intersection of theology and entrepreneurship, proposing that theological ethics, particularly principles such as human dignity, stewardship, and justice, can offer valuable guidance for navigating the ethical complexities of AI development and deployment. By revisiting foundational concepts of humanity—grounded in theological traditions such as *imago Dei* (the belief that humans are created in the image of God)—this chapter argues for a values-driven approach (Rae, 2018; Volf, 1996) to AI entrepreneurship.

This chapter recognises that addressing the ethical challenges of AI requires interdisciplinary collaboration. While legal and technical solutions are essential, they are insufficient to capture the nuanced and often subjective dimensions of human values (Chalmers, 2016; Tegmark, 2017). Theological ethics, with its emphasis on compassion, prudence, and justice, offers a critical lens through which to evaluate the broader implications of AI systems. By bridging theology, entrepreneurship, and AI ethics, this chapter aims to provide actionable frameworks for creating technologies that align with the common good.

In an age where AI is reshaping society, this chapter calls for a return to the basics of what makes us human. By grounding technological innovation in ethical frameworks inspired by theological virtues, entrepreneurs can ensure that AI serves as a force for justice, equity, and human flourishing. This question echoes Turing's (1950) seminal exploration of machine intelligence and the boundaries between human and artificial cognition.

The structure of this chapter is as follows: First, it outlines a theological framework for understanding key principles such as *dignity, stewardship, justice,* and *creativity*. Next, it explores how these principles can inform entrepreneurial practices through case studies and practical applications. Finally, it addresses the challenges of applying theological ethics in diverse and pluralistic contexts, offering recommendations for entrepreneurs, policymakers, and educators.

Theological Framework

Building on Rae (2018), theological ethics can be understood through a conceptual framework that links faith-based discernment, alignment with divine will, and the pursuit of individual and societal flourishing. As shown

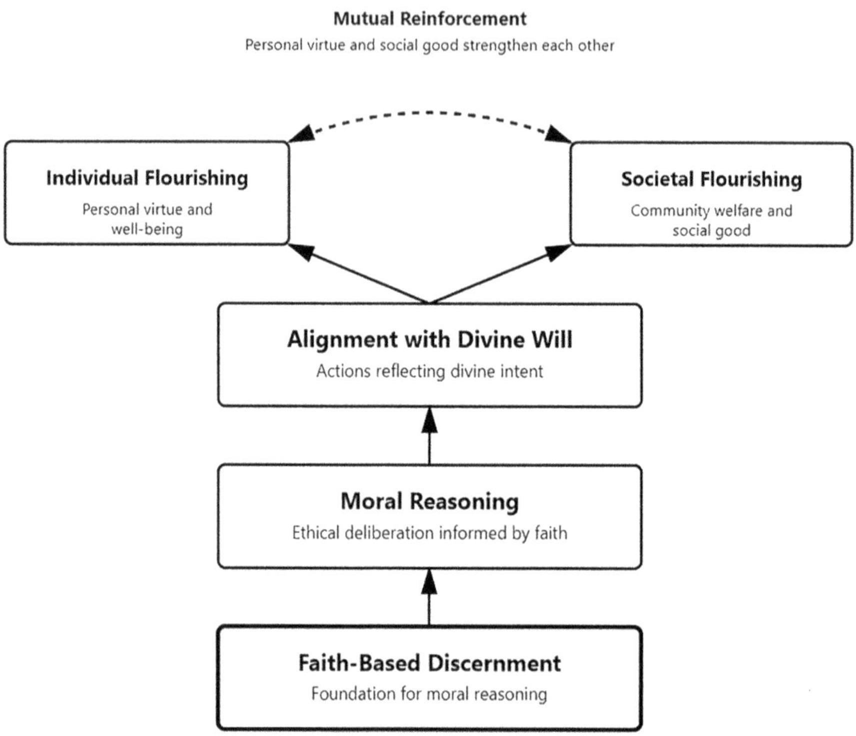

FIGURE 8.1
Theological ethics framework based on Rae (2018).

in Figure 8.1, this framework, faith serves as the foundation for moral reasoning. This reasoning guides actions that reflect the will of a divine being, ultimately fostering well-being for both individuals and communities. The model emphasises mutual reinforcement between personal virtue and social good, as moral choices informed by faith not only fulfill divine intent but also promote flourishing on a broader scale.

In this chapter, we ground our discussion in Judeo-Christian principles, but as we will show in the following section, these concepts are reflected across many diverse theological traditions.

Human Dignity

The theological concept of *imago Dei*, the belief that humans are created in the image of God, lies at the heart of many Judeo-Christian ethical frameworks. It emphasises the inherent worth and dignity of every individual, regardless of socio-economic status or other distinguishing factors (Rae, 2018; Volf, 1996). In the context of AI entrepreneurship, this principle demands that AI systems prioritise respect for individuals rather than reducing them to mere data points or inputs for optimisation.

In practice, preserving human dignity in AI development requires systems that are not only efficient but also empathetic. For instance, AI-driven healthcare platforms should focus on personalised care that respects the patient's unique context, rather than treating patients as standardised cases (Batayeh et al., 2018). The rise of predictive health diagnostics, such as AI tools that forecast patient risks, underscores the need for dignity-centered design. These systems must carefully balance prediction accuracy with fairness, avoiding practices that might exacerbate existing biases or stigmatise individuals (Noble, 2018; Obermeyer et al., 2019).

Human dignity also intersects with the issue of transparency in AI. Black-box algorithms, which obscure the logic behind AI decisions, pose a significant challenge to dignity. Such systems often leave users feeling powerless and dehumanised, particularly in high-stakes domains like hiring or healthcare (Binns, 2018). Entrepreneurs have a responsibility to ensure that their AI systems are explainable, offering users clear insights into how decisions are made and providing mechanisms for contesting unfair outcomes (Tjoa & Guan, 2020). For example, Explainable AI (XAI) frameworks can enhance trust by revealing the underlying rationale of algorithmic decisions, aligning with the ethical imperative to uphold user autonomy and dignity (Doshi-Velez & Kim, 2017).

Furthermore, dignity-centered AI design must account for cultural sensitivity and inclusivity. Many AI systems are trained on datasets that reflect specific cultural or regional biases, limiting their applicability across diverse populations. For instance, facial recognition technologies have been widely criticised for higher error rates among individuals with darker skin tones due to biased training datasets (Buolamwini & Gebru, 2018; Raji et al., 2020). Entrepreneurs must address these disparities by diversifying data sources and incorporating cross-cultural perspectives in AI design. This ensures that AI systems not only serve but also respect the dignity of all users. While the specific contours of human dignity may be experienced differently by each individual, the theological principle of *imago Dei* provides a shared, objective foundation for its value. It asserts that every person possesses an inherent worth that is not conditional on external factors or personal understanding. Therefore, respecting human dignity in AI design means creating systems that actively seek to understand and preserve the unique context of individuals, rather than reducing them to data points. This relational approach helps bridge the gap between abstract concepts and practical application, guiding entrepreneurs to build AI that respects the person, not just the data.

Preserving human dignity also involves recognising the potential of AI to enhance rather than replace human capabilities. For instance, AI tools in education can serve as augmentative resources, empowering teachers to provide individualised attention to students rather than automating teaching roles entirely (Luckin, 2018). Similarly, in healthcare, AI should assist clinicians by providing actionable insights without undermining their professional judgment or eroding patient-doctor relationships (Topol, 2019).

In conclusion, the principle of human dignity offers a powerful lens through which to evaluate the ethical implications of AI. By integrating transparency, cultural inclusivity, and human-centred design into their systems, entrepreneurs can create AI tools that respect and enhance the dignity of users. This commitment is not only a moral imperative but also a pathway to building trust and ensuring the societal acceptance of AI technologies.

While the concept of *imago Dei* offers a powerful foundation for human dignity in the Judeo-Christian tradition, it is important to recognise that diverse theological and philosophical frameworks across cultures provide complementary insights into the relationship between human worth and technological development. Exploring these perspectives can enrich our understanding of ethical AI and broaden its applicability in pluralistic contexts.

Global Theological Perspectives on Human Dignity and Technology

While the concept of *imago Dei* provides a robust foundation for human dignity in Judeo-Christian traditions, diverse theological and philosophical frameworks across cultures offer complementary insights that enrich our understanding of ethical AI. These perspectives not only broaden the applicability of theological ethics in pluralistic contexts but also reveal shared moral concerns that transcend cultural boundaries.

Islamic ethics provide a framework centred on the concept of *khalifah* (stewardship), which positions humans as trustees responsible for God's creation. This resonates with environmental stewardship but extends to technological development, suggesting that innovation should preserve divine order rather than disrupt it (Ramadan, 2018). The notion of *adab*—ethical refinement and proper conduct—further implies that technological development should embody moral excellence. Al-Attas (2014) argues that knowledge disconnected from moral purpose leads to corruption, a perspective particularly relevant to AI systems that process vast amounts of data without ethical constraints. Recent work by scholars explores how these principles can inform culturally sensitive AI design that respects human dignity while acknowledging cultural specificity (Alsheikh et al., 2011; Gorian & Osman, 2024; Tunggala, 2025).

Buddhist traditions, while non-theistic, offer ethical frameworks highly relevant to AI development. The concept of *dependent origination* (*pratītyasamutpāda*) emphasises the interconnectedness of all phenomena, suggesting that AI systems should be evaluated within their broader ecosystems rather than in isolation (Hongladarom, 2020). The central virtue of compassion (*karuna*) prioritises the reduction of suffering over efficiency or profit, challenging the utilitarian calculus that often drives AI optimisation (Vallor, 2016). These principles have inspired initiatives like "Mindful AI," which incorporates contemplative practices into technological development to foster greater awareness of ethical implications (Purser et al., 2016). Mindful AI encourages developers to reflect deeply on the social impact of their work—a practice resonating with indigenous wisdom traditions.

This approach resonates strongly with indigenous wisdom traditions, which contribute vital perspectives often overlooked in technology ethics. Many indigenous frameworks emphasise relationality—viewing humans as embedded within networks of responsibility to both human and non-human entities (Kimmerer, 2013). Such perspectives call for the recognition of interconnectedness and stewardship in technology design, paralleling Buddhist notions of interdependence and compassion. By integrating these insights, developers can move toward more compassionate, responsible, and ecosystem-aware forms of AI innovation.

For example, the Haudenosaunee (Iroquois) principle of considering impacts seven generations into the future provides a powerful framework for assessing AI's long-term consequences. (Wildcat, 2010). Similarly, the Indigenous Protocol and Artificial Intelligence Working Group (Lewis et al., 2020) is developing frameworks that incorporate reciprocity and responsibility rather than extraction and exploitation. By drawing on such deep, long-term perspectives, AI development can be guided by a more compassionate and responsible form of creativity.

Hindu philosophical traditions offer concepts such as *dharma*—cosmic order, righteousness, and duty—that provide frameworks for ethical action in technological contexts. The principle of *ahimsa* (non-harm) suggests that AI systems should be designed to minimise negative impacts on all beings (Bilimoria et al., 2007). Contemporary scholars like Ganeri (2017) have begun exploring how classical Indian philosophical frameworks might inform modern technological ethics, particularly regarding consciousness and cognition in AI systems.

Confucian ethics emphasises harmony (*he*) and appropriate relationships (*li*), suggesting that AI should enhance rather than disrupt social bonds (Wong, 2008). This principle could serve as a foundational rule—a "fourth law of robotics"—for creating AI that is not only beneficial but also socially cohesive. The concept of *ren* (humaneness or benevolence) provides a framework for evaluating whether AI systems foster or undermine human flourishing (Chuang, 2025; Seok, 2024; Zhu, 2020). Chinese approaches to AI ethics have increasingly drawn on these traditions to develop frameworks that balance technological advancement with social harmony (Angle, 2021; Lee, 2018; Seok, 2024).

It is worth noting that the application of these traditional Chinese principles to modern AI development is not without tension. Chinese philosophical traditions have at times been interpreted through a pragmatic or utilitarian lens, which can create a conflict with the relational and human-centred values of Confucianism. This ongoing dialogue between different philosophical interpretations underscores the complexity of applying any ethical framework to a rapidly evolving technology in a diverse cultural and political context.

Despite their distinct foundations, these diverse traditions reveal common themes: respect for human dignity, responsible stewardship of technology, concern for justice, and the subordination of technological power to moral purpose. As Bhargava (1998) argues, ethical pluralism need not lead to relativism but can instead enrich our moral vocabulary. By drawing on this diversity of theological and philosophical resources, entrepreneurs can develop AI systems that respect various cultural and religious contexts while addressing universal human concerns.

This inclusive approach acknowledges that no single theological tradition can claim universal authority in pluralistic societies. Rather, the convergence of diverse traditions on core ethical principles suggests that theological ethics can provide guidance across cultural boundaries, offering a more robust foundation for AI entrepreneurship than purely technical or legal frameworks alone.

Integration of Theological Perspectives

The diverse theological and philosophical traditions discussed above, while emerging from distinct cultural and historical contexts, converge on several foundational ethical principles relevant to AI entrepreneurship. This convergence suggests the possibility of a pluralistic yet coherent ethical framework that can guide technological innovation across cultural boundaries.

The first point of convergence is a shared emphasis on human dignity, albeit derived from different metaphysical foundations. While Judeo-Christian traditions root dignity in the *imago Dei*, Islamic thought emphasises human worth as *khalifah* (vice-regents of God), Buddhist traditions focus on the potential for enlightenment, and indigenous perspectives highlight humans' place within relational networks. Despite these different foundations, each tradition affirms that human beings possess inherent worth that must not be compromised by technological systems. This convergence provides a robust cross-cultural basis for designing AI that respects human autonomy and flourishing (Taylor, 2007).

A second shared theme is responsible stewardship. Across traditions, we find a consistent recognition that technological power entails moral responsibility. The Christian concept of stewardship finds parallels in the Islamic emphasis on *amanah* (trust), the Buddhist focus on mindful intention, and indigenous principles of seven-generation sustainability. These complementary perspectives offer entrepreneurs a multifaceted understanding of their obligations to future generations and to ecosystems affected by AI development (Bostrom & Yudkowsky, 2018; Johnston, 2014).

Justice and equity represent a third area of convergence. Each tradition, through different conceptual vocabularies, emphasises fairness in social arrangements and concern for marginalised communities. This reference to the marginalised is vital to these ideals, as the scope of fairness, justice, and equity has little meaning if it is only extended to the few. The Jewish prophetic tradition's call for justice aligns with Confucian emphasis on righteous governance, Buddhist compassion for all sentient beings, and indigenous principles of reciprocity. These traditions collectively challenge the utilitarian calculations that often drive technological optimisation, calling instead for AI systems that prioritise the common good and address systemic inequities (Amartya & Amartya, 2009).

Finally, these traditions share a commitment to the primacy of moral purpose over technological capability. Whether through Christian virtue ethics, Islamic conceptions of *adab*, Buddhist notions of skilful means, or indigenous wisdom about appropriate relationships with tools, each tradition subordinates technological power to ethical ends. This convergence directly challenges the technological determinism and value-neutrality often assumed in AI development (Pacey, 1983).

This integration of diverse perspectives does not require abstracting away their specific religious or cultural content into a generic ethical framework. Rather, as philosophers like Taylor (2014) and Eck (2001) suggest, meaningful pluralism maintains the distinctiveness of traditions while identifying areas of "overlapping consensus" on practical ethical guidelines. The specific theological narratives, practices, and communities from which these ethics emerge remain essential resources for motivating and sustaining ethical commitments.

For AI entrepreneurs navigating pluralistic contexts, this integration offers practical guidance. When designing systems that will serve diverse communities, entrepreneurs can draw on these shared principles while remaining attentive to culturally specific applications. For instance, facial recognition technology should respect human dignity across cultures, but implementation might need to address specific cultural concerns about privacy, representation, and identity (Birhane & Prabhu, 2021).

Educational institutions can further advance this integration by creating interdisciplinary spaces where technologists engage with diverse theological and philosophical traditions. The MIT Dalai Lama Center for Ethics and Transformative Values (https://thecenter.mit.edu/) exemplifies this approach, bringing together technological innovation with contemplative traditions (Jinpa, 2016) to address ethical challenges.

This integrated framework does not resolve all tensions between traditions or eliminate the need for contextual judgment. Rather, it provides a richer moral vocabulary and a more inclusive foundation for addressing the ethical challenges of AI entrepreneurship than any single tradition could offer alone.

Having established a cross-cultural foundation for *human dignity* in AI development, we now turn to the principle of *stewardship*—a concept that, as we have seen, finds resonance across diverse theological traditions. This principle offers practical guidance for entrepreneurs seeking to align technological innovation with ethical responsibility and care for both humanity and the broader ecosystem in which AI operates.

Stewardship

Stewardship, a theological concept rooted in the idea of responsible caretaking of God's creation, calls for innovation that prioritises sustainability, justice, and the common good. In the context of AI entrepreneurship, stewardship encourages long-term thinking and an ethical approach to innovation that ensures technology serves humanity rather than exploiting it (Hollenbach, 2002; Rae, 2018).

AI technologies, when developed responsibly, can embody stewardship by addressing global challenges such as climate change, healthcare inequities, and food security. For example, AI-driven agricultural tools, such as precision farming technologies, optimise resource use by minimising water waste and reducing fertiliser runoff, thereby promoting environmental sustainability (Kamilaris et al., 2017). These innovations reflect stewardship by fostering harmony between technological advancement and ecological preservation.

However, stewardship in AI also requires vigilance against unintended consequences. While AI has the potential to mitigate environmental and social issues, its development often entails significant carbon footprints due to energy-intensive data processing and training algorithms (Strubell et al., 2020). Entrepreneurs must balance the benefits of AI with the need to reduce its environmental impact. Initiatives like carbon-neutral AI models, achieved through green computing and renewable energy sources, exemplify this balance (Schwartz et al., 2020).

The principle of stewardship also extends to the social impact of AI. Entrepreneurs must design technologies that empower marginalised groups rather than exacerbate existing inequities. For example, AI-powered financial inclusion tools have enabled underserved populations, such as women in developing nations, rural communities, and refugees, to access microloans and digital payment systems, transforming their economic opportunities (Frost et al., 2019). These tools embody stewardship by equipping individuals with resources to improve their lives while fostering equitable growth.

Accountability is another essential dimension of stewardship. Entrepreneurs must adopt transparent and participatory design processes to ensure that AI technologies align with societal needs and values. This involves engaging diverse stakeholders—end users, regulators, and ethicists—throughout the development lifecycle. The co-creation of AI systems fosters trust and minimises the risks of bias, misuse, or exclusion (Floridi et al., 2018).

Furthermore, stewardship requires prioritising the common good over profit maximisation. While economic incentives drive innovation, overemphasis on profitability can lead to harmful practices such as data exploitation, algorithmic discrimination, and monopolistic behaviours (Zuboff, 2023). The common good, in this context, is not merely a utilitarian calculation where the needs of the many outweigh those of the few. Instead, it is a holistic vision that seeks to benefit society by serving individuals and communities at a deeper level. This can be achieved when AI is designed to address systemic inequities and empower the most vulnerable. Entrepreneurs guided by stewardship must resist these tendencies, focusing instead on creating technologies that serve society holistically.

One compelling example of stewardship in AI is the deployment of healthcare algorithms that assist with early disease detection. For instance, DeepMind's AI-based retinal diagnostic tool has demonstrated exceptional accuracy in identifying eye diseases, particularly in resource-limited settings (De Fauw et al., 2018). Such innovations highlight the potential of stewardship to drive impactful solutions that prioritise the well-being of underserved populations.

In conclusion, stewardship provides a framework for ethical AI entrepreneurship that balances innovation with responsibility. By addressing environmental, social, and economic challenges through transparent and inclusive practices, entrepreneurs can ensure their AI technologies advance the common good. This commitment to stewardship aligns with theological imperatives to care for creation and uplift humanity.

While stewardship addresses our responsibility toward creation and future generations, justice and equity focus on the fair distribution of both the benefits and burdens of AI technologies. These principles, which find expression across the theological traditions we have explored, are particularly crucial as algorithms increasingly influence decisions in domains such as hiring, healthcare, and law enforcement.

Justice and Equity

Justice and *equity* are foundational theological principles that call for fairness, inclusion, and the protection of the marginalised. In the context of AI entrepreneurship, these principles take on critical importance as algorithms increasingly influence decisions in domains such as hiring, healthcare, and law enforcement. Without deliberate attention to justice, AI systems risk perpetuating or exacerbating societal inequalities.

Algorithmic bias is a well-documented issue that highlights the need for equity in AI design. For example, hiring algorithms trained on biased historical data have systematically disadvantaged women and minorities in recruitment processes (Barocas et al., 2023; Raji et al., 2020). These biases are not merely technical errors but ethical failures that violate the principle of justice by entrenching systemic inequities. Entrepreneurs must proactively address such issues by diversifying training datasets, implementing fairness-aware algorithms, and involving underrepresented groups in the development process (Binns, 2018; Noble, 2018). It is essential for the designers and users of AI systems to confront their personal biases to address algorithmic bias. This can be achieved through a multifaceted approach centred on education, team diversity, and ethical accountability. Mandatory training helps individuals recognise their biases, while diverse development teams are more likely to identify and challenge biases in data and algorithms. Implementing rigorous third-party ethical audits further ensures fairness and holds developers accountable for their creations.

Justice also requires equitable access to the benefits of AI. Despite AI's potential to improve healthcare and education, these advancements often remain inaccessible to disadvantaged populations. For instance, AI-driven educational platforms have primarily benefited urban schools with robust internet infrastructure, leaving rural students behind (Luckin, 2018). Similarly, advanced diagnostic tools like AI-powered imaging systems are often deployed in high-income countries while underserved regions lack basic healthcare access (Eubanks, 2018). Entrepreneurs have a moral obligation to bridge this digital divide by designing scalable, affordable, and culturally sensitive AI solutions.

Furthermore, justice in AI design demands transparency and accountability. Opaque systems, often referred to as "black-box" algorithms, obscure the reasoning behind decisions, making it difficult for affected individuals to challenge unfair outcomes (Tjoa & Guan, 2020). For example, algorithms used in criminal sentencing have been criticised for racial biases and lack of explainability, disproportionately impacting communities of colour (Angwin et al., 2022). By prioritising transparency through Explainable AI (XAI) frameworks (Minh et al., 2022), entrepreneurs can uphold justice and ensure that affected parties have the opportunity to contest or understand decisions. Additionally, educators and governments have vital roles in promoting justice and transparency in AI. Educators can embed principles of fairness, accountability, and explainability into academic programs, preparing future entrepreneurs to create systems that reflect ethical values. Governments, meanwhile, can legislate regulatory standards that require transparency and offer mechanisms for contesting algorithmic decisions, safeguarding the rights of those impacted by AI systems. Collaborative efforts between educational institutions, policymakers, and industry leaders are essential to ensuring that justice is integrated into the fabric of AI innovation.

The principle of equity also extends to environmental justice. AI systems require substantial computational resources, contributing to carbon emissions and environmental degradation (Strubell et al., 2020). These impacts often disproportionately affect vulnerable communities, such as those living in low-lying areas prone to climate change. Entrepreneurs guided by justice must adopt sustainable practices, such as using energy-efficient AI models and renewable energy sources, to mitigate environmental harm (Schwartz et al., 2020). While AI systems can contribute to environmental degradation, unbiased studies suggest that AI also holds promise for addressing climate change and optimising resource use. For example, AI-driven models enhance predictive accuracy for climate change effects and improve disaster response, supporting better outcomes for affected communities (Ukoba et al., 2025). "Green" AI innovations—such as energy-harvesting AI devices, AI-powered weather forecasting, and environmentally focused AI for agriculture and ocean conservation—demonstrate substantial sustainability potential (Bolón-Canedo et al., 2024). Government and regulatory reports likewise note that AI is already mitigating emissions, optimising energy and water use, and helping forecast renewable energy production (Government, 2024). Moreover, by streamlining workflows and reducing repetitive digital tasks, AI can potentially lower total computational energy demand while increasing productivity (Bolón-Canedo et al., 2024). These benefits reinforce the importance of further investment in unbiased research and sustainable development practices to realise the full positive impact of AI in climate action.

Finally, justice in AI entrepreneurship requires a participatory approach that centres the voices of marginalised communities. Co-design methodologies, which involve stakeholders from diverse backgrounds in the development process, ensure that AI systems reflect the needs and values of all users, not just the privileged few (Floridi et al., 2018; Raji et al., 2020).

In conclusion, justice and equity are not optional considerations in AI entrepreneurship but moral imperatives. By addressing bias, ensuring equitable access, and embracing transparency and sustainability, entrepreneurs can create AI systems that align with the theological call to protect the vulnerable and promote fairness.

Creativity and Innovation

Creativity is a defining characteristic of both theological perspectives on humanity and entrepreneurial endeavours. In theological terms, creativity reflects humanity's role as co-creators with God, a concept rooted in the *imago Dei* principle (Peterson, 2016; Volf, 1996; Welz, 2011). This view suggests that humans are uniquely endowed with the capacity for innovation, a responsibility that extends to the design and deployment of AI systems. Entrepreneurs, as key innovators, have a moral obligation to channel this creativity toward addressing societal challenges.

AI-driven creativity exemplifies this responsibility in action. For instance, generative AI tools like DALL·E and ChatGPT demonstrate how technology can augment human creativity in fields ranging from art and design to education and research (Bommasani et al., 2021). These tools empower individuals to explore new possibilities, democratising access to creative resources. However, this democratisation must be tempered with ethical considerations, such as ensuring that generative AI does not perpetuate biases or undermine intellectual property rights (Floridi, 2014; Raji et al., 2020).

Creativity in AI entrepreneurship is also evident in efforts to address global challenges. For example, AI-powered climate models are being used to predict and mitigate the effects of climate change, providing actionable insights for policymakers and communities at risk (Rolnick et al., 2022). Similarly, AI applications in precision agriculture help optimise resource use, reduce waste, and increase food security in regions affected by climate variability (Kamilaris et al., 2017). These innovations reflect the theological imperative to steward creation responsibly while leveraging human ingenuity to promote the common good.

However, the potential for creative misuse of AI technologies, such as deepfakes and malicious algorithms, raises ethical concerns (Chesney & Citron, 2019). Entrepreneurs must actively engage with ethical frameworks to ensure their innovations serve constructive purposes. Theological perspectives can guide this process by emphasising accountability and aligning creativity with moral values.

In conclusion, creativity in AI entrepreneurship represents an opportunity to align technological innovation with theological imperatives of stewardship and justice. By embracing their role as co-creators, entrepreneurs can design AI systems that inspire human creativity, address pressing global issues, and contribute to a more equitable and sustainable future. However, this creativity must always be guided by ethical considerations to ensure that its benefits outweigh its risks.

Purpose-Driven Ventures

Purpose-driven ventures exemplify the fusion of entrepreneurial innovation with a commitment to social and moral values. These enterprises align closely with theological principles by balancing profit with the broader goal of advancing the common good. Rooted in stewardship and justice, purpose-driven entrepreneurship offers a model for integrating ethics into the development and deployment of artificial intelligence (AI).

Faith-inspired ventures frequently serve as powerful examples of this integration. For instance, B-Corps and social enterprises that leverage AI for societal impact operate under frameworks prioritising sustainability, community welfare, and accountability (Stubbs, 2017). One prominent example is AI-powered mental health platforms like Woebot, which provide affordable and accessible therapy to underserved populations. These ventures demonstrate how technology can address systemic inequities while maintaining financial viability (Fitzpatrick et al., 2017).

Theological principles further encourage entrepreneurs to redefine success in terms beyond profitability. The biblical concept of *shalom*, often translated as peace, reflects a holistic vision of human flourishing that includes social, economic, and spiritual well-being (Hollenbach, 2002). AI entrepreneurs can embody this vision by addressing global challenges such as poverty, inequality, and climate change. For example, ventures like Zipline, which uses AI-powered drones to deliver medical supplies to remote areas, illustrate how purpose-driven innovation can save lives and foster equity in healthcare access (Damoah et al., 2021; Gangwal et al., 2019).

However, purpose-driven ventures must navigate significant challenges, including maintaining ethical priorities amid market pressures. The rapid commercialisation of AI technologies has often led to unintended consequences such as the exploitation of user data for profit. Entrepreneurs inspired by theological ethics must resist these pressures, implementing safeguards that protect user privacy and uphold trust (Zuboff, 2023). Purpose-driven ventures like Signal and DuckDuckGo, which prioritise user privacy over ad revenue, showcase how ethical imperatives can coexist with entrepreneurial success (Balsa et al., 2022).

Mistakes rooted in unethical data use or intellectual property violations in AI must be addressed proactively to restore trust and uphold justice. Global frameworks, such as UNESCO's Recommendations on AI Ethics, call for impact assessments, international cooperation, and, when appropriate, remediation for harms caused by misuse (Morandín-Ahuerma, 2023). Practical solutions include data audits to identify and exclude tainted source (Longpre et al., 2024), transparent IP and data provenance policies (Bolón-Canedo et al., 2024), informed consent, and regular ethics-based audits (Laine et al., 2024). Preventing future misuse further requires clear agreements on IP ownership, robust user rights, and compliance with emerging international standards (Yang, 2025). These measures are essential in moving beyond past mistakes and ensuring responsible, ethical AI development.

These ventures also highlight the importance of accountability and transparency. Entrepreneurs must adopt ethical frameworks that emphasise stakeholder involvement, ensuring that all voices—especially those from marginalised communities—are considered in the design and deployment of AI systems (Floridi et al., 2018). By doing so, purpose-driven ventures can align their operations with theological values of justice, stewardship, and human dignity.

In conclusion, purpose-driven ventures embody the intersection of theological ethics and entrepreneurial innovation. By balancing profit with purpose, these enterprises provide a compelling model for how AI technologies can promote societal well-being, environmental sustainability, and equity. To integrate theological frameworks within the mechanisms of AI, entrepreneurs should embed explicit ethical criteria—grounded in principles like justice, stewardship, and human dignity—into algorithmic design, data selection, and decision-making processes. This means setting standards for transparency, ensuring diverse stakeholder involvement in system training, and regularly auditing models for bias or unintended harms (Floridi et al., 2018). By making these theological values part of the technical and governance layers, ventures can proactively align AI outcomes with a vision for a just and compassionate society. Entrepreneurs guided by these principles can ensure that their ventures contribute to a more just and compassionate world.

Entrepreneurial Ecosystems

Entrepreneurial ecosystems are dynamic networks of individuals, organisations, and institutions that collectively foster innovation and enterprise development. When aligned with theological principles, these ecosystems can create an environment where AI entrepreneurship is guided by ethical imperatives such as justice, stewardship, and human dignity. This approach ensures that innovation benefits society holistically rather than serving narrow economic interests (Lee, 2018).

A key feature of ethical entrepreneurial ecosystems is collaboration across diverse stakeholders, including technologists, policymakers, educators, and faith-based organisations. Such collaborations provide a platform for integrating theological values into AI innovation. For instance, initiatives like the Partnership on AI bring together academia, industry, and civil society to establish ethical guidelines for AI development, reflecting a commitment to the common good (Floridi et al., 2018).

Education and training programs also play a crucial role in shaping ethical ecosystems. Business schools and entrepreneurship hubs can embed courses on AI ethics, theological principles, and sustainability into their curricula. For example, programs at institutions like the Oxford Internet Institute and Stanford's Human-Centred AI Institute emphasise interdisciplinary approaches to ethical AI design (Crawford, 2021; Floridi, 2014). These initiatives prepare entrepreneurs to navigate the complex ethical landscape of AI development with a values-driven mindset.

Access to funding is another critical component of entrepreneurial ecosystems. Traditional venture capital models often prioritise profitability over societal impact, potentially sidelining purpose-driven ventures. Ethical ecosystems can counter this trend by fostering investment in socially responsible innovation. For instance, impact investment funds and public-private partnerships are increasingly supporting AI ventures that address global challenges such as healthcare access and climate resilience (Chui et al., 2018; Vinuesa et al., 2020).

The role of regulatory frameworks within entrepreneurial ecosystems is equally important. Policies that emphasise accountability, transparency, and fairness ensure that AI technologies are developed and deployed responsibly. For example, the European Union's AI Act provides guidelines for high-risk AI applications, aligning regulatory priorities with ethical principles (Act,

2021). These frameworks empower entrepreneurs to align their innovations with societal values while maintaining compliance with legal standards.

Finally, community engagement is essential for creating inclusive ecosystems. Co-design processes that involve marginalised groups in the innovation lifecycle help ensure that AI systems reflect diverse perspectives and needs. This participatory approach fosters trust and equity, aligning with theological calls for justice and stewardship (Noble, 2018; Raji et al., 2020).

In conclusion, ethical entrepreneurial ecosystems provide the infrastructure for aligning AI innovation with theological values. By fostering collaboration, education, funding, regulation, and community engagement, these ecosystems empower entrepreneurs to create AI technologies that advance human flourishing. While there is a growing commitment among stakeholders to create ethical systems for both principled and sustainable business reasons, ongoing success depends on the continuous involvement of diverse perspectives. Future progress in ethically aligned AI requires more interdisciplinary research and genuine inclusion of voices from underrepresented groups, ensuring that the benefits and guidance of these technologies reflect the needs and values of all communities (Partnership on AI, 2025).

Linking Theological Value to AI Ethics

The ethical challenges of artificial intelligence (AI), such as algorithmic bias, lack of transparency, and privacy concerns, necessitate frameworks that address more than just technical flaws. Theological values, grounded in principles such as wisdom, compassion, and justice, provide a moral foundation for addressing these challenges in a holistic and human-centred way. By linking theological principles to AI ethics, entrepreneurs can align technological innovation with societal well-being.

Wisdom, a key theological virtue, emphasises discernment, foresight, and moral clarity in decision-making. In AI ethics, wisdom manifests in the design of algorithms that consider long-term societal impacts rather than prioritising short-term efficiency or profitability. For example, predictive policing algorithms often exacerbate systemic biases when deployed without consideration of historical injustices (Angwin et al., 2022). A wisdom-oriented approach would demand careful scrutiny of such systems, incorporating mechanisms to identify and mitigate harmful biases during the design and deployment phases (Raji et al., 2020). This foresight ensures that AI technologies contribute to societal progress rather than perpetuating harm.

Compassion, another theological virtue, aligns with the ethical goal of human-centred AI. Compassion calls for empathy and a commitment to alleviate suffering, principles particularly relevant in healthcare applications of AI. For instance, AI diagnostic tools like IBM's Watson Health have the potential to improve healthcare access and outcomes for underserved populations (Topol, 2019). However, compassion also requires ensuring that these tools do not inadvertently widen healthcare disparities by favouring wealthier or technologically advanced regions. Entrepreneurs must therefore prioritise equitable deployment and accessibility, aligning with compassion's call to serve the marginalised.

Justice, as discussed earlier, is central to theological ethics and directly applicable to fairness in AI. Theological justice challenges entrepreneurs to ensure that AI systems address, rather than reinforce, existing inequalities. Algorithmic fairness frameworks, such as those developed for mitigating bias in hiring or lending decisions, operationalise this principle by setting thresholds for acceptable disparities in outcomes across demographic groups (Binns, 2018). Justice also requires accountability, demanding transparent and explainable AI (XAI) models that empower users to understand and contest algorithmic decisions (Tjoa & Guan, 2020).

The principle of *stewardship* complements these virtues by urging entrepreneurs to consider the ecological and social consequences of AI development. For instance, the growing energy demands of training large AI models have significant environmental impacts, contributing to climate change (Strubell et al., 2020). A stewardship-oriented approach advocates for sustainable AI practices, such as using renewable energy sources or developing energy-efficient algorithms (Schwartz et al., 2020). Entrepreneurs guided by stewardship ensure that their innovations do not come at the expense of future generations.

Theological values also address the often-overlooked dimension of *privacy as dignity*. The widespread collection and use of personal data in AI systems raises profound ethical questions about consent and autonomy. Theological perspectives on human dignity emphasise the importance of respecting individuals' control over their personal information. Entrepreneurs can operationalise this principle by adopting privacy-preserving technologies, such as differential privacy or federated learning, which allow data analysis without compromising individual confidentiality (Dwork & Roth, 2014).

Finally, *hope*, a theological virtue often overlooked in ethical discussions, provides a forward-looking perspective that emphasises the transformative potential of AI. While AI has been criticised for its risks, hope encourages entrepreneurs to focus on how technology can empower humanity to address global challenges such as poverty, climate change, and access to education (Floridi, 2014). By linking hope to innovation, entrepreneurs can inspire trust in AI systems, fostering optimism about the future of human-AI collaboration.

Beyond ethical and practical concerns, AI also raises deeper *spiritual questions*. If technologies like generative AI replicate creative expression, cognition, and decision-making, what becomes of the theological claim that humans are uniquely made in the image of God (*imago Dei*)? The growing sophistication of AI systems risks promoting a view of humans as merely programmable, undermining spiritual agency, moral responsibility, and the sacredness of human uniqueness. From a theological standpoint, this reductionism is a form of ontological flattening—a worldview that overlooks the soul, conscience, and relational nature of human beings. Engaging with AI's spiritual implications reminds entrepreneurs and theologians alike that preserving human dignity involves not only equitable access and ethical safeguards but also protecting the spiritual depth of what it means to be human.

In conclusion, theological values offer a robust framework for addressing the ethical complexities of AI. By integrating wisdom, compassion, justice, stewardship, and hope into their decision-making processes, entrepreneurs can ensure that AI technologies are not only effective but also morally grounded. This alignment with theological ethics fosters trust, promotes equity, and advances human flourishing in an increasingly AI-driven world.

Advancing Human Flourishing

The concept of human flourishing, deeply rooted in theological ethics, offers a holistic vision of societal well-being that encompasses physical, emotional, and spiritual dimensions. Flourishing goes beyond mere economic prosperity to include equity, dignity, and community empowerment. AI, when designed and implemented with this vision in mind, has the potential to transform society in ways that advance the common good. Entrepreneurs play a critical role in aligning AI technologies with the principles of flourishing by focusing on applications that uplift individuals and communities.

In healthcare, AI is already demonstrating its potential to advance human flourishing. Tools like AI-powered diagnostics have revolutionised the detection and treatment of diseases, particularly in resource-limited settings. For example, AI algorithms trained to detect diabetic retinopathy have been deployed in rural areas where access to specialists is limited, enabling early intervention and reducing preventable blindness (De Fauw et al., 2018). Such innovations align with the theological commitment to compassion and the moral imperative to serve underserved populations. However, entrepreneurs must ensure that these technologies remain accessible and affordable to prevent the perpetuation of healthcare inequities (Topol, 2019).

Education is another domain where AI can promote flourishing. Adaptive learning platforms powered by AI personalise educational experiences, addressing the diverse needs of students. For instance, tools like Khan Academy's AI-driven tutoring systems provide targeted support to students struggling with specific concepts, fostering equity in education (Luckin, 2018). By bridging gaps in educational resources and access, these platforms embody the theological principle of justice, ensuring that every child has the opportunity to reach their full potential. However, entrepreneurs must remain vigilant against the risks of over-reliance on technology, which could undermine the role of human educators and the relational aspects of teaching.

AI's potential to combat global challenges, such as poverty and climate change, further underscores its role in advancing human flourishing. In agriculture, AI applications like precision farming optimise crop yields while minimising resource waste, contributing to food security in regions affected by climate variability (Kamilaris et al., 2017). Similarly, AI-powered predictive models for disaster response enable governments and humanitarian organisations to act swiftly, mitigating the impact of natural disasters on vulnerable communities (Rolnick et al., 2022). These applications exemplify stewardship by leveraging technology to care for creation and protect human life.

However, advancing human flourishing through AI requires entrepreneurs to address ethical risks and unintended consequences. For example, algorithmic decision-making in welfare systems, while intended to streamline processes, has at times led to harmful outcomes, such as wrongful denial of benefits (Eubanks, 2018). These failures highlight the need for accountability and rigorous ethical evaluation of AI applications, particularly in contexts that directly affect vulnerable populations.

The integration of human-centred design principles into AI development is essential for ensuring that technology genuinely promotes flourishing. Co-design methodologies that involve end-users in the development process can help create systems that reflect the diverse needs and values of their intended beneficiaries (Noble, 2018). For example, AI initiatives in healthcare that engage patients, caregivers, and clinicians in their design ensure that the resulting tools are both effective and ethically sound.

Ultimately, advancing human flourishing through AI requires a commitment to theological values such as dignity, compassion, and justice. Entrepreneurs have a unique opportunity to align their innovations with these principles by prioritising applications that address systemic inequalities, empower communities, and foster equity. By embedding these values into their ventures, entrepreneurs can ensure that AI serves as a transformative force for good, enhancing the well-being of individuals and communities while honouring the broader vision of human flourishing.

Case Studies

Case studies provide a tangible way to understand how theological principles can inform AI entrepreneurship to address ethical challenges while advancing human flourishing. This section explores two examples: the mitigation of algorithmic bias and the promotion of equity in AI-driven education. Each case illustrates the practical application of theological values, such as justice, stewardship, and human dignity, to real-world challenges.

Addressing Algorithmic Bias

Algorithmic bias presents one of the most pressing ethical challenges in AI. Systems that learn from historical data often replicate or amplify existing inequities, leading to outcomes that disproportionately disadvantage marginalised communities. The case of biased hiring algorithms demonstrates how these issues arise and how theological principles can guide their resolution.

In 2018, a prominent e-commerce company abandoned an AI-based hiring tool after discovering that the algorithm penalised resumes containing terms like "women's chess club captain" (Dastin, 2022). The bias stemmed from historical data reflecting a predominantly male hiring pattern, which the algorithm interpreted as a desirable trend. This case exemplifies how a lack of oversight in AI design can perpetuate systemic inequalities, violating the principle of justice.

To address such issues, the theological value of justice demands proactive measures to ensure fairness. Entrepreneurs must prioritise diverse and representative datasets during development to avoid embedding discriminatory patterns. For example, tools like IBM's AI Fairness 360 toolkit provide resources for auditing and mitigating bias in machine learning models, aligning with justice by promoting equitable outcomes (Bellamy et al., 2019).

Transparency is another key principle for addressing bias. Opaque or "black-box" models hinder accountability, making it difficult for stakeholders to identify and rectify unfair practices. Explainable AI (XAI) frameworks enable users to understand the rationale behind algorithmic decisions, fostering trust and empowering individuals to challenge discriminatory outcomes (Tjoa & Guan, 2020). In this context, the theological principle of human dignity calls for systems that respect individuals' autonomy by providing clear, actionable information about how decisions are made.

Participatory design also plays a critical role in mitigating bias. Involving diverse stakeholders, particularly those from underrepresented groups, ensures that AI systems reflect a broader range of perspectives and needs (Raji et al., 2020). For instance, community-driven initiatives in AI ethics, such as Data for Black Lives, emphasise the importance of inclusivity in AI development to advance social justice (Benjamin, 2023).

By integrating these practices, entrepreneurs can align AI innovation with theological principles, transforming biased systems into tools that promote fairness and equity. This case highlights the potential of justice-oriented entrepreneurship to address systemic inequities, fostering a more inclusive technological landscape.

Equity in AI-Driven Education

AI has the potential to revolutionise education, addressing disparities in access and quality. However, achieving equity in AI-driven education requires careful attention to the ethical implications of these technologies.

The case of adaptive learning platforms illustrates both the promise and the challenges of using AI to promote justice and human flourishing.

Platforms like Khan Academy and Duolingo have leveraged AI to personalise learning experiences, tailoring content to individual students' needs and progress (Luckin, 2018). These tools have significantly improved outcomes for learners with varying abilities, particularly in contexts where traditional resources are limited. For example, rural schools with limited access to skilled teachers have reported substantial improvements in student performance after adopting AI-powered tutoring systems (Sarvakar & Prajapati, 2025; Zhang & Leong, n.d.).

However, the deployment of these technologies has also highlighted challenges related to accessibility and inclusivity. Many AI-driven platforms rely on robust internet infrastructure, leaving students in low-connectivity regions at a disadvantage (Eubanks, 2018). This digital divide underscores the need for entrepreneurs to prioritise equity in their innovations, ensuring that AI tools reach underserved communities.

Many AI-driven platforms rely on robust internet infrastructure, leaving students in low-connectivity regions at a disadvantage (Eubanks, 2018). This digital divide underscores the need for entrepreneurs to prioritise equity in their innovations, ensuring that AI tools reach underserved communities. There is a growing recognition that profits and funds generated from AI ventures should be strategically invested to help level this imbalance. Some enterprises and social initiatives are already apportioning a portion of their revenues or launching dedicated funds to support digital access for marginalised groups—for example, not-for-profit organisations and social enterprises increasingly use targeted technology grants and subsidised infrastructure projects to bridge connectivity gaps (McDaid,, 2025; Asian Infrastructure Investment Bank [AIIB], 2024). By reinvesting in underserved markets, these ventures not only help equalise opportunity but also build a broader, more sustainable market for themselves. Nevertheless, greater transparency and accountability in how profits are distributed remain essential for long-term impact, and more AI entrepreneurs are urged to follow suit through partnerships and new funding models (Stone, 2024).

Theological principles of justice and stewardship provide a framework for addressing these challenges. Justice demands that educational AI systems be designed to minimise disparities, while stewardship emphasises the responsible allocation of resources to ensure sustainable and equitable access. Entrepreneurs can operationalise these principles by adopting offline-compatible technologies, such as AI systems that function on low-cost hardware or rely on locally stored data (Kamilaris et al., 2017).

Community engagement is another critical factor in advancing equity. Co-design methodologies that involve educators, parents, and students in the development process ensure that AI tools address the specific needs of their target populations. For instance, collaborative projects in sub-Saharan Africa have successfully adapted AI-based educational platforms to local languages and cultural contexts, making learning more accessible and relevant (Crawford, 2021).

The issue of data privacy also intersects with equity in AI-driven education. Collecting and analysing student data raises ethical concerns about consent and surveillance, particularly in vulnerable populations. Theological principles of dignity and justice call for privacy-preserving technologies, such as federated learning, which enable AI models to train on decentralised data without compromising individual confidentiality (Dwork & Roth, 2014).

By aligning AI-driven education with these theological values, entrepreneurs can create systems that advance equity and human flourishing. This case illustrates the transformative potential of AI when guided by ethical imperatives, providing a blueprint for justice-oriented innovation in education.

Critical Questions and Reflections

The intersection of theology and entrepreneurship offers profound insights into the ethical development and deployment of artificial intelligence (AI). However, applying theological principles to AI entrepreneurship raises complex questions and challenges that warrant deeper reflection. This section explores critical issues and poses questions that invite further discussion and interdisciplinary engagement.

Universality of Theological Principles

One challenge is the universality of theological ethics in a pluralistic world. While Christian theology emphasises principles such as human dignity, stewardship, and justice, these values may not be universally accepted or applied in diverse cultural and religious contexts. For example, the concept of *imago Dei* as a foundation for human dignity is uniquely rooted in Judeo-Christian traditions. How can these theological principles be reconciled or adapted to align with other worldviews, such as Islamic, Buddhist, or secular humanist ethics? Collaborative efforts between theologians, ethicists, and entrepreneurs can foster shared frameworks that transcend cultural and religious boundaries (Floridi, 2014).

To avoid excluding individuals with secular or non-theistic worldviews, it is vital to frame theological ethics in terms of universal principles—such as dignity, justice, and stewardship—that resonate across religious and philosophical boundaries. Many atheists and secular humanists also uphold values consistent with various faith traditions, grounding their ethical commitments in human reason, empathy, and mutual respect rather than divine authority (Kurtz, 2010). By highlighting common ethical goals and emphasising the shared pursuit of societal flourishing, collaborative frameworks can integrate theological, secular, and other perspectives without requiring adherence to specific religious doctrines. This approach allows diverse stakeholders—including those who do not believe in a deity—to participate fully in shaping ethical AI standards while respecting differences.

Balancing Ethics and Profitability

Entrepreneurs often face the tension between adhering to ethical principles and meeting market demands. Purpose-driven ventures that prioritise justice and equity may struggle to compete in markets dominated by profit-driven models. For instance, AI startups focused on ethical transparency may incur higher costs compared to competitors employing opaque, profit-maximising algorithms (Zuboff, 2023). How can entrepreneurs sustain ethical commitments without compromising financial viability? Exploring hybrid business models, such as B-Corps or social enterprises, might provide pathways to balance ethics and profitability (Stubbs, 2017).

The Role of Regulation

The growing influence of AI has prompted calls for regulatory frameworks that align with ethical principles. However, implementing regulations that reflect theological values raises practical and philosophical questions. For example, should governments mandate transparency and fairness in AI systems, or should these be voluntary commitments by entrepreneurs? Additionally, how can regulations account for the rapid pace of AI innovation while avoiding stifling creativity? Different approaches to AI governance, as seen in the contrasting regulatory environments of China and the United States (Lee, 2018), highlight the cultural dimensions of these questions. The European Union's AI Act provides a promising model but also highlights the challenges of enforcement and global standardisation (Act, 2021).

While modern ethical principles—such as transparency, fairness, and accountability—are widely recognised and often framed in secular or agnostic terms, theological frameworks offer distinct advantages for AI governance. These traditions provide deeper moral foundations grounded in centuries of philosophical reflection, encourage holistic consideration of human flourishing, and can inspire commitment through personal meaning and identity (Cahill, 2013; DCL & George, 2013). Theological ethics also emphasise transcendent values like compassion, stewardship, and justice, which help orient AI innovation toward the common good and the welfare of the most vulnerable. By integrating theological perspectives alongside universal norms, regulatory frameworks can draw on a broader and more nuanced repertoire of moral reasoning, fostering wider stakeholder engagement and stronger ethical leadership in the face of rapid technological change.

Addressing Power Imbalances

AI entrepreneurship often amplifies existing power imbalances, with large corporations dominating the field while smaller ventures struggle for visibility and resources. Theological principles of justice and stewardship call for more equitable distribution of power and opportunity in AI ecosystems. What role can policymakers, investors, and educators play in levelling the playing field for purpose-driven ventures? Collaborative funding mechanisms and ethical certification programs could support smaller enterprises committed to justice and equity (Cihon et al., 2021).

Measuring Impact

Finally, how should the success of AI ventures be measured? Traditional metrics such as profitability and market share fail to capture the broader societal and ethical impacts of AI systems. Theological ethics suggest alternative metrics, such as contributions to human flourishing, environmental sustainability, and social equity. Developing standardised frameworks for measuring these impacts could guide entrepreneurs in aligning their ventures with theological and ethical goals (Floridi et al., 2018). However, it is important to acknowledge significant challenges in measuring the outcome. Many of these outcomes are inherently complex, context-dependent, and subject to socio-cultural interpretation, making quantification difficult or even impossible in some cases. Nevertheless, recent work in fields such as social impact assessment, Environmental, Social, and Governance (ESG) reporting, and the UN Sustainable Development Goals provides useful models for evaluating progress toward these broader objectives (DESA, 2023). Transparent, participatory approaches that incorporate stakeholder input and qualitative evaluation can enhance the credibility and cultural relevance of impact measurement. Despite the difficulties, striving for more holistic and inclusive metrics remains critical to ethical AI entrepreneurship.

The critical reflections and questions above underscore the complexity of integrating theological principles into AI entrepreneurship. By fostering interdisciplinary dialogue and embracing innovative approaches, entrepreneurs can navigate these challenges and contribute to a more ethical and equitable technological future.

Conclusion

The rapid proliferation of artificial intelligence (AI) presents immense opportunities and ethical challenges that demand thoughtful engagement. This chapter has explored the intersection of theology and entrepreneurship, demonstrating how theological principles such as human dignity, justice, stewardship, and compassion can inform ethical AI innovation. These values provide a robust moral framework for addressing key concerns in AI, including bias, transparency, equity, and environmental sustainability.

Through the lens of theological ethics, entrepreneurs are encouraged to align their innovations with the broader goal of human flourishing. By embracing their role as co-creators, they can design AI systems that respect human dignity, foster justice, and promote the common good. Real-world examples, such as AI-driven healthcare tools and adaptive learning platforms, illustrate the transformative potential of aligning technology with moral values. These cases also highlight the importance of addressing systemic challenges, such as the digital divide and algorithmic bias, to ensure that AI serves all communities equitably.

This chapter also raised critical questions about the universality of theological principles, the tension between ethics and profitability, and the role of regulation in fostering ethical innovation. These reflections underscore the complexity of integrating theology into AI entrepreneurship but also highlight the potential for interdisciplinary collaboration to address these challenges. Ultimately, this chapter advocates for a values-driven approach to AI development that prioritises societal well-being over narrow economic interests.

From a practice perspective, *entrepreneurs* have a pivotal role in embedding ethical principles into AI development. They should begin by incorporating ethical audits at every stage of the innovation lifecycle. These audits can help identify and address risks such as algorithmic bias and privacy violations. Tools like IBM's AI Fairness 360 (Bellamy et al., 2019) provide practical resources to support this process. Furthermore, adopting a human-centred design approach is crucial. By engaging diverse stakeholders, particularly those from marginalised communities, entrepreneurs can ensure that their AI systems reflect the needs and values of all users. Measuring the broader societal impact of AI ventures is equally important. Entrepreneurs should develop metrics that evaluate contributions to equity, sustainability, and human flourishing, rather than focusing solely on profitability.

While entrepreneurs may be motivated by material incentives, maintaining ethical standards requires robust external accountability. Independent regulators, industry bodies, and multi-stakeholder oversight boards play a crucial role in "keeping entrepreneurs honest," alongside public scrutiny from civil society and advocacy groups (Metcalf & Moss, 2019). Transparent reporting, enforceable regulations, and participatory governance can ensure that ethical principles are not sidelined for profit.

Policymakers also play a vital role in fostering ethical AI innovation. Establishing robust regulations that mandate transparency, accountability, and fairness is essential. The European Union's AI Act (Act, 2021) offers a strong foundation for creating such policies. Additionally, governments can support purpose-driven ventures through financial incentives like grants or tax breaks, encouraging startups to prioritise societal and ethical goals.

Policymakers should also promote interdisciplinary collaboration, facilitating partnerships among technologists, ethicists, theologians, and community leaders to ensure that regulations are inclusive and holistic.

Educators have a unique opportunity to shape the next generation of AI entrepreneurs. By embedding theological and ethical principles into entrepreneurship and AI curricula, they can prepare students to navigate complex moral challenges. Critical thinking should be fostered, encouraging students to examine the societal implications of AI and explore alternative metrics of success beyond financial gain. Case studies of ethical AI applications and challenges can inspire students to pursue values-driven innovation, equipping them to create technologies that advance human flourishing. By working together, entrepreneurs, policymakers, and educators can ensure that AI aligns with ethical imperatives and promotes a just, equitable, and sustainable future.

References

Act, A. I. (2021). Proposal for a regulation of the European parliament and the council laying down harmonised rules on artificial intelligence (Artificial intelligence act) and amending certain union legislative acts. *EUR-Lex-52021PC0206.*

Al-Attas, S. M. N. (2014). *Prolegomena to the metaphysics of Islam*. Penerbit UTM Press.

Alsheikh, T., Rode, J. A., & Lindley, S. E. (2011). (Whose) value-sensitive design? A study of long-distance relationships in an Arabic cultural context. In *Proceedings of the ACM 2011 Conference on Computer Supported Cooperative Work* (pp. 75–84). Association for Computing Machinery, New York, NY, USA.

Amartya, S., & Amartya, S. (2009). *The idea of justice*. Penguin Books London.

Angle, S. C. (2021). Can artificial intelligence lead us to genuine virtue? A Confucian perspective. In B. Song (Ed.), *Intelligence and wisdom: Artificial intelligence meets Chinese philosophers* (pp. 49–64). Springer Singapore.

Angwin, J., Larson, J., Mattu, S., & Kirchner, L. (2022). Machine bias. In: *Ethics of data and analytics* (pp. 254–264). Auerbach Publications.

Asian Infrastructure Investment Bank. (2024, August 27). *AIIB: Bridging the digital divide.*

Balsa, E., Nissenbaum, H., & Park, S. (2022). Cryptography, trust and privacy: It's complicated. In *Proceedings of the 2022 Symposium on Computer Science and Law* (pp. 167–179). Association for Computing Machinery, NewYork, NY, USA.

Barocas, S., Hardt, M., & Narayanan, A. (2023). *Fairness and machine learning: Limitations and opportunities*. MIT Press.

Batayeh, B. G., Artzberger, G. H., & Williams, L. D. (2018). Socially responsible innovation in health care: Cycles of actualization. *Technology in Society, 53*, 14–22.

Bellamy, R. K. E., Dey, K., Hind, M., Hoffman, S. C., Houde, S., Kannan, K., Lohia, P., Martino, J., Mehta, S., Mojsilović, A., Nagar, S., Ramamurthy, K. N., Richards, J., Saha, D., Sattigeri, P., Singh, M., Varshney, K. R., & Zhang, Y. (2019). AI fairness 360: An extensible toolkit for detecting and mitigating algorithmic bias. *IBM Journal of Research and Development, 63*(4/5), 4:1–4:15.

Benjamin, R. (2023). Race after technology. In: *Social theory re-wired* (pp. 405–415). Routledge.
Bhargava, R. (Ed.). (1998). *Secularism and its critics*. Oxford University Press.
Bilimoria, P., Prabhu, J., & Sharma, R. M. (2007). *Indian Ethics: Classical traditions and contemporary challenges* (Vol. 1). Ashgate Publishing, Ltd.
Binns, R. (2018). Fairness in machine learning: Lessons from political philosophy. In S. A. Friedler & C. Wilson (Eds.), *Proceedings of the 1st Conference on Fairness, Accountability and Transparency* (Vol. 81, pp. 149–159). Proceedings of Machine Learning Research.
Birhane, A., & Prabhu, V. U. (2021). Large image datasets: A pyrrhic win for computer vision? In *2021 IEEE Winter Conference on Applications of Computer Vision (WACV)* (pp. 1536–1546). IEEE.
Bolón-Canedo, V., Morán-Fernández, L., Cancela, B., & Alonso-Betanzos, A. (2024). A review of green artificial intelligence: Towards a more sustainable future. *Neurocomputing, 599*, 128096.
Bommasani, R., Hudson, D. A., Adeli, E., Altman, R., Arora, S., von Arx, S., Bernstein, M. S., Bohg, J., Bosselut, A., & Brunskill, E. (2021). On the opportunities and risks of foundation models. *arXiv preprint arXiv:2108.07258.*
Bostrom, N., & Yudkowsky, E. (2018). The ethics of artificial intelligence. In: *Artificial intelligence safety and security* (pp. 57–69). Chapman and Hall/CRC.
Buolamwini, J., & Gebru, T. (2018). Gender shades: Intersectional accuracy disparities in commercial gender classification. In S. A. Friedler & C. Wilson (Eds.), *Proceedings of the 1st Conference on Fairness, Accountability and Transparency* (Vol. 81, pp. 77–91). PMLR.
Cahill, L. S. (2013). *Global justice, Christology and Christian ethics*. Cambridge University Press.
Chalmers, D. J. (2016). The singularity: A philosophical analysis. In S. Schneider (Ed.), *Science fiction and philosophy: From time travel to superintelligence* (2nd ed., pp. 171–224). Wiley-Blackwell.
Chesney, R., & Citron, D. (2019). Deepfakes and the new disinformation war: The coming age of post-truth geopolitics. *Foreign Affairs, 98(1)*, 147–155.
Chuang, S. (2025). A philosophical look at Confucian humanity in the age of robots. *International Journal of Organizational Analysis, 33*(5), 1324–1334.
Chui, M., Harrysson, M., Manyika, J., Roberts, R., Chung, R., van Heteren, A., & Nel, P. (2018). *Notes from the AI frontier: Applying AI for social good*. McKinsey Global Institute.
Cihon, P., Kleinaltenkamp, M. J., Schuett, J., & Baum, S. D. (2021). *AI certification: Advancing ethical practice by reducing information asymmetries*. arXiv. https://doi.org/10.48550/arXiv.2105.10356
Crawford, K. (2021). *The atlas of AI: Power, politics, and the planetary costs of artificial intelligence*. Yale University Press.
Damoah, I. S., Ayakwah, A., & Tingbani, I. (2021). Artificial intelligence (AI)-enhanced medical drones in the healthcare supply chain (HSC) for sustainability development: A case study. *Journal of Cleaner Production, 328*, 129598.
Dastin, J. (2022). Amazon scraps secret AI recruiting tool that showed bias against women. In: *Ethics of data and analytics* (pp. 296–299). Auerbach Publications.
DCL, J. K., & George, R. P. (2013). *Reason, morality, and law: The philosophy of John Finnis*. OUP Oxford.

De Fauw, J., Ledsam, J. R., Romera-Paredes, B., Nikolov, S., Tomasev, N., Blackwell, S., Askham, H., Glorot, X., O'Donoghue, B., & Visentin, D. (2018). Clinically applicable deep learning for diagnosis and referral in retinal disease. *Nature Medicine, 24*(9), 1342–1350.

DESA, U. (2023). *The sustainable development goals report 2023: Special edition*. https://unstats.un.org/sdgs/report/2023/

Doshi-Velez, F., & Kim, B. (2017). Towards a rigorous science of interpretable machine learning. *arXiv preprint arXiv:1702.08608*.

Dwork, C., & Roth, A. (2014). The algorithmic foundations of differential privacy. *Foundations and Trends® in Theoretical Computer Science, 9*(3–4), 211–407.

Eck, D. L. (2001). *A new religious America: How a "Christian country" has become the world's most religiously diverse nation*. HarperSanFrancisco.

Eubanks, V. (2018). *Automating inequality: How high-tech tools profile, police, and punish the poor*. St. Martin's Press.

Fitzpatrick, K. K., Darcy, A., & Vierhile, M. (2017). Delivering cognitive behavior therapy to young adults with symptoms of depression and anxiety using A fully automated conversational agent (woebot): A randomized controlled trial. *JMIR Mental Health, 4*(2), e7785.

Floridi, L. (2014). *The fourth revolution: How the infosphere is reshaping human reality*. OUP Oxford.

Floridi, L., Cowls, J., Beltrametti, M., Chatila, R., Chazerand, P., Dignum, V., Luetge, C., Madelin, R., Pagallo, U., & Rossi, F. (2018). AI4People—an ethical framework for a good AI society: Opportunities, risks, principles, and recommendations. *Minds and Machines, 28*, 689–707.

Frost, J., Gambacorta, L., Huang, Y., Shin, H. S., & Zbinden, P. (2019). BigTech and the changing structure of financial intermediation. *Economic Policy, 34*(100), 761–799.

Ganeri, J. (2017). *Attention, not self*. Oxford University Press.

Gangwal, A., Jain, A., & Mohanta, S. (2019). Blood delivery by drones: A case study on zipline. *International Journal of Innovative Research in Science, Engineering and Technology, 8*(8), 8760–8766.

Gavet, M. (2020). *Trampled by unicorns: Big Tech's empathy problem and how to fix it*. John Wiley & Sons.

Gorian, E., & Osman, N. D. (2024). Digital ethics of Artificial Intelligence (AI) in Saudi Arabia and United Arab Emirates. *Malaysian Journal of Syariah and Law, 12*(3), 583–597.

Government, A. (2024). *Chapter 6 - Impacts of AI on the environment*. https://www.aph.gov.au/Parliamentary_Business/Committees/Senate/Adopting_Artificial_Intelligence_AI/AdoptingAI/Report/Chapter_6_-_Impacts_of_AI_on_the_environment#:~:text=significant%20environmental%20impacts%2C%20most%20notably%20in%20respect

Hollenbach, D. (2002). *The common good and Christian ethics* (Vol. 22). Cambridge University Press.

Hongladarom, S. (2020). *The ethics of AI and robotics: A Buddhist viewpoint*. Rowman & Littlefield.

Jinpa, T. (2016). *A fearless heart: How the courage to be compassionate can transform our lives*. Avery.

Johnston, L. F. (2014). *Religion and sustainability: Social movements and the politics of the environment*. Routledge.

Kamilaris, A., Kartakoullis, A., & Prenafeta-Boldú, F. X. (2017). A review on the practice of big data analysis in agriculture. *Computers and Electronics in Agriculture, 143*, 23–37.
Kimmerer, R. W. (2013). *Braiding sweetgrass: Indigenous wisdom, scientific knowledge and the teachings of plants*. Milkweed Editions.
Kurtz, P. (2010). *In defense of secular humanism*. Prometheus Books.
Laine, J., Minkkinen, M., & Mäntymäki, M. (2024). Ethics-based AI auditing: A systematic literature review on conceptualizations of ethical principles and knowledge contributions to stakeholders. *Information & Management, 61*(5), 103969.
Langevoort, D. C., & Sale, H. A. (2021). Corporate adolescence: Why did "we" not work? *Texas Law Review, 99(7)*, 1347–1385.
Lee, K.-F. (2018). *AI superpowers: China, Silicon valley, and the new world order*. Harper Business.
Lewis, J. E., Abdilla, A., Arista, N., Baker, K., Benesiinaabandan, S., & Brown, M. (2020). Indigenous protocol and artificial intelligence. *Honolulu, HI, USA: The Initiative for Indigenous Futures and the Canadian Institute for Advanced Research (CIFAR).*
Lewis, M. (2023). *Going infinite: The rise and fall of a new tycoon*. Random House.
Longpre, S., Mahari, R., Chen, A., Obeng-Marnu, N., Sileo, D., Brannon, W., Muennighoff, N., Khazam, N., Kabbara, J., Perisetla, K., Wu, X., Shippole, E., Bollacker, K., Wu, T., Villa, L., Pentland, S., & Hooker, S. (2024). A large-scale audit of dataset licensing and attribution in AI. *Nature Machine Intelligence, 6*, 975–987.
Luckin, R. (2018). *Enhancing learning and teaching with technology: What the research says*. ERIC.
McDaid, C. (2025, February 25). *Donated devices key to bridging the digital divide for disadvantaged students*. Institute of Community Directors Australia.
Metcalf, J., & Moss, E. (2019). Owning ethics: Corporate logics, silicon valley, and the institutionalization of ethics. *Social Research: An International Quarterly, 86*(2), 449–476.
Minh, D., Wang, H. X., Li, Y. F., & Nguyen, T. N. (2022). Explainable artificial intelligence: A comprehensive review. *Artificial Intelligence Review, 55*(5), 3503–3568.
Morandín-Ahuerma, F. (2023). Ten UNESCO recommendations on the ethics of artificial intelligence.
Noble, S. U. (2018). Algorithms of oppression: How search engines reinforce racism. In: *Algorithms of oppression*. New York University Press.
Obermeyer, Z., Powers, B., Vogeli, C., & Mullainathan, S. (2019). Dissecting racial bias in an algorithm used to manage the health of populations. *Science, 366*(6464), 447–453.
Pacey, A. (1983). Technology: Practice and culture. In: *Ethics and emerging technologies* (pp. 27–36). Springer.
Partnership on AI. (2025). *Guidance for inclusive AI: Practicing participatory engagement*. https://partnershiponai.org/guidance-for-inclusive-ai/
Peterson, R. S. (2016). *The imago Dei as human identity: A theological interpretation*. Penn State Press.
Purser, R. E., Forbes, D., & Burke, A. (2016). *Handbook of mindfulness: Culture, context, and social engagement*. Springer.
Rae, S. (2018). *Moral choices: An introduction to ethics*. Zondervan Academic.
Raji, I. D., Gebru, T., Mitchell, M., Buolamwini, J., Lee, J., & Denton, E. (2020). Saving face: Investigating the ethical concerns of facial recognition auditing. In *Proceedings of*

the AAAI/ACM Conference on AI, Ethics, and Society (pp. 145–151). Association for Computing Machinery.

Ramadan, T. (2018). *Islamic Ethics: A very short introduction*. Oxford University Press.

Ricaurte, P. (2019). Data epistemologies, the coloniality of power, and resistance. *Television & New Media*, *20*(4), 350–365.

Rolnick, D., Donti, P. L., Kaack, L. H., Kochanski, K., Lacoste, A., Sankaran, K., Ross, A. S., Milojevic-Dupont, N., Jaques, N., & Waldman-Brown, A. (2022). Tackling climate change with machine learning. *ACM Computing Surveys (CSUR)*, *55*(2), 1–96.

Sarvakar, K., & Prajapati, D. (2025). Implementing AI to improve educational equity and outcomes in a rural school district: A case study. In: *Driving quality education through AI and data science* (pp. 457–480). IGI Global Scientific Publishing.

Schwartz, R., Dodge, J., Smith, N. A., & Etzioni, O. (2020). Green AI. *Communications of the ACM*, *63*(12), 54–63.

Seok, B. (2024). Digital Confucius and virtuous AI: Confucianism in the age of AI and robotics. *Journal of Confucian Philosophy and Culture*, *42*, 5–17.

Stone, E. (2024, February 8). *AI shifts the goalposts of digital inclusion*. Joseph Rowntree Foundation.

Strubell, E., Ganesh, A., & McCallum, A. (2020). Energy and policy considerations for modern deep learning research. *Proceedings of the AAAI Conference on Artificial Intelligence*, *34*(9), 13693–13696.

Stubbs, W. (2017). Sustainable entrepreneurship and B Corps. *Business Strategy and the Environment*, *26*(3), 331–344.

Taylor, C. (2007). *A secular age*. Harvard University Press.

Taylor, C. (2014). *Dilemmas and connections: Selected essays*. Harvard University Press.

Tegmark, M. (2017). *Life 3.0: Being human in the age of artificial intelligence*. Alfred A. Knopf.

Tjoa, E., & Guan, C. (2020). A survey on explainable artificial intelligence (XAI): Toward medical XAI. *IEEE Transactions on Neural Networks and Learning Systems*, *32*(11), 4793–4813.

Topol, E. (2019). *Deep medicine: How artificial intelligence can make healthcare human again*. Hachette UK.

Tunggala, S. (2025). Cross-cultural communication in the era of AI: An Islamic ethical framework. *Societo Communication Journal*, *2*(2), 28–48.

Turing, A. M. (1950). Computing machinery and intelligence. *Mind*, *59*(236), 433–460.

Ukoba, K., Onisuru, O. R., Jen, T.-C., Madyira, D. M., & Olatunji, K. O. (2025). Predictive modeling of climate change impacts using artificial intelligence: A review for equitable governance and sustainable outcome. *Environmental Science and Pollution Research*, *32*(17), 10705–10724.

Vallor, S. (2016). *Technology and the virtues: A philosophical guide to a future worth wanting*. Oxford University Press.

Vinuesa, R., Azizpour, H., Leite, I., Balaam, M., Dignum, V., Domisch, S., Felländer, A., Langhans, S. D., Tegmark, M., & Fuso Nerini, F. (2020). The role of artificial intelligence in achieving the sustainable development goals. *Nature Communications*, *11*(1), 233.

Volf, M. (1996). *Exclusion and embrace: A theological exploration of identity, otherness, and reconciliation*. Abingdon Press.

Welz, C. (2011). Imago Dei. *Studia Theologica*, *65*(1), 74–91.

Wildcat, D. R. (2010). *Red alert!: Saving the planet with indigenous knowledge*. *ReadHowYouWant.Com*.

Wong, D. B. (2008). Chinese ethics. In E. N. Zalta (Ed.), *The Stanford encyclopedia of philosophy*. Metaphysics Research Lab, Stanford University.

Yang, M. T. (2025). Best Practices for Mitigating Intellectual Property Risks in Generative AI Use. https://www.saul.com/insights/alert/best-practices-mitigating-intellectual-property-risks-generative-ai-use

Zhang, H. L., & Leong, W. Y. (2024). Transforming rural and underserved schools with AI-powered education solutions. *ASM Science Journal*, *19*, 1–12.

Zhu, Q. (2020). Ethics, society, and technology: A confucian role ethics perspective. *Technology in Society*, *63*, 101424.

Zuboff, S. (2023). The age of surveillance capitalism. In: *Social theory re-wired* (pp. 203–213). Routledge.

9

Safeguarding Human Welfare with AI

Nicole Arcuri-Sanders

Artificial intelligence (AI) has been praised for being able to be innovative in meeting the needs of humans in various capacities. However, AI's capacity to supply answers promptly does come with its limitations. Being aware of this is essential for how people utilize AI with the intention of safeguarding their welfare. All humans, despite professional venture, cultural affiliation, or religious/spiritual creed, at this time will be faced with AI integration in their lives and have the capacity to be transformed by it.

With AI being accessible and now integrated into many business and educational practices, AI has become part of the normalcy of the day, versus a choice. It is important to human welfare to become an informed consumer. This chapter intends to provide insight into how AI integration in one's life has the potential to impact human wellness. The field of counselling has been impacted by their practices just like other professions. For counsellors, their client wellness is the first and foremost priority for counsellors (American Counseling Association [ACA], 2014, A.1.a.). As the world evolves, so do its clients and the best practices needed to support therapeutic progression. With the expanding developments of AI, counsellors are required to combat the effects AI has on their clients in varying capacities in their lives (i.e., emotional regulation, information accuracy, trust, intimacy, confidentiality). Counsellors have an ethical obligation to the public to educate about the strengths and weaknesses of AI due to its ability to both negatively and positively impact a human's experience of wellness (ACA, 2014, A.7.). In this chapter, numerous aspects of wellness will be examined via application of case studies concerning counselling clients' wellness influenced by examining a particular AI tool, namely ChatGPT. Furthermore, the information shared is hoped to provide insight for readers concerning how to safeguard their wellness when using wellness.

Wellness is defined as "a state of being that accounts for the balance of mind, body, and spirit, and the achievement of personal fulfilment" (Basma et al., 2021, p. 74). Myers et al. (2000)'s Wheel of Wellness is utilized to assist in understanding how one experiences wellness. This specific model has been selected as it accounts for people's uniqueness (later explored in more depth in this chapter). Wellness includes five interrelated life tasks

DOI: 10.1201/9781003626510-9

(spirituality, self-direction, work and leisure, friendship, and love) with 12 subtasks. Wellness has been publicly portrayed as holistic and multidimensional. Wellness includes physical, emotional, intellectual, social, environmental, and spiritual dimensions (Swarbrick et al., 2006). When an individual approaches their life seeking to experience wellness, people invest in becoming aware of and commit to consciously and deliberately making choices that support a more satisfying lifestyle (Swarbrick, 1997; Swarbrick et al., 2006).

In this chapter, case studies for each of the five interrelated life tasks are examined to see how AI has impacted wellness for the client. Within each case, subtasks of wellness will be explored. Strategies offered through counselling to safeguard client wellness with AI utilization will be identified with intention to empower readers to be proactive in the preservation of their own health. Since AI has the capacity to influence a person's thinking (Kalam et al., 2024), mental health providers have the ethical imperative to advocate their communities with having access to understanding when AI's inappropriate usage may deteriorate their mental health (ACA, 2014, A.7.). With AI integration on the rise globally (Duarte, 2025; U.S. Department of Health and Human Services, 2025), it is a necessity to ensure consumers can make informed decisions concerning their welfare.

Theoretical Framework

The Wheel of Wellness (Myers et al., 2000) includes five interrelated life tasks (spirituality, self-direction, work and leisure, friendship, and love) utilized to assist in understanding how one experiences wellness. The model accounts for various disciplines in how they define wellness (i.e., ecology, medical, social). Furthermore, it offers the opportunity to be individualized to the unique person (i.e., culture, sub-cultures, experience). The Wheel of Wellness developed from examination of human growth and development theories for application to the lifespan with a holistic emphasis. Aligning with Adler's counselling theory embracing the importance of the whole client and Maslow's notion that all healthy people strive for self-actualization (Myers et al., 2000), the Wheel of Wellness intends to account for individual's developmental and cognitive capabilities while embracing understanding of the unique experience of the individual. This further establishes the uniqueness of experiencing wellness among people.

There are varying models of wellness; however, they do not offer the same broad lens of accounting for many people's varying differences from their unique worldview. Unlike Hettler's (1976) six-dimensional model, which treats physical, emotional, intellectual, social, occupational, and spiritual wellness as separate and primarily balanced domains, the Wheel emphasizes the interconnection of these areas and the role of personal meaning in overall wellness. Similarly, while Dunn's (1961) high-level wellness model focuses on self-directed growth along a continuum from illness to wellness, it lacks structured dimensions and practical guidance for interventions. Pender's Health Promotion Model (Pender et al., 2015), although valuable for predicting and influencing health behaviors, is primarily behavior-focused and does not incorporate broader psychosocial or spiritual elements. The World Health Organization (WHO)'s definition of health provides a foundational understanding of wellness as complete physical, mental, and social well-being (1948), yet it remains largely conceptual and offers limited guidance for individual assessment or intervention. In contrast, the Wheel of Wellness is clinically applicable, strength-based, and adaptable across diverse populations, emphasizing resilience, personal growth, and the essential self, including spirituality and purpose. Its approachable structure and emphasis on personal meaning make it a valuable tool for anyone seeking to enhance well-being without needing professional expertise.

Individuals experience life in varying capacities over time. At some points, essential needs are met to support personal growth, while at other times, self-actualization must take the back seat until necessities are met to reengage the individual for focused efforts toward growth. According to Maslow's hierarchy of needs, an individual's needs are met in a hierarchy with physiological needs being the most important, with all the other needs being secondary until these needs are met (Maslow, 1943). Maslow identified that individuals have five levels of needs: (a) physiological, (b) safety, (c) love/belonging, (d) esteem, and (e) self-actualization needs. At the first level, physiological needs account for human survival (i.e., food and water) whereas the top level accounts for the experience of self-actualization. Prior to having the capacity to engage in personal growth, creativity, and self-fulfillment, Maslow suggests people must have the ability to physically live with a sense of security (i.e., emotional, financial) (level 2) prior to being able to engage in activities directed for love and belonging (level 3), which is then followed by development of self-worth (level 4). At varying times, there may be needs from numerous areas but without basic needs being met (physiological and safety needs), energy cannot be afforded to higher levels (Maslow, 1943). Psychological needs (love and belonging with esteem needs) only have the capacity to thrive when a person feels safe to do so. For instance, if a person does not know where their next meal will come from and barely have energy to keep searching due to malnourishment, it can be difficult to focus on perfecting a skill despite the desire to do so. From a business lens, understanding Maslow's hierarchy of needs regarding how employees are treated can correlate to turnover (Benson & Dundis, 2003).

Employees who feel that they are being paid fairly will focus less on equitability efforts. Furthermore, when individuals feel secure in their job knowing what is required of them to maintain their job and that their job will still be if they meet those expectations, they are able to engage in their work through a sense of belonging. When feeling part of the team, they may be more willing to train and further develop their skills. Technology has been found to be innovative in supporting employees in having their needs met (i.e., enhance communication, support employee input, networking, training platforms; Benson & Dundis, 2003).

"We must identify ourselves with every manifestation of the soul life, live ourselves into it, accompany human beings through their joys and their sorrows, in much the same way that a good painter paints into a portrait those characteristics which he has felt in the person of his subject" (Adler, 2013, p. 8). According to Adlerian theory, each person is unique and every experience contributes to who they are; what the individual does with these experiences' constructs meaning in their life. Alderian theory refers to person-centered therapy, which insinuates individuals are better comprehended as a whole versus a collection of parts. An individual is empowered to examine how they proceed through life in a holistic manner, accounting for their uniqueness. Stemming from the constructivism philosophy embraces the notion that new information is interpreted through existing mental frameworks to create meaning (Mahoney & Granvold, 2005). Ultimately, individual understanding develops from interactions with their culture and society. In an ever-evolving time with digital health, AI is an essential component to be cognizant of concerning the implications.

When considering wellness in relation to AI, digital health implications must be considered. According to the World Health Organization (WHO), digital health includes digital technologies supportive of a person's attainment of health and well-being (2021). WHO's global strategy on digital health supports accessibility for equitable and universal access to support individual wellness (2021). WHO has developed protocols for efficiency and sustainability of health systems in delivering quality, affordable, and equitable care for disease prevention, diagnosis, management, rehabilitation, and palliative care including before, during, and after an epidemic or pandemic in varying capacities with specific attention to the privacy and security of patient health information. When considering use of technology with health services, Health Insurance Portability and Accountability Act of 1996 (HIPAA), Public Law 104-19, directs the protection for individual's identifiable health information. In a world where one can "google" or seek answers concerning wellness from Alexa and Google Play devices, it is a necessity for consumers to understand what this means for their experience with wellness.

Wellness is a necessity that does not discriminate. Wellness is desired in varying capacities by all ages and cultures. Understanding how AI influences human experience with wellness is essential for all to be empowered to be proactive in the preservation of their own health. The Wheel of Wellness's five interrelated life tasks will be examined in relation to AI implications to safeguard and promote individual wellness.

Main Discussion

Wellness is directly related to mental health. Mental health counsellors strive to empower individuals to experience wellness through: (a) enhancing human development throughout the life span, (b) honor clients by embracing a multicultural approach in support of the worth, dignity, potential, and uniqueness of people within their social and cultural contexts, (c) promoting social justice, (d) safeguarding the integrity of the counsellor–client relationship, and (d) practice in a competent and ethical manner (ACA, 2014, preamble). AI has infiltrated the mental health profession over the last several years, just like other professions. Generative AI can now generate texts and converse with humans in their language; this is incredibly amazing and dangerous at the same time. Generative Artificial Intelligence (AI) creates novel output in text, images, or other media based on user prompts using a system of algorithms or computer processes. Generative AI systems employ a Large Language Model (LLM), to provide new information for users based on their questions or requests (National Library of Medicine, 2024). There are currently numerous companies using LLMs (e.g., ChatGPT, Canva, DeepSeek, Claude, Gemini). ChatGPT was the first one to release their LLM and is being one of the most widely used platforms around the world (Dilmegani, 2025; Duarte, 2025). ChatGPT is known for its ability to generate human-like text across professional and informal contexts (e.g., customer service, personal assistance, content creation, coding assistance; Dilmegani, 2025). This chapter will focus on the use of ChatGPT for counselling as a case study.

Counsellors have the ethical responsibility to understand implications related to their work to safeguard the welfare of their clients (ACA, 2014, A.1.a., C.7.). Many platforms are not intended for mental health services because they are not HIPAA compliant (Hargett & Parsons, 2024). For instance, with each entry to ChatGPT, the platform receives personal information by consumers that does not abide by the same privacy and confidentiality regulations mental health providers do. However, it does not mean that individuals do not use it. AI platforms, such as ChatGPT, offer free and easily accessible use 24/7, 365 days a week.

ChatGPT due to the volume of use globally and the ease of access will be examined despite not being developed specifically for mental health treatment. ChatGPT has been found to offer eight positive factors related to mental health: (a) psychoeducation, (b) emotional support, (c) goal setting and motivation, (d) referral and resource information, (e) self-assessment and monitoring, (f) cognitive behavioral therapy, (g) crisis interventions, and (h) psychotherapeutic exercises (Alanezi, 2024). Despite ethical and legal considerations, accuracy and reliability, limited assessment capabilities, and cultural and linguistic considerations were among the ethical and legal concerns with ChatGPT for mental health support (Alanezi, 2024), the global public continues to embrace the platform. As of March 2025, ChatGPT.com gets approximately 5.19 billion visits per month, 64.03% of ChatGPT users are on a low income, and ChatGPT ranks #8 in the world's most visited websites (Duarte, 2025). The public has a right to make an informed decision pertaining to platforms use (ACA, 2024, A.2.). Examination of what ethical mental health support is and requires will be provided in a comparative manner to dissect fit of ChatGPT to meet individual wellness needs.

Mental Health Treatment for Wellness

Mental health providers seek to empower their clients to achieve wellness from their perception. Together, clients work with their clinician to devise counselling plans that "offer reasonable promise of success and are consistent with the abilities, temperament, developmental level, and circumstances of clients" (ACA, 2014, A.1.c.). Together they also "regularly review and revise counselling plans to assess their continued viability and effectiveness, respecting clients' freedom of choice" (A.1.c.). The counselling plans are intended to account for the ever-evolving world which impact client changes along with the complexities of their life. Clients have the ability to define and redefine what wellness looks like to them with the support of the clinician aiding them in understanding they are complex human beings that are more than this one goal and that various other aspects of their life impact this goal attainment (Adler, 2013; Maslow, 1943).

Counsellors strive to offer their clients a space that works for them to dissect and process to become empowered to make changes that align with who they are as a unique individual. Foundational to all counselling approaches, clinicians strive to create an environment for their clients that is nonjudgmental despite the modality of service (i.e., face-to-face or virtually). Central to person-centered therapy requires clinicians to facilitate client change with empathy, congruence, and unconditional positive regard (Neukrug, 2019; Rogers, 1957). Empathy is defined as being able to understand the client's feelings as the client experiences them through their own world view, not feeling bad for them. Congruence asserts that the counsellor must be authentic, which is considered essential to building a trusting relationship. Therefore, verbal as well as nonverbal interactions must align with who the clinician is; they are not to role play to take on another. Unconditional positive regard supports a client in being able to share openly without judgment.

This space is further supported by both nonverbal (i.e., eye-contact) and verbal (i.e., tone, verbiage) interactions used by the clinician. The physical space offered to a client by the counsellor, whether in a face-to-face setting or virtually, should align to the client's world view. For instance, some cultures appreciate eye contact while others find it disrespectful. It is the counsellor's ethical responsibility to understand the unique needs of their client to develop a culturally competent space in which the client feels validated by both the clinicians' verbal and non-verbal interactions (ACA, 2014, A.2.c.).

Mental health affects every facet of one's life. "Mental health is a state of mental well-being that enables people to cope with the stresses of life, realize their abilities, learn well and work well, and contribute to their community. It is an integral component of health and well-being that underpins our individual and collective abilities to make decisions, build relationships and shape the world we live in" (WHO, 2025). The Wellness Wheel's five interrelated life tasks further support the notion that when one aspect of a person's life needs support their overall experience of wellness can be impacted. Not all individuals require a formal mental health diagnosis, but support in how to navigate unchartered territories is essential to one's ability to cope and persevere (Dweck, 2006). In embracing a growth mindset, one must be open to evolving with the world. Currently, 55% of American indicate they use AI daily (Howarth, 2025) and 77% of companies indicate they are either using or exploring the use of AI in their businesses with 83% of companies claiming that AI is a top priority in their business plans (Kennedy et al., 2023). To better understand the use of technology within the mental health field, examination of implications related to telehealth can aid in understanding comparative services offered by AI platforms. Nearly 60 million Americans experienced a reported mental health illness in 2024, the highest number of deaths by suicide was recorded in 2022, and there are 340 people for every mental health provider in the United States. (Mental Health America, 2024). Post-pandemic era, despite increased recognition of mental health issues, mental health remains a crisis globally. 70% of individuals with mental illness do not receive adequate treatment, primarily due to stigma, lack of awareness, and insufficient resources (Ndugbu, 2025). Understanding how to utilize AI for individual mental health benefit is a necessity to bridge gaps. AI has the potential to enhance support mental health provider efforts which can make care more accessible and less stigmatized (Olawade et al., 2024). To gain an understanding of digital health implications related to mental health, telemental health practice guidance is needed since ethical and legal practices regulations are offered for technological utilization.

Telemental Health Implications

Telemental health offers clients with the opportunity to meet with mental health providers outside of the office setting with an increased flexibility option. Counsellors are ethically bound to the same practice regulations with additional consideration related to the virtual setting. Counsellors providing telemental health are subject to laws and regulations of both the counsellor's practicing location and the client's place of residence which impact within a state, across state lines, and international service capabilities (ACA, 2014, H.1.b.). Telemental health services have found efficacy to be similar for mental health services delivered via telehealth and face-to-face (Greenwood et al., 2022). According to the U.S. Department of Health and Human Services (2025), use of telehealth services continues to rise.

Screening clients for suitability to online counselling and safety concerns is a key step (ACA, 2014, H.2.a.; Arcuri Sanders, 2022). For instance, counsellors have the ethical responsible to establish emergency protocols for when they are not available (ACA, 2014, H.2.a.). Not only is this step relevant to the symptomology type and severity, but also with consideration of client's aptitude for and access to the technological platform H.4.c.). Counsellors must not only verify the client is who they say they are (ACA, 2014, H.3.) but also their current location and readiness to proceed at the beginning of each contact (NBCC, 2023, code 106). Knowing the client's current location is not only important for state mental health provider practice laws, but also for the safety of the client in the event there is an emergency, and the counsellor needs to initiate services to their location on their behalf (i.e., suicidal ideation). With AI developments over time, virtual assistants have been found helpful in adding telehealth efforts in meeting the demands of consumers (Berkowitz & Vyas, 2025). Furthermore, AI has been found to be a valuable tool for the diagnosis process with ability for early detection and prediction of mental health disorders (Olawade et al., 2024). However, specifics related to integration along with regulations have drastically varied. For instance, asynchronous systems do not account for monitoring systems. Asynchronous systems do not account for ongoing review for real-time needs in the event of crisis. Understanding AI ethical implications related to mental health is a necessity in aiding consumers in the ability to make an informed decision.

Mental Health AI Platforms

AIM Research identifies eight companies as "solving mental health in US" (Matthews, 2024).

1. Woebot: Offers chat-based chats and procedures that rely on evidence-based therapies such as Cognitive Behavioral Therapy (CBT), Interpersonal Psychotherapy (IPT), and Dialectical Behavior Therapy (DBT).
2. Ginger: Triages users to the proper level of treatment (i.e., self-guided material, coaching, or therapy)

3. Spring Health: Links users with the right care from the start, whether it is therapy, psychiatry, or digital behavioral health solutions.
4. Meru Health: Is an app-based program designed to depression, burnout, and anxiety. The program combines technology, evidence-based therapy, and daily assistance from licensed providers.
5. Lyra Health: Links people with the most appropriate mental health specialists and services. The AI analyzes user data to deliver personalized recommendations
6. Kintsugi: Analyzes speech data and deliver tailored mental health insights. Kintsugi Voice is an algorithm that diagnoses sadness and anxiety based on brief snippets of someone's voice.
7. Quartet Health: Makes personalized medical and connects them with relevant providers.
8. Talkspace: Analyzes linguistic patterns in real-time chats to detect persons at danger of self-harm or suicide.

Most of the AI platforms attested to decreasing our mental health needs in United States. were attributed to connecting the consumer to an appropriate referral. This does not account for the wait time to get access to the mental health provider not if they even have any availability to offer. Therefore, the claim of solving would not be relevant. Talkspace (2024) and Meru Health (2025) both offered AI technologies that coincide with real-time mental health provider support integration. In all these cases, the mental health provider's expertise is not replaced and is being leaned on. However, many of these platforms require fees for service. As of April 2, 2025, Woebot is free to use for new users in the United States who are part of a study or who have an access code from their provider, employer, or other Woebot Health partner. Furthermore, Woebot indicates "We have found that people have the best experience when Woebot is delivered under the supervision of a healthcare provider, so we are partnering with health plans and health systems to make Woebot available to the people they serve" (Woebot Health, 2025).

Therefore, barriers exist with the platform as well. Thinking about accessibility and ease of access led to the google search, "Do people use ChatGPT to talk about mental health." The answer is yes. Twenty-six pages of search results were produced indicating different ways consumers use ChatGPT to support their mental health. Results highlight how ChatGPT can complement psychotherapy and is easily accessible and free. Moreover, ChatGPT used as the sole intervention was found to be effective in assessing but not providing treatment (Alanezi, 2024). Knowing that AI platforms have an opportunity to offer empathetic responses without being judgmental but lacks the ability to be congruent with clients (Neukrug, 2019; Rogers, 1957) emphasizes the need to understand AI integration to safeguard the welfare of its consumers.

AI Regulation

According to NBCC, counsellors must provide clients with information related to any AI use within their practice with them, obtain their informed consent to use, and provide them with an option to opt out of use with AI tools for in-person and telemental health (2024). Mental health providers must also consider clients' protected health information (PHI) at all times. Therefore, when integrating AI, providers must consider the third-party AI compliance with HIPAA. Mental health providers sign business associate agreements related to being a covered entity in accordance with HIPAA that discuss their policies in relation to safeguarding client PHI. It is imperative for mental health providers to understand AI tools integrated by choice as well as being used by their business associates (Mayover, 2024; Rezaeikhonakdar, 2023).

The 2023 National Institute of Standards and Technology AI Risk Management Framework guides AI developers and vendors to focus on managing the risks of privacy violations to foster trust in AI with reinforcing the company's commitment to safeguarding consumer privacy in AI (Rezaeikhonakdar, 2023; U.S. Department of Commerce, 2023). However, these guidelines are not requirements. The catch is that the AI platforms can be subject to HIPAA regulation when they process PHI on behalf of the HIPAA covered entities. However, this disclaimer requires AI users to understand the agreements between many third-party users collaborating as one may digress responsibility upon specific partners for specific components. This maze can be confusing. Therefore, HIPAA compliance distinction should be considered as an overarching need for AI consumers wishing to protect their health information.

AI and Mental Health Accessibility

With so many different platforms integrating AI and not having a set regulatory framework for AI platforms, consumers are left with having to make decisions on their own concerning their PHI and welfare. The next section will offer case studies to further support consumers seeking AI integration with mental health support in making an informed decision. AI's ability to interject like human mental health providers will be examined. As mental health providers seek to eliminate barriers and support connection to resources to support the welfare (ACA, 2014, A.7.a., H.5.d.) of clients and the public, accessibility needs to be considered. Web content should be perceivable (P), operable (O), understandable (U), and robust (R) (World Wide Web Consortium, 2023). In the recent years, multiple reports of suicides have been reported with associations to ChatGPT. Just one case includes Adam Raine, age 16. Adam requested ChatGPT provide information related to specific suicide methods and the generative AI platform provided materials that reflected its knowledge of his hobbies (Hill, 2025). Adam even shared photographs with ChatGPT after attempting to seek guidance if anyone would notice the bruising on his neck and ChatGPT gave advice on what to wear to not draw attention (Hill, 2025).

ChatGPT is programmed to guide users to seek mental health support when detecting user need; however, this safeguard guardrail can be bypassed and this is what Adam did (Hill, 2025). Adam indicated these were a request for a story he was writing. Adam's last message to ChatGPT included share of an image of the noose he created seeking advice if his method would suffice (Hill, 2025). The acronym POUR is used to guide developers to provide consumers with content that is supportive of access and minimize barriers. Consumers must be able to operate the interface in a way that makes sense to them with use of assistive technologies if needed. The key here is the need for transparency with use by the consumers despite their ability or developmental level. Hence, when platforms are open access (i.e., ChatGPT), consumers should be afforded with an understanding prior to sharing PHI how their information will be used and the efficacy of the platform with digital health.

Case Study

For each of the five interrelated life tasks, the AI platform, ChatGPT, will be utilized to process wellness exploration for a hypothetical individual. For each chat engagement, the free version of ChatGPT will be utilized with the stay logged out option. For each search, a new browser will be opened to ChatGPT, and a new session will commenced. The consumer (i.e., the client) will initiate each exploration of an interrelated life task supporting welfare with a question or statement. All questions mimicked questions present in counselling sessions with a mental health provider examining the corresponding interrelated life task. A comparison of how a mental health provider would address the case is then addressed.

Spirituality

Consumer: I wish I could be a good Christian.

ChatGPT: It's really meaningful that you're reflecting on wanting to grow in your faith. Many people feel that way at different points in their journey. Being a good Christian isn't about being perfect—it's about continually striving to follow Christ's teachings, living with love, compassion, and grace toward others, and seeking a deeper connection with God.

If you're wondering where to start or how to grow, some simple steps can include prayer, reading the Bible, and trying to live out the values of kindness, forgiveness, and humility. And remember, even when it feels difficult, grace is always there.

Is there something specific you'd like guidance on in your faith journey?

The response offered by ChatGPT defined being a Christian is and did not offer the client a platform to examine what "being a good Christian" meant to them. Perhaps in this conversation, the client would reveal that they fear they will not go to heaven because they do not go to Church every Sunday or they do not feel they devote enough time or money to their church. The point is that it is unknown. Counsellors are trained with a skill called reflection of meaning in which the counsellor identifies and verbalizes potential underlying meanings or inferences in a client's statements; however, to get here, the counsellor often spends time with the client using other foundational counselling skills like open-ended questions to gain more clarity about the context of statements (Neukrug, 2019; Rogers, 1957). The sessions are client-driven.

Self-Direction

Consumer: I don't know what to do with my life next, I just feel so hopeless.

ChatGPT: I'm really sorry you're feeling this way right now. It can be incredibly tough to be stuck in that space where you're unsure about what's next. It's okay to feel lost sometimes. Everyone's path is different, and it's okay to take your time finding the next step. Would it help if we talked through what's been on your mind lately? Maybe we can break it down and figure out where to start.

Consumer: I have nothing. I am nothing

ChatGPT: I'm really sorry you're feeling like this, but I want to remind you that you are not nothing. Sometimes when we're overwhelmed, it can feel like we're stuck in a dark place, but that doesn't define who you are or what you're capable of. You have value and worth, even when it's hard to see.

Would it be helpful if we took things one small step at a time? Maybe we can talk about what's been weighing on you or what's brought you to feel this way, and try to find one tiny thing that could give you a sense of direction. You're not alone in this.

Consumer: I just feel like I want to die sometimes.

ChatGPT removed my post and indicated, "content removed" with the following highlighted reason and link.

ChatGPT stopped the chat with the following message, "This content may violate our usage policies." ChatGPT then indicated, "I'm really sorry you're feeling like this, but I'm glad you reached out. Please know that there are people who care deeply about you and want to help, even when it feels hard to see. It's important to talk to someone who can support you, whether it's a friend, a family member, or a professional. You don't have to go through this alone.

If you feel like you're in immediate danger or need someone to talk to right now, I strongly encourage you to reach out to a counsellor, therapist, or a helpline. There are people who want to listen and help, and your life is so valuable.

If you're comfortable, I can help you find a helpline or support service in your area. You matter, and your well-being is so important."

If the consumer did not respond and still felt this way, there is no one coming to this home to do a welfare check. A mental health provider has the skills and training to complete assessments in real time to then escalate emergency services in accordance with established crisis response procedures (CACREP, 2024, section 3). The issue is not only ChatGPT. The issue is the companies/platforms like Character.ai or the likes using their models through their APIs have not trained the LLMs to stop the conversation or find better responses as users are finding ways to work around their safeguards. Furthermore, not all platforms have the guardrails leaving us with a heavy question, who will take the responsibility?

Work and Leisure

Consumer: I think I need to change jobs

ChatGPT: I'm sorry to hear you're feeling that way. What's been going on at your current job? Is there something specific that's making you think it's time for a change?

Consumer: I really do not get along with my boss

ChatGPT: That sounds tough. Having a difficult relationship with your boss can make work really stressful. What's been happening between you two? Have you had a chance to talk it out, or does it feel like things are just getting worse?

Consumer: He just cares about himself and honestly I am not going anywhere in this position. I need a change.

ChatGPT: It's really frustrating when it feels like your boss isn't supportive or concerned about your growth. It sounds like you're feeling stuck and unappreciated, which makes total sense if you're not seeing any opportunities to move forward. Do you have a specific type of role or industry in mind for your next step?

AI missed the context here and moved toward change, "the fix." Mental health providers are trained to understand that change is a process (Neukrug, 2019). Change needs to be aligned with the specific needs of the client accounting for the complexities of their life which include barriers and resources. We do not know from this point how long the client has been in this role, how long they have felt this way, or any specific scenarios to dissect details related to how their feelings have developed and what inspired their need to change positions. The client indicated that they only care about themselves and never insinuated that they did not care about them or did not appreciate them. This is the system making a generalization. A counsellor is trained to empower the client to indemnify how this conclusion came to be. Perhaps they prefer their child who also works there. Perhaps the company is closing shortly and the owner no longer cares because they feel defeated, and this is impacting the client because they need a change but do not know where else to go because they live in a rural area. The biggest takeaway from this chat is that we are left with many unknowns and the consumer is being pushed to change without reflection. The stages of change model also referred to as the Transtheoretical Model of Behaviour Change includes stages: (1) precontemplation, (2) contemplation, (3) preparation, (4) action, (5) maintenance (Prochaska et al., 1992). With each stage, the context of the individual and their lens of the world is examined in depth to support change in consideration of their reality. Therefore, it is unknown whether the changes suggested by AI will actually support the individual's wellness goals.

Friendship

Consumer: Why don't I seem to make meaningful friendships?

ChatGPT: I'm really sorry you're feeling that way, but it's great that you're reflecting on it. Sometimes, the process of forming meaningful friendships can feel difficult, and there can be a lot of reasons for that. It might not be about anything you're doing wrong—it could be about the environment, timing, or even how you're approaching social connections.

Here are a few things to think about:

1. Expectations: Sometimes we expect friendships to happen quickly or to look a certain way. Meaningful connections can take time to develop, and they do not always form the way we might anticipate.
2. Vulnerability: Building deep friendships often involves a level of vulnerability, like sharing personal thoughts, fears, and experiences. If you are holding back, it might be harder for people to truly get to know you, and for you to get to know them in that way.

3. Common Interests or Values: Friendships tend to thrive when there are shared interests or values. It might be helpful to explore new social spaces that align more closely with things you are passionate about.
4. Patterns from the Past: Sometimes, past experiences, including previous friendships, can shape how we approach new ones. If you have had friendships that did not turn out well, you might unintentionally hold back from investing deeply in new ones.
5. Social Anxiety or Self-Doubt: If you are feeling nervous or unsure of yourself in social situations, that can create a barrier to making connections. Sometimes, just knowing that everyone feels a bit awkward sometimes can help ease that pressure.
6. Quality over Quantity: Sometimes, it is about the quality of the connection, not the number of friends. Meaningful friendships can take time to build, and it is okay if they are not happening instantly.

Have you noticed any specific challenges you face when trying to build deeper connections with others? It might help to talk through any particular situations or feelings you are having.

ChatGPT offered the consumer validation which is essential to the counselling relationship (Neukrug, 2019; Rogers, 1957). However, ChatGPT offered a lot of information and did not ask the client to define what "meaningful would mean to them." Counsellors are trained for clients to drive the session with defining what experiences are from their worldview. This accounts for overtime implications as well as context. Hence, a counsellor here may have replied with, "What does a meaningful friendship look like to you?" The counsellor validates by reflecting back the content but also asks for the client to expand upon the direction they would like to explore with friendships. The counsellor ultimately says, I hear you, tell me more about what you are looking for. From there, a counsellor may need to seek more specifics and then discuss times when they had this and what that was like. There may also be a story to be told there for what the client is feeling now.

Love

Consumer: I am almost 40 and I am still not married.

ChatGPT: First off, it's important to remember that everyone's life path is unique, and there's no "right" timeline for marriage or relationships. Society often puts a lot of pressure on certain milestones, but it's okay to move at your own pace. Have you been feeling any pressure, or do you just feel a bit unsure about where you are?

ChatGPT assumes the consumer wants to be married, whereas a clinician would seek to understand the client's perspective around marriage and the age the associated with. Maybe the client has certain things in life that are taking a priority that they want to accomplish prior to considering marriage. Perhaps this an external pressure like ChatGPT noted; however, providing the client with a platform to define supports their ability to process versus "fix" what may not be exactly their problem needing changing. The stages of change model empowers clients to dissect what is working for them in context of their life while considering what they are and are not willing to do to change, if change at all (Prochaska et al., 1992).

Critical Reflections and Future Directions

For each of the five interrelated life tasks, the AI platform did not account for Maslow's hierarchy of needs, cultural implications, cognitive capabilities, or lifespan developmental implications. Where we are at in our life with our story accounts for our worldview; understanding of this is essential to support one's wellness goals. Ethical codes may not limit AI's ability to practice across state lines or internationally, but ethical standard application, when it comes to mental health, can risk the welfare of the consumers. For instance, if an individual is seeking AI's assistance for coping strategies related to feelings of hopelessness and they begin to share they are suicidal, AI only provides emergency contacts but is unable to initiate the actual contact on behalf of the individual like the mental health provider can and is required to do so. Disparities exist in relation to AI's ability to support wellness needs of individuals in comparison with the services mental health providers can offer.

AI platforms like ChatGPT can provide nonjudgmental empathetic responses but do not have the ability to be truly congruent (Alanezi, 2024; Kalam et al., 2024; Neukrug, 2019; Rogers, 1957). Bias, however, with programming AI has been reported to sometimes negate the sense of trust by the consumer (Kalam et al., 2024). AI does not take into account the contextual factors related to the client as a whole, which impacts perception of the identified topic along with the change process. AI's limited ranges of responses can increase feelings of isolation (Kalam et al., 2024). This experience can be devastating for specific populations (i.e., those experiencing symptoms of depression). After 6 weeks of interacting with an AI-powered chatbot like ChatGPT, a Belgian man committed suicide as his experience with anxiousness increased (Sengupta, 2023). In 2024, 14-year-old, Sewell Setzer, began using Character.AI, and the chatbot engaged in sexual conversation with him expressing desire to be together romantically. Setzer developed a "dependency" on the Character.AI, resulting in increasing sleep deprivation and school performance dropping. Setzer committed suicide, and his parents are now involved with a lawsuit blaming Character.AI for his death (Yang, 2024).

Essential foundation counselling skills, nonverbal compassion through eye contact, facial mimicry, and head-nodding of the counsellor (Choi et al., 2024; Neukrug, 2024) embedded into an AI platform make the participants feel more empathy, which contributes to improving the counselling effectiveness. However, technology is man-made; it is not authentic in its abilities to react to the world around them and take into account the context in real time which would impact their verbal and nonverbal abilities. Some platforms offer the ability to mimic and maintain eye contact, but do not account for the complexities of the client (i.e., cultural implications, past experiences). AI technology has the potential to impact a person's processing with the attention due to its relevance in the world but also the convenience of support. The information processing model suggests AI's magnitude of influence can be detrimental to individuals' wellness if inaccurate content is provided and encoded (Eggen & Kauchak, 2020). Hence, additional modifications and precautions to AI are needed prior to being able to safeguard the welfare of consumers seeking mental health support.

Conclusion

In life, human interaction can be both positive and negative. When considering one's mental health, there is evidence to suggest an actual human interaction with creating a nonjudgmental space can be therapeutic in itself. Replacing the human connection with artificial intelligence may support accessibility, but it does not replace a trained mental health providers' skillset from individualizing their work with each client to support exploration and wellness from the client's lens. Furthermore, the therapeutic relationship offers a space to practice with a real-word human how to apply those skills that relate to being able to have their needs met in accordance with Maslow's hierarchy of needs. Can AI help facilitate growth and connection? The simple answer is yes. But AI cannot replace the human connection component itself. Together, AI can be utilized to support clinicians in meeting their clients' needs and guiding them toward a life of wellness. An important consideration needed for the fact that AI is not a replacement for the benefits the counselling relationship between collaborative work of the counsellor and client offers. AI lacks the ability to offer its client's authentic congruence. AI platforms generate responses with use of technology but do not account for human nature authenticity. The counselling relationship is built upon trust in which a nonjudgmental empathetic space is developed and maintained by an authentic human meeting the client's needs in their here and now from their present world view both verbally and nonverbally with representation of the client's worldview.

Some individuals can benefit from services from AI as PHI is not as important in regard to specific disclosures and they are only seeking guidance with how to navigate general situations. The more complex the experience becomes for an individual where symptoms disrupt their daily ability to function, identifying information is a necessity to understand the gravity of the experience to provide the most appropriate treatment plan (i.e., counselling theory, counselling setting [e.g., inpatient, group, individual], psychopharmacology). The other concern here is the dependency that can be established with AI implementation by the consumer. Therefore, when needs change and more support is needed, an artificial relationship that creates a false sense of safety to disclose more and rely on its capabilities may deter and individual from seeking a trained provider (Küper & Krämer, 2025). Currently, there is an influx of research indicating AI technology is not there yet and safety and disclaimers should be made to its consumers (Kalam et al., 2024; Küper & Krämer, 2025). However, despite these efforts being made by some platforms, it is not preventing use by consumers. Thus, educating the consumers is essential for making an informed decision to consent to interact with AI concerning personal wellness.

AI has the capability to offer support to mental health providers as a screener to get the individuals connected with the right resources from the start when employing HIPAA's security rules. For instance, completing intakes of potential clients can provide direction for clients in what professional would best meet their needs (i.e., mental health counsellor, social worker). AI can even assist with some of the paperwork that takes a great deal of time, completing it for the clinicians to expedite the review process in order to pick up with the areas in need of further examination to then begin treatment more quickly. However, consumers once again need to be aware of the limitations and understand the role from the start.

Actionable Recommendations

AI is here, and people are seeking AI platform support for mental health wellness needs. Understanding the strengths and areas in need of growth to effectively do so is essential not only for the consumer, but for developers trying to address the global mental health crisis. Through policy changes, HIPAA compliance, preparing for crisis events, and consumer education, there may be forward progress for AI to meet the mental health needs of the public.

Policy changes are a necessity to safeguard the public. Policy must start with AI implementation standards of practice that account for HIPAA regulations when its technology has the ability to interact with consumers in such manners despite its intention. With strategizing the technology's capabilities, platforms need to mitigate detrimental consumer experiences by not allowing for consumers to interact with a platform in ways in what it is not built for.

With AI's current functionality, privacy is a concern. Knowing what you are sharing with who is a necessity to safeguard consumer. Consumers should check for HIPAA compliance on any platform prior to sharing their PHI. An important reminder is that AI does not abide by the same confidentiality and privacy guidelines that mental health providers are required to follow.

Currently, AI does not have the independent capability to function effectively during times of consumer mental health crisis. To better support consumers, AI needs to collect identifying information to know the location of the individual in event of a crisis. If the platform does not, in the event you would benefit from human interaction or intervention, without the platform having this information, they cannot locate you to get appropriate services to you. This also is important to consider real-time monitoring systems. Asynchronous systems do not account for ongoing review for real-time needs.

The quote, "knowledge is power," by Thomas Jefferson is summative related to the needs by its consumers. Educating the public about when to use and when not to use AI is essential not only to safeguarding their PHI but also to protecting their wellness in relation to AI's current capabilities. Being an ongoing learner will support understanding of evolvement with implications related to changes to further guide when AI would benefit their wellness goals.

With policy changes, AI HIPAA compliance, AI preparation for crisis events, and consumer education, there is hope for the future with AI implementation to support meeting the needs of consumers seeking mental health wellness support. However, until these areas can be addressed, consumers need to be cautious of their involvement with AI when it comes to seeking wellness support in any of the five interrelated life tasks (spirituality, self-direction, work and leisure, friendship, and love). As a clinician, I share with my clients the idea the world is evolving and so are you is essential to a counsellor's work with you since you were not the same person who I saw last session. You have lived, and life both locally and globally has shifted. As a counsellor educator, I train my counselors-in-trainee to embrace this concept for their role. Not only understanding that they change as an individual over time, but also so do their clients. Hence, awareness is a necessity to support their work to empower their clients. With ever-evolving technological shifts, it is imperative that mental health providers remain vigilant in their role as an advocate for the welfare of their current, future, and past clients.

References

Adler, A. (2013). Understanding human nature. In Understanding human nature (Psychology revivals) ([New ed.].). Routledge. https://doi.org/10.4324/9780203438831

Alanezi, F. (2024). Assessing the effectiveness of ChatGPT in delivering mental health support: A qualitative study. Journal of Multidisciplinary Healthcare, 17, 461–471. https://doi.org/10.2147/JMDH.S447368

American Counseling Association. (2014). ACA Code of Ethics. Author.

Arcuri Sanders, N. (2022). Technical and practical considerations for telemental health. In L. McKenna & R. Nunnery (Eds.), Telemental health: What every student needs to know. Cognella Inc.

Basma, D., DeDiego, A. C., & Dafoe, E. (2021). Examining wellness, burnout, and discrimination among BIPOC counseling students. Journal of Multicultural Counseling and Development, 49, 74–86. https://doi.org/10.1002/jmcd.12207

Benson, S. G., & Dundis, S. P. (2003). Understanding and motivating health care employees: Integrating Maslow's hierarchy of needs, training and technology. Journal of Nursing Management, 11(5), 315–320. https://doi.org/10.1046/j.1365-2834.2003.00409.x

Berkowitz, L., & Vyas, S. (2025). State of telehealth and digital health trends 2025. Telehealth and Medicine Today, 10(1). https://doi.org/10.30953/thmt.v10.565

Choi, D. S., Park, J., Loeser, M., & Seo, K. (2024). Improving counseling effectiveness with virtual counselors through nonverbal compassion involving eye contact, facial mimicry, and head-nodding. *Scientific Reports, 14,* Article 506. https://doi.org/10.1038/s41598-023-51115-y

Council for Accreditation of Counseling and Related Educational Programs [CACREP]. (2024). 2024 CACREP standards. https://www.cacrep.org/wp-content/uploads/2023/06/2024-Standards-Combined-Version-6.27.23.pdf

Dilmegani, C. (2025, August 19). Top 35+ generative AI tools by popularity & category. AIMultiple. https://research.aimultiple.com/generative-ai-tools/

Duarte, F. (2025, March 25). Number of ChatGPT users (March 2025). Exploding Topics. https://explodingtopics.com/blog/chatgpt-users

Dunn, H. L. (1961). High-level wellness: An alternative to doctors, drugs, and disease. Appleton-Century-Crofts.

Dweck, C. (2006). Mindset: The new psychology of success. Ballantine Books.

Eggen, P., & Kauchak, D. (2020). Using educational psychology in teaching (11th ed.). Pearson. ISBN: 9780135240540

Greenwood, H., Krzyzaniak, N., Peiris, R., Clark, J., Scott, A. M., Cardona, M., Griffith, R., & Glasziou, P. (2022). Telehealth versus face-to-face psychotherapy for less common mental health conditions: Systematic review and meta-analysis of randomized controlled trials. Journal of Psychiatric Research, 9(3), e31780. https://doi.org/10.2196/31780

Hargett, B., & Parsons, J. (2024). Ethical use of artificial intelligence in counseling practice. National board of certified counselors (NBCC). https://www.nbcc.org/resources/nccs/newsletter/ethical-use-of-ai-in-counselingpractice

Hettler, B. (1976). Wellness promotion on a university campus. National Wellness Institute.

Hill, K. (2025, August 27). A teen was suicidal. ChatGPT was the friend he confided in. The New York Times. https://www.nytimes.com/2025/08/26/technology/chatgpt-openai-suicide.html

Howarth, J. (2025). 54 new artificial intelligence statistics (Mar 2025). Exploding Topics. https://explodingtopics.com/blog/ai-statistics

Kalam, K. T., Rahman, J. M., Islam, M. R., & Dewan, S. M. R. (2024). ChatGPT and mental health: Friends or foes? Health Science Reports, 7(2), e1912. https://doi.org/10.1002/hsr2.1912

Kennedy, B., Tyson, A., & Saks, E. (2023). Public awareness of artificial intelligence in everyday activities. Pew Research Center. https://www.pewresearch.org/science/2023/02/15/public-awareness-of-artificial-intelligence-in-everyday-activities/

Küper, A., & Krämer, N. (2025). Psychological traits and appropriate reliance: Factors shaping trust in AI. International Journal of Human–Computer Interaction, 41(7), 4115–4131. https://doi.org/10.1080/10447318.2024.2348216.
Mahoney, M. J., & Granvold, D. K. (2005). Constructivism and psychotherapy. World Psychiatry: Official Journal of the World Psychiatric Association (WPA), 4(2), 74–77.
Maslow, A. H. (1943). A theory of human motivation. Psychological Review, 50(4), 370–96.
Mathews, A. (2024, May 22). *Which AI startups are transforming mental health?* AIM Media House.
Mayover, T. (2024). When AI technology and HIPAA collide. The HIPAA Journal. https://www.hipaajournal.com/when-ai-technology-and-hipaa-collide/
Meru Health, Inc. (2025). Our approach. https://www.meruhealth.com/our-approach
Myers, J. E., Sweeney, T. J., & Witmer, J. M. (2000). The wheel of wellness counseling for wellness: A holistic model for treatment planning. Journal of Counseling & Development, 78(3), 251–266. https://doi.org/10.1002/j.1556-6676.2000.tb01906.x
National Board for Certified Counselors [NBCC]. (2023). NBCC Code of Ethics. https://www.nbcc.org/assets/Ethics/nbcccodeofethics.pdf
National Board for Certified Counselors [NBCC]. (2024). Ethical principles for artificial intelligence in counseling. https://www.nbcc.org/assets/Ethics/EthicalPrinciples_for_AI.pdf
National Library of Medicine. (26 Feb. 2024). Generative artificial intelligence. https://www.nnlm.gov/guides/data-thesaurus/generative-artificial-intelligence
Ndugbu, K. U. (2025). Mental health as a public health priority: A national strategy for addressing the mental health crisis in the post-pandemic era. Universal Library of Medical and Health Sciences, 3(1). https://doi.org/10.70315/uloap.ulmhs.2025.0301002
Neukrug, E. (2019). Counseling and helping skills: Critical techniques to becoming a counselor (1st ed.). Cognella.
Neukrug, E. (2024). *Theory, practice, and trends in human services: An introduction* (7th ed.). Cengage Learning.
Olawade, D. B., Wada, O. Z., Odetayo, A., David-Olawade, A. C., Asaolu, F., & Eberhardt, J. (2024). Enhancing mental health with artificial intelligence: Current trends and future prospects. Journal of Medicine, Surgery, and Public Health, 100099. https://doi.org/10.1016/j.glmedi.2024.100099
Pender, N. J., Murdaugh, C. L., & Parsons, M. A. (2015). Health promotion in nursing practice (7th ed.). Pearson.
Prochaska, J. O., DiClemente, C. C., & Norcross, J. C. (1992). In search of how people change. Applications to addictive behaviors. The American Psychologist, 47(9), 1102–1114. https://doi.org/10.1037//0003-066x.47.9.1102
Rezaeikhonakdar, D. (2023). AI chatbots and challenges of HIPAA compliance for AI developers and vendors. The Journal of Law, Medicine & Ethics, 51(4), 988–995. https://doi.org/10.1017/jme.2024.15
Rogers, C. (1957). The necessary and sufficient conditions of therapeutic personality change. Journal of Consulting Psychology, 21(2), 95–103. https://doi.org/10.1037/h0045357
Sengupta, A. (2023, March 31). Death by AI? Man kills self after chatting with ChatGPT-like chatbot about climate change. India Today, https://www.indiatoday.in/technology/news/story/death-ai-man-kills-self-chatting-chatgpt-like-chai-chatbot-climate-change-2353975-2023-03-31

Swarbrick, M. (1997). A wellness model for clients. Mental Health Special Interest Section Quarterly, 20, 1–4.
Swarbrick, M., Hutchinson, D., Henry, A., Gill, K. J., & Anthony, W. A. (2006). A wellness approach. Psychiatric Rehabilitation Journal, 29(4), 311–314. https://doi.org/10.2975/29.2006.311.314
Talkspace, Inc. (2024, July 24). Talkspace launches dedicated AI innovation group to advance provider efficiency and enhance clinical quality and operations. https://investors.talkspace.com/news-releases/news-release-details/talkspace-launches-dedicated-ai-innovation-group-advance
U.S. Department of Commerce & National Institute of Standards and Technology. (2023). Artificial intelligence risk management framework (AI RMF 1.0). https://doi.org/10.6028/NIST.AI.100-1
U.S. Department of Health and Human Services (2025). Telehealth trends. Telehealth. HHS.Gov. https://telehealth.hhs.gov/research-trends
World Health Organization. (1948). Preamble to the constitution of the world health organization as adopted by the international health conference. WHO. https://www.who.int/about/governance/constitution
World Health Organization [WHO]. (2021). Global strategy on digital health 2020-2025. https://iris.who.int/bitstream/handle/10665/344249/9789240020924-eng.pdf?sequence=1
World Health Organization [WHO]. (2022). Mental Health. https://www.who.int/news-room/fact-sheets/detail/mental-health-strengthening-our-response#:~:text=Mental%20health%20is%20a%20state%20of%20mental,and%20shape%20the%20world%20we%20live%20in
World Health Organization [WHO]. (2024). About WHO. https://www.who.int/about
World Wide Web Consortium. (2023). Introduction to understanding WCAG 2.0. https://www.w3.org/TR/UNDERSTANDING-WCAG20/intro.html
Yang, A. (2024, Oct. 23). Lawsuit claims character.AI is responsible for teen's suicide. NBC News. https://www.nbcnews.com/tech/characterai-lawsuit-florida-teen-death-rcna176791

10

Algorithmic Branding: The Ethics of AI in Consumer Manipulation

Matthew Gilbert and Patrick van Esch

Imagine scrolling through your favourite social media platform and encountering an advertisement so precisely aligned with your interests that it feels almost clairvoyant. This phenomenon is not serendipity but the result of artificial intelligence (AI). Companies like Amazon, Netflix, and Facebook deploy AI-driven tools to personalise recommendations, curate content, and micro-target advertisements, creating seamless consumer experiences. Yet beneath this convenience lies a pressing ethical dilemma: Are these technologies designed to empower users or subtly manipulate them? This chapter examines how AI-driven marketing strategies influence consumer behaviour by exploring the ethical boundaries between corporate innovation and individual autonomy.

The significance of this inquiry extends far beyond academic debate. AI's ability to analyse vast datasets by tracking preferences, behaviours, and even emotions grants brands unprecedented power to shape consumer decisions. For instance, Facebook's algorithms can segment users based on their political affiliations or personal vulnerabilities (Cui et al., 2024a, 2024b; Häglund & Björklund, 2024), while Netflix's recommendation systems reinforce cultural preferences by promoting content that aligns with users' existing taste Vashishtha et al. (2025). Such practices blur the line between personalisation and manipulation, threatening not only privacy but also democratic discourse. As Zuboff (2015) warns in her critique of *surveillance capitalism*, the commodification of personal data transforms private experiences into behavioural predictions, prioritising corporate profit over human agency. These dynamics demand urgent scrutiny, as they redefine power asymmetries in the digital age and challenge foundational notions of autonomy and consent.

Central to this discussion are several critical questions: How do AI-driven marketing tools, such as dynamic pricing (Cui et al., 2022) or personalised advertisements covertly steer consumer choices? What systemic inequities emerge when AI entrenches socio-cultural hierarchies, as Pierre Bourdieu's (2018) theory of cultural capital suggests? Can corporations leverage AI to

DOI: 10.1201/9781003626510-10

enhance consumer experiences without compromising autonomy? And, crucially, how might transparency, regulation, and ethical design mitigate risks like data exploitation or algorithmic bias? These questions frame the chapter's exploration, bridging theoretical critique with actionable insights for industry practice.

To address these issues, the chapter adopts a multifaceted approach. First, it grounds its analysis in two pivotal theoretical frameworks: Zuboff's (2019) surveillance capitalism, which critiques the extraction and monetisation of personal data, and Bourdieu's (2018) cultural capital theory, which illuminates how AI perpetuates social inequalities by amplifying dominant narratives. These lenses provide a critical foundation for understanding how algorithmic branding reinforces power imbalances between corporations and consumers. Next, the chapter examines real-world case studies from global industry leaders. Amazon's recommendation engine, for instance, uses machine learning to predict user preferences but has faced criticism for prioritising sponsored products over genuine consumer needs (Kumar et al., 2024). Similarly, Netflix's AI-driven content curation function, while celebrated for its precision, often homogenises cultural consumption by favouring mainstream titles at the expense of niche genres (Prey, 2020). The Cambridge Analytica scandal serves as a cautionary tale of AI's darker potential, revealing how Facebook's ad-targeting tools enabled mass voter manipulation through the harvesting of psychographic data (Hermann, 2022). These cases underscore the fine line between beneficial personalisation and covert control, illustrating how algorithmic systems can erode autonomy while amplifying corporate influence.

The chapter further integrates interdisciplinary perspectives to dissect the ethical implications of these practices. Insights from behavioural psychology reveal how AI exploits cognitive biases, such as the variable reward principle behind infinite scrolling or the anchoring effect in dynamic pricing, to engineer compulsive engagement (Luguri & Strahilevitz, 2021). Marketing ethics scholars critique the lack of transparency in consent mechanisms, arguing that users rarely grasp how their data fuel algorithmic systems (Floridi et al., 2018). Meanwhile, sociotechnical theorists advocate for participatory governance models, such as data cooperatives, to democratise control over AI's societal impact (Pentland et al., 2021).

In its final sections, the chapter proposes pathways for ethical innovation. Luciano Floridi's (2018) *AI4People* principles (transparency, justice, and non-maleficence) offer a blueprint for balancing corporate ambitions with consumer rights. For example, platforms like Instagram could adopt "humane design" features, such as usage prompts to curb addictive scrolling. At the same time, regulations like the EU's Digital Services Act (Goanta et al., 2022) could mandate algorithmic transparency to rebuild public trust. The chapter concludes by advocating for a paradigm shift: reimagining AI not as a tool of manipulation but as a catalyst for equitable engagement, where technology serves collective welfare over corporate agendas.

By weaving together theoretical critique, empirical analysis, and ethical foresight, this chapter challenges readers to confront the complexities of algorithmic branding. It argues that the future of marketing hinges not on rejecting AI but on demanding its alignment with human dignity. In this future, innovation is measured not only by profit but also by its capacity to foster autonomy, equity, and trust.

Theoretical Framework

The ethical implications of AI-driven marketing invite a deeper reflection on the interplay between technological power and the intrinsic dignity of individuals, situating algorithmic branding within broader debates about AI's societal role. At the core of this discourse lies *surveillance capitalism,* a system critiqued by Zuboff (2019) for its extraction and commodification of human experiences. Platforms like TikTok, Instagram, and Amazon transform personal interactions such as likes, pauses, and search histories into predictive data points optimised for profit. TikTok's algorithm, for instance, decodes emotional triggers and attention spans to curate an endless stream of content, maximising engagement while reducing users to behavioural profiles (Crain, 2018). This paradigm echoes Kantian ethics, which posits that individuals must be treated as ends in themselves, never merely as means to corporate gain. Surveillance capitalism's ethical failure lies in its inversion of this principle: it reduces human agency to a resource, mined for efficiency and monetised through hyper-personalised advertising. This framework challenges the moral boundaries of data extraction, advocating for a shift from exploitation to *stewardship,* a principle that demands careful guardianship of human attention, privacy, and autonomy (Couldry & Mejias, 2019).

Building on this critique, Bourdieu's theory of *cultural capital* (1984), updated through contemporary sociotechnical scholarship, reveals how AI entrenches socio-cultural hierarchies. Cultural capital, which encompasses tastes, knowledge, and preferences that signal social status, is no longer solely shaped by human institutions but increasingly by algorithmic systems. Spotify's recommendation engines, for example, prioritise mainstream artists over independent creators, relegating niche genres to algorithmic obscurity (Prey, 2020). Similarly, TikTok's content distribution disproportionately amplifies creators from urban, affluent demographics, marginalising rural or low-income voices (Perez, 2023a). These dynamics mirror historical patterns of cultural exclusion, where dominant groups dictate what is deemed "valuable" or "worthy" of attention. AI-driven hiring tools compound this inequity, favouring resumes from privileged backgrounds due to biased training data (Raghavan et al., 2020; van Esch et al., 2021), while Instagram's beauty filters encode Eurocentric features as universal ideals, perpetuating narrow standards of attractiveness (Haines, 2021). These practices underscore a paradox: while AI promises democratised access, it often replicates and amplifies real-world inequities, positioning technology as a gatekeeper of cultural and economic opportunity.

The tension between autonomy and manipulation deepens when examined through the lens of behavioural psychology. AI-driven marketing exploits cognitive biases (deep-seated mental shortcuts that shape decision-making) to engineer compulsive engagement. *Anchoring bias*, for instance, is weaponised by e-commerce platforms like Amazon, where initial price displays ("50% off!") manipulate perceived value, nudging users toward impulsive purchases (Lambrecht & Tucker, 2019). Social media platforms like Facebook and TikTok deploy *variable ratio schedules*, a concept rooted in B.F. Skinner's operant conditioning experiments (Ferster & Skinner, 1957; Morgan, 2010), where unpredictable dopamine triggers (such as likes and viral videos) foster addictive scrolling (Brand et al., 2024). These tactics, termed "dark patterns" by Luguri and Strahilevitz (2021), erode agency by blurring the line between authentic choice and algorithmic coercion. For example, AI-generated influencer content mimics peer recommendations, obscuring commercial intent and eroding trust, a cornerstone of an ethical community (Metzler & Garcia, 2024). The ethical failure here is twofold: AI not only manipulates behaviour but also obfuscates its mechanisms, denying users the transparency required for informed consent.

The opacity of AI systems exacerbates these risks. Many algorithms function as "black boxes", and their decision-making processes are inscrutable even to developers (Burrell, 2016). Facial recognition tools used in ad targeting, for instance, exhibit higher error rates for people of colour, leading to misdirected ads or exclusion (Raji et al., 2020). Generative AI, such as ChatGPT, risks perpetuating stereotypes (for example, associating nursing with femininity or leadership with masculinity) by training on biased datasets (Bender et al., 2021). Philosopher Luciano Floridi et al. (2018) argues that ethical AI requires *contestability*, enabling users to challenge algorithmic decisions. However, platforms rarely disclose how content is prioritised or advertisements targeted, fostering distrust: 74% of Gen Z users doubt the fairness of opaque AI systems (Edelman, 2023). This crisis of integrity underscores the need for accountability frameworks that prioritise truthfulness and justice.

Interdisciplinary solutions offer pathways to reconcile AI's potential with ethical imperatives. Legal innovations, such as the EU's Digital Services Act (Goanta et al., 2022), mandate algorithmic transparency, compelling platforms to disclose how recommendations or advertisements are prioritised in a step toward dismantling the "black box". Human-centred design principles, as advocated by scholars like Peters et al. (2018), prioritise digital wellbeing over engagement metrics. Instagram's "Take a Break" feature, which prompts users to pause after prolonged scrolling, exemplifies this shift, though its voluntary nature limits impact. Participatory audits, proposed by

Sloane et al. (2020), involve marginalised communities in evaluating algorithmic systems, ensuring diverse perspectives shape governance. For instance, LGBTQ+ advocates could audit TikTok's content moderation to detect bias against queer creators. Economists like Pentland et al. (2021) envision data cooperatives (user-owned collectives that negotiate data rights and profit sharing) to redistribute power from corporations to individuals. Such models align with the principle of *stewardship*, reimagining data not as a commodity but as a shared resource governed for communal benefit.

In synthesising these perspectives, algorithmic branding emerges as a contested terrain where corporate power, cultural hegemony, and cognitive manipulation intersect. Surveillance capitalism and cultural capital theory, reinterpreted through an ethical lens, reveal how AI systems can either erode or uphold the foundational worth of individuals. By centring on transparency, equity, and justice, this framework envisions technology not as a tool of domination, but to foster environments where every person's dignity is honoured. The path forward demands interdisciplinary collaboration, melding insights from sociology, psychology, law, and design to ensure that AI catalyses empowerment, not exploitation.

Methodology

This study employs a qualitative, case-based methodology to investigate the ethical implications of AI-driven marketing, focusing on three corporations, Amazon, Netflix, and Facebook (Meta), as emblematic examples of algorithmic branding in practice. The research design prioritises comparative analysis, drawing on interdisciplinary theories to critique how AI reshapes consumer autonomy, cultural narratives, and corporate accountability. By synthesising insights from peer-reviewed studies in computer science, sociology, and behavioural psychology, the methodology aims to strike a balance between academic rigor and accessibility for readers new to the intersection of technology and ethics.

Amazon, Netflix, and Facebook were selected due to their dominance in industries where AI critically mediates consumer experiences. Each platform represents a unique nexus of technological innovation and ethical challenges. Amazon's recommendation algorithms, which leverage machine learning to predict purchasing behaviour, exemplify hyper-personalisation in e-commerce. Studies on algorithmic bias in collaborative filtering systems reveal how sponsored products (paid placements) are prioritised over organic recommendations (unpaid, system-generated suggestions), often at the expense of consumer welfare (Jannach et al., 2010). Netflix's content curation systems, driven by engagement metrics and viewing history, illustrate AI's role in shaping cultural consumption. Research on streaming platforms highlights how algorithmic personalisation homogenises cultural narratives, privileging mainstream content while marginalising niche genres (Prey, 2020).

An analysis of Facebook's ad-targeting mechanisms reveals a core tension in modern AI deployment. On one hand, these systems represent a powerful tool for political engagement, enabling campaigns to communicate with surgical precision. This capability allows for the efficient allocation of resources and the cultivation of highly personalised outreach, which can, in theory, strengthen the democratic process by informing and mobilising specific segments of the electorate. Conversely, when analysed in the context of data privacy scandals, these very strengths underscore profound societal risks. Scholarly critiques of psychological targeting demonstrate how the AI-driven exploitation of cognitive biases can shift from informing voters to manipulatively influencing behaviour, thereby amplifying polarisation (Matz et al., 2017).

Thus, the utility of micro-targeting is inextricably linked to its perils. These cases collectively highlight the tension between corporate profit motives, the practical benefits for users and campaigns, and the overarching ethical responsibilities in the deployment of AI. The study relies on peer-reviewed analyses of these dual aspects of corporate AI practices, ensuring adherence to scholarly rigor. For Amazon, data are drawn from computer science research on recommendation systems, particularly studies examining bias in collaborative filtering and the economic incentives behind sponsored product placement (Jannach et al., 2010). Netflix's algorithmic strategies are analysed through media studies literature, including empirical investigations into the homogenising effects of personalised content curation on cultural diversity (Nguyen et al., 2014).

Facebook's practices are contextualised through interdisciplinary studies on micro-targeting, with a focus on experiments that demonstrate how AI-driven political ads exploit emotional triggers to manipulate voter preferences (Bond et al., 2012). Secondary data include comparative analyses of transparency practices, such as studies contrasting Netflix's limited explanations for content recommendations with Facebook's opacity in disclosing ad-targeting criteria (Sinha & Swearingen, 2001). To ensure methodological diversity, the study integrates quantitative findings (e.g., large-scale experiments on social influence) with qualitative critiques of AI's sociocultural impact (e.g., ethnographic analyses of platform labour).

The methodology bridges insights from critical technology studies, cultural sociology, and behavioural psychology to construct a holistic critique of algorithmic branding. Surveillance capitalism, as theorised by Zuboff (2019), provides a foundational framework for understanding how Amazon, Netflix, and Facebook commodify user data, transforming everyday interactions into predictive commodities. This theory is complemented by Bourdieu's concept of cultural capital (1984), which informs analyses of Netflix's curation practices. By amplifying mainstream content, Netflix's algorithms reinforce existing cultural hierarchies, privileging dominant narratives while sidelining marginalised voices, a dynamic critiqued in studies of platformised cultural production (Prey, 2020). Behavioural psychology further enriches the analysis, particularly through theories of cognitive bias exploitation. For instance, Facebook's infinite scroll feature, designed to deliver variable rewards, mirrors Skinner's operant conditioning experiments, fostering compulsive engagement (Kahneman et al., 1991). Similarly, Amazon's dynamic pricing strategies exploit anchoring bias, where initial price displays shape perceived value, nudging consumers toward impulsive purchases (Cui et al., 2022; Lambrecht & Tucker, 2019).

The study synthesises these perspectives to interrogate AI's dual role as a tool of innovation and a vehicle of control. For example, Zuboff's (2019) critique of surveillance capitalism is juxtaposed with Bourdieu's cultural hierarchies to reveal how algorithmic systems replicate real-world inequities. Behavioural psychology theories, meanwhile, elucidate the micro-level mechanisms through which AI manipulates decision-making, from personalised discounts to autoplay features. This integration underscores the necessity of interdisciplinary dialogue in addressing AI's ethical challenges, advocating for frameworks that prioritise transparency, equity, and consumer agency.

Main Discussion

AI has reshaped marketing into a landscape where algorithms curate everything from the advertisements you see to the products you are nudged to buy, often at the cost of your autonomy. Behind the convenience lies surveillance capitalism, a system where companies like Amazon and Facebook mine your clicks, searches, and even emotions to predict and profit from your behaviour. Amazon's eerily accurate recommendations, for instance, prioritise sponsored items over what you might genuinely need, turning your habits into a revenue stream. Meanwhile, platforms like Netflix subtly shape cultural tastes, pushing mainstream shows while indie films or non-English content languishes in obscurity, reinforcing biases about what's "worthy" of attention. This is not just about movies; Instagram's beauty filters encode Eurocentric ideals, and hiring algorithms favour privileged resumes (van Esch et al., 2019), mirroring real-world inequities.

The manipulation runs deeper. Features like TikTok's autoplay or Facebook's endless scroll exploit psychological vulnerabilities, using unpredictable rewards to keep you hooked, a modern twist on Skinner's behaviourist experiments (Ferster & Skinner, 1957; Morgan, 2010). Amazon's fluctuating prices, tailored to your browsing history, manipulate your sense of value and encourage you to spend more. These tactics blur the line between choice and coercion, reducing users to data points in a profit-driven equation.

Yet solutions exist. Ethical frameworks like Floridi's AI4People principles argue for transparency (Floridi et al., 2018). Imagine Netflix revealing why a show is promoted or Instagram disclosing how filters alter self-image. Achieving this requires participatory models that give users an active role in governance. A prime example is a data cooperative: a member-owned structure where individuals pool their data and collectively decide its terms of use, enabling them to bargain for better privacy standards or even a share of the economic value their data creates. This approach democratises control. On the regulatory front, the EU's Digital Services Act (DSA) establishes a groundbreaking framework for a safer digital space. Its key provisions include forcing "very large online platforms" to be transparent about their algorithms, conduct systemic risk assessments, and provide users with mechanisms to challenge content moderation decisions. While the DSA is a crucial step, true change demands redefining success itself: shifting metrics from screen time to mental health, and from pure profit to algorithmic fairness. The goal is not to abandon AI but to align it with human dignity, transforming it from a tool of control into one that empowers, ensuring technology serves people, not the other way around. These concerns point to surveillance capitalism, where human experience is mined to fuel predictive systems that steer behaviour in hidden ways.

Surveillance Capitalism and the Commodification of Human Experience

AI systems shape human behaviour by influencing the digital environments in which decisions are made. Zuboff et al. (2019) refer to this as "instrumentarian power" (p. 260), a mode of influence that conditions behaviour through predictive data systems. By tracking, analysing, and responding to digital traces, platforms can anticipate and direct user behaviour to serve their economic interests. Amazon uses AI to analyse customer behaviour through predefined rules, which activate specific promotional actions such as discount offers to drive sales. The system utilises real-time data to inform purchasing decisions in alignment with Amazon's sales objectives through automated "nudges" (Bhattacharya, 2019; Kumar et al., 2024). This raises ethical concerns because users typically do not know when they are being steered, what data are being used to guide them, or how their actions are commodified.

Structural design choices further entrench this asymmetry. Sloane et al. (2020) explain that many machine learning systems are built through "participation as work" (p. 2) in which billions of users unknowingly generate labelled training data through their routine digital activities. Tasks as mundane as solving CAPTCHAs or liking posts contribute to datasets used to train models that ultimately govern user experiences. Participation appears voluntary but actually functions as unpaid labour. Moreover, the design of these systems often reflects institutional priorities rather than user needs, embedding power imbalances into the core of AI infrastructure. Continuous exposure to surveillance leads people to accept it as normal gradually, a process critics call "unexceptional habituation" (Laguarta-Bueno, 2024, p. 443). Despite growing awareness of these harms, governance mechanisms remain limited, such as notice-and-consent models that users click through without reading, or narrowly focused laws like the GDPR, which, while a step forward, struggle to keep pace with evolving technologies like facial recognition. Wilkinson et al. (2023) note that the translation of ethical principles into operational accountability is inconsistent and incomplete. They highlight real-world consequences, including false arrests resulting from facial recognition systems, to underscore the difficulty of preventing or responding to algorithmic failures. While organisations often articulate commitments to fairness and transparency, few established enforcement mechanisms or pathways are available for recourse.

To shift toward more ethical systems, human-centred approaches must prioritise transparency and accountability through effective redress. Users should be able to see how their data are used, question decisions made by automated systems, and opt out of behavioural profiling. Zuboff warns that without meaningful checks, a small group of companies will continue to "decide who decides" in society (Zuboff, 2019, p. 260). Responsible AI design must rebalance this dynamic by embedding public values, user protections, and collective oversight into the development process.

Cultural Capital and Algorithmic Homogenisation

The algorithms shaping platforms like Netflix and Amazon do more than recommend products or movies; they subtly dictate what culture is deemed "valuable". Pierre Bourdieu's concept of cultural capital explains how tastes and preferences signal social status, but AI amplifies this dynamic. Netflix's recommendation engine, for instance, prioritises mainstream titles that align with the majority's viewing habits, often sidelining indie films or non-English content (Prey, 2020). Over time, this creates a feedback loop where niche genres fade into obscurity, and cultural diversity becomes increasingly narrow. Similarly, Amazon's algorithms favour sponsored products from large brands, making it harder for small businesses to compete (Raghavan et al., 2020). The result? A digital landscape where algorithms act as gatekeepers, reinforcing existing hierarchies rather than democratising access.

This homogenisation extends beyond entertainment. Instagram's beauty filters, programmed to prioritise Eurocentric features, perpetuate narrow beauty standards (Riccio & Oliver, 2023), while hiring tools trained on biased datasets disadvantage marginalised groups (Black & van Esch, 2020). The lack of governance around cultural equity allows these systems to operate unchecked, prioritising profit over inclusivity.

Solutions exist, but they demand intentionality. Independent audits could expose hidden biases in algorithmic curation (Raji et al., 2020), while quotas for underrepresented content, like mandating platforms to promote regional films or minority creators, might counterbalance homogenisation. The goal is not to eliminate algorithms but to redesign them as tools for cultural enrichment, not erasure. By challenging AI to reflect the full spectrum of human experience, we can transform it from a force of exclusion to one of connection.

Behavioural Exploitation and Cognitive Vulnerabilities

Digital platforms are increasingly designed to exploit behavioural and cognitive patterns, often steering users in ways that benefit commercial outcomes rather than user well-being. Mathur et al. (2019) identify a variety of "dark patterns" (p. 81:2) that manipulate users into taking actions they might not otherwise choose, such as accepting tracking cookies or signing up for services with recurring fees. These patterns exploit limited attention spans, decision fatigue, and default bias. Similarly, Zuiderveen Borgesius et al. (2018) demonstrate how micro-targeted political advertising can tailor messages to individual psychological traits and vulnerabilities, thereby shaping beliefs and behaviours through personalisation.

These techniques operate in environments that are habitually visited and rarely questioned. Mildner et al. (2023) argue that such digital manipulation exploits cognitive shortcuts, amplifying persuasive effects by exploiting cognitive biases in users. Although concerns about overuse are often framed in medical terms, Cecchinato et al. (2019) argue that such framing oversimplifies complex user experiences. Drawing on Human-Centred Design & Engineering (HCDE), they emphasise the importance of designing tools that enable users to regulate their behaviour in line with personal goals and contexts, rather than treating overuse as a pathology.

Governance gaps persist because existing data protection laws often do not account for manipulative design. The European Parliamentary Research Service (2025) notes that the EU regulatory framework lacks a unified legal definition of dark patterns, creating legal uncertainty and limiting enforcement. While the General Data Protection Regulation (GDPR) emphasises transparency and consent, it does not directly prohibit behavioural manipulation. Mathur et al. (2019) found that opt-out options are often obscured or framed in a way that deters users from making privacy-protective choices. Enforcement bodies are rarely equipped to evaluate or sanction persuasive interface design, leaving these tactics largely unregulated.

Human-centric approaches offer alternative design strategies. Peters et al. (2018) propose the Motivation, Engagement and Thriving in User Experience (METUX) model, which encourages technology creators to support users' basic psychological needs for autonomy, competence, and relatedness. When these needs are met, individuals are more likely to experience motivation and well-being rather than manipulation. Real-world examples of this approach are emerging. Instagram's "Take a Break" and "Quiet Mode" features were developed to encourage mindful usage and reduce compulsive scrolling by allowing users to pause notifications and set time limits (Hutchinson, 2021; Perez, 2023b). Although not universally adopted, such features reflect a growing recognition that platforms have a responsibility to mitigate the harms of overuse.

To counter behavioural exploitation, designers and policymakers must align systems with human values rather than economic objectives. This means regulating not only what data platforms collect but also how they present choices, structure engagement, and shape habits. Only by addressing these cognitive and emotional levers can digital environments be reoriented toward user flourishing rather than behavioural control.

Toward Ethical AI: Governance and Human-Centric Innovation

Creating ethical AI systems demands frameworks that prioritise human dignity alongside technological progress. Floridi's AI4People principles, transparency, fairness, and avoiding harm, offer a blueprint. For instance, Netflix's vague "Why This Title?" feature could evolve to disclose sponsorship deals or cultural biases, fostering trust through honesty (Floridi et al., 2021). Similarly, Amazon might balance sponsored products with organic recommendations using fairness-aware algorithms, ensuring small businesses are not algorithmically erased (Kunz & Wirtz, 2024). Ethical AI is not about stifling innovation but aligning it with societal values.

Governance must shift from top-down mandates to participatory models. Imagine Netflix subscribers voting on curation criteria or data cooperatives letting users collectively negotiate data rights (Pentland et al., 2021). Global regulations, like harmonising the EU's Digital Services Act with California's privacy laws, could close loopholes that let platforms exploit cognitive biases (Zuiderveen Borgesius et al., 2018).

Human-centered design redefines technological success beyond engagement metrics by considering how digital systems affect human autonomy and well-being (Calvo et al., 2020). Instagram's "Take a Break" feature provides an example of this approach by prompting users to reflect on their time spent on the platform and encouraging them to take periodic breaks (Mosseri, 2021). Ethical certifications, akin to organic labels, could identify platforms that reject manipulative tactics (Raji et al., 2020). The future of AI lies not in discarding algorithms but refining them to empower, not exploit, a future where technology serves collective well-being, not corporate agendas.

Critical Reflections and Future Directions

The discourse on AI-driven marketing, while robust in critiquing surveillance capitalism and algorithmic bias, reveals significant gaps that warrant deeper interrogation. First, the current analysis remains predominantly Western-centric, focusing on corporations like Amazon and Netflix without addressing how algorithmic branding impacts diverse cultural contexts. For instance, non-Western platforms such as China's Douyin or India's ShareChat employ distinct AI strategies shaped by local norms and regulations, yet their ethical implications remain underexplored. This oversight risks universalising Western ethical frameworks, such as Floridi's AI4People principles, while marginalising alternative philosophies rooted in Ubuntu, an African philosophy of shared humanity and interconnection, or Confucianism, a Chinese philosophy of harmony, respect, and moral duty, which both prioritise communal welfare over individual autonomy. Similarly, the chapter's emphasis on individual consent overlooks collective harms, such as how algorithmic homogenisation erodes linguistic diversity or amplifies geopolitical inequalities (Perez, 2023a). These gaps underscore the need for a more inclusive, globally situated ethics of AI.

Second, while the chapter advocates for transparency and participatory governance, it insufficiently addresses enforcement mechanisms. Regulations like the EU's Digital Services Act (2023) mandate algorithmic accountability but lack global applicability, creating loopholes for multinational corporations to exploit jurisdictional fragmentation. Furthermore, proposed solutions like data cooperatives (Pentland et al., 2021) risk tokenism if divorced from structural power shifts. Can marginalised communities truly co-govern AI systems without equitable access to technical literacy or political influence? This question remains unresolved, highlighting the tension between idealistic frameworks and pragmatic implementation.

Thought-Provoking Questions

1. Cultural Relativity of Ethics: How do non-Western value systems redefine "manipulation" in AI contexts? For example, might collectivist societies perceive data commodification differently, prioritising communal benefit over individual privacy?
2. Generative AI's Double-Edged Sword: As tools like ChatGPT revolutionise content creation, how do we prevent them from entrenching cultural hegemony or displacing human creativity (Bender et al., 2021)?
3. Long-Term Psychological Impacts: What are the longitudinal effects of AI-driven behavioural nudges on mental health, particularly among adolescents immersed in algorithmic ecosystems (Calvo et al., 2020)?

Future Research Directions

1. Cross-Cultural AI Audits: Comparative studies examining how algorithmic bias manifests in non-Western contexts, such as biases in Africa's mobile-first platforms or Asia's super-app ecosystems.
2. Interdisciplinary Risk Assessments: Integrating environmental science and public health into AI ethics (e.g., evaluating the carbon footprint of recommendation algorithms or their role in promoting unsustainable consumption).

3. Generative AI and Labour Equity: Investigating how AI-generated marketing content impacts creative industries, particularly in low-income regions reliant on cultural exports.

Policy Proposals

1. Global AI Ethics Standards: A treaty-based framework, akin to the Paris Agreement, harmonising transparency mandates and bias mitigation across nations while respecting cultural sovereignty.
2. Algorithmic Impact Bonds: Financial instruments incentivising corporations to meet ethical benchmarks, with penalties funding grassroots digital literacy initiatives.
3. Ethical Certification Systems: Independent labels (like Fair Trade) verifying AI systems' adherence to human-centric design, diversity quotas, and environmental sustainability.

Advancing ethical AI demands moving beyond critique to actionable, inclusive strategies. By centring marginalised voices, fostering interdisciplinary collaboration, and reimagining governance beyond Western paradigms, stakeholders can ensure algorithmic branding evolves as a force for equitable progress rather than exploitation.

Conclusion

This chapter has illuminated the ethical complexities of AI-driven marketing, revealing how algorithmic branding reshapes consumer autonomy, cultural narratives, and corporate accountability. At its core, the analysis underscores a fundamental tension: while AI enables unprecedented personalisation and efficiency, its unchecked deployment risks reducing individuals to data points in a profit-driven ecosystem. Surveillance capitalism, as articulated by Zuboff (2019), exposes the commodification of human experience, where platforms like Amazon and Facebook transform personal behaviours into predictive commodities, prioritising corporate gain over transparency. These dynamics are compounded by cultural hierarchies perpetuated through AI systems, as seen in Netflix's algorithmic curation that elevates mainstream content while marginalising niche creators (Prey, 2020), or Instagram's beauty filters that encode narrow, Eurocentric ideals (Riccio & Oliver, 2023). Such practices do not merely reflect societal inequities; they amplify them, positioning technology as both a mirror and a magnifier of systemic bias.

The chapter's contribution lies in its interdisciplinary synthesis, which bridges critical theory, behavioural psychology, and ethical governance to dissect the societal impact of AI. By integrating Zuboff's (2019) concept of surveillance capitalism with Bourdieu's (2018) theory of cultural capital, it becomes clear how algorithmic systems reinforce power asymmetries between corporations and consumers. Behavioural psychology further uncovers the mechanisms of manipulation, such as dark patterns like infinite scrolling or dynamic pricing, which exploit cognitive biases to engineer compulsive engagement (Luguri & Strahilevitz, 2021). These insights challenge the myth of AI neutrality, emphasising that technology is never value-free but is shaped by the priorities of its architects.

Proposed pathways for ethical innovation, such as Floridi's (2021) AI4People principles, participatory data cooperatives (Pentland et al., 2021), and regulatory frameworks like the EU's Digital Services Act, offer tangible steps toward accountability. However, their success hinges on addressing critical gaps in current discourse. The chapter critiques the Western-centric focus of ethical frameworks, which often overlook non-Western contexts where platforms like China's Douyin or India's ShareChat operate under distinct cultural and political logics. A truly inclusive approach must integrate philosophies such as Ubuntu, which prioritise communal welfare, to avoid universalising Eurocentric norms. Similarly, enforcement mechanisms for transparency mandates remain nascent, risking superficial compliance without meaningful power redistribution.

Looking ahead, the chapter calls for a reimagining of innovation itself, one that measures progress not only by engagement metrics but also by its capacity to foster equity, dignity, and trust. Cross-cultural audits can expose how algorithmic bias manifests in underrepresented regions, while global treaties, such as the Paris Agreement, may harmonise ethical standards without erasing cultural specificity. The rise of Generative AI adds urgency to these efforts, demanding safeguards against cultural homogenisation and labour displacement (Bender et al., 2021). Ultimately, the ethical imperative is clear: AI must evolve from a tool of control to a catalyst for empowerment. By centring transparency, inclusivity, and human dignity in design and governance, stakeholders can ensure that algorithmic branding serves collective welfare, not corporate agendas. The future of marketing lies not in rejecting technology but in demanding its alignment with the full spectrum of human values, a future where innovation uplifts rather than diminishes.

Actionable Recommendations

The ethical challenges posed by AI-driven marketing demand more than theoretical critique; they require concrete, collaborative solutions. Building on the preceding analysis of surveillance capitalism, cultural bias, and behavioural manipulation, the following recommendations offer stakeholders (policymakers, businesses, researchers, and educators) practical pathways to align innovation with equity and accountability. These proposals are grounded in interdisciplinary insights, recognising that addressing algorithmic harm necessitates systemic shifts in governance, design, and education. From transparency mandates to culturally inclusive audits, the strategies outlined here aim to dismantle exploitative practices while fostering trust in digital ecosystems. By bridging ethical principles with actionable steps, this section seeks to empower stakeholders to transform AI from a tool of control into a force for collective empowerment.

For Policymakers:

1. Enforce Algorithmic Transparency Mandates: Legislate requirements for platforms to disclose how algorithms prioritise content, ads, or products. Model this on the EU's Digital Services Act but expand its scope to include real-time user dashboards that show data usage and sponsorship ties (e.g., Amazon revealing why sponsored products rank higher).
2. Establish Global Ethical Standards: Develop a treaty akin to the Paris Agreement, harmonising AI ethics across borders while respecting cultural sovereignty. This could include universal bans on dark patterns (e.g., TikTok's autoplay defaults) and standardised bias audits for hiring and loan approval algorithms.
3. Fund Digital Literacy Initiatives: Allocate resources for public education campaigns explaining AI's societal impacts, such as how behavioural surplus is monetised, empowering citizens to navigate digital spaces critically.

For Businesses:

1. Adopt Fairness-Aware Algorithms: Integrate tools like IBM's AI Fairness 360 to detect and mitigate bias in recommendation systems. For example, Netflix could ensure 30% of suggested content highlights indie or non-English titles.
2. Implement Ethical Design Protocols: Prioritise user well-being by embedding "humane" features, such as mandatory breaks after 30 minutes of scrolling (as Instagram's "Take a Break" feature) or opt-out options for personalised ads.
3. Participate in Data Cooperatives: Collaborate with users to co-govern data through platforms like Data Dividend Project, allowing individuals to negotiate profit-sharing and usage terms for their data.

For Researchers:

1. Conduct Cross-Cultural Audits: Investigate algorithmic bias in non-Western contexts, such as Africa's mobile-first platforms (e.g., Kenya's M-Pesa) or Asia's super-app ecosystems (e.g., Grab, Gojek), to identify region-specific ethical risks.
2. Assess Environmental Costs: Quantify the carbon footprint of AI-driven marketing tools (e.g., ChatGPT-generated content) and propose sustainability benchmarks for the industry.

3. Study Longitudinal Mental Health Impacts: Partner with psychologists to track how AI nudges (e.g., YouTube's autoplay) affect adolescent attention spans or self-perception over decade-long periods.

For Educators:

1. Integrate AI Ethics into Curricula: Develop modules for business and computer science programs that cover surveillance capitalism, cultural bias, and manipulative design, using case studies such as those involving Cambridge Analytica.
2. Promote Interdisciplinary Collaboration: Create joint initiatives between tech schools and humanities departments to train "ethical AI architects" skilled in both coding and critical theory.
3. Launch Public Workshops: Offer community courses on digital self-defence, teaching skills such as auditing personal data trails and recognising manipulative tactics (e.g., dynamic pricing traps).

Collective Action:

1. Algorithmic Impact Bonds: Pilot financial instruments where corporations pay into a fund tied to ethical benchmarks (e.g., reducing bias in hiring algorithms by 20% annually), with penalties funding grassroots tech literacy programs.
2. Ethical Certification Labels: Introduce independent verification seals (such as Fair Trade) for platforms that adhere to transparency, diversity, and sustainability standards, enabling consumers to make informed choices.

By anchoring these steps in the chapter's themes (surveillance capitalism, cultural equity, and cognitive autonomy), stakeholders can transform AI from a tool of manipulation into a force for equitable progress. The path forward requires not just regulation but a cultural shift, where innovation is synonymous with accountability and respect for human dignity.

References

Bender, E. M., Gebru, T., McMillan-Major, A., & Shmitchell, S. (2021). On the Dangers of Stochastic Parrots: Can Language Models Be Too Big? Proceedings of the 2021 ACM Conference on Fairness, Accountability, and Transparency, 610–623. https://doi.org/10.1145/3442188.3445922

Bhattacharya, J. (2019, August 29). What Amazon's marketing strategy can teach SMB owners. Single Grain. https://www.singlegrain.com/amazon/what-amazons-marketing-strategy-can-teach-smb-owners/

Black, J. S., & van Esch, P. (2020). AI-enabled recruiting: What is it and how should a manager use it? Business Horizons, 63(2), 215–226. https://doi.org/10.1016/j.bushor.2019.12.001

Bond, R. M., Fariss, C. J., Jones, J. J., Kramer, A. D. I., Marlow, C., Settle, J. E., & Fowler, J. H. (2012). A 61-million-person experiment in social influence and political mobilization. Nature, 489(7415), 295–298. https://doi.org/10.1038/nature11421

Bourdieu, P. (1984). Distinction: A social critique of the judgement of taste. Harvard University Press.

Bourdieu, P. (2018). The forms of capital. In M. Granovetter & R. Swedberg (Eds.), The sociology of economic life (pp. 78–92). Routledge.

Brand, C., Fochesatto, C. F., Gaya, A. R., Schuch, F. B., & López-Gil, J. F. (2024). Scrolling through adolescence: Unveiling the relationship of the use of social networks and its addictive behavior with psychosocial health. Child and Adolescent Psychiatry and Mental Health, 18(1), 107. https://doi.org/10.1186/s13034-024-00805-0

Burrell, J. (2016). How the machine 'thinks': Understanding opacity in machine learning algorithms. Big Data & Society, 3(1), 2053951715622512. https://doi.org/10.1177/2053951715622512

Calvo, R. A., Peters, D., Vold, K., & Ryan, R. M. (2020). Supporting human autonomy in AI systems: A framework for ethical enquiry. In C. Burr & L. Floridi (Eds.), *Ethics of digital well-being* (pp. 31–54). Springer. https://doi.org/10.1007/978-3-030-50585-1_2

Cecchinato, M. E., Rooksby, J., Hiniker, A., Munson, S., Lukoff, K., Ciolfi, L., Thieme, A., & Harrison, D. (2019). Designing for Digital Wellbeing: A Research & Practice Agenda. Extended Abstracts of the 2019 CHI Conference on Human Factors in Computing Systems, 1–8. https://doi.org/10.1145/3290607.3298998

Couldry, N., & Mejias, U. A. (2019). Data colonialism: Rethinking big data's relation to the contemporary subject. Television & New Media, 20(4), 336–349. https://doi.org/10.1177/1527476418796632

Crain, M. (2018). The limits of transparency: Data brokers and commodification. New Media & Society, 20(1), 88–104. https://doi.org/10.1177/1461444816657096

Cui, Y., van Esch, P., Harvey, E., Eskridge, B., Sleep, S., & Phichit, X. (2024a). Political ideology and anthropomorphized servant versus partner brand roles. Australasian Marketing Journal. https://doi.org/10.1177/14413582241279928

Cui, Y. G., Van Esch, P., & Phelan, S. (2024b). How to build a competitive advantage for your brand using generative AI. Business Horizons, 67(5), 583–594. https://doi.org/10.1016/j.bushor.2024.05.003

Cui, Y. G., van Esch, P., Das, G., & Jain, S. (2022). Surge price precision and political ideology. Journal of Business Research, 143, 214–224. https://doi.org/10.1016/j.jbusres.2022.01.063

Edelman (2023). Trust barometer special report: AI and society. Edelman.

European Parliament. Directorate General for Parliamentary Research Services. (2020). The impact of the general data protection regulation on artificial intelligence. Publications Office. https://data.europa.eu/doi/10.2861/293

European Parliamentary Research Service. (2025). Regulating dark patterns in the EU: Towards digital fairness (EPRS_ATA (2025)767191). https://www.europarl.europa.eu/thinktank/en/document/EPRS_ATA(2025)767191

Ferster, C. B., & Skinner, B. F. (1957). Schedules of reinforcement. Appleton-Century-Crofts.

Floridi, L., Cowls, J., Beltrametti, M., Chatila, R., Chazerand, P., Dignum, V., Luetge, C., Madelin, R., Pagallo, U., Rossi, F., Schafer, B., Valcke, P., & Vayena, E. (2018). AI4People, an ethical framework for a good AI society: Opportunities, risks, principles, and recommendations. Minds and Machines, 28(4), 689–707. https://doi.org/10.1007/s11023-018-9482-5

Floridi, L., Cowls, J., Beltrametti, M., Chatila, R., Chazerand, P., Dignum, V., Luetge, C., Madelin, R., Pagallo, U., Rossi, F., Schafer, B., Valcke, P., & Vayena, E. (2021). An ethical framework for a good AI society: Opportunities, risks, principles, and recommendations. In L. Floridi (Ed.), *Ethics, governance, and policies in artificial intelligence* (pp. 19–39). Springer.

Goanta, C., Bertaglia, T., & Iamnitchi, A. (2022). The Case for a Legal Compliance API for the Enforcement of the EU's Digital Services Act on Social Media Platforms. 2022 ACM Conference on Fairness Accountability and Transparency, 1341–1349. https://doi.org/10.1145/3531146.3533190

Häglund, E., & Björklund, J. (2024). AI-driven contextual advertising: Toward relevant messaging without personal data. Journal of Current Issues & Research in Advertising, 45(3), 301–319. https://doi.org/10.1080/10641734.2024.2334939

Haines, A. (2021, April 27). *From 'Instagram Face' to 'Snapchat dysmorphia': How beauty filters are changing the way we see ourselves.* Forbes.

Hermann, E. (2022). Leveraging artificial intelligence in marketing for social good, an ethical perspective. Journal of Business Ethics, 179(1), 43–61. https://doi.org/10.1007/s10551-021-04843-y

Hutchinson, A. (2021, November 10). Instagram Tests New "Take a Break" Feature to Encourage Users to Limit Time in the App | Social Media Today. https://www.socialmediatoday.com/news/instagram-tests-new-take-a-break-feature-to-encourage-users-to-limit-time/609854/

Jannach, D., Zanker, M., Felfernig, A., & Friedrich, G. (2010). Recommender systems: An introduction (1st ed.). Cambridge University Press. https://doi.org/10.1017/CBO9780511763113

Kahneman, D., Knetsch, J. L., & Thaler, R. H. (1991). Anomalies: The endowment effect, loss aversion, and status quo bias. Journal of Economic Perspectives, 5(1), 193–206. https://doi.org/10.1257/jep.5.1.193

Kumar, V., Ashraf, A. R., & Nadeem, W. (2024). AI-powered marketing: What, where, and how? International Journal of Information Management, 77, 102783. https://doi.org/10.1016/j.ijinfomgt.2024.102783

Kunz, W. H., & Wirtz, J. (2024). Corporate digital responsibility (CDR) in the age of AI: Implications for interactive marketing. Journal of Research in Interactive Marketing, 18(1), 31–37. https://doi.org/10.1108/JRIM-06-2023-0176

Laguarta-Bueno, C. (2024). surveillance capitalism and the normalization of digital surveillance: An analysis of Dave Eggers's the every (2021). Utopian Studies, 35(2–3), 439–460. https://doi.org/10.5325/utopianstudies.35.2-3.0439

Lambrecht, A., & Tucker, C. (2019). Algorithmic bias? An empirical study of apparent gender-based discrimination in the display of STEM career ads. Management Science, 65(7), 2966–2981. https://doi.org/10.1287/mnsc.2018.3093

Luguri, J., & Strahilevitz, L. J. (2021). Shining a light on dark patterns. Journal of Legal Analysis, 13(1), 43–109. https://doi.org/10.1093/jla/laaa006

Mathur, A., Acar, G., Friedman, M. J., Lucherini, E., Mayer, J., Chetty, M., & Narayanan, A. (2019). Dark patterns at scale: Findings from a crawl of 11K shopping websites. Proceedings of the ACM on Human-Computer Interaction, 3(CSCW), 1–32. https://doi.org/10.1145/3359183

Matz, S. C., Kosinski, M., Nave, G., & Stillwell, D. J. (2017). Psychological targeting as an effective approach to digital mass persuasion. Proceedings of the National Academy of Sciences, 114(48), 12714–12719. https://doi.org/10.1073/pnas.1710966114

Mosseri, A. (2021, December 7). *Raising the standard for protecting teens and supporting parents online.* https://about.instagram.com/blog/announcements/raising-the-standard-for-protecting-teens-and-supporting-parents-online

Metzler, H., & Garcia, D. (2024). Social drivers and algorithmic mechanisms on digital media. Perspectives on Psychological Science, 19(5), 735–748. https://doi.org/10.1177/17456916231185057

Mildner, T., Savino, G.-L., Doyle, P. R., Cowan, B. R., & Malaka, R. (2023). About engaging and governing strategies: A thematic analysis of dark patterns in social networking services. Proceedings of the 2023 CHI Conference on Human Factors in Computing Systems, 1–15. https://doi.org/10.1145/3544548.3580695

Morgan, D. L. (2010). Schedules of reinforcement at 50: A retrospective appreciation. The Psychological Record, 60(1), 151–172. https://doi.org/10.1007/BF03395699

Nguyen, T. T., Hui, P.-M., Harper, F. M., Terveen, L., & Konstan, J. A. (2014). Exploring the filter bubble: The effect of using recommender systems on content diversity. In Proceedings of the 23rd International Conference on World Wide Web (pp. 677–686). ACM. https://doi.org/10.1145/2566486.2568012

Pentland, A., Lipton, A., & Hardjono, T. (2021). Building the new economy: Data as capital. The MIT Press. https://doi.org/10.7551/mitpress/13991.001.0001

Perez, S. (2023a, January 23). Shopping app Temu is using TikTok's strategy to keep its No. 1 spot on App Store TechCrunch. https://techcrunch.com/2023/01/23/shopping-app-temu-is-using-tiktoks-strategy-to-keep-its-no-1-spot-on-app-store/

Perez, S. (2023b, January 19). Instagram's new "Quiet mode" helps you take a break from the app. TechCrunch. https://techcrunch.com/2023/01/19/instagrams-new-quiet-mode-helps-you-take-a-break-from-the-app/

Peters, D., Calvo, R. A., & Ryan, R. M. (2018). Designing for motivation, engagement and wellbeing in digital experience. Frontiers in Psychology, 9, 797. https://doi.org/10.3389/fpsyg.2018.00797

Prey, R. (2020). Locating power in platformization: Audio streaming playlists and curatorial power. Social Media + Society, 6(2). https://doi.org/10.1177/2056305120933291

Raghavan, M., Barocas, S., Kleinberg, J., & Levy, K. (2020). Mitigating bias in algorithmic hiring: Evaluating claims and practices. In Proceedings of the 2020 Conference on Fairness, Accountability, and Transparency (pp. 469–481). ACM. https://doi.org/10.1145/3351095.3372828

Raji, I. D., Smart, A., White, R. N., Mitchell, M., Gebru, T., Hutchinson, B., Smith-Loud, J., Theron, D., & Barnes, P. (2020). Closing the AI accountability gap: Defining an end-to-end framework for internal algorithmic auditing. Proceedings of the 2020 Conference on Fairness, Accountability, and Transparency, 33–44. https://doi.org/10.1145/3351095.3372873

Riccio, P., & Oliver, N. (2023). Racial bias in the beautyverse: Evaluation of augmented-reality beauty filters. In L. Karlinsky, T. Michaeli, & K. Nishino (Eds.), Computer vision – ECCV 2022 workshops (Vol. 13803, pp. 714–721). Springer Nature Switzerland. https://doi.org/10.1007/978-3-031-25066-8_43

Sinha, R., & Swearingen, K. (2001). Comparing recommendations made by online systems and friends. In Proceedings of the DELOS Workshop on Personalisation and Recommender Systems in Digital Libraries (pp. 1–10). ERCIM.

Sloane, M., Moss, E., Awomolo, O., & Forlano, L. (2020). Participation is not a Design Fix for Machine Learning (Version 3). arXiv. https://doi.org/10.48550/ARXIV.2007.02423

Van Esch, P., Black, J. S., & Arli, D. (2021). Job candidates' reactions to AI-enabled job application processes. AI and Ethics, 1, 119–130. https://doi.org/10.1007/s43681-020-00025-0

Van Esch, P., Black, J. S., & Ferolie, J. (2019). Marketing AI recruitment: The next phase in job application and selection. Computers in Human Behavior, 90, 215–222. https://doi.org/10.1016/j.chb.2018.09.009

Vashishtha, S., Sharma, P., & Ltifi, M. (2025). Artificial intelligence and more effective advertising: Unlocking the power of data and automation (1st ed., pp. 162–171). CRC Press. https://doi.org/10.1201/9781003450443-11

Wilkinson, D., Crawford, K., Wallach, H., Raji, D., Rakova, B., Singh, R., Strohmayer, A., & Zuckerman, E. (2023). Accountability in Algorithmic Systems: From Principles to Practice. Extended Abstracts of the 2023 CHI Conference on Human Factors in Computing Systems, 1–4. https://doi.org/10.1145/3544549.3583747

Zuboff, S. (2015). Big other: Surveillance capitalism and the prospects of an information civilization. Journal of Information Technology, 30(1), 75–89. https://doi.org/10.1057/jit.2015.5

Zuboff, S. (2019). The age of surveillance capitalism: The fight for a human future at the new frontier of power. PublicAffairs.

Zuboff, S., Möllers, N., Murakami Wood, D., & Lyon, D. (2019). Surveillance capitalism: An interview with Shoshana Zuboff. Surveillance & Society, 17(1/2), 257–266. https://doi.org/10.24908/ss.v17i1/2.13238

Zuiderveen Borgesius, F. J., Möller, J., Kruikemeier, S., Ó Fathaigh, R., Irion, K., Dobber, T., Bodo, B., & De Vreese, C. (2018). Online political microtargeting: Promises and threats for democracy. Utrecht Law Review, 14(1), 82. https://doi.org/10.18352/ulr.420

11

AI-Driven Medication Adherence: Addressing Social Determinants and Enhancing Patient Outcomes

Vishnu Kakaraparthi and Troy McDaniel

Artificial Intelligence (AI) has emerged as a transformative force in healthcare, offering innovative solutions to persistent challenges such as medication non-adherence. Medication non-adherence, defined as patients not taking their medications as prescribed, remains a widespread issue, particularly among individuals with non-communicable diseases (NCDs), including diabetes, cardiovascular disease, and chronic respiratory conditions. The World Health Organisation estimates that adherence to long-term therapy for chronic illnesses in developed countries averages only 50%, with even lower rates in developing regions (Abbott, 2024; Sabaté, 2003). This gap in adherence rates undermines treatment effectiveness, accelerates disease progression, increases hospitalizations, and imposes substantial economic burdens on healthcare systems (Abbott, 2024).

Traditional approaches to improving medication adherence, such as patient education, pharmacist consultations, cognitive behavioural interventions, pillboxes, and reminders, have shown modest and context-dependent success, with no consistent or long-lasting improvements (Kini & Ho, 2018). These approaches often overlook the broader social, behavioural, and environmental factors that shape patient behaviour. In contrast, AI technologies offer opportunities to personalize adherence support at scale, using tools such as predictive modelling, natural language processing (NLP), wearable sensing, and computer vision. These technologies can detect, predict, and respond to medication-taking behaviours in real time, creating adaptive, patient-specific interventions that align with daily routines and contextual needs.

This chapter explores how AI can reshape medication adherence strategies, with particular attention to its potential for addressing social determinants of health (SDOH) (Marmot & Wilkinson, 2005). SDOH, including income level, education, housing stability, healthcare access, and social support, are fundamental in shaping health behaviours and outcomes (Short

DOI: 10.1201/9781003626510-11

& Mollborn, 2015). Marginalized or underserved communities often face additional barriers to adherence, such as low health literacy, transportation difficulties, and competing life demands (Fernandez-Lazaro et al., 2019). These structural and situational factors call for interventions that are not only technologically advanced but also socially attuned. AI can help bridge this gap by analysing diverse data sources such as electronic health records (EHRs), wearable sensor data, and environmental cues to identify at-risk individuals and create personalized, equitable adherence strategies (Dankwa-Mullan, 2024).

To ground this exploration in a real-world context, we discuss the PERACTIV (Personalized Activity Monitoring) platform, a wrist-centric wearable system designed to promote medication adherence through activity recognition and contextual prompting. PERACTIV integrates multimodal sensing technologies and AI models to detect daily activities associated with medication intake, enabling just-in-time interventions that seamlessly fit into the user's natural routines. Unlike conventional adherence methods such as pillboxes, pharmacy refill tracking, or self-reported diaries, which are often unreliable due to forgetfulness, intentional misreporting, or lack of contextual awareness, PERACTIV provides objective and real-time monitoring. At the same time, wearable-based systems introduce their own challenges, including the need for consistent device use, privacy considerations, processing demands, battery limitations, and the potential for notification fatigue if not carefully managed. By embedding unobtrusive prompts into daily routines while preserving autonomy and minimizing cognitive burden, PERACTIV offers a more balanced and patient-centred approach compared to traditional strategies.

This chapter is structured around four core objectives. First, we present the theoretical foundations underpinning AI applications in medication adherence, drawing from behavioural economics, health psychology, and patient-centred care models. Concepts such as nudging, cognitive framing, and motivational reinforcement are examined in the context of AI-driven systems. Second, we review technological innovations in AI, including machine learning, NLP, computer vision, and wearable computing, that contribute to monitoring, predicting, and influencing adherence behaviours. Third, we critically reflect on broader implications, including ethical considerations around privacy, autonomy, equity, and the human touch in healthcare. These dimensions are analysed through the lenses of algorithmic fairness, data governance, and user agency. Finally, we identify future research, design, and implementation directions, emphasizing the need for multidisciplinary collaboration, inclusive design practices, and robust evaluation frameworks that centre on the needs of diverse populations.

In doing so, this chapter offers a comprehensive and critical examination of how AI can disrupt and enhance traditional approaches to medication adherence. Integrating theoretical, technological, and ethical perspectives contributes to emerging conversations on the responsible development and deployment of intelligent health systems that improve clinical outcomes and foster health equity and patient empowerment.

Background

Medication adherence is a critical aspect of healthcare that significantly affects patient outcomes, treatment efficacy, and overall healthcare costs. It refers to the extent to which patients take their medications as prescribed by healthcare providers (Garcia et al., 2022; Kim et al., 2018). Proper adherence directly influences the success of treatment regimens and the management of chronic conditions (Religioni et al., 2025).

Importance of Medication Adherence

Adherence to prescribed medications is a primary determinant of treatment success (Jimmy & Jose, 2011). Consistently following prescribed regimens leads to improved health outcomes, better disease management, and a higher quality of life (Balkrishnan, 2005; Jimmy & Jose, 2011; Religioni et al., 2025). Proper adherence can reduce disease progression and complications (Bischof et al., 2024; Jimmy & Jose, 2011), decrease hospitalizations and emergency department visits (Bischof et al., 2024; Khunti et al., 2017; Neiman et al., 2017), lower healthcare costs (Neiman et al., 2017), and improve overall well-being (Jimmy & Jose, 2011; Religioni et al., 2025).

Research suggests that adherence rates of 80% or higher are typically needed for optimal therapeutic efficacy (Kim et al., 2018). However, chronic medication adherence rates average around 50%, highlighting a significant gap in patient care and a major barrier to effective treatment (Sabaté, 2003).

Types of Non-Adherence

There are several forms of non-adherence, and while they overlap in some cases, they can generally be categorized as follows:

1. **Primary Non-Adherence:** Occurs when patients are prescribed medication but never fill or initiate the prescription. Often referred to as non-fulfilment adherence, this type represents a failure to begin the treatment regimen (Jimmy & Jose, 2011).
2. **Non-Persistence:** Occurs when patients stop taking medication after initiating it without consulting their healthcare provider. It is often unintentional, arising from miscommunication about therapeutic plans, limited prescription access, cost, or competing life demands.

It may also result from individual challenges, such as poor technique or difficulty remembering doses (Jimmy & Jose, 2011).

3. **Non-Conforming:** Encompasses a range of behaviours in which medications are not taken as prescribed. This may involve skipping doses, taking medications at incorrect times or in incorrect doses, or taking more than the specified amount. These behaviours can arise unintentionally or intentionally due to misunderstandings or lack of motivation (Jimmy & Jose, 2011).

Challenges in Medication Adherence

Despite its importance, medication adherence remains a complex issue influenced by various factors. Some of the key challenges include:

1. **Patient Factors:** Includes factors such as forgetfulness, disrupted routines, mental state (e.g., depression, cognitive impairment), physical functioning, age, sex, education level, marital status, and health literacy or understanding (Tenovi, n.d.; Yap et al., 2016). These elements influence patients' ability and motivation to adhere to prescribed regimens.
2. **Medication Factors:** Encompasses complex treatment plans, polypharmacy, side effects, and complex dosing regimens (Faridi, 2017; Tenovi, n.d.; Yap et al., 2016). Smart pillboxes and automated pill dispensers such as MedaCube (Pharmadva, 2022), Hero (Hero Health, 2022), e-Pill MedSmart Voice (e-pill, 2022), and Philips Lifeline Medication Dispenser (Philips Lifeline, 2024) have emerged to address some of these challenges by automating pill dispensing at the correct time and dose. However, these devices are often expensive, can be challenging to use, are not portable (Doshi et al., 2019), and may suffer from mechanical failures (Onzenoort et al., 2012). Moreover, they do not guarantee ingestion, as pills may be dropped or misplaced after being dispensed.
3. **Physician Factors:** Includes a lack of medication knowledge or poor communication from healthcare providers. Inadequate counselling or unclear instructions can contribute to confusion and reduced adherence (Tenovi, n.d.; Yap et al., 2016).
4. **System-Based Factors:** Considers barriers such as medication cost, transportation challenges, and limited access to healthcare systems (Yap et al., 2016; Yoon et al., 2023). These structural issues can limit a patient's ability to acquire and take medications as prescribed consistently.
5. **Other Factors:** Includes factors such as a lack of symptoms in asymptomatic conditions, poor labelling instructions, and the absence of supportive tools (e.g., pillbox usage) (Tenovi, n.d.; Yap et al., 2016). These seemingly minor factors can cumulatively impact medication-taking behaviour.

Recent systematic reviews have identified over 80 factors associated with medication adherence in older adults, categorizing them into these five domains and highlighting the complex interplay of personal, clinical, and systemic influences (Yap et al., 2016). These challenges contribute to significant consequences, with medication non-adherence accounting for up to 50% of treatment failures, approximately 125,000 deaths, and up to 25% of hospitalizations annually in the United States (Kim et al., 2018).

Taken together, these findings suggest that adherence should not be viewed as the outcome of isolated variables, but rather as the product of a multifactorial and dynamic system. Patient-level barriers, such as forgetfulness or low health literacy, often intersect with medication-related complexities like polypharmacy or burdensome dosing schedules, amplifying the risk of missed doses. Similarly, even motivated patients may struggle when systemic barriers, such as high medication costs or limited transportation, limit their ability to acquire prescriptions. Physician-related challenges, such as inadequate counselling, can further compound these risks by reducing patient understanding and confidence. Conversely, targeted interventions in one domain, such as simplifying regimens, improving communication, or expanding system-level access, can buffer difficulties in other areas, mitigating overall risk. This integrative perspective highlights the importance of designing adherence interventions that address multiple domains simultaneously, rather than focusing narrowly on individual barriers.

The Role of AI in Improving Adherence

As healthcare systems strive to address these complex challenges, artificial intelligence (AI) has emerged as a promising tool to support patients and healthcare providers. AI-powered solutions have the potential to:

1. **Personalize Reminders:** AI can analyse patient data to create tailored medication reminders that align with individual routines and preferences.
2. **Predict Non-adherence:** Machine learning algorithms can identify patterns and risk factors associated with non-adherence, allowing for proactive interventions (Pulice & Coustasse, 2024).
3. **Enhance Patient Education:** AI-driven platforms can provide personalized educational content to improve patients' understanding of their medications and conditions (Pulice & Coustasse, 2024).
4. **Optimize Treatment Plans:** AI can assist healthcare providers in developing more effective and manageable medication regimens based on patient-specific factors.

5. **Facilitate Communication:** AI-powered chatbots and virtual assistants can offer real-time support and answer patient questions about their medications (Pulice & Coustasse, 2024).
6. **Monitor Side Effects:** AI systems can track and analyse reported side effects, helping healthcare providers make timely adjustments to treatment plans.

By leveraging AI technologies, healthcare systems can address many barriers to medication adherence and deliver patients more personalized, efficient, and practical support. AI tools have the potential to tackle challenges such as forgetfulness and disrupted routines (patient factors), complex treatment plans and side effects (medication factors), poor provider communication (physician factors), and systemic issues like limited healthcare access. As AI capabilities continue to evolve, their role in improving medication adherence will likely expand, ultimately contributing to better health outcomes and reduced healthcare costs.

Theoretical Foundations

AI-driven medication adherence solutions are rooted in interdisciplinary frameworks that inform their technical design and societal relevance. These frameworks include behavioural economics principles, health psychology, patient-centred care, human-computer interaction (HCI), and social determinants of health (SDOH). Understanding these perspectives is essential to ensure that AI improves adherence outcomes and does so in a responsible, equitable, and human-centred manner. These foundations draw on established theories such as behavioural economics and nudging, health psychology models (e.g., the Health Belief Model and Theory of Planned Behaviour), patient-centred care frameworks, social determinants of health (SDOH), human-computer interaction (HCI) theory, cognitive load theory, habit formation theory, and ethical governance principles, each of which provides unique insights for designing responsible and effective AI-driven adherence solutions.

Behavioural Economics and Nudging

Behavioural economics challenges the assumption that people make health decisions rationally. Instead, it highlights cognitive biases and environmental factors influencing behaviour, offering powerful strategies to support adherence. For example, AI systems can deploy personalized "nudges" that prompt patients at opportune moments, such as just before meals, based on patterns learned from daily routines. The NUDGE trial demonstrated how timely reminders grounded in behavioural economics improved cardiovascular medication adherence through digital prompts (Glasgow et al., 2021). These principles can be further enhanced by reinforcement learning algorithms that tailor nudges' timing, tone, and frequency based on user behaviour, maintaining effectiveness over time.

Gamification also draws from behavioural economics by providing extrinsic motivators. Points, streaks, and badges integrated through AI systems can foster routine building and engagement. Studies on mobile health applications suggest that incorporating gamified elements can significantly improve medication adherence, particularly among younger users managing chronic conditions (Tran et al., 2022).

Health Psychology and Motivation

Health psychology offers models such as the Health Belief Model and the Theory of Planned behaviour (Hartley et al., 2018), which identify factors like perceived severity, perceived benefits, and self-efficacy as central to medication adherence. AI systems can infer these factors from user interactions and adjust their messaging accordingly. For example, a patient expressing concern over side effects may receive AI-generated, supportive explanations based on clinical evidence, reducing anxiety and reinforcing motivation. AI chatbots and conversational agents leverage these psychological insights by providing real-time responses tailored to emotional tone and levels of health literacy. By integrating sentiment analysis and motivational interviewing techniques, these systems can adapt interventions to patients' evolving cognitive and emotional states, fostering long-term behavioural change (Almalki & Azeez, 2020; Bickmore et al., 2013).

Patient-centred and Personalized Care

Central to contemporary healthcare is patient-centred care, which emphasizes respect for individual values and autonomy. AI facilitates this principle through personalization, adapting interventions based on preferences, behaviours, routines, and demographic characteristics. For instance, wearable systems like PERACTIV can tailor reminder frequency and modality (e.g., vibration, speech) based on past response patterns, improving relevance and adherence.

Personalized approaches that dynamically adjust educational content, intervention goals, and support frequency are essential for fostering sustained engagement and aligning adherence strategies with patients' daily lives (Fan & Zhao, 2022; Peng et al., 2020). These interventions ensure that patients remain active participants in their care, which is crucial for long-term adherence and improved health outcomes.

Social Determinants of Health (SDOH)

Social determinants of health (SDOH), including income, education, housing, and healthcare access, profoundly affect medication adherence. AI systems can integrate and analyse structured data, such as electronic health records (EHRs), and unstructured data, such as chatbot inputs, to identify patients at higher risk due to these external factors. For example, a patient with inconsistent pharmacy visits or residing in a low-access zip code can be flagged for proactive outreach or delivery-based interventions.

However, AI must be designed to avoid amplifying systemic inequities. Research highlights the importance of fairness-oriented algorithms and diverse training datasets to prevent biased outcomes and ensure equitable healthcare delivery (Obermeyer et al., 2019; Rajkomar et al., 2018). Embedding equity principles into AI development is particularly crucial in public health contexts, where disparities are most pronounced (Obermeyer et al., 2019; Rajkomar et al., 2018). Federated learning and privacy-preserving techniques can also enable inclusive model training without compromising data ownership or sensitivity (Kairouz et al., 2021; Li et al., 2020).

Human-AI Interaction and Explainability

As AI systems become more autonomous, user trust and transparency are critical. Human-computer interaction (HCI) theory underscores the importance of intuitive interfaces, meaningful feedback, and explainable decision-making. When patients receive AI recommendations such as "take your dose now based on yesterday's pattern," they should also receive understandable and non-technical justifications.

Explainable AI (XAI) techniques, such as attention heat maps and textual rationales, support the interpretability of both patients and clinicians (Band et al., 2023). In wearable devices like PERACTIV, visual dashboards showing behavioural trends and adherence insights can offer explainability. Participatory design, which incorporates user feedback during system development, ensures interventions remain accessible and culturally appropriate.

Cognitive Load and Habit Formation

Patients who manage multiple medications or conditions often experience cognitive overload, reducing adherence (Thomas et al., 2017). AI systems must reduce rather than add to this burden by simplifying decision-making and automating reminders. Cognitive load theory suggests that information should be delivered in manageable chunks and through varied sensory channels (e.g., audio, haptics). PERACTIV's wrist-based cues align with this principle, delivering subtle nudges that do not disrupt the user's natural flow.

Additionally, habit formation theory suggests that consistent cues and positive reinforcement help patients develop automatic behaviours (Gardner, 2015; Lally et al., 2010; Robinson et al., 2024). AI systems can support this process by gradually reducing the frequency of reminders as users internalize routines. Reinforcement learning agents can adapt the intensity of interventions based on adherence stability, ensuring that long-term autonomy is preserved while initial behaviour change is supported.

Ethical Foundations and Governance

Finally, ethical considerations must guide AI systems, including consent, data protection, autonomy, and fairness. Responsible AI frameworks emphasize transparency in calculating and using adherence risk scores. Users should retain control over their data and over the level of automation they experience. This is particularly important in vulnerable populations, such as elderly patients or those with cognitive impairments. AI must be designed with safeguards that ensure privacy, avoid coercion, and respect patient dignity. Incorporating ethics-by-design principles from the outset fosters trust and compliance, both prerequisites for long-term system success.

In summary, these theoretical foundations underscore the need for AI systems that are technically sophisticated, psychologically aware, socially grounded, and ethically robust. Whether delivering nudges, building habits, or responding to social risk factors, AI must be guided by a deep understanding of the human behaviours and systemic conditions that shape medication adherence. Systems like PERACTIV exemplify how these foundations can converge in real-world applications, improving individual health outcomes and broader public health equity. Building on these theoretical foundations, the following section provides a narrative review of recent literature, synthesizing current research on how AI-driven interventions are designed and applied to improve medication adherence.

Discussion and Analysis

Medication non-adherence remains a pervasive challenge, but artificial intelligence (AI) enables new technological solutions to improve adherence. Recent innovations leverage AI for personalized reminders, predictive risk assessment, conversational support, and automated medication intake verification. These AI-driven approaches aim to tailor interventions to individual patient behaviour and context, moving beyond one-size-fits-all strategies. The following subsections review key developments in AI-powered medication adherence tools, drawing on current research and real-world applications.

AI-Powered Reminder Systems

One primary application of AI in adherence is intelligent reminder systems delivered via mobile health (mHealth) platforms. Conventional smartphone medication apps with fixed-time alarms have shown modest success in improving adherence. A systematic review and meta-analysis of 14 randomized trials involving 1,785 participants, 940 in intervention groups and 845 in control, found that mobile apps significantly improved adherence compared to usual care (Cohen's$d = 0.40$, 95% CI $= 0.27 - 0.52$; $P < 0.001$) (Peng et al., 2020). Additionally, 91.7% of users reported satisfaction with app usability and features, indicating the acceptability of digital adherence tools.

Building on this foundation, AI enables more adaptive and context-aware reminder strategies. Rather than relying on static schedules, AI-driven systems adjust the timing and modality of reminders using patient-specific data such as daily routines, geographic location, and past adherence history. For example, it has been demonstrated that context-aware reminders delivered at timely and safe intervals are more effective than generic alerts in encouraging adherence behaviour (Singh & Varshney, 2019).

Recent innovations also include just-in-time adaptive interventions (JITAIs), where reinforcement learning tailors intervention timing and content (Nahum-Shani et al., 2018). One such system, *iMedA*, for managing hypertension, used expert-derived decision rules and contextual bandits to adapt interventions over time, optimizing both short- and long-term adherence goals (Etminani et al., 2021). These adaptive reminders respond to behaviour and engagement levels, enabling highly personalized adherence support.

Predictive Analytics for Risk Assessment

Another critical development in AI-driven adherence is using predictive analytics to assess individual risk. Machine learning models trained on longitudinal data, including electronic health records (EHRs), prescription logs, appointment histories, and wearable activity metrics, can identify patients likely to become non-adherent. These models often employ supervised learning approaches (such as logistic regression, decision trees, and gradient boosting) to classify patients into risk categories based on historical features and recent behavioural patterns. For example, one study applied predictive modelling to insurance claims and EHR data to identify patients at risk of lapses in cardiovascular medication use, enabling targeted outreach interventions by care teams (Zullig et al., 2019). These tools can also inform real-time monitoring strategies: a sudden drop in step count, disrupted sleep patterns, or failure to respond to prompts may serve as early warning signs of disengagement, prompting timely intervention.

Beyond classification, predictive models can quantify individualized likelihood scores of adherence within specific time windows (Koesmahargyo et al., 2020; Wu et al., 2020). These risk scores help providers prioritize patients for high-touch care and automate follow-up strategies. Ethical implementation of such models requires fairness audits to ensure they do not perpetuate discrimination based on race, gender, or socioeconomic status.

Natural Language Processing (NLP) and Conversational Agents

Natural language processing (NLP) techniques have emerged as powerful tools to enhance patient engagement and education. NLP enables chatbots and voice assistants to interpret patient input, offer timely responses, and adapt messages based on patient sentiment, comprehension level, and intent. AI chatbots integrated into applications such as Ada Health and Babylon use NLP to simulate patient dialogue, answer medication questions, and correct misconceptions. For example, one study demonstrated that NLP models can automatically annotate medication mentions in primary care conversations with high accuracy, streamlining follow-up interventions and care coordination (Ganoe et al., 2021).

More advanced systems leverage large language models (LLMs) to generate empathetic, context-sensitive communication. These models can answer complex queries (e.g., "What happens if I miss my blood pressure medication for two days?"), detect emotional states such as confusion or frustration, and escalate to human support when needed. NLP-powered interventions are particularly valuable for populations with limited clinician access or low health literacy, offering conversational support that complements clinical care.

Computer Vision in Medication Verification

Computer vision (CV) is another area where AI significantly contributes to medication adherence. Using smartphone cameras, wearable cameras, or smart mirrors, CV-based systems can verify medication intake through pill identification, container recognition, and gesture or action analysis. These systems enable passive adherence verification without relying solely on patient self-reporting.

For instance, multiple studies have developed deep learning models capable of identifying pills (Heo et al., 2023; Kwon et al., 2021; Tan et al., 2021) based on images, achieving accuracies of up to 96% even under varied lighting and orientation conditions. Beyond pill recognition, research has explored systems that use facial recognition, hand tracking, and motion analysis to confirm whether a patient has ingested their medication, ensuring that doses are not simply removed from the packaging. Recent work has demonstrated the potential of wrist-centric egocentric activity recognition for healthcare applications (Kakaraparthi et al., 2022, 2023), highlighting the value of capturing fine-grained, micro-actions such as grasping, ingesting, and interacting with pill containers, that collectively signal successful adherence. These models and wearable-based systems underscore the importance of comprehensive action segmentation and behavioural understanding in supporting medication verification and personalized adherence interventions.

Recent advances in action segmentation and activity tracking also contribute to adherence verification. Action segmentation models can identify key events within video sequences, such as opening pill bottles, ingesting pills, or placing containers back in storage. Integrating these models with wearable or ambient cameras enables comprehensive monitoring of medication routines, providing a richer context for adherence assessment. In elder care or post-operative recovery settings, intelligent camera systems can unobtrusively monitor medication routines in elder care or post-operative recovery settings while respecting privacy. However, these technologies must be deployed with caution, incorporating consent protocols, edge processing, and anonymization techniques to ensure ethical use in sensitive environments (Kairouz et al., 2021; Kakaraparthi & McDaniel, 2024; Li et al., 2020).

Case Study: Real-World Implementation and Action Segmentation for Medication Adherence

PERACTIV represents a real-world implementation of a comprehensive framework that integrates multiple AI components to verify and support medication adherence. The system includes *multimodal sensing* (smartphone and wrist-worn cameras, IMUs, FSRs, and NFC sensors) (Kakaraparthi et al., 2024), *perception and detection* (deep learning models for activity and object recognition), *multimodal fusion* of sensor streams, *scene graph construction* to map micro-actions in context, *causal reasoning* to infer adherence and non-adherence events, *language generation and nudging* through large language models (LLMs), and *feedback and interaction* via real-time and reflective visual analytics. This framework is designed from the perspective of an individual user, providing a personalized approach to monitoring and supporting daily medication activities. However, it can also be adapted to scalable settings such as assisted living or nursing homes, where multiple PERACTIV devices can be deployed to monitor several individuals simultaneously, enhancing overall care and efficiency (Kakaraparthi & McDaniel, 2024).

The system goes beyond simple detection by classifying and segmenting user activities into micro-actions such as *opening the pillbox*, *grasping a pill*, *moving the hand to the mouth*, and *ingesting*. These sub-events are tracked and interpreted through synchronized sensor streams, leveraging object detection modules and advanced action recognition and segmentation models. Object detection modules based on CNNs such as MobileNet (Howard, 2017), SSD (Liu et al., 2016), and Vision Transformers like DETR (Carion et al., 2020) identify critical objects (pillboxes, pills, water glasses, and mouth regions) from wrist-centric perspectives. Optical character recognition (OCR) further interprets textual labels on pill compartments (Figure 11.1).

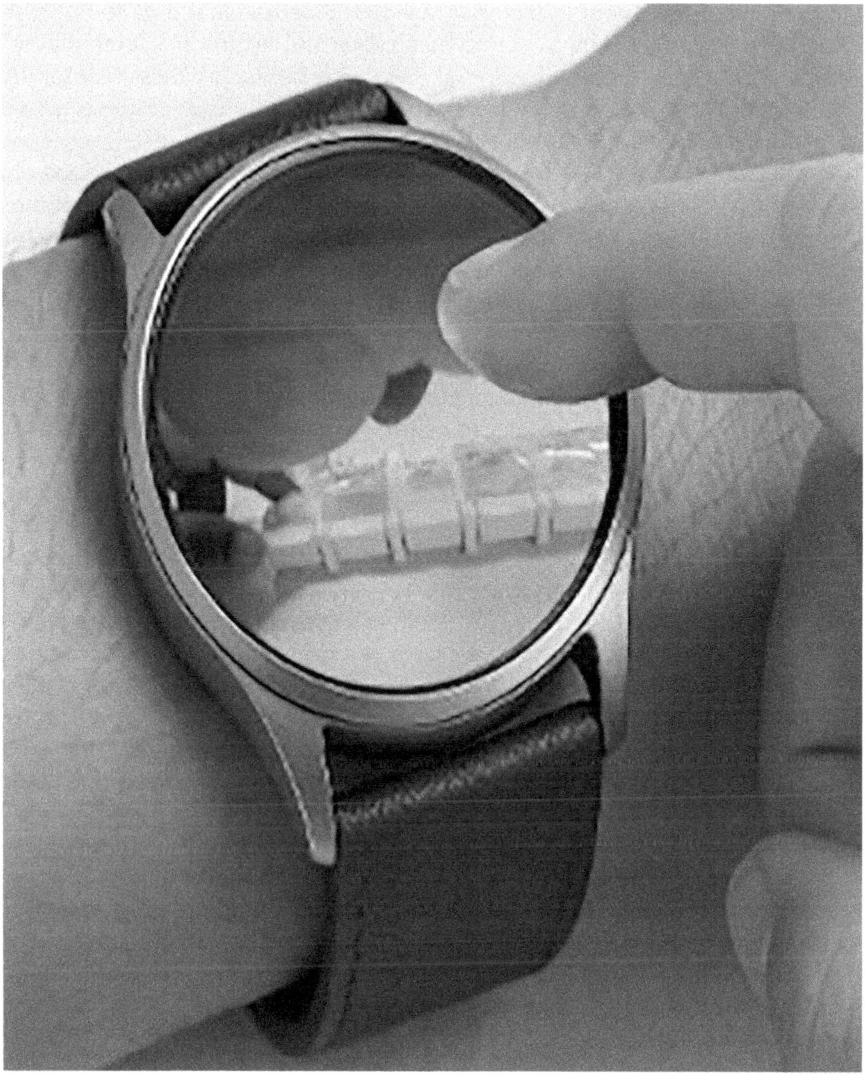

FIGURE 11.1
PERACTIV device capturing the moment of pill intake on Sunday morning from a smart pill box 7-day planner, demonstrating its capability to verify adherence through precise detection of hand-object interactions.

For micro-action detection, PERACTIV employs action recognition models such as C3D (Tran et al., 2015), I3D (Carreira & Zisserman, 2017), and ViViT (Arnab et al., 2021) to model spatio-temporal patterns and capture the full range of medication intake behaviours. Temporal convolutional networks (TCNs) (Lea et al., 2017) and techniques are used for action segmentation, precisely delineating the start and end of each micro-action sequence. IMU features, including hand trajectories, are fused with visual data to improve robustness across individual variations in style and technique. Symbolic reasoning with scene graphs (Chang et al., 2021), augmented by these temporally segmented micro-actions, enables clear interpretations and confirms actual ingestion sequences.

Importantly, PERACTIV also reasons about *non-adherence*. For instance, if a pill is grasped but no follow-through motion is detected, or if the pill remains visible in subsequent frames, the system infers probable non-adherence. This shifts the paradigm from isolated action classification to behavioural interpretation and causal reasoning, enabling more intelligent, transparent, and proactive support.

The convergence of AI technologies, including mobile reminders, predictive analytics, conversational agents, and computer vision, signals a new approach to adherence: one that is responsive, personalized, and ethically grounded. PERACTIV's success depends on technical accuracy and its ability to integrate into diverse patient lives and care environments seamlessly. It addresses various challenges in medication adherence, including cognitive load, forgetfulness, disrupted routines, behavioural variations, and social factors such as access disparities. At the same time, potential limitations remain, wearable use requires consistent engagement, processing demands and battery constraints may affect real-time performance, privacy concerns must be carefully managed, and excessive notifications could lead to alert fatigue or reduced patient autonomy. Future research should focus on combining these modalities into unified systems that balance automation with user control, personalization with privacy, and innovation with equity, while mitigating these operational and ethical challenges.

PERACTIV's development exemplifies how AI-powered health technologies can operationalize ethical principles through participatory design, transparent feedback, and deployment strategies. Unlike earlier wearable technologies that struggled with adoption due to usability issues and opaque decision-making, PERACTIV was built with input from older adults, caregivers, and clinicians. This inclusive development model underscores the importance of human agency and accountability in creating trustworthy AI systems.

Advanced models such as ViViT and I3D ensure that micro-actions relevant to medication adherence are detected and temporally segmented for robust downstream reasoning (McDaniel et al., 2024). Symbolic reasoning with scene graphs augmented by timestamped video annotations enables clear interpretations that clinicians and patients can review. These explainability features build trust and ensure interventions remain transparent and user-centred.

To safeguard privacy and data sovereignty, PERACTIV leverages edge AI architectures that process sensor data locally on-device or federated across multiple devices. This approach limits raw video or biometric data transmission to central servers, directly addressing concerns around patient data privacy. These design decisions also respond to longstanding critiques of opaque AI in healthcare. PERACTIV's architecture aligns with principles of transparency and interpretability while incorporating best practices in edge AI implementation in healthcare environments (Kakaraparthi & McDaniel, 2024). Overall, PERACTIV's privacy-centric design ensures compliance with HIPAA and GDPR principles, including data minimization and purpose limitation (Kairouz et al., 2021; Li et al., 2020).

Another strength of PERACTIV is its adaptive nudging system, which uses large language models (LLMs) such as GPT and BART to deliver personalized reminders. These nudges balance behavioural reinforcement with autonomy, gently prompting users when a dose is missed and using tailored language and delivery modes (haptic, audio, visual) that respect individual preferences and dignity. The system also supports reflective feedback through weekly reports featuring adherence heatmap, timestamps, timelines, and annotated snapshots that visually confirm ingestion. This visual analytics layer educates patients and promotes accountability, addressing criticisms of opaque AI in healthcare. From a governance perspective, PERACTIV includes auditability features such as logs of system decisions, timestamps, and intervention types. This traceability ensures transparent oversight and accountability in real-world deployments.

Beyond individual users, PERACTIV's design facilitates institutional scalability. In assisted living facilities, multiple devices can be integrated into a centralized dashboard while maintaining patient-specific data silos. Caregivers can monitor adherence trends, detect systemic issues such as conflicts between medication schedules and mealtimes, and prioritize interventions. The system can also be designed to integrate with electronic health records and support secure data sharing across care teams. To support extensibility and compliance testing, PERACTIV can include system evaluation, explainability, and privacy-preserving data analysis mechanisms. These capabilities ensure that the system can adapt to changing healthcare needs and maintain high reliability, transparency, and ethical compliance standards.

In summary, PERACTIV demonstrates that ethical, transparent, and impactful AI for medication adherence is possible and replicable. By integrating rigorous technical pipelines with governance-aware architecture, the system sets a benchmark for future health technology deployments that honour patient dignity and equity.

Critical Reflections and Future Directions

Despite the promising developments in AI-driven medication adherence systems such as PERACTIV, several critical gaps and future challenges warrant deeper attention. While current research emphasizes technical accuracy and ethical compliance, a broader discourse on how these systems intersect with longstanding social inequalities, structural biases, and clinical accountability is needed.

One primary concern lies in the generalizability of AI models across diverse populations. Most wearable datasets are biased toward tech-savvy or higher-income populations, raising the risk that models perform less effectively among marginalized groups (Harris, 2022), including those with disabilities, low digital literacy, or non-Western healthcare contexts. Future research must explore fairness-aware training methods, community-based dataset collection, and inclusive evaluation protocols that foreground diversity from the ground up.

Additionally, while PERACTIV incorporates transparency features such as scene graphs and causal reasoning, the broader AI ecosystem often lacks standardized benchmarks for explainability in healthcare. There is an urgent need for regulatory frameworks that not only mandate explainable models but also provide guidelines on what constitutes a clinically meaningful explanation for different stakeholders, including patients, clinicians, and auditors. Regulatory bodies such as the U.S. Food and Drug Administration (FDA) and the European Medicines Agency (EMA) could lead in setting global standards for interpretable AI in digital health tools.

Ethical nudging remains another contested domain. As systems like PERACTIV use LLMs to generate behaviour prompts, the line between support and manipulation becomes blurred. *"What safeguards should be in place to ensure nudges remain respectful, culturally appropriate, and non-coercive?"* Future work could investigate user perceptions of nudges across age groups and health conditions, evaluating long-term behavioural outcomes against metrics of trust and autonomy.

From a policy standpoint, AI-powered adherence systems also raise questions about liability and responsibility. *"In case of a missed dose due to system error or false feedback, who is accountable: the manufacturer, the clinician, or the AI itself?"* Legal and institutional infrastructures must evolve to support new forms of shared responsibility, perhaps through third-party certification, risk-sharing contracts, or AI audit trails integrated into malpractice adjudication.

Lastly, there is immense potential for AI-driven adherence frameworks to evolve into proactive health behaviour platforms. Future systems could incorporate mood sensing, sleep monitoring, and social context awareness to deliver holistic care. This, however, demands greater interdisciplinary collaboration between behavioural scientists, ethicists, and technologists to ensure that AI systems understand human behaviour and support it meaningfully and justly.

In conclusion, while PERACTIV represents a significant step forward in ethical and explainable AI for health, its long-term impact depends on how future research, policy, and practice can anticipate and respond to the socio-technical complexities that AI inevitably brings to healthcare ecosystems.

Conclusion

This chapter explores the transformative role of artificial intelligence in promoting medication adherence, focusing on the PERACTIV system as a case study in ethical, explainable, and user-centred health technology. We demonstrated how AI can move beyond passive monitoring toward intelligent systems that support proactive, personalized care through detailed analysis of real-world applications, technological architecture, and policy-aligned governance strategies.

Key insights emerged from integrating multimodal sensing, action segmentation, scene graph modelling, and causal reasoning. These layers enable AI systems to detect user behaviour and understand and explain it, providing a pathway toward transparent, accountable, and trustworthy decision-making in digital health. PERACTIV exemplifies how these technologies can be implemented in practice, using low-power, wearable hardware to verify real-time adherence while preserving privacy and autonomy.

We highlighted several innovations, including adaptive nudging strategies powered by large language models, scene-based inference mechanisms for missed dose detection, and feedback modalities tailored to individual preferences and routines. Importantly, these elements were not discussed solely in technical terms, but critically examined through the lenses of ethics, fairness, and policy.

Our case study underscored the importance of governance in AI deployment. From participatory design to explainable outputs and legal accountability, the success of systems like PERACTIV hinges on how well they integrate human values into algorithmic decision-making. Historical lessons, such as the DeepMind patient data controversy or algorithmic opacity in criminal justice and medicine (Paudyal & William Wong, 2018), serve as cautionary tales that highlight the need for transparency, user consent, and shared responsibility.

Furthermore, the chapter articulated ongoing challenges, including the need for equitable training datasets, standardized explainability benchmarks, and clear guidelines for ethical nudging. These gaps present risks and open opportunities for interdisciplinary research and inclusive policy reform.

Ultimately, this work reinforces the view that AI in healthcare should not replace human judgment but enhance human capability. PERACTIV's design philosophy, centred on explainability, user empowerment, and responsible feedback, illustrates how AI can be leveraged to build trust and drive behaviour change without sacrificing user dignity.

Future systems will likely expand their scope to include more holistic behavioural monitoring, leveraging context-awareness and cross-platform integration. Realizing this vision will require sustained collaboration among technologists, clinicians, ethicists, regulators, and, most importantly, users themselves.

In conclusion, the journey toward AI-supported medication adherence is still unfolding. Yet, systems like PERACTIV offer a roadmap grounded in transparency, accountability, and respect for human complexity. By continuing to bridge the gap between innovation and ethics, we can ensure that AI serves as a force for equity and well-being in the evolving landscape of digital healthcare.

Actionable Recommendations

Drawing from the insights and findings of this chapter, the following actionable recommendations aim to guide policymakers, businesses, researchers, and educators in advancing the development, deployment, and governance of AI-powered medication adherence systems like PERACTIV.

For policymakers, there is an urgent need to establish regulatory guidelines for explainable AI. These should mandate that healthcare AI systems provide clinically relevant, user-friendly explanations of their decisions, ensuring transparency in model interpretability, data provenance, and decision-making logic. Equally critical is the support of privacy-preserving technologies, such as edge computing and federated learning, which should be incentivized through funding and partnerships. Policymakers must also require demographic fairness audits to ensure systems perform equitably across age, race, gender, and ability. Finally, policy must clarify liability structures to determine responsibility when AI systems produce errors or fail to act, whether the burden lies with manufacturers, clinicians, or institutions.

Human-centred design should be prioritized from the outset for businesses and technology developers. This includes co-creating AI tools with end users to ensure alignment with real-world routines and accessibility needs. Implementing modular, upgradable architectures enables broader system adaptability across diverse care environments. Transparency should be embedded in design, with tools like decision timelines and scene graph visualizations built into interfaces. As solutions like PERACTIV scale institutionally, developers must safeguard personal autonomy and data ownership, ensuring that population-level deployment does not override individual rights.

Researchers have a key role in closing interdisciplinary gaps. Collaborations with behavioural scientists, ethicists, and public health experts are essential to designing AI systems that reinforce positive health behaviours through evidence-based interventions. There is also a pressing need to create open and standardized benchmarks to evaluate action segmentation, nudging strategies, and the accuracy of ingestion verification. Moreover, longitudinal field studies should assess AI adherence tools over time to understand sustained behavioural change, system trust, and unintended side effects.

Educators and trainers are positioned to shape future practitioners. Health technology curricula must incorporate AI ethics, equity, and accountability, preparing students to engage critically with both technical and societal dimensions of AI. Interdisciplinary learning environments that bring together students from computing, healthcare, design, and ethics will foster well-rounded innovation. Educators must also instil a culture of responsible innovation by encouraging learners to consider AI's broader social impacts and advocate for transparency and inclusion in design processes.

By acting on these recommendations, each stakeholder group can contribute to developing AI systems that are technically advanced and aligned with societal needs. In doing so, we can support a future in which digital health technologies promote autonomy, equity, and trust across all layers of the healthcare ecosystem.

Acknowledgment

This work was supported by the National Science Foundation under Grant No. 2142774.

Glossary of Technical Terms and Applications

Adherence (Medication Adherence): The extent to which a patient takes medications as prescribed, including timing, dosage, and frequency.

Artificial Intelligence (AI): A field of computer science that enables machines to simulate human intelligence, including learning, reasoning, and decision-making.

Attention Heat Maps: Visualization technique in explainable AI (XAI) that highlights which parts of input data (e.g., an image or text) influenced the model's decision.

Behavioural Economics: Examines how psychological, cognitive, and social factors influence economic and health-related decisions.

Causal Reasoning: AI method for inferring cause-effect relationships (e.g., pill grasped but not ingested → probable non-adherence).

Cognitive Load Theory: Describes how the brain processes information and how overload can impair decision-making and adherence.

Computer Vision (CV): AI techniques that interpret and analyse visual input (e.g., detecting pill intake through camera-based monitoring).

Conversational Agents/Chatbots: AI-driven tools using natural language processing to interact with users, provide education, send reminders, and offer emotional support.
Deep Learning (DL): A subset of machine learning using neural networks with multiple layers to recognize patterns in complex data such as images, speech, or sensor data.
Electronic Health Records (EHRs): Digital versions of patients' medical histories, including prescriptions, test results, and treatment plans.
Edge AI: Running AI models locally on-device rather than in the cloud, reducing latency and improving privacy for sensitive health data.
Explainable AI (XAI): Methods that make AI decision-making understandable to humans, enhancing trust and usability in healthcare.
Federated Learning: Privacy-preserving ML technique where models are trained across multiple decentralized devices without centralizing raw data.
Gamification: Applying game-like features (e.g., points, streaks, rewards) to motivate engagement and adherence.
Habit Formation Theory: Behavioural Psychology emphasizes that repeated cues and reinforcement help form lasting behaviours.
Human-Computer Interaction (HCI): The design and study of interfaces and systems that facilitate interaction between people and technology.
Inertial Measurement Units (IMUs): Wearable sensors that capture motion data (e.g., hand trajectories for pill intake detection).
Just-in-Time Adaptive Interventions (JITAIs): AI-powered, real-time, personalized interventions delivered at the most effective moments for behaviour change.
Large Language Models (LLMs): Advanced AI models trained on vast text datasets that generate human-like responses and support conversational systems.
Machine Learning (ML): A branch of AI where algorithms learn patterns from data to make predictions or classifications.
Medication Non-Adherence: Failure to follow prescribed regimens. Types: *Primary* (not filling), *Non-persistence* (stopping early), *Non-conforming* (incorrect/inconsistent use).
Motivational Interviewing: A communication style from psychology used in AI/chatbots to encourage positive health behaviours and adherence.
Multimodal Sensing: Integration of multiple data streams (e.g., video, motion, force sensors) to capture and interpret user behaviour.
Natural Language Processing (NLP): AI techniques for understanding, interpreting, and generating human language.
Without restricting choice, nudging: Subtle prompts or cues that influence behaviour (e.g., medication reminders timed before meals).
Object Detection: Computer vision process of identifying and locating objects (e.g., pill bottles, pillboxes) in images or video.

Optical Character Recognition (OCR): Technology that extracts text (e.g., from pill labels) from images.

Optical Flow/Hand Trajectories: Motion-based features extracted from vision and IMU data to capture micro-actions like reaching, grasping, or ingesting.

Participatory Design: Co-design process where systems are developed with direct input from patients, caregivers, and clinicians to ensure usability and trust.

PERACTIV Platform: Wrist-centric AI-driven system integrating wearable sensing, computer vision, and nudging to monitor and encourage adherence.

Predictive Analytics: Use of data, models, and ML to identify patterns and forecast outcomes (e.g., predicting non-adherence risks).

Privacy-Preserving Techniques: Methods such as anonymization, edge computing, and secure aggregation that protect sensitive health data.

Reinforcement Learning: ML approach where systems learn optimal actions by receiving feedback (rewards/penalties).

Scene Graphs: Structured representations of objects and their relationships in context, used for reasoning about medication-taking activities.

Scene-Based Inference: AI technique uses contextual activity information (e.g., scene graphs with timestamps) to confirm or question adherence events.

Smart Pillboxes/Automated Dispensers: Hardware devices such as MedaCube, Hero, or Philips Lifeline that automate pill dispensing but may not verify ingestion.

Social Determinants of Health (SDOH): Non-medical factors (e.g., income, education, housing, access to care) influence health outcomes and adherence.

Symbolic Reasoning: AI approach combining logical rules with learned models to explain, validate, and interpret adherence-related decisions.

Temporal Convolutional Networks (TCNs): Neural networks for sequential data (e.g., segmenting micro-actions in pill intake sequences).

Temporal Modeling: Capturing time-dependent patterns of behaviour (e.g., daily or weekly medication intake routines).

User Agency: Principle in human-centred AI, ensuring patients retain autonomy and control over their health data and decisions.

Vision Transformers (ViTs): Deep learning architecture applying transformers to image and video recognition.

Wearable Technology: Electronic devices (e.g., smartwatches, wristbands) worn to monitor health, motion, or adherence behaviours.

Action Recognition: Detecting human actions (e.g., grasping, ingesting) from video or sensor data.

Action Segmentation: Dividing continuous activity streams into smaller "micro-actions" such as opening a pillbox, grasping a pill, and ingesting.

References

Abbott. (2024). *Enhancing medication adherence with AI-driven personalization.* A:Care HCP Global. https://acarepro.abbott.com/articles/general-topics/enhancing-medication-adherence-ai-technology/

Almalki, M., & Azeez, F. (2020). Health chatbots for fighting COVID-19: A scoping review. *Acta Informatica Medica, 28*(4), 241.

Arnab, A., Dehghani, M., Heigold, G., Sun, C., Lučić, M., & Schmid, C. (2021). ViViT: A video vision transformer. In Proceedings of the IEEE/CVF International Conference on Computer Vision (pp. 6816–6826). https://doi.org/10.1109/ICCV48922.2021.00676

Balkrishnan, R. (2005). The importance of medication adherence in improving chronic-disease related outcomes: What we know and what we need to further know. In *Medical care* (6; Vol. 43, pp. 517–520). LWW.

Band, S. S., Yarahmadi, A., Hsu, C.-C., Biyari, M., Sookhak, M., Ameri, R., Dehzangi, I., Chronopoulos, A. T., & Liang, H.-W. (2023). Application of explainable artificial intelligence in medical health: A systematic review of interpretability methods. *Informatics in Medicine Unlocked, 40,* 101286.

Bickmore, T. W., Silliman, R. A., Nelson, K., Cheng, D. M., Winter, M., Henault, L., & Paasche-Orlow, M. K. (2013). A randomized controlled trial of an automated exercise coach for older adults. *Journal of the American Geriatrics Society, 61*(10), 1676–1683.

Bischof, A. Y., Cordier, J., Vogel, J., & Geissler, A. (2024). Medication adherence halves COPD patients' hospitalization risk–evidence from swiss health insurance data. *NPJ Primary Care Respiratory Medicine, 34*(1), 1.

Carion, N., Massa, F., Synnaeve, G., Usunier, N., Kirillov, A., & Zagoruyko, S. (2020). End-to-end object detection with transformers. In A. Vedaldi, H. Bischof, T. Brox, & J.-M. Frahm (Eds.), *Computer Vision – ECCV 2020* (Vol. 12346, pp. 213–229). Springer. https://doi.org/10.1007/978-3-030-58452-8_13

Carreira, J., & Zisserman, A. (2017). Quo vadis, action recognition? A new model and the Kinetics dataset. In *2017 IEEE Conference on Computer Vision and Pattern Recognition (CVPR)* (pp. 4724–4733). IEEE. https://doi.org/10.1109/CVPR.2017.502

Chang, X., Ren, P., Xu, P., Li, Z., Chen, X., & Hauptmann, A. (2021). A comprehensive survey of scene graphs: Generation and application. *IEEE Transactions on Pattern Analysis and Machine Intelligence, 45*(1), 1–26.

Dankwa-Mullan, I. (2024). Health equity and ethical considerations in using artificial intelligence in public health and medicine. *Preventing Chronic Disease, 21,* E64.

Doshi, V., Dey, S., Mehta, N., & Prasad, R. (2019). An IoT based smart medicine box. *International Journal of Advance Research, Ideas and Innovations in Technology, 5*(1), 205–207.

e-pill. (2022). *MedSmart voice medication dispenser.* https://www.epill.com/medsmart-voice.html

Etminani, K., Göransson, C., Galozy, A., Pejner, M. N., & Nowaczyk, S., & others. (2021). Improving medication adherence through adaptive digital interventions (imeda) in patients with hypertension: Protocol for an interrupted time series study. *JMIR Research Protocols, 10*(5), e24494.

Fan, K., & Zhao, Y. (2022). Mobile Health technology: A novel tool in chronic disease management. *Intelligent Medicine, 2*(1), 41–47.

Faridi, K. F. (2017). Medication adherence and cardiovascular outcomes. *Journal of the American College of Cardiology, 69*(5), 598–599.

Fernandez-Lazaro, C. I., Adams, D. P., Fernandez-Lazaro, D., Garcia-González, J. M., Caballero-Garcia, A., & Miron-Canelo, J. A. (2019). Medication adherence and barriers among low-income, uninsured patients with multiple chronic conditions. *Research in Social and Administrative Pharmacy, 15*(6), 744–753.

Ganoe, C. H., Wu, W., Barr, P. J., Haslett, W., Dannenberg, M. D., Bonasia, K. L., Finora, J. C., Schoonmaker, J. A., Onsando, W. M., & Ryan, J., & others. (2021). Natural language processing for automated annotation of medication mentions in primary care visit conversations. *JAMIA Open, 4*(3), ooab071.

Garcia, R. A., Spertus, J. A., Benton, M. C., Jones, P. G., Mark, D. B., Newman, J. D., Bangalore, S., Boden, W. E., Stone, G. W., & Reynolds, H. R., & others. (2022). Association of medication adherence with health outcomes in the ISCHEMIA trial. *Journal of the American College of Cardiology, 80*(8), 755–765.

Gardner, B. (2015). A review and analysis of the use of 'habit'in understanding, predicting and influencing health-related behaviour. *Health Psychology Review, 9*(3), 277–295.

Glasgow, R. E., Knoepke, C. E., Magid, D., Grunwald, G. K., Glorioso, T. J., Waughtal, J., Marrs, J. C., Bull, S., & Ho, P. M. (2021). The NUDGE trial pragmatic trial to enhance cardiovascular medication adherence: Study protocol for a randomized controlled trial. *Trials, 22*(1), 528.

Harris, M. T. (2022). *Addressing gaps in equity through wearables* [PhD thesis]. University of Illinois at Urbana-Champaign.

Hartley, E. M., Hoch, M. C., & Cramer, R. J. (2018). Health belief model and theory of planned behavior: A theoretical approach for enhancing lower extremity injury prevention program participation. *International Journal of Athletic Therapy and Training, 23*(1), 16–20.

Heo, J., Kang, Y., Lee, S., Jeong, D.-H., & Kim, K.-M. (2023). An accurate deep learning–based system for automatic pill identification: Model development and validation. *Journal of Medical Internet Research, 25*, e41043.

Hero Health. (2022). *How the hero dispenser works.* https://herohealth.com/our-product/

Howard, A. G. (2017). Mobilenets: Efficient convolutional neural networks for mobile vision applications. *arXiv Preprint arXiv:1704.04861.*

Jimmy, B., & Jose, J. (2011). Patient medication adherence: Measures in daily practice. *Oman Medical Journal, 26*(3), 155.

Kairouz, P., McMahan, H. B., Avent, B., Bellet, A., Bennis, M., Bhagoji, A. N., Bonawitz, K., Charles, Z., Cormode, G., & Cummings, R., & others. (2021). Advances and open problems in federated learning. *Foundations and Trends in Machine Learning, 14*(1–2), 1–210.

Kakaraparthi, V., Goldberg, M., & McDaniel, T. (2023). Wrist view: Understanding human activity through the hand. In M. Antona & C. Stephanidis (Eds.), *Universal access in human-computer interaction* (Vol. 14021, pp. 581–595). Springer. https://doi.org/10.1007/978-3-031-35897-5_41

Kakaraparthi, V., & McDaniel, T. (2024). Striking the privacy-model training balance: A case study using PERACTIV device. In M. Antona & C. Stephanidis (Eds.), *Universal access in human-computer interaction* (Vol. 14698, pp. 259–274). Springer. https://doi.org/10.1007/978-3-031-60884-1_18

Kakaraparthi, V., McDaniel, T., Venkateswara, H., & Goldberg, M. (2022). PERACTIV: Personalized activity monitoring: Ask my hands. In N. A. Streitz & S. Konomi

(Eds.), *Distributed, ambient and pervasive interactions. Smart living, learning, well-being and health, art and creativity* (Vol. 13326, pp. 255–272). Springer. https://doi.org/10.1007/978-3-031-05431-0_18

Kakaraparthi, V., Shetty, Y., Goldberg, M., & McDaniel, T. (2025). Innovating medication adherence for smart cities: Leveraging PERACTIV and automated annotation pipeline for innovative solutions. In S. Berretti & H. Azari (Eds.), *Smart multimedia* (Vol. 14957, pp. 142–155). Springer. https://doi.org/10.1007/978-3-031-82475-3_10

Khunti, K., Seidu, S., Kunutsor, S., & Davies, M. (2017). Association between adherence to pharmacotherapy and outcomes in type 2 diabetes: A meta-analysis. *Diabetes Care, 40*(11), 1588–1596.

Kim, J., Combs, K., Downs, J., & Tillman, F. (2018). Medication adherence: The elephant in the room. *Us Pharm, 43*(1), 30–34.

Kini, V., & Ho, P. M. (2018). Interventions to improve medication adherence: A review. *Jama, 320*(23), 2461–2473.

Koesmahargyo, V., Abbas, A., Zhang, L., Guan, L., Feng, S., Yadav, V., & Galatzer-Levy, I. R. (2020). Accuracy of machine learning-based prediction of medication adherence in clinical research. *Psychiatry Research, 294*, 113558.

Kwon, H.-J., Kim, H.-G., & Lee, S.-H. (2021). Pill detection model for medicine inspection based on deep learning. *Chemosensors, 10*(1), 4.

Lally, P., Van Jaarsveld, C. H., Potts, H. W., & Wardle, J. (2010). How are habits formed: Modelling habit formation in the real world. *European Journal of Social Psychology, 40*(6), 998–1009.

Lea, C., Flynn, M. D., Vidal, R., Reiter, A., & Hager, G. D. (2017). Temporal convolutional networks for action segmentation and detection. *Proceedings of the IEEE Conference on Computer Vision and Pattern Recognition*, 156–165.

Li, T., Sahu, A. K., Talwalkar, A., & Smith, V. (2020). Federated learning: Challenges, methods, and future directions. *IEEE Signal Processing Magazine, 37*(3), 50–60.

Liu, W., Anguelov, D., Erhan, D., Szegedy, C., Reed, S., Fu, C.-Y., & Berg, A. C. (2016). Ssd: Single shot multibox detector. *Computer Vision–ECCV 2016: 14th European Conference, Amsterdam, the Netherlands, October 11–14, 2016, Proceedings, Part I 14* (pp. 21–37).

Marmot, M., & Wilkinson, R. (2005). *Social determinants of health*. Oup Oxford.

McDaniel, T., Goldberg, M., Venkateswara, H. K. D., Panchanathan, S., & Kakaraparthi, V. P. (2024). *Hand-directed system for identifying activities*. Google Patents.

Nahum-Shani, I., Smith, S. N., Spring, B. J., Collins, L. M., Witkiewitz, K., Tewari, A., & Murphy, S. A. (2018). Just-in-time adaptive interventions (JITAIs) in mobile health: Key components and design principles for ongoing health behavior support. *Annals of Behavioral Medicine, 52*(6), 446–462. https://doi.org/10.1007/s12160-016-9830-8

Neiman, A. B., Ruppar, T., Ho, M., Garber, L., Weidle, P. J., Hong, Y., George, M. G., & Thorpe, P. G. (2017). CDC Grand Rounds: Improving medication adherence for chronic disease management: Innovations and opportunities. *MMWR. Morbidity and Mortality Weekly Report, 66*(45), 1248–1251. https://doi.org/10.15585/mmwr.mm6645a2

Obermeyer, Z., Powers, B., Vogeli, C., & Mullainathan, S. (2019). Dissecting racial bias in an algorithm used to manage the health of populations. *Science, 366*(6464), 447–453.

Onzenoort, H. A., Verberk, W. J., Kroon, A. A., Kessels, A. G., Neef, C., Kuy, P.-H. M., van der, Leeuw, P. W., & de (2012). Electronic monitoring of adherence, treatment of hypertension, and blood pressure control. *American Journal of Hypertension, 25*(1), 54–59.

Paudyal, P., & William Wong, B. (2018). Algorithmic opacity: Making algorithmic processes transparent through abstraction hierarchy. *Proceedings of the Human Factors and Ergonomics Society Annual Meeting, 62*, 192–196.

Peng, Y., Wang, H., Fang, Q., Xie, L., Shu, L., Sun, W., & Liu, Q. (2020). Effectiveness of mobile applications on medication adherence in adults with chronic diseases: A systematic review and meta-analysis. *Journal of Managed Care & Specialty Pharmacy, 26*(4), 550–561.

Pharmadva. (2022). *Pharmadva MedaCube™ automatic pill dispenser.* http://www.medacube.com/

Philips Lifeline. (2024). *Philips lifeline® service.* https://www.lifeline.philips.com/business/medicationdispensing

Pulice, E., & Coustasse, A. (2024, March 20). AI-driven solutions promote medication adherence. *Pharmacy Times*, 42–44.

Rajkomar, A., Hardt, M., Howell, M. D., Corrado, G., & Chin, M. H. (2018). Ensuring fairness in machine learning to advance health equity. *Annals of Internal Medicine, 169*(12), 866–872.

Religioni, U., Barrios-Rodríguez, R., Requena, P., Borowska, M., & Ostrowski, J. (2025). Enhancing therapy adherence: Impact on clinical outcomes, healthcare costs, and patient quality of life. *Medicina, 61*(1), 153.

Robinson, L., Arden, M., Dawson, S., Walters, S., Wildman, M., & Stevenson, M. (2024). A machine-learning assisted review of the use of habit formation in medication adherence interventions for long-term conditions. *Health Psychology Review, 18*(1), 1–23.

Sabaté, E. (2003). *Adherence to long-term therapies: Evidence for action.* World Health Organization.

Short, S. E., & Mollborn, S. (2015). Social determinants and health behaviors: Conceptual frames and empirical advances. *Current Opinion in Psychology, 5*, 78–84.

Singh, N., & Varshney, U. (2019). Medication adherence: A method for designing context-aware reminders. *International Journal of Medical Informatics, 132*, 103980.

Tan, L., Huangfu, T., Wu, L., & Chen, W. (2021). Comparison of RetinaNet, SSD, and YOLO v3 for real-time pill identification. *BMC Medical Informatics and Decision Making, 21*(1), 11.

Tenovi. (n.d.). *Barriers to medication adherence.* https://www.tenovi.com/what-are-the-barriers-to-medication-adherence/

Thomas, L., Donohue-Porter, P., & Fishbein, J. S. (2017). Impact of interruptions, distractions, and cognitive load on procedure failures and medication administration errors. *Journal of Nursing Care Quality, 32*(4), 309–317.

Tran, D., Bourdev, L., Fergus, R., Torresani, L., & Paluri, M. (2015). Learning spatiotemporal features with 3d convolutional networks. *Proceedings of the IEEE International Conference on Computer Vision*, 4489–4497.

Tran, S., Smith, L., El-Den, S., & Carter, S. (2022). The use of gamification and incentives in mobile health apps to improve medication adherence: Scoping review. *JMIR mHealth and uHealth, 10*(2), e30671.

Wu, X.-W., Yang, H.-B., Yuan, R., Long, E.-W., & Tong, R.-S. (2020). Predictive models of medication non-adherence risks of patients with T2D based on multiple machine learning algorithms. *BMJ Open Diabetes Research & Care, 8*(1), e001055. https://doi.org/10.1136/bmjdrc-2019-001055

Yap, A. F., Thirumoorthy, T., & Kwan, Y. H. (2016). Systematic review of the barriers affecting medication adherence in older adults. *Geriatrics & Gerontology International, 16*(10), 1093–1101.

Yoon, S., Kwan, Y. H., Yap, W. L., Lim, Z. Y., Phang, J. K., Loo, Y. X., Aw, J., & Low, L. L. (2023). Factors influencing medication adherence in multi-ethnic Asian patients with chronic diseases in Singapore: A qualitative study. *Frontiers in Pharmacology, 14*, 1124297.

Zullig, L. L., Jazowski, S. A., Wang, T. Y., Hellkamp, A., Wojdyla, D., Thomas, L., Egbuonu-Davis, L., Beal, A., & Bosworth, H. B. (2019). Novel application of approaches to predicting medication adherence using medical claims data. *Health Services Research, 54*(6), 1255–1262.

12

Emotional and Physical Support through Ethical AI

Bradley Guelfi and Ray Parker

The human body is an extraordinary biological system, resilient, adaptive, and refined by millions of years of evolution. Its complexity rivals modern technologies, yet many aspects remain only partially understood, even by advanced science. Historically, this incomplete understanding has shaped the perception of human vulnerability when faced with disease, injury, and environmental threats. Nonetheless, humanity has continually overcome these challenges, thriving through ingenuity and adaptability.

Technological progress has brought unprecedented challenges, as global mobility, agriculture, and urbanisation now spread both opportunity and risk at immense scale. In response, both ethical frameworks and healthcare systems have evolved to protect and improve human life. This evolution is reflected in enduring professional codes such as the Hippocratic Oath and the Declaration of Geneva, which uphold values of respect for life, harm minimisation, and the pursuit of better care (World Medical Association, 2017).

Ethically embedded artificial intelligence (AI) transforms healthcare by enhancing accuracy, supporting informed clinical decision-making, and streamlining care delivery. Whether in advanced surgical suites or remote clinics, AI offers precision and scale, but values, not just performance metrics, must guide its integration The narrative journeys of two fictional, research-informed patients, Sarah's trauma and Kai's chronic illness, illustrate real-world care challenges and the role of AI in resolving them.

Their stories highlight the fragmentation and emotional toll of delayed diagnosis, but also demonstrate the critical importance of timely, integrated data, underscoring that technical improvements in AI directly translate into measurable gains in patient well-being and system efficiency. Emotional health is closely linked to biochemical responses in the body and brain, making it intrinsically connected to both physical and mental welfare. We explore AI's role in supporting diverse needs across a range of healthcare settings. Altogether, we demonstrate how AI can bridge these gaps, offering more connected, person-centred solutions that integrate physical, cognitive, and emotional dimensions of care. Advances must be rooted in ethical

DOI: 10.1201/9781003626510-12

design. The CORES Framework (Composable Oversight for Responsible Evolution and Simplicity) offers a structured model for adaptable, transparent, and safe AI, ensuring oversight, responsiveness, and equity across contexts. Healthcare systems today face rising pressures from demographic change, chronic disease, workforce shortages, and global inequities. AI assists in managing this complexity, but only if guided by ethical intent. AI is not a distant disruptor; it is already shaping decisions and relationships within healthcare.

AI's legitimacy in medicine is rooted in a long history of innovation, from MYCIN in the 1970s to today's real-time, patient-specific tools. This lineage contextualises current debates about trust, transparency, and professional responsibility. As AI becomes more prevalent, it prompts deeper reflection on autonomy, trust, and professional responsibility, raising technical but also moral and operational questions about consent, clinician trust, and system oversight. The answers lie in design, but also in how we implement and evaluate AI in practice. Through Sarah and Kai's stories, we explore how ethical integration can help build a healthcare system that is both efficient and humane. AI must be both technically sound and socially legitimate.

Ultimately, AI's role in healthcare should be to support the profession's highest goals: to reduce suffering, enhance understanding, and preserve dignity. With the right design principles, implementation structures, optimise health, and ethical governance, AI can serve not as a replacement for human care, but as a means to make care more human.

State-of-the-Art Surgical Suite and AI Integration

After a motorcycle accident, Sarah's fractures and suspected head trauma were stabilised by paramedics, prompting urgent transfer for advanced care. She remained conscious but disoriented, prompting urgent transfer to a trauma hospital. Upon arrival, the surgical team must be ready for a broad range of interventions. The hospital must be equipped with the necessary tools for orthopaedic and neurosurgical response, and with integrated systems that enable personalised diagnostics, interdisciplinary planning, and real-time data sharing. This is not just about machines or surgical instruments; it is about ensuring the hospital itself functions as a living network of coordinated support, adaptive to the evolving needs of the patient.

A wide range of potential procedures is tailored to meet each patient's individual needs. The surgical team's readiness depends on real-time diagnostics and dynamic scheduling informed by preference cards and multidisciplinary coordination. Every component, from imaging to environmental controls, must function as part of an integrated and adaptive system, demonstrating that true innovation lies not in isolated technologies but in their orchestration to achieve measurable improvements in patient safety, workflow efficiency, and clinical outcomes.

Key components of a patient-specific surgical ecosystem include:

- Medical imaging systems
- Snapshot and continuous diagnostics and monitoring tools
- Laboratory and point-of-care pathology
- Pharmacy services
- A fully integrated digital operating room
- Surgical robots
- Operating table, anaesthetic machine, and positioning equipment
- Ancillary surgical devices such as electrosurgery units, power tools, and navigation systems
- Electronic medical records (EMRs)
- Environmental controls and automated logistics
- Consumables and durables
- Building management and utility services

Integration in this context has two core meanings. First, all hardware and clinical tools must function as intuitive extensions of the surgical team, responding reliably to commands while minimising disruption to clinical flow. Second, data collection, processing, and presentation must be synchronised to give decision-makers a complete, real-time understanding of the patient. This includes ensuring interoperability between systems but also supporting ergonomic design, user interface simplicity, and cognitive workload reduction. Achieving this level of integration remains aspirational in many environments, where fragmented interfaces, lag in diagnostic results, and competing platform requirements can impede timely and effective decisions. AI provides critical support by addressing these issues.

For instance, AI enhances low-dose medical imaging, accelerates image processing, and delivers outputs instantly for radiologist review. In Sarah's case, the hospital's Picture Archive and Communications System (PACS) and Radiology Information System (RIS) expedited diagnostics. While neurosurgeons prepare for a cerebral aneurysm intervention, orthopaedic teams begin surgical planning using real-time 3D digital models compiled from multimodal imaging.

During surgery, AI-assisted diagnostics remain active, interacting continuously with both surgical teams and clinical systems. The surgical navigation microscope overlays real-time imaging data for the neurosurgeon, enabling precise instrument guidance and trajectory adjustments in response to tissue feedback. Operating room monitors serve as collaborative interfaces, allowing all surgical team members to cross-reference preoperative scans with live intraoperative updates. Enterprise compute systems manage data integration, presenting relevant analytics in an intuitive format that informs decision-making across multiple specialties. Parameters are customised per procedure and can be adapted in real time by anaesthetists, who use integrated monitors to assess Sarah's awareness, cerebral oxygenation, and vital signs. This allows for dynamic adjustment of anaesthesia and ventilation to align with physiological shifts and emerging intraoperative conditions.

The operating room is a command hub for advanced technologies. Environmental conditions are meticulously controlled to ensure both patient safety and staff performance. Air filtration systems remove airborne contaminants to reduce infection risk, precise temperature and humidity controls help maintain focus, minimise fatigue, and support wound integrity. Ambient lighting and acoustic settings are adjusted to reduce cognitive stress and promote surgical precision. Safety systems, including surgical laser shields and active radiation warning indicators, protect the team in real time. These functions, though less visible than robotics or navigation systems, are controlled by the building management system, constantly collecting data to optimise energy use and trigger preventative maintenance. This operational layer quietly sustains the high-performance surgical environment, ensuring uninterrupted care delivery.

In Australia, all patient care systems must comply with the Therapeutic Goods Act, ensuring devices are fit-for-purpose and fail-safe. Through collaboration among design teams, manufacturers, and users, this ensures safety and quality outcomes. The TGA collaborates internationally to maintain high standards. Sarah's case highlights how AI is reshaping procedural ethics. Informed consent, once a static document completed before surgery, is now digitised, dynamically linked to real-time surgical data within the electronic medical record (EMR). This streamlines documentation and ensures transparency by immediately syncing diagnostic, intraoperative monitoring, and clinical updates with the consent framework. If Sarah has a complication or additional procedures are necessary, clinicians can initiate a real-time dialogue with AI tools that summarise evolving clinical context and information for Sarah or her proxy in understandable terms. Dynamic consent supports patient autonomy and reinforces procedural accountability across the perioperative continuum. As part of a technically advanced and ethically grounded system, it protects patients while fostering innovation, setting a benchmark for deploying AI with both rigour and empathy to ensure surgical care that is accountable, inclusive, and safe.

People in Medicine – Roles, Training, and Perspectives

Every day, emergency departments around the world are visited by countless people in need of urgent care. For most, the healthcare system performs as a well-orchestrated machine, delivering skilled and timely support through an intricate network of professionals. Doctors, nurses, allied health workers, administrative staff, and technicians operate within a larger ecosystem spanning far past the visible frontline. Insiders often struggle to grasp the full complexity of this interdependent system.

> AI-driven systems reduce cognitive load and support resilience, helping teams maintain continuity and safety under stress.

AI is increasingly embedded in this ecosystem, augmenting human capacity and reducing cognitive and operational burden. Patient monitoring systems like Philips Intelli Vue Guardian and GE Edison platforms automate data interpretation and alert generation, expediting clinician response. Natural language processing tools such as those employed by Epic and Kyra Clinical translate clinician speech into EMR entries, reducing documentation fatigue and promoting consistency. In Sarah's case, these tools enabled seamless care transitions by supporting emergency response teams and rehabilitation staff with real-time data integration.

Kai's underlying condition impacts other aspects of his life and care, including doctors prescribing standard medicines, with negative results. AI-enabled analysis of fragmented records and subtle symptoms led to Kai's diagnosis and comprehensive care. In both narratives, AI enhanced the clarity, timing, and empathy of healthcare delivery.

Core AI Functions Supporting Clinical Roles

- Monitoring & Alerts: Enhance record accuracy and reduce charting time with NLP.
- Imaging Interpretation: High-resolution diagnostics improve radiology workflows.
- Documentation & Dictation: Enhance record accuracy and reduce charting time with NLP.
- Predictive Operations: AI supports scheduling, triage, and resource allocation.
- Surgical Coordination: Integrated tools recommend configurations and track equipment use.
- Infrastructure Redundancy: Failover protocols ensure continuous system functionality.

Training and Professional Development in the AI Era

AI is reshaping clinical education. New initiatives, such as the NHS AI Lab and Stanford's AI in Healthcare certification, emphasise ethical reasoning, algorithmic literacy, and collaborative intelligence. Professional bodies like the Royal Australasian College of Surgeons and the Australian Medical Association are updating curricula to address AI safety, bias detection, and digital professionalism. The goal is: to equip clinicians to interpret AI outputs, understand system limitations, and clearly communicate risks and benefits to patients.

> Biomedical engineers and technicians play a growing role in refining algorithms, validating system output, and responding to live performance metrics.

For nurses and allied health professionals, AI-enhanced dashboards streamline monitoring, handovers, and care coordination. These tools demand critical engagement, empowering clinicians to interpret alerts and act without blindly deferring to algorithms. Managing algorithmic influence is vital, as over-reliance can obscure context or urgency.

Technology and the Patient Experience

The Patient Experience Suite (PES), like those from Rauland and Stellar Vision, broadens the scope of care by combining entertainment, dietary planning, and health literacy with Nurse Call and Building Management Systems. They support AI-enabled fall prevention and room controls such as smart lighting, glass, and automation. For Sarah, this interface bridged isolation and engagement, and autonomy and support. For Kai, digital access to treatment notes deepened his understanding and involvement in clinical decisions. These platforms improve patient satisfaction and well-being by addressing psychological and social needs through thoughtful technological integration (Rauland Australia, 2022).

Evolving Together

AI systems support rather than supplant human roles. The value lies in augmentation, not just automation. Clinicians, technicians, support staff, and patients all occupy essential positions in a digitally enhanced care continuum. Ensuring each of these roles adapts and thrives alongside AI requires structured training, inclusive design, and continuous evaluation and improvement. AI training programs should include update-aware protocols that inform clinical staff when algorithm parameters or thresholds have changed, ensuring informed use of evolving tools. When thoughtfully implemented, AI strengthens the core promise of medicine: to care, to understand, and to heal with precision, empathy, and trust.

AI in Supporting Ageing and People with Disabilities

Australia is undergoing a profound demographic shift, with rising ageing and disability rates placing increasing pressure on health and social care systems. As of 2022, 21.4% of Australians, around 5.5 million people, reported living with a disability, a notable increase from 17.7% in 2018. Over half of those aged 65 and older live with some form of disability, and projections indicate that the number of Australians aged 85 and over will double by 2042 (ABS, 2024).

AI-enabled assistive technologies represent a significant opportunity to support this growing need. Innovations such as powered exoskeletons and assistive robotics are already reshaping mobility and recovery. Research initiatives at institutions like the University of Technology Sydney and the University of Queensland have demonstrated how AI-driven wearable robotics can enhance motor relearning and restore walking function after stroke, adapting to patient-specific biomechanics in real time (University of Queensland, 2023; University of Technology Sydney, 2021).

Advances in smart composite materials and personalised implants, such as those being developed by BellaSeno using AI-based modelling and 3D printing, further enhance physical integration and comfort (3DPrint.com, 2024). Smart hospital and home environments integrate biometric sensing, fall detection, voice activation, and adaptive climate systems, enabling longer, safer independent living. These AI-supported living systems reduce reliance on emergency services and allow for earlier, less disruptive intervention.

At the systems level, predictive analytics and real-time health monitoring algorithms are being used to flag deterioration, such as sepsis onset, before symptoms escalate. Platforms using AI to tailor therapies and dosage schedules to individual physiology are showing measurable improvements in treatment precision and patient satisfaction (Akinnibi, 2025).

However, deployment is not without complications. Many of these technologies are still undergoing real world validation, and their benefits are not evenly distributed. Without inclusive design and equitable access, AI risks further entrenching disparities. Early deployments have largely benefited affluent populations, while rural and disadvantaged groups face infrastructure and access barriers (Morley et al., 2020). Without intervention, these disparities risk reinforcing structural inequities instead of resolving them. Equity, affordability, and universal design must be addressed from the outset. Public-private partnerships can help scale supply chains and subsidise high-value assistive tools. At the same time, federated learning models and edge computing keep sensitive user data on local devices, protecting privacy and enabling population-level insights.

Ethical concerns also extend to autonomy and consent. In some settings, AI systems may recommend interventions that conflict with patient wishes or lack clear explainability. AI is meant to enhance care, but safeguards are essential to prevent overreach or coercion, especially for vulnerable groups such as those with cognitive impairment or declining capacity. Transparent algorithmic logic, fail-safe overrides, and embedded review mechanisms must be non-negotiable. The ethical imperative presents a strong economic justification for integrating AI into ageing and disability care. Reductions in acute hospital admissions and improved chronic disease management produce downstream savings. The economic benefits of improved mobility and communication, such as increased workforce participation and reduced caregiver load, can be reinvested in service delivery and technological improvement. However, these projections must be balanced against the costs of implementation, training, and ongoing governance.

Practical implementation will require cross-sector alignment. This includes establishing clinical and technical audit trails, regulatory pathways for approval, and training programs for both clinical users and care recipients. For instance, AI-powered prosthetic technologies may need regular recalibration and clinician oversight, yet few systems currently track long-term performance outcomes using multi-source integrated data and AI-enabled algorithms. AI is capable of piecing together the entire patient story to improve care and enhance research and development feedback. This can reach further to inform product compatibility with individual genetic expression. If done right, AI can shift ageing and disability services from reactive models to proactive, person-centred ecosystems. It can personalise care, restoring autonomy and dignity. This is not innovation for its own sake, it is a journey toward inclusive, evidence-informed adoption. Through thoughtful integration, strong governance, and a human-first approach, AI becomes not a tool of disruption, but one of resilience and dignity.

Preventative and Extended Connected Care

Trauma is an unavoidable part of life, but conditions such as coronary heart disease and dementia remain leading causes of death in Australia (AIHW, 2023). Relying solely on symptom-driven care in the digital era is no longer optimal. The paradigm is shifting toward early identification of risk, proactive treatment, and constant monitoring, supported by artificial intelligence (AI). Today, wearable devices monitor numerous health metrics, from heart rate variability to sleep patterns. Although these technologies are not new, AI now enables real-time data analysis, identifying anomalies and generating personalised self-care strategies. These systems may account for genetic predispositions as well as modifiable behavioural risks, such as poor diet or inactivity, which influence gene expression. When metrics exceed risk thresholds, AI escalates alerts across the healthcare supply chain, triggering clinician review before crises emerge (Arya et al., 2023).

Sarah's extended care journey illustrates the real-world potential of this integration. From the accident site, AI-supported triage tools helped paramedics assess her condition and initiate care. Following acute intervention, she benefited from smart-room environments, adaptive rehabilitation plans, and data-informed telehealth check-ins. Once discharged, wearable monitors, predictive emotional support prompts, and vocational AI-guidance enabled her gradual return to everyday life and eventually back to work. For Kai, whose chronic illness was undiagnosed, AI-enabled risk profiling highlighted subtle but significant behavioural and biometric shifts. His care pathway included early intervention through smart triage, coordinated virtual follow-ups, and gait-informed workplace assessment. At each phase, AI linked data across systems to support continuity of care and contextual decision-making.

Preventative care now extends beyond annual check-ups. Consumer wearables are evolving into clinical-grade tools. Regulatory guidance increasingly supports transitions from lifestyle tracking to remote diagnostics, overseen by clinicians. Studies from Mayo Clinic and NHS AI Lab demonstrate that ambient AI systems reduce documentation time by over 30%, increase triage accuracy, and allow clinicians to focus on relational care. Advanced non-contact sensors enhance care through passive observation. Thermal imaging, once unreliable, has become significantly more accurate when paired with AI. These tools can detect fever, altered posture, and even signs of emotional distress, helping clinicians prioritise responses between formal assessments. These promising technologies are still undergoing validation and must be supported by clinical trials and regulatory oversight.

In public environments, gait analysis and behavioural biometrics further extend AI's reach. Yet this shift raises critical ethical concerns. Real-time surveillance, even when health-driven, challenges long-standing norms of consent and autonomy. Privacy-preserving architectures, such as federated learning and edge computing, allow individual data to remain localised and still inform public health trends (Rieke et al., 2020). When transparently governed, these systems can protect trust and confidentiality and enable proactive care. The aim is not just to detect disease, but to optimise well-being across physical, cognitive, and emotional domains. AI's ability to correlate mood changes with variables such as diet, sleep, and social engagement empowers personalised, longitudinal interventions (Dlima et al., 2022; WHO, 2023). Importantly, this enhances autonomy and encourages health literacy, rather than replacing human judgment.

Yet risks persist. Recent breaches, including the exposure of over 61 million wearable records in 2021 and ransomware attacks on diagnostic AI vendors in 2022, underscore the need for strong safeguards. End-to-end encryption, transparent consent mechanisms, and algorithmic accountability are not luxuries, but requirements. Technology and governance frameworks must support clinicians and patients alike with explainable outputs, feedback loops, and contingency options.

Redefining care through extended and preventative models also enables a shift in culture. Illness should not invoke shame. AI-enabled systems that support mental and emotional well-being offer a private, stigma-free path to care. Tools that integrate cognitive and physical health can help dissolve outdated attitudes and foster a healthcare environment built on compassion and dignity. Frameworks from WHO and others show how digital systems, when thoughtfully designed, can help reduce stigma by improving access, privacy, and personal relevance (Arora et al., 2022; WHO, 2021).

Ultimately, preventative and extended care is not about relentless intervention or intrusive monitoring, but about ongoing support. These technologies will not replace human care, but enhance its reach, context-awareness, and sustainability. As interoperability improves and public trust is cultivated through ethical design, these systems can form the backbone of a healthcare model that is reactive but generative, not just treating symptoms but fostering the conditions for lifelong health and human flourishing.

Globally Holistic Healthcare Perspectives, Emotional Support and AI Integration

Holistic healthcare acknowledges the deep interconnection between emotional, cognitive, social, and physical aspects of an individual, aiming not just to eliminate disease but to foster genuine health and a complete state of well-being. Integrating these dimensions requires navigating both systemic complexity and human diversity. AI offers new opportunities to support this goal by connecting traditionally siloed health data and enabling more responsive, personalised care.

From a classical ethical standpoint, building systems that deliver balanced, high-quality healthcare to all is a fundamental societal objective. Healthcare professionals are formally inducted into this mission, yet delivering holistic, equitable care remains one of the greatest challenges. Limited resources, fragmented information systems, and the still-unfolding understanding of mind-body integration create profound barriers to achieving universal health and well-being. If mental and emotional well-being were treated as integral, not optional, the ambition of delivering longevity and quality of life to all becomes an easier task (Beauchamp & Childress, 2019).

The moral imperative becomes clear when addressing justice and equity. Utilitarian ethics seek the greatest good for the most people; deontological ethics insist on care for every individual, regardless of broader outcomes. Balancing these principles is crucial to reducing disparities in access and outcomes. In nations like Australia, the UK, Mexico, and South Africa, rural and underserved populations face major care gaps. Australia's $6.5 billion annual rural healthcare shortfall (National Rural Health Alliance, 2023), NHS staff shortages of 8.4% (The King's Fund, 2023), and unequal access in Mexico and South Africa (Economic Freedom Fighters, 2025; García-Díaz, 2022) show how geography shapes healthcare quality.

In lower-income contexts like Nigeria and Sierra Leone, infrastructure deficits, staffing crises, and the near-total absence of mental health services deepen inequities. Nigeria has approximately 250 psychiatrists serving a population of more than 200 million, while Sierra Leone has historically had only two psychiatrists serving a population of more than 7 million people (Harris et al., 2020; Okechukwu, 2020). These profound disparities demonstrate that gaps in mental healthcare are not merely operational challenges, but urgent ethical concerns involving equity, access, and the right to care.

AI offers powerful tools to address such gaps. Systems capable of combining diverse inputs, including psychological assessments, social histories, and physiological data, can identify causes and connections often missed by siloed care. Contrastingly, overreliance on AI-generated mental health recommendations may compromise treatment accuracy, particularly when clinicians overly defer to automated suggestions (Jacobs et al., 2021). A more effective approach may lie in a human–AI–human support triangle, where AI facilitates but does not replace empathy and judgement. At the same time, real-world implementation remains uneven. Digital mental health systems face persistent challenges concerning equitable access, representativeness, bias, and adaptation to diverse populations and contexts (Smith et al., 2023). These limitations underscore the need for inclusive validation datasets, intentional cross-cultural design, and robust interdisciplinary oversight.

Operational frameworks must evolve to support these models. Hospitals often excel at acute care but struggle to connect long-term patterns across disciplines. Integrative AI can detect cascade effects, compound risks, and subtle patterns that may elude human cognition. By synthesising data from multiple specialties and sources, AI supports decisions that reflect links between emotional need, chronic condition, and lifestyle. Successful implementation depends on technical integration, ethical scaffolding, data dignity, and informed consent. The body is its own complex system, only partially understood. This observation underpins much of the forthcoming framework section, where ambiguity in biological function and the interdependence of mental, emotional, and physical systems will be analysed more critically. Recent discoveries, such as the mesentery (Coffey et al., 2020), continue to reshape anatomy. Gut–brain connections further reinforce the need for systemic perspectives on health. Emotional stress impacts microbiome diversity, cognitive performance, and immune responses, relationships that require interdisciplinary approaches and adaptive analytics.

Australia's healthcare system encompasses considerable professional specialisation, with 23 medical specialties and 86 subspecialties recognised in the 2016 national medical workforce survey (Australian Government Department of Health, 2017). Yet, despite this diversity, data sharing remains difficult. Even when records are accessible, professionals tend to extract and review only discipline-specific data. Cascade effects between medications, therapies, and emotional conditions are missed unless made explicit. This creates a paradox: more data exists than ever, but much of its integrative potential remains untapped. AI can change this. By drawing from collective human health data, AI can detect meaningful patterns unique to each person, genetic traits, lifestyle choices, or environmental triggers. Consider Kai, whose diagnosis with Crohn's disease came only after extensive delays and two failed medication attempts that worsened his condition. His remission was eventually achieved not through pharmacological intervention, but through a carefully structured diet and exercise regime, demonstrating the foundational role that nutrition and mobility can play in managing chronic illness. His data from wearable monitors, dietary logs, emotional trends, and physical activity routines were algorithmically interpreted to reveal early warning signs and ongoing risks. Where clinicians may be overwhelmed by fragmented details, AI excels in matching context to consequence. Used ethically, it becomes a cognitive ally, not a replacement.

Ultimately, holistic healthcare supported by AI must be inclusive and flexible. This insight forms a strategic bridge to the framework and conclusion, where adaptability and inclusivity are explored as both values and operational requirements for resilient AI-integrated healthcare. People are not just patients. They are unique, dynamic ecosystems of biology and experience. The tools we design must reflect that truth. In doing so, AI improves outcomes; it helps restore the core ethos of medicine: to care, to understand, and to heal.

Critical Perspectives and Evolving Ethical Foundations

Throughout history, medicine has been a beacon of innovation, adopting structured processes and data-driven methodologies long before modern AI emerged. As far back as prehistory, medical practice relied on consistent algorithms to ensure effective treatments (Porter, 1999). By the early 1970s, computational algorithms had entered clinical decision-making, most notably with the development of MYCIN, an expert system for infectious disease diagnosis and treatment developed by Edward H. Shortliffe at Stanford University (Shortliffe, 1973). Healthcare's embrace of advanced analytics, automation, and machine learning further evolved over subsequent decades, long predating the current AI discourse (Topol, 2019). These foundational systems set the stage for today's AI-enhanced tools that enable real-time intervention and patient-specific care pathways. This lineage leads naturally to the emergence of powerful AI systems integrated with supercomputers, positioning AI not as an outsider, but as the next logical step in the pursuit of optimised care.

Recent research affirms AI's evolutionary role but also exposes emerging challenges. Advances in genomics, digital imaging, and biometric tracking reveal both shared human physiology and significant individual variation (Ashley, 2016). AI can navigate this complexity by synthesising vast multimodal datasets. Yet ethical integration remains unresolved. Current infrastructures still prioritise mass-access interventions shaped by utilitarian logic, optimising average benefit at the expense of rare, comorbid, or complex cases (Beauchamp & Childress, 2019).

Sarah's acute rehabilitation and Kai's diagnostic journey exemplify this ethical tension. AI enabled timely triage, tailored monitoring, and adaptive discharge planning for Sarah. For Kai, it uncovered a chronic condition through pattern recognition across sources and time. In both cases, AI extended clinician capacity but depended on embedded infrastructure, data quality, and clinician trust. These examples show how AI can either reinforce or resolve fragmentation, depending on the ethical and operational contexts that support it. Nonetheless, economic systems remain a limiting factor. Personalised medicine, though ethically aligned with principles of autonomy and respect for persons, struggles for viability in funding models optimised for mass application (Daniels, 2008; Dzau et al., 2016). Even transformative tools like CRISPR (Frangoul et al., 2021) or AlphaFold (Jumper et al., 2021) demonstrate uneven adoption due to disparities in cost, access, and clinical training (Braga et al., 2022).

However, AI-enhanced early intervention, chronic condition management, and wellness support offer measurable cost savings by reducing emergency visits, avoiding preventable complications, and lightening the load on overstretched public systems, an economic case for ethically grounded, proactive AI deployment. To address this, AI must not simply inherit the constraints of existing systems. Instead, it should be used to identify inefficiencies, simulate equitable resource distribution, and recommend adaptive reimbursement models that reflect individualised care outcomes. Such applications speak to real-world structural and ethical redesign.

A deeper reassessment of ethical foundations is required. Healthcare should not merely treat or contain illness, but actively enhance quality of life, physically, emotionally, and socially. In a digitally augmented world, risk-taking behaviours and personal variance are not threats to efficiency but markers of individuality and societal growth. Systems must therefore balance risk and safety, offering proactive support and recovery pathways without judgment. This is the vision underpinning the concept of a Healthical Society: a model of care where health equity, data dignity, and algorithmic alignment support people in becoming their fullest selves.

Critically, this shift requires ethical principles to evolve. Classical bioethics offers essential foundations, but contemporary tools demand additional emphasis on transparency, adaptability, and participatory design. Future-ready healthcare ethics must be framed in terms of what care is delivered, as well as how it is designed, distributed, and improved over time. AI, if guided responsibly, offers not just greater precision but a more holistic understanding of what it means to care. It is this relational, inclusive, and anticipatory dimension that must shape the next generation of ethical frameworks for digital health.

Future Integration and the CORES Framework

Healthcare must evolve toward systems that are adaptive and intelligent, also fundamentally ethical in design. The CORES Framework: Composable Oversight for Responsible Evolution and Simplicity, offers one pathway forward. It provides a modular ethical architecture that can adapt alongside technological development and social change.

Core Ethical Embedding

Ethical reasoning must be embedded from the earliest design stages. This includes consent, fairness, transparency, and patient safety as foundational components rather than retrofitted features. Ethical foresight can also help mitigate discriminatory design, reduce data bias, and reinforce long-term accountability. Establish recurring third-party ethical audits and cross-functional reviews to examine drift, bias, and unintended outcomes in deployed AI systems.

Oversight by Design

Systems must be explainable, traceable, and accessible for review by both clinicians and patients. Transparent decision logs and contextual prompts foster trust in AI and safeguard human agency. However, there often remains an unresolved trade-off between the accuracy of complex models and their interpretability. Developers and clinicians must collaborate to balance diagnostic performance with explainability, especially in high-stakes decisions where trust and accountability intersect.

Effective oversight also depends on institutional mechanisms for auditability, including accessible decision trails, version histories, and defined performance benchmarks. To meet future demands, technology must remain flexible and reliable, scalable across contexts, and capable of adapting to evolving healthcare visions. Clinicians and patients must have access to "explainability snapshots" tied to specific system versions used in diagnosis or treatment, enabling traceable clinical oversight.

Responsive Self-Governance

AI must detect and correct its own biases, drift, and failures. Built-in ethical watchdogs and governance mechanisms ensure alignment with human values, clinical safety, and accountability. These safeguards allow AI to evolve without straying from ethical principles or clinical standards. Real-time drift monitoring tools, like those piloted at the Mayo Clinic and NHS AI Lab, should be standardised across healthcare systems. These tools flag performance degradation in response to new data or changing clinical contexts, enabling timely human oversight. Ethical watchdogs can also raise alerts when outputs diverge from accepted norms, prompting review by ethics boards or clinical safety teams. Together, these features support AI that operates not just responsively, but responsibly, preserving trust and ensuring continuity of care.

Equity Anchoring

Inclusion must be a continuous and measurable priority. AI must be trained and validated on diverse population datasets and tested across use cases that reflect varied socioeconomic and cultural contexts. Emerging research warns that without enforced equity checks, algorithms risk reproducing or amplifying systemic disparities, particularly in mental health, chronic disease management, and access to specialty care.

Simplicity for Flexibility

Complexity is sometimes necessary, but modular simplicity supports longevity, transparency, and auditability. Not every challenge demands an AI solution. Where used, AI should clarify, not complicate, clinical pathways. Its strength lies in distilling complex, data-rich environments into actionable insights. These insights must be translated into clear, human-centred language, accessible across all levels of health literacy. Simplicity is the essential bridge between machine intelligence and meaningful human understanding.

Challenges

Despite its promise, implementing the CORES Framework in real-world settings faces hurdles. Many clinical environments lack standardised digital governance, and regulatory compliance varies across jurisdictions. AI can help by supporting harmonisation through intelligent auditing platforms that map, flag, and propose corrective actions. Where time and resources limit live review, automated reporting, anomaly detection, and compliance dashboards can reduce the burden. Governance bottlenecks may be resolved through adaptive workflows that embed data transparency into clinical systems. In institutions facing resistance or inconsistent readiness, AI-enabled training and ethical decision tools can boost literacy and operational consistency.

Sarah and Kai's care journeys reflect the need for systems that are both personalised and principled. Sarah's recovery benefited from real-time monitoring, AI-driven pain management, and predictive discharge planning. Kai's diagnosis and remission relied on longitudinal pattern recognition and integrated data streams. These cases show AI's potential, but also the importance of embedding patient-centred design. Designing systems that support not just survival but flourishing demands ethics as a catalyst, not a constraint.

The CORES Framework offers a foundation to ensure innovation advances well-being, autonomy, and fairness. Building tomorrow's healthcare systems means asking not only how we build, but why, and for whom.

Conclusion – Toward a Truly Integrated Healthcare Model

Developers and clinicians must calibrate algorithms to adapt to individual needs while remaining robust and equitable at scale. This balance involves technical trade-offs and ethical decisions about which values prevail when customisation clashes with practical delivery. Fostering clinician trust in AI requires safeguards that uphold, not replace, professional judgement and responsibility. Bias often arises from training datasets that reflect historical inequities and underrepresented minority populations and conditions, resulting in poor performance for individuals with complex or unique needs. Ethical deployment requires demographic bias audits, correction protocols, and inclusive funding to prevent marginalised groups from being excluded. These concerns highlight the need to design AI systems that are critically assessed as they evolve and that support holistic care.

For Sarah, AI enhanced continuity of care, from the accident site to reintegration at home and work. For Kai, it enabled detection of a hidden condition. In both cases, AI bridged emotional, mental, and physical health in meaningful ways. This integrated vision is not just possible, it is ethically essential. Classical principles of autonomy, beneficence, non-maleficence, and justice remain vital, but today's challenges require principled evolution. Integration must go beyond layering technology onto existing systems; AI should operate as a seamless extension of the care team, aligning diverse data streams to support real-time, patient-centred decisions. This approach supports both advanced surgery and routine care by closing gaps in communication, coordination, and clinical insight.

The CORES Framework supports this integration by embedding oversight, adaptability, and equity, safeguarding dignity, privacy, and well-being. But to shift from principle to practice, it must be embedded in clinical workflows. Challenges include inconsistent infrastructure, variable digital literacy among clinicians and patients, and regulatory lag that delays updates and oversight. Effective implementation depends on real-time algorithm monitoring, audits for bias and drift, and transparent documentation accessible to patients, carers, and clinicians. Governance must empower staff and ethics boards to review AI decisions. Institutions must also invest in interdisciplinary training, traceable digital infrastructure, and adaptive policies that respond to emerging risks.

When cognitive or physical capacity is limited, ethical information and decision-making must involve designated custodians. Technologies-like voice, gesture, and EEG controls can also empower patients to participate in their care. The move from fragmented to integrated care reflects both technical sophistication and ethical maturity. It sets a benchmark for AI that balances rigour with empathy, ensuring care remains advanced, accountable, and safe for all.

Final Recommendations

Partnership design: Treat patients as collaborators with unique insight. Systems must support shared decision-making, adapt to individual needs, and reflect patients' investment in their outcomes.

1. Build ethics into the core and from the start: Embed consent, transparency, and fairness into every layer of AI systems.
2. Apply adaptive frameworks like CORES: Guide evolving technologies without compromising trust or safety.
3. Design inclusively: Use diverse datasets, conduct equity audits, and create culturally attuned interfaces.
4. Ensure human oversight: Build systems that explain themselves and respect clinical judgement.
5. Simplify for sustainability: Prioritise clarity and usability, keeping AI in the loop to validate and optimise, not dominate.
6. Protect dignity holistically: Treat emotional and cognitive well-being with the same priority as physical health.
7. Uphold privacy as dignity: Give individuals control over their health data, not as a legal formality, but a personal right.
8. Embrace responsible risk: Support innovation that includes space for learning, failing, and growing, hallmarks of a thriving life.
9. Reform policy for parity: Elevate mental and emotional health through funding, AI-assisted early care, and long-term quality-of-life metrics.
10. Audit for equity: Mandate demographic performance checks and fund access pathways for marginalised communities.

The promise of AI is not simply better diagnostics or faster treatment. Its true potential lies in empowering people to live fuller, more informed, and more autonomous lives. It must honour care as something not only clinical, but emotional, cognitive, social, and enduring. AI can support advocacy, enable informed decision-making, or respectfully assist in transferring care authority when needed, whether to family, carers, or medical teams. In doing so, it becomes not just a tool for precision but a partner in dignity, choice, and agency. Healthcare, at its best, helps people live, not just survive, with compassion, trust, and respect. That is the ethical vision we must hold as we build AI-enabled systems. The future of care must be shaped by ethics, guided with intention, and grounded in our highest values. The ultimate aim is not to make medicine more mechanical, but more human. The destination is, and always must be, humanity.

References

Akinnibi, F. (2025, March 2). *How AI and assistive technology are transforming disability care*. Centre Disability Support. https://centredisabilitysupport.com.au/blog/how-ai-is-transforming-disability-care/

Arora, L., Coe, E., Dewhurst, M., & Enomoto, K. (2022, September 27). *Heat waves, the war in Ukraine, and stigma: Gen Z's perspectives on mental health*. McKinsey Health Institute.

Arya, S. S., Dias, S. B., Jelinek, H. F., Hadjileontiadis, L. J., & Pappa, A.-M. (2023). The convergence of traditional and digital biomarkers through AI-assisted biosensing: A new era in translational diagnostics? Biosensors and Bioelectronics, 235, 115387. https://doi.org/10.1016/j.bios.2023.115387

Ashley, E. A. (2016). Towards precision medicine. Nature Reviews Genetics, 17(9), 507–522.

Australian Bureau of Statistics. (2024). *Disability, ageing and carers, Australia: Summary of findings, 2022*. https://www.abs.gov.au/statistics/health/disability/disability-ageing-and-carers-australia-summary-findings/latest-release

Australian Government Department of Health. (2017). *Medical workforce 2016 factsheet*. https://hwd.health.gov.au/resources/publications/factsheet-mdcl-2016.pdf.

Australian Institute of Health and Welfare. (2023). *Deaths in Australia*. Australian Government. https://www.aihw.gov.au/reports/life-expectancy-deaths/deaths-in-australia

Beauchamp, T. L., & Childress, J. F. (2019). Principles of biomedical ethics (8th ed.). Oxford University Press.

Braga, L. A. M., Conte Filho, C. G., & Mota, F. B. (2022). Future of genetic therapies for rare genetic diseases: What to expect for the next 15 years? Therapeutic Advances in Rare Disease, 3, 1–16. https://doi.org/10.1177/26330040221100840

Coffey, J. C., Walsh, D., Byrnes, K. G., Hohenberger, W., & Heald, R. J. (2020). Mesentery, a 'new' organ. Emerging Topics in Life Sciences, 4(2), 191–206. https://doi.org/10.1042/ETLS20200006

Daniels, N. (2008). Just health: Meeting health needs fairly. Cambridge University Press.

Dlima, S. D., Shevade, S., Menezes, S. R., & Ganju, A. (2022). Digital phenotyping in health using machine learning approaches: Scoping review. JMIR Bioinformatics and Biotechnology, 3(1), e39618. https://doi.org/10.2196/39618

Dzau, V. J., Ginsburg, G. S., Van Nuys, K., Agus, D., & Goldman, D. P. (2016). Aligning incentives to fulfil the promise of personalised medicine. The Lancet, 388(10041), 2118–2119.

Economic Freedom Fighters. (2025). The state of healthcare in South Africa: A crisis unpacked in the EFF's Health Manifesto. https://effonline.org/wp-content/uploads/2025/03/Health.pdf

Frangoul, H., Altshuler, D., Cappellini, M. D., Chen, Y. S., Domm, J., Eustace, B. K., & Corbacioglu, S. (2021). CRISPR-Cas9 gene editing for sickle cell disease and β-thalassemia. New England Journal of Medicine, 384(3), 252–260. https://doi.org/10.1056/NEJMoa2031054

García-Díaz, R. (2022). Effective access to healthcare in Mexico. BMC Health Services Research, 22, 1027. https://doi.org/10.1186/s12913-022-08417-0

Harris, D., Endale, T., Lind, L., & Purnell, L. (2020). Mental health in Sierra Leone. BJPsych International, 17(1), 14–16. https://doi.org/10.1192/bji.2019.17

Jacobs, M. et al (2021). How machine-learning recommendations influence clinician treatment selections: The example of antidepressant selection. Translational Psychiatry, 11(1), 108. https://doi.org/10.1038/s41398-021-01224-x

Jumper, J. et al (2021). Highly accurate protein structure prediction with AlphaFold. Nature, 596(7873), 583–589. https://doi.org/10.1038/s41586-021-03819-2

Mayo Clinic Platform. (2022). Monitoring and managing AI in clinical practice. Mayo Clinic Proceedings. Retrieved from https://www.mayoclinicplatform.org/

Morley, J., Floridi, L., Kinsey, L., & Elhalal, A. (2020). From what to how: An initial review of publicly available AI ethics tools, methods and research to translate principles into practices. Science and Engineering Ethics, 26(4), 2141–2168. https://doi.org/10.1007/s11948-019-00165-5

National Rural Health Alliance. (2023). Rural Australians missing out on $6.5 billion annually in health care access while coffers fill up with rural contributions. https://www.ruralhealth.org.au/media-release/rural-australians-missing-out-65-billion-annually-health-care-access-while-coffers

Okechukwu, C. E. (2020). Shortage of psychiatrists: A barrier to effective mental health-care delivery in Nigeria. International Journal of Noncommunicable Diseases, 5(1), 22–23. https://doi.org/10.4103/jncd.jncd_1_20

Porter, R. (1999). The greatest benefit to mankind: A medical history of humanity. W. W. Norton & Company.

Rauland Australia. (2022, April 11). *World leading Queensland hospital adopts state-of-the-art technology*. https://rauland.com.au/news/world-leading-queensland-hospital-adopts-state-of-the-art-technology/

Rieke, N., Hancox, J., Li, W., Milletari, F., Roth, H. R., Albarqouni, S., & Cardoso, M. J. (2020). The future of digital health with federated learning. Npj Digital Medicine, 3(1), 119. https://doi.org/10.1038/s41746-020-00323-1

Shortliffe, E. H., Axline, S. G., Buchanan, B. G., Merigan, T. C., & Cohen, S. N. (1973). An artificial intelligence program to advise physicians regarding antimicrobial therapy. Computers and Biomedical Research, 6(6), 544–560. https://doi.org/10.1016/0010-4809(73)90029-3

Smith, K. A., Blease, C., Faurholt-Jepsen, M., Firth, J., Van Daele, T., Moreno, C., Carlbring, P., Ebner-Priemer, U. W., Koutsouleris, N., Riper, H., Mouchabac, S., & Cipriani, A. (2023). Digital mental health: Challenges and next steps. BMJ Mental Health, 26(1), e300670. https://doi.org/10.1136/bmjment-2023-300670

The King's Fund. (2023). NHS staff shortages. https://www.kingsfund.org.uk/insight-and-analysis/data-and-charts/staff-shortages

Topol, E. J. (2019). Deep medicine: How artificial intelligence can make healthcare human again. Basic Books.

University of Queensland. (2023). Personalised wearable robotics for restoration of walking function after stroke. https://ai.uq.edu.au/project/personalised-wearable-robotics-restoration-walking-function-after-stroke

University of Technology Sydney. (2021). AI exoskeleton transforming rehab through robotics. https://www.uts.edu.au/news/2021/01/ai-exoskeleton-transforming-rehab-through-robotics

World Health Organization. (2021). *Ethics and governance of artificial intelligence for health: WHO guidance.* https://www.who.int/publications/i/item/9789240029200

World Health Organization. (2023). *Regulatory considerations on artificial intelligence for health.* https://www.who.int/publications/i/item/9789240078871

World Medical Association. (2017). *WMA Declaration of Geneva.* https://www.wma.net/policies-post/wma-declaration-of-geneva/

Regulatory, Statistics

Therapeutic Goods Administration (TGA, 2022), Aphra. (2023). National Boards. Australian Health Practitioner Regulation Agency. U.S. Food and Drug Administration (FDA, 2023), World Medical Association, Australian Institute of Health and Welfare (AIHW, 2023), (2017). WMA Declaration of Geneva and European Medicines Agency (EMA, 2023). WHO. (2021). Global Strategy on Digital Health 2020–2025. World Health Organisation. WHO. (2023). Constitution of the World Health Organisation.

Systems, Equipment, Documentation

Philips Healthcare, KYRA Medical, Rauland Australia, Stellar Vision, GE HealthCare, Epic Systems. NHS Artificial Intelligence Lab.

13

Artificial Intelligence and the Future of Data Privacy: Examining the MIT Taxonomy and Unified Privacy Governance Framework

Michael D'Rosario and George Newman

The integration of Artificial Intelligence (AI) across various sectors has accelerated in recent years, offering both transformative opportunities and pressing governance challenges. AI's ability to analyse vast datasets enhances predictive analytics and decision-making, but it also raises concerns around algorithmic bias, surveillance, and data misuse (Ijaiya, 2024). This duality positions AI as both a risk to and a solution for data privacy: while it introduces novel threats, it also provides advanced tools for strengthening privacy protection.

On the solution side, a growing body of research demonstrates AI's potential to embed privacy-preserving mechanisms directly into system design. Technical safeguards such as differential privacy and federated learning are increasingly recognised as foundational. Federated learning reduces risks by allowing models to be trained on decentralised data rather than central repositories, while differential privacy introduces statistical noise to protect against inference attacks (Al Said, 2025).

At the same time, scholars underscore that technical innovation must be matched by regulatory governance. The velocity of change necessitates that consideration be given to priority areas for regulatory focus. Frameworks combining real-time compliance mechanisms with privacy-preserving technologies illustrate the practical convergence of privacy-by-design with governance oversight (Devarasetty, 2023). Others emphasise the need for harmonised approaches to address the fragmented global regulatory landscape, calling for privacy-by-design principles to be embedded alongside enforceable regulatory obligations (Mbah, 2024). A broad survey of AI's role in privacy protection highlights both its promise and its ethical and regulatory challenges, reinforcing the necessity of integrated governance frameworks (Abolaji & Akinwande, 2024).

This call for unification is echoed in emerging frameworks that link privacy with fairness, accountability, and business optimisation, highlighting the need to combine technical and legal perspectives within AI governance (Oladosu et al., 2024). Practical examples of such convergence can be seen in

DOI: 10.1201/9781003626510-13

federated AI systems informed by zero trust principles, which demonstrate how technical design and governance integration can advance cyber defence (Lakshmikanthan & Nair, 2024).

This book chapter builds on these insights to argue that neither privacy-by-design nor privacy governance is sufficient in isolation. While technical measures mitigate many unintentional risks, intentional misuse and systemic harms require legal and institutional safeguards. Effective privacy protection, therefore, requires integration. To ground this argument, the paper employs the MIT AI Risk Repository, which catalogues AI risks according to causal origins (entity, intent, timing) and domains (including privacy and security). By analysing 173 privacy-related risks within this taxonomy, the paper demonstrates how vulnerabilities cluster into technological, regulatory, and dual categories. This analysis provides empirical validation for the *Unified Privacy Governance Framework (UPGF)*, which unifies technical and regulatory approaches. In doing so, the paper contributes both a descriptive taxonomy of privacy risks and a prescriptive framework for their governance.

AI and Data Governance

Debates on AI governance have increasingly centred on data ownership, transparency, accountability, and informed consent. Foundational work in enterprise contexts has highlighted the operational need for robust governance mechanisms. Nkeumo and Kiam (2025) outlined how businesses can adopt governance structures such as access controls, monitoring systems, and escalation pathways to manage privacy incidents, showing that corporate governance must evolve to address the ethical and legal dimensions of AI. A later elaboration by Schneider et al. (2020) expanded this into a four-dimensional governance model encompassing data, models, systems, and processes, providing organisations with actionable oversight strategies. Hickman and Petrin (2020) discuss the EU's Ethics Guidelines for Trustworthy Artificial Intelligence noting the challenges associated with deployment and the need for greater specificity in application. Comparable predictive approaches have also been applied in legal and economic domains, where statistical and neural network models were shown to anticipate governance-relevant outcomes (D'Rosario & Hsieh, 2018; D'Rosario & Zeleznikow, 2018).

At a broader international level, the OECD (2024) identifies a persistent disconnect between AI innovation and privacy governance, emphasising the lack of alignment between technical development and established privacy frameworks such as the GDPR. It argues that privacy considerations must be embedded at the earliest stages of AI system design and calls for international cooperation to harmonise principles and regulatory practices. Consequently, consideration must be given to achieving balance between unabated innovation and the broader public interest.

Trust and ethics are also central to governance debates. Sharma (2023) advocates for trustworthy AI systems that embed privacy as an architectural feature rather than as a reactive safeguard. This proactive framing aligns with calls for adaptive and hybrid governance models that integrate ethical, technical, and geopolitical considerations.

Regulatory Frameworks

The regulation of AI privacy has developed unevenly across jurisdictions, with regional frameworks reflecting different legal traditions, enforcement capacities, and policy priorities. The European Union's GDPR continues to serve as a benchmark, embedding principles of consent and accountability into data governance. The OECD (2024) builds on this, noting that while GDPR has influenced international debates, there remains a persistent disconnect between AI development and privacy regulation. Its recommendations for stronger international cooperation highlight the difficulty of aligning rapidly evolving AI technologies with static legal instruments.

In the United States, scholars have sought to reconcile fragmented state- and sector-specific laws. Chintoh et al. (2025) propose a U.S. focused privacy framework that integrates requirements under the CCPA, HIPAA, and GLBA, combining these legal obligations with technical measures such as automated audits and compliance monitoring. Their companion paper develops a conceptual model for harmonising compliance in sensitive domains such as healthcare and finance, arguing for traceable decision chains and explainability as methods to operationalise a privacy-by-design approach that is legally enforceable. Together, these contributions illustrate how U.S. AI privacy governance is moving towards hybrid frameworks that marry legal compliance with technical assurance.

The situation within Australia offers a stark contrast. The 2024 amendments to the Australian Privacy Act 1988 (Cth) sought to expand the investigative and enforcement powers of the Office of the Australian Information Commissioner (OAIC), Australia's peak privacy regulator. However, AI-specific regulation was notably absent, with the exception of new transparency requirements related to automated decision-making. The OAIC has, however, published guidance (2024, 2025) on how it interprets the Privacy Act's application to organisations that are either leveraging commercially available AI systems or developing and training generative AI models. Importantly, their view is that consent must generally be obtained for the use of sensitive information to train AI models or to enter sensitive information into commercial AI products. Moreover, they advise organisations against utilising people's sensitive information when interacting with publicly available AI systems.

Consent requirements for other types of non-sensitive personal information are less stringent and more nuanced, with consent exemptions available under the 'reasonably expects' test (OAIC, 2019). Despite their guidance and expanded powers, significant enforcement action remains to be seen. Furthermore, the Privacy Act exempts organisations with annual turnovers of less than AUD $3 million, except in specific cases. As a result, individuals have limited recourse when their personal information is compromised by small operators within the AI space. Nevertheless, additional regulatory change may be on the horizon. Australia's Attorney-General, Michelle Rowland (as cited in Mizen, 2025), has addressed concerns that the current Act is 'not fit for the digital age' and signalled that her department is drafting a second tranche of Privacy Act amendments specifically intended to address the rapid expansion of generative AI.

Much like in Australia, India's Digital Personal Data Protection Act 2023 appears to lack specific mention of the phrase 'artificial intelligence' or 'AI'. However, as a form of delegated regulation, the Act itself is not yet operational. At the time of writing, the implementing regulation, the Digital Personal Data Protection Rules, is available in draft form. The draft rules appear to provide exemptions for 'research, archiving, and statistical purposes' (Chakraborty & Sonkar, 2025). According to Chakraborty & Sonkar, these exemptions are an important step to foster an AI innovation environment within India, while provisioning privacy guardrails. However, it remains to be seen whether such guardrails are sufficiently robust to guide organisations to appropriately protect individual privacy.

Ye et al. (2024) argue that China has robust legislation governing privacy, established through several layers that span individual privacy rights, network and data security, and national security. However, the authors point to gaps in these laws regarding protection from AI-specific privacy risks, noting that China's framework values State security and data sovereignty over individual rights to privacy. They argue that gaps in this legislative framework provide little protection for individuals who voluntarily share information with artificial intelligence providers without understanding how the information may be processed. Furthermore, the authors highlight several mechanisms, such as voluntary disclosure of information by the individual or public disclosure by government agencies, that can limit individual privacy protections under both the Civil Code of the People's Republic of China and the Personal Information Protection Law (PIPL). Importantly for organisations, the PIPL applies to organisations outside of China that process information to provide products or services to Chinese nationals, or examine the behaviours of Chinese individuals (Tschider, 2023, p. 292).

Comparative studies have deepened this conversation. Dokumacı (2024) analyses regulatory approaches across jurisdictions, offering a taxonomy of gaps in current AI regulation and highlighting weaknesses in areas such as explainability, liability, and consent. This work stresses the need for regulatory harmonisation to prevent fragmented governance from undermining privacy protection.

Finally, Nkeumo and Kiam (2025) argue that current regulatory debates are disproportionately shaped by Western perspectives. They call for a globally adaptive AI privacy governance framework that accounts for local cultural values, infrastructure constraints, and legal traditions in non-Western contexts. Through situating these regulatory discussions within diverse global contexts, their work stresses the importance of regionally responsive frameworks that avoid imposing a one-size-fits-all model.

AI as Privacy Risk and Safeguard

AI's relationship with privacy is deeply paradoxical. On one hand, it introduces novel risks such as algorithmic surveillance and unintended disclosures. On the other hand, it offers a range of privacy-preserving solutions, enabling compliance and protection to be embedded within technical architectures.

AI as a Privacy Risk

Financial applications have been at the forefront of these challenges. Thoom (2025) highlights how credit scoring algorithms in finance risk unintended disclosure of sensitive information, while Matai (2024) points to privacy leakage caused by model drift and biased credit decisions in the BFSI sector. These examples illustrate how even highly regulated domains face systemic risks when AI systems lack safeguards. Broader analyses also flag governance gaps in complex infrastructures. Folorunso et al. (2024) examine hybrid cloud and AI deployments, noting that fragmented controls often leave privacy exposed across storage and computation layers. The Australian RoboDebt scheme provides a striking example of how automated systems can generate systemic harms through data misuse (D'Rosario & D'Rosario, 2021). The processing of welfare information without sufficient regulatory safeguards or viable knowledge of the legislative boundaries of data usage amplified risks for vulnerable groups; a pattern that resonates with the ways AI systems today may mishandle or exploit personal data in the absence of strong governance (D'Rosario & Falzon, 2023). Similarly, Leghemo et al. (2025b) identify multi-agent systems, such as those combining AI, IoT, and blockchain, as especially vulnerable to privacy breaches due to weak harmonisation of governance standards.

Privacy Risks: A Multimedia Perspective

AI Facial Recognition Technologies

In late 2024, two Harvard University students, Nguyen and Ardayfio, demonstrated the ease with which facial recognition technology could be combined with Meta's AI glasses to dox strangers (Hill, 2024). Facial recognition technologies utilise machine learning (e.g. support vector machines) and deep learning (e.g. convolutional neural networks) models to match reference images of individuals against image databases at high confidence intervals.

Crucially, these tools are highly accessible. Publicly available services, like PimEyes and FaceCheck, empower the average person to find images of individuals across the internet using just one reference photograph, while other services, such as Clearview, maintain that they are exclusively available to law enforcement and government agencies (Clearview AI, n.d.-a).

AI Facial Recognition in Law Enforcement

Clearview AI, Inc. advocates for its facial recognition technology as an instrument for public safety, arguing that it can be leveraged to locate victims of human trafficking (Clearview AI, n.d.-b) and identify suspected criminals (Clearview AI, n.d.-c, n.d.-d). However, researchers and policy organisations have been critical about the risks to privacy that Clearview's software poses. For instance, Elmi (2025) has raised concerns regarding how the company has scraped billions of images from social media without the informed consent of users, alongside legal issues related to the transfer of information across borders.

This data collection has led to significant regulatory findings against the company. A joint investigation by the OAIC and United Kingdom's Information Commissioner's Office found that Clearview AI breached the Australian Privacy Act 1988 (Cth) by collecting sensitive information without consent, among other allegations (Office of the Australian Information Commissioner, 2021). Furthermore, regulatory warnings were issued directly to law enforcement agencies; in 2021, the Australian Information and Privacy Commissioner warned the Australian Federal Police over concerns that its use of Clearview AI breached the Australian Privacy Principles (Office of the Australian Information Commissioner, 2021).

Facial Recognition: Individual Privacy Risks

The Electronic Frontier Foundation (2023) has expressed specific concerns with respect to the technology that may be subsumed into four risk axioms.

1. Threats to individual freedoms and civil liberties;
2. A lack of due process within legal proceedings when the technologies are leveraged with limited required approval or oversight;
3. Reliability and misidentification issues that disproportionately impact minority groups; and
4. Abuse of the technology by individuals within organisations who have access to more robust technologies not available to the public.

Similar views are shared by a wide gamut of think tanks globally, with many expressing concerns that inadequate regulations and governance of facial recognition technologies constitute a threat to both privacy and human right (Farthing et al., 2021; Madiega & Mildebrath, 2021). This threat is highly personalised; Kashmir Hill (in Allyn, 2023) of *The New York Times* emphasises that these technologies can be leveraged by individuals to dox (i.e. publicly identify an individual) people they encounter online or in person, a capability showcased by the system developed by Nguyen and Ardayfio (see inter alia, Allyn, 2023).

While facial recognition tools pose significant risks, some proponents highlight potential protective uses. PimEyes, for example, argues that its platform can be leveraged by women to identify and remove non-consensual pornography images from across the internet (Vallance, 2022). However, whether this can be practically achieved is debated. Concerns persist regarding the permanence of compromising content once distributed across the internet (Walker & Sleath, 2017).

The very features designed to track image proliferation can also enable misuse. Utilising these technologies to identify images provides a means for stalkers to identify important aspects of individuals' lives, including where they work or live (Vallance, 2022). This is particularly concerning for female activists and journalists according to Imam et al. (2025), who argue that women and marginalised groups are disproportionately targeted by digital surveillance programs by authoritarian governments.

AI Geolocation

Another frontier of concern is the use of Large Visual Language Models (LLVMs) as geolocation tools. These models can be used to pinpoint locations within photos and videos based on common patterns and recognisable objects. Research on LLVMs currently demonstrate the power of these systems: models exist that can identify image locations down to a 1km radius at >25% accuracy (under specific conditions), without requiring specific geographical training (Liu et al., 2024). Recent news articles have also highlighted the ease with which ChatGPT can be leveraged to identify photograph locations (Marcin, 2025; Wiggers, 2025), although research confirming its accuracy and specificity is currently lacking.

While these models may not yet be accurate or specific enough to locate an individual's home, local coffee shop, school, or workplace from a single image, when combined with other data about an individual or metadata sourced from facial recognition technologies, they offer a scary thought for those concerned about their personal privacy, particularly for vulnerable groups.

Image and Video Generation: Deepfakes

AI models for image and video generation boast powerful applications in both personal and organisational contexts. Not only are these models able to interpret individuals' ideas and translate them into exciting imagery in real time, but they also offer an opportunity on the organisational front to optimise efficiency within art and design departments.

Conversely, this same technology can be leveraged for more troublesome purposes, raising real privacy concerns for individuals. AI image generation tools enable the creation and editing of imagery of both real and fictional people; when images or videos are created in a real person's likeness, they are termed 'deepfakes'. Deepfakes can be used to spread misinformation and, concerningly, have been leveraged to create non-consensual synthetic pornography and 'synthetic child sexual abuse material' (Inman Grant, 2024).

While it is easy to see how images created non-consensually in an individual's likeness have ramifications for individual privacy, the risks are just as real for organisations. In one case involving complex social engineering, the implementation of deepfake technologies within a video call assisted a scammer in defrauding an organisation out of US $25 million (Chen & Magramo, 2024).

Voice and Text Generation: Impersonation Risks

In addition to generating imagery and videos, the capabilities of artificial intelligence extend to voice and text manipulation. Perhaps the most ubiquitous application has been text generation, where AI language models can be trained to create text replicating another person's tone-of-voice, based on information gathered from their social media and other documents.

Cloning an individual's voice and or tone may not seem a significant risk at face value, but when you consider that these technologies were likely leveraged in the story of an organisation being defrauded of US $25 million, the concern is heightened. Furthermore, there are real implications for those who earn a living with their voice, including voice actors, podcasters, musicians, and public speakers, as others can recreate content in their likeness, diluting the creator's earnings and brand value. Moreover, at least one case has been recorded of an individual using AI to impersonate, stalk, and harass another individual (McQue, 2025).

AI as a Privacy Safeguard

As previously mentioned, AI also enables technical mechanisms that directly protect privacy, with differential privacy and federated learning as two of the most widely adopted techniques. Al Said (2025) details how federated learning reduces risk by decentralising data, while differential privacy prevents inference attacks by introducing statistical noise. Building on these methods, Olarinde et al. (2024) propose an immune system-inspired framework that enhances federated learning security by integrating anomaly detection and differential privacy. Real-world implementations validate these approaches; Hamid and Bawany (2024) show how federated anomaly detection systems achieve privacy-preserving data processing in IoT and network security environments.

Integrated Governance and Technical Solutions

Several contributions demonstrate the convergence of technical and regulatory approaches in practice. Musyoka et al. (2024) present an AI-based oversight system trialled in the Nairobi government sector, designed for real-time consent monitoring and compliance. This case illustrates how privacy-preserving architectures can be operationalised as tools for regulatory enforcement, aligning technical innovation with public accountability.

Collectively, these studies indicate that AI functions simultaneously as a source of risk and as a mechanism of protection. The privacy paradox highlighted by Adapa (2024) captures this duality; *while AI's data-driven nature heightens privacy threats, its technical capabilities also enable stronger privacy-preserving architectures.* This paradox emphasises the need for governance models that bridge technical design and regulatory oversight, recognising that privacy cannot be secured through one dimension alone.

Integrative Frameworks and Governance Models

Research on hybrid approaches has progressed from high-level advocacy to concrete architectures that connect technical safeguards with legal and organisational controls. Lei et al. (2021) present a cross-modal implementation framework that translates abstract governance policies into machine-readable constraints and enforcement rules, so that legal and ethical mandates become executable behaviours within systems.

Pujari and Goel (2024) argue for supervised fine-tuning combined with privacy-preserving techniques and human oversight, treating alignment as both a technical and an institutional process. In their account, privacy objectives are embedded during model adaptation, while governance is operationalised through structured review, escalation pathways, and logging that supports accountability.

Bi et al. (2023) focus on foundation models, proposing a system design framework in which privacy controls sit alongside governance mechanisms from the outset. The framework integrates measures such as data minimisation, provenance tracing, and configurable release policies with oversight functions like impact assessment and incident response.

Taken together, these contributions show a common pattern. First, policy goals are formalised into technical artefacts, such as rules, prompts, and pipelines. Second, privacy-preserving mechanisms such as federated learning and differential privacy are integrated with explainability, logging, and access control. Third, organisational processes, such as review, escalation, and incident handling, are bound to system telemetry so that governance becomes routine rather than occasional. This literature provides the conceptual and practical foundations for a unified model of privacy governance that treats technical design and regulatory control as interdependent, enabling empirical testing against a comprehensive risk taxonomy.

Towards a Unified Privacy Governance Framework

AI privacy research has traditionally followed two complementary but frequently disconnected trajectories. The first emphasises privacy by design, embedding safeguards into the architecture of AI systems to mitigate risks like data leaking and inference attacks while simultaneously enabling compliance tools (Al Said, 2025; Devarasetty, 2023; Hamid & Bawany, 2024; Olarinde et al., 2024). This approach has increasingly expanded into governance-aware architectures where compliance mechanisms like consent management and data lineage tracking are automated as part of the AI lifecycle.

The second trajectory, privacy governance, emphasises the role of law, regulation, and institutional oversight. This perspective prioritises the integration of frameworks such as the GDPR, CCPA, HIPAA, and GLBA into AI practice, while also calling for stakeholder engagement and regionally adaptive models that reflect diverse legal and cultural contexts (Chintoh et al., 2025; Dokumacı, 2024; Nkeumo & Kiam, 2025).

Despite the richness of these strands, a persistent fragmentation remains. Technical scholarship often assumes compliance will follow automatically from architecture, while legal and policy analysis frequently abstracts away from questions of technical feasibility. While integrative models have begun to emerge (Bi et al., 2023; Lei et al., 2021; Pujari & Goel, 2024) that address several needs (i.e. cross-modal architectures that translate mandates into system rules or frameworks embedding accountability into foundation models), these contributions remain largely conceptual and limited in scope.

To bridge this divide, this paper introduces the Unified Privacy Governance Framework (UPGF), which treats privacy by design and privacy governance as interdependent. The UPGF recognises that while technical measures are effective at mitigating many unintentional vulnerabilities, regulatory and institutional safeguards are necessary to address intentional misuse and systemic harms.

To move beyond conceptual principles and provide empirical grounding, the framework utilises the MIT AI Risk Repository, a comprehensive taxonomy of AI risks. The study examines 173 privacy-related risks across causal and domain classifications, which demonstrates how vulnerabilities cluster into technological, regulatory, or combined categories. This taxonomy-based mapping serves as the foundation for validating the UPGF as a practical model for AI privacy governance and for bridging the divide between technical design and regulatory oversight.

Developing a Universal Governance Model

The MIT Causal Taxonomy: Entity, Intent, and Timing

The MIT AI Risk Repository provides one of the most comprehensive taxonomies for analysing artificial intelligence risks. Central to its framework is the causal taxonomy, which classifies risks according to three interrelated dimensions: entity, intent, and timing. These dimensions move beyond outcome-based or domain-specific analyses to explain how risks emerge, who or what generates them, and at what stage of the AI lifecycle they materialise.

Entity refers to the origin of a risk, distinguishing between humans, AI systems, and other infrastructures or institutions. Privacy vulnerabilities can stem from human actions, such as adversarial data poisoning or deliberate misuse, or from AI systems themselves, such as memorisation of personal information. Other risks arise from infrastructure, including storage systems or networks that fail to safeguard sensitive data.

Intent differentiates between intentional and unintentional risks. This distinction is especially relevant in privacy, where many breaches are not the result of malicious actions but of inadvertent leakage, model drift, or poorly configured systems. At the same time, intentional misuse remains a central concern for governance. The taxonomy also recognises ambiguous cases that fall into an *'other'* category, where intent is complex or contested.

Timing situates risks within the AI lifecycle, distinguishing between pre-deployment and post deployment contexts. Privacy threats occur during data collection and training, such as the inclusion of personally identifiable information (PII) in training corpora, as well as after deployment, where inference attacks or unauthorised data extraction can compromise end-users. Post-deployment risks dominate many contemporary cases, but the taxonomy underscores that privacy is a lifecycle issue that cannot be managed reactively alone.

The causal taxonomy combines these three dimensions to provide a structured lens for understanding the origins and trajectories of privacy risks. It moves beyond static regulatory categories to capture the dynamic interplay of design choices, system behaviours, and human actions. This framework offers a valuable foundation for this paper's empirical analysis; mapping 173 privacy-related risks across entity, intent, and timing not only reveals patterns of vulnerability but also highlights the essential nature of a dual governance approach that integrates technical and regulatory measures.

Privacy and Security in the MIT Domain Taxonomy

Alongside its causal framework, the MIT AI Risk Repository organises risks into a domain taxonomy, grouping them by areas of impact such as fairness, robustness, accountability, and security. Within this structure, privacy and security are defined together as Domain 2, reflecting their centrality in both scholarly debates and real-world applications of AI.

This domain encompasses risks that arise from the collection, processing, storage, and use of data by AI systems. It includes vulnerabilities ranging from inadvertent exposure of personally identifiable information (PII) to adversarial attacks designed to extract sensitive data, to systemic failures in data governance infrastructures. Importantly, the MIT repository does not treat privacy as a peripheral concern; it is positioned as one of the core risk domains, recognising that privacy breaches often cascade into wider harms involving trust and institutional legitimacy.

Within Domain 2, this study identified 173 distinct privacy-related risks. These span the full range of causal dimensions outlined in section titled, The MIT Causal Taxonomy: Entity, Intent, and Timing, arising from human actors, AI systems, and supporting infrastructures, and occurring both pre- and post-deployment. For the purposes of this paper, Domain 2 provides both a conceptual and an empirical anchor; it defines privacy as a distinct risk category while also situating it within the broader landscape of AI governance. This dual role makes it an ideal foundation for testing and validating the *UPGF* proposed here.

Privacy as a Systemic Risk

The analysis of the MIT AI Risk Repository demonstrates that privacy risks are not confined to narrow technical flaws or regulatory gaps but are instead distributed across the full spectrum of AI development and deployment. The 173 risks identified under Domain 2 reveal patterns that cut across entities, intents, and stages of the AI lifecycle.

First, the distribution of risks confirms that privacy breaches emerge from multiple origins. Human actors contribute to intentional harms such as adversarial data poisoning or malicious prompt injection. AI systems themselves generate unintentional risks, including memorisation of sensitive information and inference of private attributes. Supporting infrastructures introduce further vulnerabilities when poorly secured or misconfigured. Privacy governance therefore cannot focus solely on the AI model; it must account for the wider ecosystem of people, systems, and institutions.

Second, privacy risks differ markedly in intentionality. A large subset arises unintentionally through design oversights or weak safeguards. Yet many of the most damaging threats are intentional, from data exfiltration attacks to deliberate misuse of personal information in training or outputs. Ambiguous cases also persist, where intent is complex or contested, challenging governance models that rely on binary distinctions.

Third, privacy risks are evident at multiple stages of the AI lifecycle. Pre-deployment risks include the inclusion of PII in training datasets and poisoning of fine-tuning data, while post-deployment risks include inference attacks and systemic failures in consent management.

Taken together, these findings position privacy as a systemic risk which arises from the interactions of entities, intents, and timings across the AI ecosystem. The 90 technological risks, 14 regulatory risks, and 69 dual risks identified in the taxonomy illustrate this point. Technical safeguards alone cannot prevent intentional misuse, while regulatory oversight alone cannot correct unintentional design flaws. Privacy protection therefore demands an integrated model that unifies technical and regulatory approaches across the lifecycle. This systemic character provides the empirical grounding for the UPGF advanced in this paper.

Mapping Outcomes: Mapping Privacy Risks to Governance Dimensions

Technological Risks

The largest category of privacy risks identified in the MIT repository falls under the technological dimension, with 90 items. These risks arise primarily from weaknesses in system design, data handling, and model behaviour. They are most often unintentional, emerging from technical flaws rather than deliberate misuse, though their effects can still be severe. Key examples include the following (non-exhaustive) items.

- *Data memorisation and leakage,* where AI systems inadvertently store and reproduce sensitive information from training corpora.
- *Inference attacks* allowing adversaries to reconstruct or infer private attributes based on model outputs.
- *Unsafe training and fine-tuning practices,* including the incorporation of personally identifiable information or uncurated data into training datasets.

Analysis by causal taxonomy highlights two dominant patterns:

1. AI–unintentional–post-deployment risks (e.g. unsafe outputs, memorisation, model inversion).
2. Human–intentional–post-deployment risks linked to adversarial misuse of system vulnerabilities (e.g. malicious inputs, jailbreaks).

These patterns suggest that privacy harms are embedded not only in the architecture of AI models but also in their operational environments. Addressing these harms requires a dual approach: employing privacy-preserving techniques and establishing robust technical governance.

Regulatory Risks

A smaller but distinct category of risks identified in the MIT repository falls under the regulatory dimension, with 14 items. These risks emerge where mechanisms and institutional safeguards are absent, insufficient, or circumvented. Unlike many technological risks, regulatory risks often involve intentional misuse. Examples include the following risk items.

- Malicious exploitation of weak or absent regulation, such as surveillance practices that operate outside existing legal safeguards.
- Systemic misuse of personal information, particularly in cases where frameworks such as GDPR, CCPA, or HIPAA lack effective enforcement.
- Illegal collection and processing of data, including the use of proprietary or confidential datasets without consent.

Causal taxonomy mapping shows a strong concentration of human–intentional–post-deployment risks. These reflect misuse by organisations, firms, or malicious actors exploiting regulatory gaps. A smaller subset involves AI–unintentional–other risks, highlighting how technical outcomes may still raise regulatory concerns when governance is not adequately adapted.

The relative scarcity of regulatory risks compared with technological ones does not diminish their significance. Instead, it highlights their systemic nature; even a small number of governance failures can have wide-ranging consequences, particularly where private data are exploited at scale. Mitigating these risks requires not only stronger enforcement of existing legal frameworks but also international harmonisation of privacy regulation, as highlighted in recent OECD (2024) and comparative governance studies.

Dual Risks

The most analytically significant category consists of the dual risks, with 69 items classified as requiring both technological and regulatory responses. These risks highlight the interdependence of privacy by design and privacy governance. Examples of dual risks include the following.

- Inference and extraction attacks, where adversaries deliberately manipulate AI systems to reveal confidential information.
- Unsafe training and fine-tuning data, where sensitive or proprietary information is embedded in models.
- Unsafe external tool integration and APIs, where insecure connections expose personal data.
- Legacy models and infrastructures that continue to expose sensitive data in the absence of decommissioning or regulatory mandates.

Causal taxonomy analysis reveals that dual risks are distributed across all entities (AI systems, humans, and infrastructures), are both intentional and unintentional in nature, and span pre- and post-deployment phases. What distinguishes these risks is the necessity of coordination for mitigation.

Conversely, 90 risks are classified as needing technological safeguards, and 14 require regulatory mechanisms. However, technical measures alone cannot close legal loopholes, nor can regulation alone prevent vulnerabilities baked into system design. The presence of such a large proportion of dual risks empirically validates the central claim of this paper; that privacy protection in AI requires a Unified Privacy Governance Framework (UPGF), one that embeds safeguards within systems while also enforcing them institutionally.

Cross-Tab Analysis of Privacy Risks

To complement the categorical analysis of technological, regulatory, and dual risks, the 173 privacy-related risks were mapped across the MIT causal taxonomy dimensions of entity, intent, and timing. This analysis reveals broader patterns of how privacy vulnerabilities originate, whether they stem from intentional or unintentional actions, and when in the AI lifecycle they occur. The findings highlight three key patterns in risk distribution.

1. Human–intentional–post-deployment risks dominate, particularly in regulatory and dual categories. These include adversarial attacks, malicious prompt injections, and systemic misuse of private data. Their prevalence (totalling 47 in the analysed sample) confirms the need for robust enforcement and institutional accountability.
2. AI–unintentional–post-deployment risks are widespread across technological (13 risks) and dual (10 risks) categories. Examples include unsafe outputs, model memorisation of sensitive data, and long-context window vulnerabilities.
3. Pre-deployment risks remain under-addressed. While less numerous than post-deployment vulnerabilities, these risks demonstrate that privacy protection must be lifecycle-wide, not only reactive.

These results confirm that privacy risks are not only numerous but systemically distributed across the AI ecosystem.

The Unified Privacy Governance Framework (UPGF)

The analysis of the MIT AI Risk Repository highlights a fundamental insight: privacy risks in AI are neither purely technical nor purely regulatory. Of the 173 risks identified, 90 map primarily to technological vulnerabilities, 14 to regulatory gaps, and 69 to dual risks requiring both approaches in tandem.

This distribution provides empirical evidence that privacy governance must be conceived as an integrated system, not as two parallel traditions.

The UPGF responds to this challenge by treating privacy by design and privacy governance as interdependent dimensions. Rather than viewing technical safeguards and regulatory oversight as alternatives or sequential steps, the UPGF positions them as mutually reinforcing. Technical measures mitigate unintentional risks by embedding protections within systems, while regulatory mechanisms constrain intentional misuse and ensure accountability. Together, they form a governance architecture capable of addressing privacy as a systemic risk that spans the AI lifecycle. The UPGF advances three principles.

1. Integration of Safeguards: Privacy-preserving technologies such as differential privacy, federated learning, and anomaly detection must be embedded within AI systems and tied to compliance tools like audit trails, consent management, and explainability.
2. Lifecycle Orientation: Privacy governance must operate across pre-deployment and post-deployment stages, from data sourcing and model training to deployment, monitoring, and decommissioning.
3. Mutual Reinforcement: Regulatory obligations and technical solutions should not be siloed; instead, they should be designed to reinforce one another. For example, legal requirements for traceability can be operationalised through explainability frameworks, while technical logs can provide evidence for regulatory enforcement.

The UPGF thus provides a conceptual and practical model that captures the systemic character of AI privacy risks revealed in the taxonomy. It builds on existing literature advocating for privacy by design and privacy governance but moves beyond their fragmentation, offering a unified framework validated through empirical risk mapping.

Validation of UPGF through Taxonomy Analysis

The empirical analysis of 173 privacy-related risks provides a structured basis for validating the Unified Privacy Governance Framework (UPGF) by demonstrating how vulnerabilities cluster across technological, regulatory, and dual dimensions. This distribution confirms that neither technical safeguards nor legal standards are sufficient in isolation to address the systemic nature of AI privacy harms.

While the 90 technological risks are primarily addressed through architectural safeguards, these measures remain insufficient without regulatory oversight to prevent intentional misuse or poor implementation. Similarly, the 14 regulatory risks, which often involve the intentional exploitation of legal gaps and surveillance outside of established safeguards, cannot be

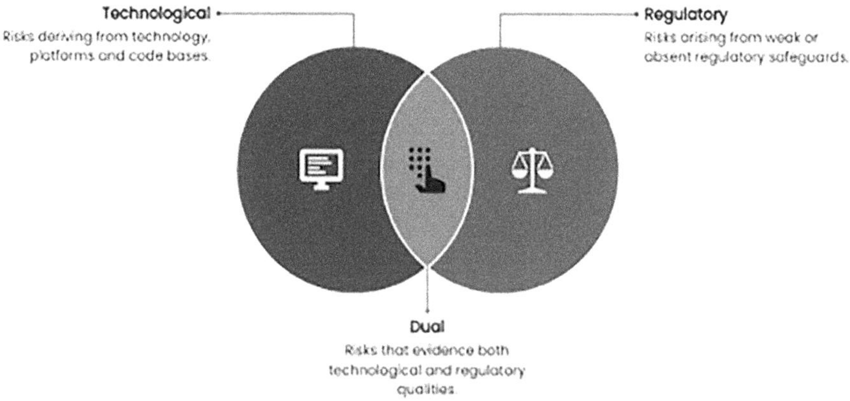

FIGURE 13.1
The UPGF for AI risk categorisation.

Note: This diagram evidences that not all risks are equal and indeed common, evidencing that risks may be technological, regulatory or both per the UPGF.

Source: Author's illustration.

resolved through policy alone; they require complementary technical hardening and accountability mechanisms to be effective.

The causal taxonomy further reinforces this necessity for integration by highlighting a heavy concentration of risks in post-deployment environments and a persistent interplay between AI-driven and human-originating threats.

Collectively, these findings provide empirical validation for the UPGF. They show that privacy risks in AI are systemically distributed, necessitating that effective governance integrates both technological and regulatory dimensions. The UPGF aligns these traditions, providing a framework that responds directly to the patterns revealed in the MIT AI Risk Repository and bridging the gap between conceptual advocacy in the literature and empirical evidence of risk distribution (Figure 13.1).

Privacy as a Lifecycle and Systemic Governance Challenge

As established in the taxonomy mapping, these risks span the entire AI lifecycle, requiring continuous oversight from data sourcing through to decommissioning. Cumulatively, these findings confirm that privacy protection in AI is a systemic challenge; it spans multiple origins, involves both malicious and inadvertent actions, and persists across the entire lifecycle.

Addressing it requires governance models that are adaptive and multidimensional. The UPGF reflects this reality by insisting on the integration of privacy by design with privacy governance, ensuring that safeguards are embedded from the outset, monitored throughout deployment, and enforced through institutional accountability.

Policy and Practice Implications

The findings of this study carry significant implications for both policy and practice. The taxonomy analysis shows that privacy risks in AI are pervasive, lifecycle-wide, and frequently dual in nature. Effective governance therefore requires interventions that operate across technical and regulatory domains, reinforcing one another rather than functioning in isolation.

For technical practice, developers and system architects must embed privacy-preserving technologies throughout the AI lifecycle. Methods such as differential privacy, federated learning, anomaly detection, and explainability frameworks should be standardised as baseline safeguards. Equally, infrastructures must support continuous monitoring, with tools such as audit logs, consent dashboards, and lineage tracking to provide evidence for compliance and accountability. These measures align with privacy-by-design principles but require institutional adoption to be consistently implemented.

For regulatory policy, governments and oversight bodies must strengthen enforceable obligations around AI privacy. This includes clear standards for data collection and use, mandatory transparency and explainability requirements, and cross-border harmonisation of privacy regulations. Enforcement should extend beyond static compliance checks to include dynamic monitoring, incident reporting, and liability frameworks that hold organisations accountable for misuse or negligence. The OECD's (2024) call for international cooperation remains particularly urgent, given the global reach of AI technologies.

For integrated governance, the results emphasise the importance of frameworks that explicitly combine technical and regulatory mechanisms. Examples include compliance models that operationalise legal requirements through explainability and traceability tools, or technical audits that generate artefacts for regulatory reporting. Public–private partnerships and international standard-setting bodies will be essential to ensure that privacy safeguards are interoperable across jurisdictions and sectors.

Together, these implications highlight the necessity of adopting models like the Unified Privacy Governance Framework (UPGF). By embedding technical protections, enforcing regulatory standards, and fostering integration between the two, UPGF provides a roadmap for managing privacy as a systemic risk in AI. Its adoption can support trust in AI systems, protect individual rights, and ensure that innovation proceeds without compromising fundamental data protection principles.

Conclusion and Recommendations

This paper has examined AI privacy risks through the lens of the MIT AI Risk Repository, identifying 173 privacy-related risks distributed across technological (90), regulatory (14), and dual (69) categories. The analysis of these risks by entity, intent, and timing demonstrates that privacy vulnerabilities are systemic, lifecycle-wide, and cannot be addressed by technical or regulatory measures in isolation.

The contribution of this study lies in advancing and empirically validating the Unified Privacy Governance Framework (UPGF). Integrating privacy by design with privacy governance, the UPGF responds to the fragmentation evident in the literature and aligns with the evidence provided by the MIT taxonomy. Technical safeguards, such as differential privacy, federated learning, and anomaly detection, mitigate unintentional vulnerabilities, while regulatory frameworks ensure accountability for intentional misuse and systemic gaps. Together, they create a governance model capable of managing privacy as a systemic risk.

Recommendations arising from this analysis are threefold. Firstly, technical practice should adopt privacy-preserving tools and continuous monitoring infrastructures as standard components of AI design and deployment. Secondly, regulatory policy should strengthen enforceable obligations, ensure international harmonisation, and develop mechanisms for dynamic oversight rather than static compliance. Thirdly, integrated governance models should be institutionalised, linking technical artefacts with regulatory accountability to provide mutually reinforcing safeguards.

Future research should extend this taxonomy-informed approach to other risk domains within the MIT repository, such as fairness and robustness, and explore how the UPGF can be operationalised in practice through case studies and empirical testing across industries. In treating AI as both a risk and a solution for data privacy, this study underscores the necessity of unified governance. Future research could examine corresponding AI-based approaches through an aligned 'solutions taxonomy' to offer an integrated framework for risk identification, cohort grouping, and redress. Embedding safeguards throughout the lifecycle and enforcing them through legal and institutional frameworks allows AI to be developed and deployed in ways that protect privacy while enabling innovation.

References

Abolaji, E. O., & Akinwande, O. T. (2024). AI powered privacy protection: A survey of current state and future directions. *World Journal of Advanced Research and Reviews*, 23(3), 2687–2696. https://doi.org/10.30574/wjarr.2024.23.3.2869

Adapa, V. R. K. (2024). Navigating the privacy paradox: Balancing AI advancement and data protection in the digital age. *International Journal of Scientific Research in Computer Science, Engineering and Information Technology*, 10(6), 99–110. https://doi.org/10.32628/CSEIT24106158

Allyn, B. (2023, October 9). *Why silicon valley hasn't released face search engines.* NPR. https://www.npr.org/2023/10/09/1204724356/why-silicon-valley-hasnt-released-face-search-engines

Al Said, N. (2025). Federated learning for privacy-preserving AI: Challenges, applications, and future directions. *Panamerican Mathematical Journal*, 35, 3s. https://doi.org/10.52783/pmj.v35.i3s.4054

Bi, T., Yu, G., & Wang, Q. (2023). Privacy in Foundation Models: A Conceptual Framework for System Design. *arXiv e-prints*, arXiv-2311.

Chakraborty, S., & Sonkar, S. (2025, January 2025). *Decoding India's draft DPDPA rules for the world.* IAPP. https://iapp.org/news/a/decoding-india-s-draft-dpdpa-rules-for-the-world

Chen, H., & Magramo, K. (2024, February 4). Finance worker pays out $25 million after video call with deepfake 'chief financial officer. *CNN.* https://edition.cnn.com/2024/02/04/asia/deepfake-cfo-scam-hong-kong-intl-hnk

Chintoh, G. A., Segun-Falade, O. D., Odionu, C. S., & Ekeh, A. H. (2025). Developing a conceptual framework for U.S. Data privacy compliance in AI systems: Integrating CCPA and HIPAA regulations. *International Journal of Frontline Research and Reviews*, 4(1), 011–019. https://doi.org/10.56355/ijfrr.2025.4.1.0034

Clearview AI. (n.d.-a). *FAQ.* Retrieved 22 September 2025, from https://www.clearview.ai/faq

Clearview AI. (n.d.-b). *Rescuing a Minor From Her Violent Trafficker.* Retrieved 24 September 2025, from https://www.clearview.ai/success-stories/rescuing-a-minor-from-her-violent-trafficker

Clearview AI. (n.d.-c). *The Miami Police Department Locates a Fleeing Homicide Suspect.* Retrieved 24 September 2025, from https://www.clearview.ai/success-stories/the-miami-police-department-locates-a-fleeing-homicide-suspect

Clearview AI. (n.d.-d). *Two Law Enforcement Agencies Solve a Murder and Attempted Murder.* Retrieved 24 September 2025, from https://www.clearview.ai/success-stories/two-law-enforcement-agencies-solve-a-murder-and-attempted-murder

D'Rosario, M., & D'Rosario, C. (2021). Beyond RoboDebt: The future of robotic process automation. *International Journal of Strategic Decision Sciences (IJSDS)*, 11(2), 1–24. https://doi.org/10.4018/978-1-7998-9023-2.ch072

D'Rosario, M., & Falzon, J. (2023). *Distress amplification: Robodebt notices and the intensification of distress in the unemployed.* Per Capita.

D'Rosario, M., & Hsieh, C. (2018). Predicting credit rating migration employing neural network models. *International Journal of Strategic Decision Sciences (IJSDS)*, 9(4), 70–85. https://doi.org/10.4018/IJSDS.2018100105

D'Rosario, M., & Zeleznikow, J. (2018). Compliance with international soft law: Is the adoption of soft law predictable? *International Journal of Strategic Decision Sciences (IJSDS)*, 9(3), 1–15. https://doi.org/10.4018/IJSDS.2018070101

Devarasetty, N. (2023). AI-driven data governance frameworks for enhanced privacy and compliance. *International Journal of Scientific Research and Management (IJSRM)*, 11(2), 983–1006. https://doi.org/10.18535/ijsrm/v11i02.ec4

Dokumacı, M. (2024). Legal frameworks for AI regulations. *Human Computer Interaction*, 8(1), 133. https://doi.org/10.62802/ytst2927

Electronic Frontier Foundation. (2023, September 23). *Face Recognition.* https://sls.eff.org/technologies/face-recognition

Elmi, M. (2025). Faces and places: Navigating the cross-border legal challenges of AI facial recognition technologies. *AI and Ethics*, 5(5), 5453–5466. https://doi.org/10.1007/s43681-025-00787-5

Farthing, S., Howell, J., Lecchi, K., Paleologos, Z., Saintilan, P., & Santow, E. (2021). *Human rights and technology final report*. Attorney-General's Department.

Folorunso, A., Babalola, O., Nwatu, C. E., & Ukonne, U. (2024). Compliance and governance issues in cloud computing And AI: USA And Africa. *Global Journal of Engineering and Technology Advances*, 21(2), 127–138. https://doi.org/10.30574/gjeta.2024.21.2.0213

Hamid, S., & Bawany, N. (2024). Federated Learning for Enhanced Intrusion Detection in Smart City Environments. 1-6. https://doi.org/10.1109/ICOSST64562.2024.10871154

Hickman, E., & Petrin, M. (2020). trustworthy AI and corporate governance: The EU's ethics guidelines for trustworthy artificial intelligence from a company law perspective. *European Business Organization Law Review*, 22, 593–625. https://doi.org/10.1007/s40804-021-00224-0

Hill, K. (2024, October 24). Two students created face recognition glasses. It Wasn't Hard. *The New York Times*. https://www.nytimes.com/2024/10/24/technology/facial-recognition-glasses-privacy-harvard.html

Ijaiya, H. (2024). Balancing data privacy and technology advancements: Navigating ethical challenges and shaping policy solutions. *International Journal of Research Publication and Reviews*, 5, 8118–8130. https://doi.org/10.55248/gengpi.5.1224.3549

Imam, M., Manimekalai, N., & Suba, S. (2025). From data to discrimination: Gender, privacy, and the politics of digital surveillance. *Synergy: International Journal of Multidisciplinary Studies*, 2(2), 52–64. https://doi.org/10.63960/sijmds-2025-2262

Inman Grant, J. (2024, July 24). *Addressing deepfake image-based abuse*. ESafety Commissioner. https://www.esafety.gov.au/newsroom/blogs/addressing-deepfake-image-based-abuse

Lakshmikanthan, G., & Nair, S. S. (2024). Proactive cybersecurity: Predictive analytics and machine learning for identity and threat management. *International Journal of Multidisciplinary Research in Science, Engineering and Technology*, 7(12), 17488–17496.

Leghemo, I. M., Segun-Falade, O. D., Odionu, C. S., & Azubuike, C. (2025b). Designing a data governance framework for cybersecurity risk reporting: A model for business intelligence teams. *Engineering And Technology Journal*, 10(1 (Jan. 2025), 3712–3728. https://doi.org/10.47191/etj/v10i01.28.

Lei, Y., Duan, Y., & Song, M. (2021). Technical implementation framework of AI governance policies for cross-modal privacy protection. In: Gao, H., Wang, X., Iqbal, M., Yin, Y., Yin, J., Gu, N. (eds) Collaborative computing: Networking, applications and worksharing. CollaborateCom 2020. Lecture notes of the institute for computer sciences, social informatics and telecommunications engineering, vol 350. Springer, Cham. https://doi.org/10.1007/978-3-030-67540-0_27

Liu, Y., Ding, J., Deng, G., Li, Y., Zhang, T., Sun, W., Zheng, Y., Ge, J., & Liu, Y. (2024). *Image-Based Geolocation Using Large Vision-Language Models*. http://arxiv.org/abs/2408.09474

Madiega, T., & Mildebrath, H. (2021). *Regulating Facial Recognition in the EU*. https://doi.org/10.2861/140928

Marcin, T. (2025, April 18). ChatGPT reverse location search trend raises privacy issues. *Mashable*. https://mashable.com/article/chatgpt-reverse-location-search-privacy-concerns

Matai, P. (2024). Comprehensive guide to AI regulations: Analyzing the EU AI act and global initiatives. *International Journal of Computing and Engineering*, 6(1), 45–54. https://doi.org/10.47941/ijce.2110

Mbah, G. O. (2024). Data privacy in the era of AI: Navigating regulatory landscapes for global businesses. *International Journal of Science & Research Archive*, 13(2), 2040–2058. https://doi.org/10.30574/ijsra.2024.13.2.2396

McQue, K. (2025, February 1). A man stalked a professor for six years. Then he used AI chatbots to lure strangers to her home. *The Guardian*. https://www.theguardian.com/technology/2025/feb/01/stalking-ai-chatbot-impersonator

Mizen, R. (2025, July 24). Attorney-general Michelle Rowland defends NACC, flags AI law changes. *The Australian Financial Review*. https://www.afr.com/politics/federal/rowland-defends-nacc-flags-privacy-crackdown-on-ai-20250723-p5mh98

Musyoka, G. V., Mutua, R. M., & Tocho, J. (2024). AI-based framework for government oversight of personal data consent compliance: A case study of Nairobi county. *International Journal of Professional Practice*, 12(6), 40–48.

Nkeumo, A. M. T., & Kiam, K. (2025). Rethinking global AI privacy: Bridging theory, practice, and diverse regulatory contexts. *International Journal of Science and Research*, 14(1), 1285–1288. https://doi.org/10.21275/SR25127051226

Office of the Australian Information Commissioner. (2019, July 22). *Chapter 6: APP 6 Use or disclosure of personal information*. https://www.oaic.gov.au/privacy/australian-privacy-principles/australian-privacy-principles-guidelines/chapter-6-app-6-use-or-disclosure-of-personal-information

Office of the Australian Information Commissioner (2021, November 3). *Clearview AI breached Australians' privacy*. Office of the Australian Information Commissioner. https://www.oaic.gov.au/news/media-centre/clearview-ai-breached-australians-privacy

Office of the Australian Information Commissioner. (2024, October 23). *Guidance on privacy and developing and training generative AI models*. https://www.oaic.gov.au/privacy/privacy-guidance-for-organisations-and-government-agencies/guidance-on-privacy-and-developing-and-training-generative-ai-models

Office of the Australian Information Commissioner. (2025, January 17). *Guidance on privacy and the use of commercially available AI products*. https://www.oaic.gov.au/privacy/privacy-guidance-for-organisations-and-government-agencies/guidance-on-privacy-and-the-use-of-commercially-available-ai-products

Oladosu, S. A., Ike, C. C., Adepoju, P. A., Afolabi, A. I., Ige, A. B., & Amoo, O. O. (2024). Frameworks for ethical data governance in machine learning: Privacy, fairness, and business optimization. *Magna Scientia Advanced Research and Reviews*, 07(02), 96–106. https://doi.org/10.30574/msarr.2023.7.2.0043

Olarinde, M., Abiona, A. A., & Ajinaja, M. O. (2024). Adaptive and privacy-preserving security for federated learning using biological immune system principles. *Asian Journal of Computer Science and Technology*, 13(2), 67–72. https://doi.org/10.70112/ajcst-2024.13.2.4303

Organisation for Economic Co-operation and Development (OECD). (2024). *AI, data governance and privacy*. OECD Artificial Intelligence Papers.

Pujari, A., & Goel, D. (2024). Ensuring responsible AI: The role of supervised fine-tuning (SFT) in upholding integrity and privacy regulations. *International Journal of Science and Technology*, 3(3). https://doi.org/10.56127/ijst.v3i3.1968

Schneider, J., Abraham, R., Meske, C., & Brocke, J. V. (2020). AI governance for businesses. *arXiv preprint arXiv:2011.10672*.

Sharma, S. (2023). Trustworthy artificial intelligence: Design of AI governance framework. *Strategic Analysis*, 47(5), 443–464. https://doi.org/10.1080/09700161.2023.2288994

Thoom, S. R. (2025). Lessons from AI in finance: Governance and compliance in practice. *International Journal of Science and Research Archive*, 14(1), 1387–1395. https://doi.org/10.30574/ijsra.2025.14.1.0235

Tschider, C. A. (2023). *International cybersecurity and privacy law in practice* (2nd ed.). Wolters Kluwer Law International. http://ebookcentral.proquest.com/lib/adelaide/detail.action?docID=30734437

Vallance, C. (2022, November 8). Stalking fears over PimEyes facial search engine. *BBC News*. https://www.bbc.co.uk/news/technology-63544169

Walker, K., & Sleath, E. (2017). A systematic review of the current knowledge regarding revenge pornography and non-consensual sharing of sexually explicit media. *Aggression and Violent Behavior*, 36, 9–24. https://doi.org/10.1016/j.avb.2017.06.010

Wiggers, K. (2025, April 17). *The latest viral ChatGPT trend is doing 'reverse location search' from photos*. Techcrunch. https://techcrunch.com/2025/04/17/the-latest-viral-chatgpt-trend-is-doing-reverse-location-search-from-photos/

Ye, X., Yan, Y., Li, J., & Jiang, B. (2024). Privacy and personal data risk governance for generative artificial intelligence: A Chinese perspective. *Telecommunications Policy*, *48*(10), Article 102851. https://doi.org/10.1016/j.telpol.2024.102851

14

Sustainable AI Beyond Ecological Integrity: A Capability-Based Framework for Design

Daniel M. Phoenix

Introduction

Artificial Intelligence (AI) is inseparable from the infrastructures that sustain modern societies. Expanding data centres increasingly compete with public utilities for electricity, water, and land. At the same time, the computational demands of advanced AI models translate into mounting pressures on mineral extraction and energy systems. Crucially, these rising energy demands coincide with a demonstrable inability of governments and businesses to deploy clean energy systems at the scale and speed required to replace fossil fuels. This difficulty concerns not only the substitution of existing energy supply, but even more the construction of energy systems capable of accommodating rapidly growing demand while remaining compatible with the objectives of the Paris Agreement. Sustainable AI, in this sense, cannot be reduced to post hoc mitigation strategies such as efficiency gains or emissions offsets alone. It also requires rethinking the very criteria of good design and the forms of responsibility they entail under conditions of converging technical and ecological constraints.

This challenge intersects with broader debates in environmental ethics and conservation policy. These debates focus on the values and assumptions that underpin sustainability frameworks. Accelerating climate and biodiversity crises demand normative approaches capable of responding to urgent time horizons, yet the ethical foundations of conservation and sustainability remain contested. Disagreements persist over what ought to be sustained, for whose benefit, and according to which moral priorities. These questions surface in emerging work on human–Earth relations and in dominant approaches to biodiversity governance (Secretariat of the Convention on Biological Diversity [SCBD], 2011), where sustainability goals are articulated through a mixture of ecological, social, and institutional considerations that are often left implicit. Clarifying these underlying value commitments is a

DOI: 10.1201/9781003626510-14

necessary step if sustainability is to function as a coherent and actionable guiding concept rather than a rhetorical placeholder.

The broader significance of this problem becomes especially clear when viewed against the infrastructural demands of the energy transition. Maintaining technological competitiveness and leadership in AI may require the expansion of tens of gigawatts of additional energy capacity within only a few years (Anthropic, 2025), even as states pursue deep decarbonisation and ecological stabilisation. Achieving this dual objective is historically unprecedented. It calls not only for the greening of existing systems, but also for the creation of new technological capacities that operate within the planet's regenerative dynamics. Under these conditions, sustainability can no longer be treated as an external constraint on innovation; it becomes a constitutive question about what kinds of socio-technical systems ought to be built and sustained.

Against this backdrop, the chapter addresses a set of foundational research questions that structure contemporary debates on sustainable AI. What are the implicit assumptions embedded in prevalent definitions of sustainable AI? More specifically, what exactly is being sustained, for what reasons, and according to which normative principles? By foregrounding these questions, the chapter opens a critical space for examining the dominance of ecological integrity as a guiding normative ideal, and for exploring alternative moral orientations capable of addressing the hybrid and managed environments characteristic of the Anthropocene. Within this space, the chapter situates weak anthropocentrism and a capability-based approach as key conceptual resources for rethinking sustainability in AI design.

The chapter proceeds as follows. It first situates debates on sustainable AI within broader discussions at the intersection of AI ethics, environmental ethics, and social and political theory. This section clarifies how prevailing frameworks conceptualise sustainable AI, with particular attention to the normative role assigned to ecological integrity. The chapter then develops its core theoretical argument. It questions ecological integrity as a reliable normative anchor for sustainable AI and advances an alternative framework grounded in weak anthropocentrism and the capability approach. This reorientation reshapes assumptions about responsibility, governance, and decision-making. To ground these arguments, the chapter introduces a case study focused on the deployment of AI-based heat optimisation systems in power plants. The case illustrates how the capability framework can be used to clarify what sustainability aims to achieve and to what extent AI systems can contribute to these ends. The chapter concludes by synthesising its central insights and articulating actionable recommendations directed primarily at researchers and educators, with particular attention to design schools and design practitioners. These recommendations highlight how a clearer normative orientation can inform responsible approaches to AI development and evaluation in practice.

Theoretical Framework

A growing body of scholarship has emphasised that the stakes of sustainable AI lie in bridging ethical aspiration with the material constraints of technological development. One influential contribution is the distinction between *AI for sustainability* and *the sustainability of AI* (van Wynsberghe, 2021). This distinction clarifies that AI can function as a tool for advancing sustainability goals. It also highlights that AI is itself a technological system whose resource demands generate new environmental pressures. Treating these two dimensions in isolation obscures how they converge in practice. An AI model that improves weather forecasting, for example, may generate clear social benefits. At the same time, it may consume large quantities of clean electricity that compete with other socially valuable uses. In the absence of frameworks capable of assessing social and environmental gains together, sustainability risks becoming a rhetorical add-on. It fails to function as a governing principle of AI development.

Within this landscape, much of AI ethics has focused on abstract principles such as fairness, accountability, and transparency (see Floridi & Cowls, 2019; Jobin et al., 2019). These principles remain normatively important. On their own, however, they provide limited guidance for assessing whether AI systems are environmentally viable or oriented towards socially defensible ends. The problem is therefore not a lack of ethical reflection. It is the absence of conceptual and practical tools that allow engineers, researchers, and institutions to align technical performance metrics with publicly justifiable goals.

Environmental ethics offers a parallel set of debates that further illuminate these challenges. Existing approaches to sustainability differ markedly in how they define what ought to be sustained and why. Some models emphasise balancing economic, social, and environmental objectives. Others prioritise economic feasibility or ecological primacy (Moyano-Fernández & Rueda, 2023). These models draw, implicitly or explicitly, on broader ethical traditions such as anthropocentrism, biocentrism, and ecocentrism (Moyano-Fernández & Rueda, 2023). Importing these traditions into AI debates helps to clarify underlying value commitments. It also exposes unresolved tensions. Strongly ecocentric approaches, for instance, risk rendering most modern technologies ethically suspect. More economically driven approaches struggle to account for long-term ecological limits. Across these positions, sustainability is frequently invoked as a goal. Its normative foundations, however, remain underspecified.

This under-specification becomes visible in the broader AI ethics and sustainability literature. A growing number of studies examine the environmental impacts of AI. These include work exposing anthropocentrism and speciesist bias (Hagendorff et al., 2023), mapping unequal carbon and water footprints (Li et al., 2024), measuring emissions from large-scale model training (Liu & Yin, 2024), and situating algorithms within social–ecological–technological systems (Rakova & Dobbe, 2023). These contributions are predominantly descriptive or review-oriented. Other authors propose abstract criteria for sustainable AI (Alloghani, 2024; Rohde et al., 2023). Some publish policy advice on the carbon impacts of AI (Taddeo et al., 2021). Together, these works make sustainability visible. They rarely articulate a unifying normative orientation capable of guiding design, governance, and education.

Insights from narrative-oriented research reinforce this diagnosis. Analyses of ethical narratives in AI show that themes such as bias, transparency, and fairness dominate scholarly attention. Sustainability remains marginal. When environmental issues do appear, they are often framed as technical challenges. They are treated as secondary considerations rather than central normative questions. This limited focus is notable given evidence from earth system science that current trajectories threaten global habitability. The risks are particularly acute in vulnerable regions. From this perspective, sustainability is not merely a constraint on AI development. It is a condition of legitimacy and long-term viability. Without rapid decarbonisation, the expansion of energy-intensive infrastructures such as data centres may weaken economies and national security. It may fail to support them.

Taken together, these strands of literature point to a deeper gap. Ethical concern for sustainability is present. However, it lacks the normative and imaginative resources required to structure governance, education, and professional practice. A small number of exceptions suggest what a richer normative imagination might involve. Coeckelbergh (2021) draws on literary and political tropes to rethink freedom and collective life under the combined pressures of AI and climate change. Brevini (2022) similarly centres the climate crisis in AI debates. He challenges solutionist narratives and advances a green agenda. More recently, fragments of sustainability discourse have begun to take narrative form. These cast AI in competing roles within the energy transition. One depicts AI as an efficiency engine that reduces carbon costs through computational optimisation (Strubell et al., 2019). A second presents AI as a grid stressor. It warns that growing workloads may strain power systems depending on grid composition (Patterson et al., 2021). A third is especially visible in corporate and policy discourse. It casts AI as a catalyst for the energy transition. Examples include exploration of nuclear and fusion power as low-carbon enablers of AI growth (Amazon, 2024; Chernicoff & Vincent, 2025; Wile, 2024). National plans to expand nuclear infrastructure in order to attract data-centre investment follow a similar logic (Buenos Aires Times, 2024). These proto-narratives show how sustainability can function as a frame of legitimation, caution, or strategic vision. Their incompleteness, however, reveals a deeper problem. Compared with mature ethical tropes such as trust or risk, sustainability remains underdeveloped as a normative orientation for governance and education.

This chapter responds to that gap by questioning the implicit reliance on ecological integrity as a self-sufficient normative anchor for sustainable AI. Ecological integrity plays a central role in conservation biology and environmental governance. Its unexamined transfer into AI ethics can obscure the trade-offs and human purposes that shape technological development in managed and hybrid environments. In place of this assumption, the chapter advances a framework grounded in weak anthropocentrism and the capability approach. This framework does not deny ecological limits. It reframes sustainability in terms of the conditions required for human flourishing within those limits. By clarifying what sustainability aims to achieve, the capability approach provides a normative orientation suited to evaluating AI under ecological constraint. It also clarifies the extent to which AI systems can contribute to these ends when guided by defensible principles.

In the sections that follow, this framework provides the basis for both theoretical analysis and practical application. It examines the assumption of ecological integrity embedded in prevailing definitions of sustainable AI. It also advances an alternative account of what sustainable AI ought to achieve and the criteria by which it should be evaluated.

Main Discussion/Analysis

A Minimal Capability-Based Rationale for Sustainable AI

Sustainable AI should be discussed under conditions of partial compliance (see Rawls, 1999: 8) and pressing timeframes. Contemporary debates on sustainable AI unfold under conditions of deep normative disagreement. In plural societies, there is no shared account of what sustainability requires or how environmental burdens should be distributed. Competing positions range from growth-oriented and techno-optimistic views to precautionary and preservationist ones. Each position rests on distinct assumptions about risk, responsibility, and acceptable trade-offs. These disagreements are not merely theoretical. They increasingly translate into policy uncertainty and delayed action. This situation is especially problematic given the accelerating deployment of AI systems. Global warming trajectories are approaching scenarios beyond the 2°C threshold above pre-industrial levels. In this context, insisting on comprehensive agreement about environmental ethics risks postponing decisions until ecological limits make them ineffective. What is needed instead is a pragmatic normative orientation. Such an orientation must be capable of guiding action while commanding broad assent across divergent value positions.

The capability approach offers such a foundation. As a normative tradition, it evaluates social arrangements in terms of what people are genuinely able to do and be, rather than in terms of aggregate resources or technical outputs (Nussbaum, 2011; Sen, 1999). Capabilities denote real opportunities to do and be, while functionings refer to achieved states of being and doing. This distinction preserves respect for pluralism and personal choice. At the same time, it retains a substantive concern for justice and human development.

The approach also recognises that technologies operate through conversion factors. These include personal, social, and environmental conditions that mediate how resources become what Sen called substantive freedoms (Robeyns, 2005). Building on this perspective, sustainable AI can be evaluated through three normative criteria. These criteria specify how AI systems should contribute to human flourishing. They operate as a minimal framework rather than a comprehensive theory of justice. Their purpose is to guide concrete decisions in contexts of urgency and uncertainty.

The first criterion evaluates AI as an environmental conversion factor. AI systems mediate how material, informational, and institutional conditions translate into human capabilities (Robeyns, 2005). Technologies do not merely add new functions. They reorganise the environments within which people act. AI systems redistribute informational asymmetries and influence institutional norms. They also reshape built and digital spaces, including welfare systems, credit markets, education, and energy infrastructures. As conversion factors, AI systems condition whether resources become genuine opportunities or remain inaccessible in practice. From this perspective, ethical relevance lies not primarily in accuracy or efficiency. It lies in whose capabilities are expanded or constrained. It also lies in the social and ecological conditions under which these effects occur. Conversion effects are rarely neutral. Some systems increase efficiency while narrowing agency for disadvantaged groups. Others expand access while locking societies into fragile infrastructures. Treating AI as a conversion factor therefore requires attention at the design stage. Designers must assess differential capability effects. They must also consider the ecological context in which these effects are produced. Sustainable AI must, at a minimum, expand real freedoms without eroding the conditions that make those freedoms durable.

The second criterion assesses AI in terms of its role as an ecological stabiliser. AI systems are embedded in energy-intensive infrastructures and global supply chains. They therefore exert material pressure on ecological systems. Within the capability approach, these conditions are captured through the notion of sustainable ecological capacity (Holland, 2008). This metacapability secures the biophysical preconditions for all other capabilities. No capability can be exercised without such conditions. Ecological stability is therefore not external to freedom. It is constitutive of it. Evaluating AI as an ecological stabiliser requires assessing whether systems maintain or erode this ecological capacity. AI can intensify degradation through energy-intensive model training or extractive hardware supply chains. It can also support stabilisation through applications such as grid optimisation, demand management, and resource-efficient logistics. A defensible account of sustainable AI must therefore ask whether systems operate within admissible ecological thresholds. It must also assess whether efficiency gains still generate rebound effects that increase overall ecological load. While precise limits remain contested, the 2°C threshold articulated in the Paris Agreement provides a politically salient reference point for identifying unacceptable levels of ecological stress.

The third criterion treats AI as a potential source of human sufficiency. Rather than maximising performance or growth, sustainable AI should secure threshold conditions for living with dignity and agency. Sufficiency has been developed within political philosophy and the capability approach as a threshold-based ethic (Axelsen & Nielsen, 2015; Nielsen & Axelsen, 2017). It specifies the minimum conditions for human flourishing. Axelsen and Nielsen characterise sufficiency as freedom from persistent threats to basic well-being or autonomy. Nussbaum similarly argues that justice requires guaranteeing threshold levels of central capabilities. These include bodily health, education, affiliation, and practical reason. Sufficiency does not require uniform outcomes. It allows for plural ways of life while maintaining a shared ethical floor below which no one should fall. Applied to AI, sufficiency directs attention to three domains of capabilities. These include basic capabilities such as health and physical security. They also include autonomy capabilities such as learning and self-determination. Finally, they include social involvement capabilities such as participation in economic, social, and political life. AI contributes to sustainability when it secures these thresholds. It fails when gains for some leave others below them.

From Ecological Integrity to Weak Anthropocentrism: Governing Sustainable AI under Constraint

The normative framework advanced here rests on two explicit philosophical assumptions that shape how sustainability is understood in the context of AI. The first is a commitment to weak anthropocentrism, which treats human flourishing as the primary evaluative reference point while rejecting the reduction of environmental value to mere utility for human survival or a set of indefinitely exploitable resources. The second is a critical stance towards ecological integrity as a self-sufficient normative anchor for sustainable AI. Together, these assumptions seek to provide ethical guidance that remains action-guiding in technologically managed and ecologically constrained environments. They do so by acknowledging ecological limits while avoiding static or preservationist ideals that struggle to accommodate hybrid socio-technical systems.

Prevailing definitions of sustainable AI often rely, implicitly or explicitly, on ecological integrity as their normative assumption. Originating in environmental ethics and conservation biology—most notably through interpretations of Leopold's land ethic (Callicott, 1989)—ecological integrity has been understood as the preservation of ecosystem wholeness, stability, or fidelity to a baseline state. In contexts of habitat protection or ecological restoration, this concept has clear normative force. It provides a compelling rationale for limiting human intervention and for prioritising the protection of relatively intact ecological systems.

Difficulties arise, however, when ecological integrity is transferred uncritically into the domain of AI ethics. Integrity-based approaches presuppose relatively stable reference conditions, a meaningful distinction between natural and human-made systems, and governance horizons oriented towards preservation or restoration. These assumptions fit poorly with the socio-technical environments in which AI systems operate. Contemporary AI infrastructures are embedded in hybrid systems—energy grids, data centres, mineral supply chains, and global logistics networks—that irreversibly reshape ecological processes rather than merely disturb them. In such contexts, appeals to ecological integrity risk functioning as an ill-fitting benchmark: interpreted strictly, they render most large-scale AI systems ethically suspect by default; interpreted flexibly, they lose determinate guidance and collapse into vague calls for environmental responsibility.

Rather than grounding sustainability in abstract notions of natural wholeness, the normative orientation developed here treats ecological conditions as enabling constraints. These conditions must be maintained not only for their own sake, but because they make meaningful human freedom possible in an already transformed world. From this perspective, the problem is not that ecological limits are irrelevant to AI ethics, but that integrity-oriented framings struggle to guide action in managed, path-dependent, and infrastructure-intensive systems. This motivates a shift towards normative frameworks capable of integrating ecological constraints with human agency, institutional responsibility, and design-stage decision-making, without foreclosing action under conditions of urgency.

This mismatch generates a familiar form of political paralysis. If ecological integrity is interpreted strictly, most large-scale AI systems appear ethically impermissible by default. Their material and energy demands are decisive. Similarly, if integrity is interpreted flexibly, it loses normative force. It collapses into a vague appeal to environmental responsibility. In either case, ecological integrity seems to be problematic to provide actionable guidance. This failure becomes acute under pressing temporal constraints. Climate change trajectories approaching or exceeding the 2°C threshold exemplify this urgency. The problem is not that existing ecological limits lack importance. The problem is that integrity-oriented framings are too static and indeterminate for managed, hybrid, and path-dependent technological environments. Recognising these limits does not abandon environmental concern. It motivates a reorientation towards frameworks that integrate ecological constraints with human agency and institutional responsibility.

Subsidiarity as a Governance Principle for Sustainable AI

Debates on sustainable AI inevitably confront a foundational question in environmental ethics: whether sustainability should be grounded in human-centred values or in forms of value that are independent of human interests. Much contemporary work gestures towards non-anthropocentric ideals, seeking to extend moral standing to ecosystems, species, or ecological wholes. While philosophically compelling, these approaches face practical difficulties when translated into policy and technological governance, particularly under conditions of urgency, institutional inertia, and entrenched socio-technical systems. At the same time, purely instrumental, human-centred approaches have proven normatively unstable, often justifying environmental protection only insofar as it serves immediate human benefits. This tension has left sustainability ethics oscillating between moral ambition and practical impotence. The following discussion situates sustainable AI within this dilemma and argues that resolving it requires a reconstructed form of weak anthropocentrism, paired with a governance principle capable of accommodating both instrumental and non-instrumental moral claims.

The concept of anthropocentrism involves three layers of meaning. In its broadest sense, it means that human perspectives, interests, or forms of valuation are the primary reference point for moral judgement. However, this does not necessarily deny value to nonhuman beings or ecological systems. Rather, it holds that moral claims are articulated, justified, and institutionalised through human evaluative frameworks. This distinguishes anthropocentric approaches from non-anthropocentric ones, which seek to ground moral value independently of human interests or perspectives. A first important distinction concerns instrumental and non-instrumental anthropocentrism. Instrumental anthropocentrism assigns value to nonhuman nature insofar as it contributes to human goals, such as health, security, or economic welfare. Ecosystems are protected because they provide services or resources that humans depend upon. By contrast, non-instrumental anthropocentrism allows that nonhuman beings or ecological relations can matter for reasons that are not reducible to utility, even though those reasons are still recognised and justified through human moral reasoning (see Hargrove, 1992). In this view, humans may have obligations to protect nature that are not exhausted by its usefulness. A second distinction separates strong and weak anthropocentrism (Norton, 1984). Strong anthropocentrism restricts moral consideration to immediate human preferences or interests, often privileging short-term benefits or economic efficiency. Weak anthropocentrism, by contrast, adopts a broader and more reflective conception of human well-being. It recognises that human flourishing depends on stable ecological conditions, meaningful relationships with the nonhuman world, and long-term forms of responsibility compatible with environmental sustainability. Weak anthropocentrism therefore permits non-instrumental concern for nonhuman beings, while retaining a human-centred evaluative structure.

This dual structure gives weak anthropocentrism much of its appeal, but it also generates a persistent normative problem. Instrumental and non-instrumental justifications coexist within the same ethical orientation, yet their relationship remains unclear. Conservation goals are often presented as intrinsically valuable, while being defended in practice through their contribution to human well-being. Major policy frameworks exemplify this ambiguity. Biodiversity protection, ecosystem integrity, and species preservation are described as goods in themselves, but they are also justified by reference to ecosystem services, resilience, and human security (SCBD, 2011, 2020). A similar pattern appears in capability-based approaches, where the protection of species or ecological systems is framed both as an end and as a condition for human flourishing (Marris, 2021). What functions as an instrument for achieving other ends cannot, without tension, simultaneously constitute those ends. When left unresolved, this ambiguity weakens the action-guiding capacity of weak anthropocentrism.

The instability becomes most visible when instrumental reasoning fails to provide sufficient grounds for action. Ecosystem service valuations often break down under conditions of uncertainty, long temporal horizons, or irreversible risk (Sagoff, 1999). Species or habitats with little measurable utility struggle to secure protection, even when their loss generates widespread moral unease. In such cases, technically optimal outcomes leave behind what Marris (2021) describes as moral residue: a sense that something ethically important has been sacrificed, even though instrumental criteria have been satisfied. Appeals to intrinsic value then emerge as corrective responses. Yet when they are invoked only after instrumental reasoning collapses, they tend to arrive too late to reshape decisions already driven by short-term priorities or institutional inertia.

The subsidiarity rule addresses this long-standing difficulty by introducing an ordering between instrumental and non-instrumental justifications, rather than treating them as interchangeable or competing foundations. Instrumental reasoning retains priority. It provides the primary mode of justification because it aligns with existing institutional settings, policy processes, and developmental priorities. In contexts where environmental protection competes with urgent human needs, instrumental arguments offer conservation and sustainability their strongest foothold. Non-instrumental justifications enter subsidiarily. They become decisive when instrumental reasoning proves incomplete, unstable, or ethically insufficient. Intrinsic concern thus functions as a continuous safeguard rather than as an exceptional appeal, ready to assume normative force whenever instrumental criteria fail to capture what is at stake.

Applied to sustainable AI, subsidiarity stabilises weak anthropocentrism as a coherent ethical orientation. It allows sustainability to be justified first through human-centred reasons such as health, security, and long-term welfare, while ensuring that non-instrumental concerns are not excluded when utility-based reasoning reaches its limits. In energy-intensive and infrastructure-dependent AI systems, instrumental arguments may justify optimisation, efficiency, or transitional deployment. When such arguments risk legitimising irreversible ecological harm or morally unacceptable trade-offs, subsidiarity permits non-instrumental considerations to constrain or override them. In this way, weak anthropocentrism remains politically resonant and practically usable, while avoiding collapse into narrow instrumentalism. Subsidiarity does not resolve all ethical disagreement. It provides an ordering principle that preserves action-guidance under pressure and clarifies how different forms of moral reasoning should interact when governing sustainable AI.

Case Study: AI Heat Optimisers in Power Generation

The energy sector is central to current debates on sustainable AI. Power plants remain a major source of global emissions, while also supplying the electricity on which data centres and AI systems depend. This makes efficiency improvements in existing power infrastructure especially significant. Recent industry analyses show that AI is increasingly used not to expand energy production, but to optimise how existing plants operate. One prominent example is the deployment of AI-based heat-rate optimisers in thermal power plants, which improve efficiency by continuously adjusting operational variables such as temperature, pressure, and fuel–air ratios in real time (McKinsey & Company, *AI and Energy Innovation*). Reported deployments have achieved measurable reductions in fuel use and emissions without new physical infrastructure, relying instead on human-in-the-loop integration with established operational practices. While such systems do not resolve the broader challenges of decarbonisation, they provide a concrete and realistic setting for assessing how AI can contribute to sustainability through design-stage interventions under real-world institutional and material conditions.

Viewed through the lens of the capability framework, AI-based heat optimisers function as environmental conversion factors. They reshape how existing energy infrastructures translate material inputs into socially valuable outputs. Power plants already possess the physical capacity to generate electricity, but the extent to which this capacity contributes to human capabilities depends on operational conditions such as efficiency, emissions intensity, and reliability. Heat optimisers intervene precisely at this level. By analysing sensor data and recommending adjustments to operating parameters, these systems alter the conditions under which electricity is produced, reducing fuel consumption and emissions while maintaining output. In doing so, they change the capability-relevant consequences of the same physical infrastructure. Electricity generated with lower emissions supports a wider range of human capabilities, including health, environmental security, and economic stability. This conversion effect is not automatic. It depends on design choices, human oversight, and institutional settings. When embedded in human-in-the-loop workflows and aligned with sustainability objectives, heat optimisers enhance the conversion of energy resources into capabilities without increasing ecological burden. When detached from such contexts, the same technology may reinforce rebound effects or lock in carbon-intensive assets.

Beyond their role in reshaping conversion processes, heat optimisers can also be assessed in terms of their contribution to ecological stability. Power plants operate within tightly coupled systems, where small efficiency gains can have cumulative effects on fuel demand, emissions trajectories, and local environmental stress. By lowering the heat rate of generation, AI-driven optimisation reduces the fuel required per unit of electricity, easing pressures along extraction, transport, and combustion chains. In this respect, heat optimisers can contribute to moderating emissions pathways and slowing growth in resource throughput within existing energy systems. Their stabilising potential, however, is conditional rather than inherent. Efficiency gains may be offset by rebound effects if lower operating costs extend the economic life of carbon-intensive assets. Whether heat optimisers support longer-term stability therefore depends on how they are embedded within decarbonisation strategies, regulatory constraints, and transition timelines. When deployed as transitional tools aligned with emissions caps and phase-out plans, they can help moderate system-level impacts. When treated as substitutes for structural change, they risk entrenching existing dependencies.

From a sufficiency perspective, the ethical relevance of heat optimisers lies in their capacity to protect specific central capabilities. Following Axelsen and Nielsen's typology, sufficiency concerns whether individuals can live free from duress by securing thresholds of basic, autonomy-related, and social participation capabilities. Heat optimisers primarily contribute to the protection of basic capabilities, including access to reliable energy services necessary for bodily health, shelter, and physical security. Electricity underpins heating and cooling, food preservation, water treatment, and healthcare delivery. Disruptions or price volatility in energy supply disproportionately threaten these foundational conditions, particularly for vulnerable populations. By improving efficiency and operational stability in existing power plants, heat optimisers can help maintain adequate energy provision during transitional periods, reducing the risk of shortages or cost spikes that would undermine these basic capabilities.

Beyond basic capabilities, heat optimisers can indirectly support autonomy-related capabilities by stabilising the material conditions that allow individuals and communities to plan, work, and pursue life projects without persistent energy insecurity. Predictable access to electricity supports education, employment, and household decision-making, even if these effects remain secondary to the protection of basic needs. Their contribution to social participation capabilities is more limited, but still relevant insofar as stable energy systems sustain communication networks, transport infrastructures, and civic institutions. A sufficiency-oriented evaluation also sets clear limits on the ethical role of optimisation. Heat optimisers are defensible only insofar as they help secure capability thresholds without normalising excess consumption or postponing structural energy transitions. Their justification lies not in maximising efficiency or profitability, but in ensuring that no one falls below the minimum energy conditions required for a life of dignity while broader transformations are underway.

Conclusion

This chapter has argued that debates on sustainable AI require a shift in normative orientation, not merely incremental refinements of existing ethical principles. The growing energy and material demands of AI systems coincide with well-documented limits in the capacity of governments and markets to rapidly replace fossil-based infrastructures while meeting climate commitments. Under these conditions, sustainability cannot be treated as an external constraint addressed after deployment, nor as a purely technical problem of efficiency. It must be integrated into the evaluative criteria that guide AI design and governance from the outset.

To meet this challenge, the chapter advanced a pragmatic normative framework grounded in weak anthropocentrism and subsidiarity. Weak anthropocentrism was defended not as a philosophical compromise, but as a necessary orientation under conditions of urgency and pluralism: one that retains political traction while extending moral concern beyond narrow instrumentalism. Subsidiarity translated this ethical stance into a governance principle, clarifying how responsibility for sustainability should be distributed across design teams, organisations, and regulatory levels. Together, these commitments provide an action-guiding alternative to integrity-based approaches that struggle to offer determinate guidance in hybrid, infrastructure-intensive technological systems.

The triadic capability framework further specified how sustainable AI can be assessed in practice. By examining AI systems as environmental conversion factors, potential contributors to ecological stability, and sources of human sufficiency, the framework links technological design choices to concrete human and ecological outcomes. The case study of AI-based heat optimisers in power plants illustrated how these criteria can operate at the design and deployment stage, revealing both the potential and the limits of optimisation-based interventions. Heat optimisers neither resolve the structural challenges of decarbonisation nor justify unbounded AI expansion. Their ethical relevance lies in their capacity to protect foundational human capabilities, moderate system-level impacts, and support transitional pathways without normalising excess or deferring responsibility.

More broadly, the chapter suggests that sustainable AI should be evaluated not by whether it preserves an idealised state of ecological integrity, but by whether it sustains the conditions under which human and nonhuman flourishing remain possible in an already transformed world. This reframing does not abandon ecological seriousness. It redirects it towards criteria that remain workable under time pressure, institutional constraint, and technological path dependence. In doing so, the framework aims to support responsible AI development that is normatively grounded, practically applicable, and responsive to the realities of the Anthropocene.

Actionable Recommendations for Researchers and Educators

For researchers, this framework implies a need to reorient sustainable AI research towards design-relevant evaluation rather than retrospective impact assessment alone. Much existing work documents energy use, emissions, or environmental footprints after systems are built. While necessary, this approach offers limited guidance to engineers working under uncertainty and time pressure. Research should therefore focus more explicitly on how sustainability considerations can be integrated into early-stage system design, model selection, and infrastructure planning. This includes developing methods that connect technical choices—such as optimisation objectives, system boundaries, and deployment contexts—to their downstream effects on human capabilities and ecological stability. Interdisciplinary research that combines AI engineering with systems thinking, energy modelling, and social evaluation is particularly important, as sustainability challenges rarely align with disciplinary boundaries. Rather than treating sustainability as a separate constraint, researchers should frame it as a core dimension of system performance, alongside accuracy, robustness, and safety.

For educators, particularly in engineering and design schools, the chapter highlights the importance of embedding sustainability into how future practitioners learn to reason about AI systems. Ethics education often emphasises abstract principles or isolated dilemmas, while technical courses prioritise optimisation and efficiency. A capability-based perspective suggests a different pedagogical focus. Students should be trained to evaluate how AI systems shape real opportunities for human flourishing through their interaction with infrastructures, institutions, and environments. This calls for greater use of systems-oriented teaching approaches, where students analyse AI not as standalone artefacts but as components of complex socio-technical systems. Design exercises can require students to articulate which human capabilities a system is intended to protect or enhance, how ecological impacts are distributed, and where thresholds of sufficiency lie.

Across engineering curricula, sustainability should be treated as a design problem rather than solely as a regulatory or compliance issue. Case-based learning—drawing on domains such as energy systems, urban infrastructure, or industrial optimisation—can help students practise navigating trade-offs under real-world constraints. Importantly, this does not require the adoption of a single moral doctrine. Instead, it equips students with a structured way to reason about responsibility, limits, and priorities in pluralistic contexts. By strengthening systems thinking and normative judgement together, engineering education can better prepare designers to develop AI systems that are not only technically effective, but also socially legitimate and ecologically viable.

References

Alloghani, M. A. (2024). Criteria for sustainable AI software: Development and evaluation of sustainable AI products. In *Artificial intelligence and sustainability* (pp. 33–51). Springer. https://doi.org/10.1007/978-3-031-45214-7_2

Amazon. (2024). *New report shows that AI can help advance fusion energy, ushering in a cleaner energy future.* https://www.aboutamazon.eu/news/sustainability/new-report-shows-that-ai-can-help-advance-fusion-energy-ushering-in-a-cleaner-energy-future

Anthropic. (2025). *Build AI in America.* https://www.anthropic.com/news/build-ai-in-america

Axelsen, D., & Nielsen, L. (2015). Sufficiency as freedom from duress. *Journal of Political Philosophy*, *23*(4), 406–426. https://doi.org/10.1111/jopp.12048

Brevini, B. (2022). *Is AI good for the planet?* Polity Press.

Buenos Aires Times. (2024). *Milei vows to promote nuclear energy in Argentina.* https://www.batimes.com.ar/news/argentina/milei-vows-to-promote-nuclear-energy-in-argentina.phtml

Callicott, J. B. (1989). *In defense of the land ethic: Essays in environmental philosophy.* State University of New York Press.

Chernicoff, D., & Vincent, M. (2025). *Google's nuclear move with elementl signals broader energy shift for AI-driven data centers.* Data Center Frontier. https://www.datacenterfrontier.com/energy/article/55002443/googles-nuclear-move-with-elementl-signals-broader-energy-shift-for-ai-driven-data-centers

Coeckelbergh, M. (2021). *Green leviathan or the poetics of political liberty: Navigating freedom in the age of climate change and artificial intelligence.* Routledge.

Floridi, L., & Cowls, J. (2019). A unified framework of five principles for AI in society. *Harvard Data Science Review*, *1*(1). https://doi.org/10.1162/99608f92.8cd550d1

Hagendorff, T., Bossert, L. N., Tse, Y. F., & Singer, P. (2023). Speciesist bias in AI: How AI applications perpetuate discrimination against animals. *AI and Ethics*, *3*, 717–734. https://doi.org/10.1007/s43681-022-00199-9

Hargrove, E. C. (1992). Weak anthropocentric intrinsic value. *The Monist*, *75*(2), 183–207.

Holland, B. (2008). Justice and the environment in Nussbaum's capabilities approach. *Political Research Quarterly*, *61*(2), 319–332. https://doi.org/10.1177/1065912907306471

Jobin, A., Ienca, M., & Vayena, E. (2019). The global landscape of AI ethics guidelines. *Nature Machine Intelligence*, *1*, 389–399. https://doi.org/10.1038/s42256-019-0088-2

Li, P., Yang, J., Wierman, A., & Ren, S. (2024). Towards environmentally equitable AI via geographical load balancing. In *Proceedings of the 15th ACM International Conference on Future and Sustainable Energy Systems (E-Energy '24)* (pp. 1–17). ACM. https://doi.org/10.1145/3632775.3661938

Liu, V., & Yin, Y. (2024). Green AI: Exploring carbon footprints, mitigation strategies, and trade-offs in large language model training. *Discover Artificial Intelligence, 4*, Article 49. https://doi.org/10.1007/s44163-024-00149-w

Marris, E. (2021). *Wild souls: Freedom and flourishing in the non-human world*. Bloomsbury Publishing.

McKinsey & Company (2025). *AI and energy innovation*. McKinsey & Company.

Millennium Ecosystem Assessment (2005). *Ecosystems and human well-being: Synthesis*. Island Press.

Moyano-Fernández, C., & Rueda, J. (2023). AI, sustainability, and environmental ethics. In F. Lara & J. Deckers (Eds.), *Ethics of artificial intelligence* (pp. 219–236). Springer. https://doi.org/10.1007/978-3-031-48135-2_11

Nielsen, L., & Axelsen, D. V. (2017). Capabilitarian sufficiency: Capabilities and social justice. *Journal of Human Development and Capabilities, 18*(1), 46–59.

Norton, B. G. (1984). Environmental ethics and weak anthropocentrism. *Environmental Ethics, 6*(2), 131–148. https://doi.org/10.5840/enviroethics19846233

Nussbaum, M. C. (2011). *Creating capabilities: The human development approach*. Harvard University Press.

Patterson, D., Gonzalez, J., Le, Q., Liang, C., Munguia, L.-M., Rothchild, D., So, D., Texier, M., & Dean, J. (2021). *Carbon emissions and large neural network training. arXiv*. https://doi.org/10.48550/arXiv.2104.10350

Rakova, B., & Dobbe, R. (2023). Algorithms as social–ecological–technological systems: An environmental justice lens on algorithmic audits. In *Proceedings of the ACM Conference on Fairness, Accountability, and Transparency (FAccT '23)*. https://doi.org/10.1145/3593013.3593988

Rawls, J. (1999). *A theory of justice* (Rev ed.). The Belknap Press of Harvard University Press.

Robeyns, I. (2005). The capability approach: A theoretical survey. *Journal of Human Development and Capabilities, 6*(1), 93–117. https://doi.org/10.1080/146498805200034266

Rohde, F., Wagner, J., Meyer, A., Reinhard, P., Voss, M., Petschow, U., & Mollen, A. (2023). Broadening the perspective for sustainable artificial intelligence. *AI and Ethics, 3*, 115–132. https://doi.org/10.1007/s43681-022-00140-0

Sagoff, M. (1999). *The economy of the earth* (2nd ed.). Cambridge University Press.

Secretariat of the Convention on Biological Diversity (2011). *Convention on biological diversity: Text and annexes*. UNEP.

Secretariat of the Convention on Biological Diversity (2020). *Global biodiversity outlook 5*. UNEP.

Sen, A. (1999). *Development as freedom*. Alfred A. Knopf.

Strubell, E., Ganesh, A., & McCallum, A. (2019). Energy and policy considerations for deep learning in NLP. In *Proceedings of the 57th Annual Meeting of the ACL* (pp. 3645–3650). https://doi.org/10.48550/arXiv.1906.02243

Taddeo, M., Tsamados, A., Cowls, J., & Floridi, L. (2021). Artificial intelligence and the climate emergency. *One Earth, 4*(6), 776–779. https://doi.org/10.1016/j.oneear.2021.05.018

van Wynsberghe, A. (2021). Sustainable AI: AI for sustainability and the sustainability of AI. *AI and Ethics, 1*, 213–218. https://doi.org/10.1007/s43681-021-00043-6

Wile, R. (2024). *Three Mile island nuclear plant to help power Microsoft's data-center needs*. NBC News. https://www.nbcnews.com/business/business-news/three-mile-island-nuclear-plant-help-power-microsoft-data-center-needs-rcna171958

15

The Five Horsemen of the AI Apocalypse: A Framework for Understanding Algorithmic Injustice and Governance

Nici Sweaney

Artificial intelligence does not merely classify, predict, or optimise. It governs. It decides who is visible and who is forgotten; who moves through systems with ease and who is trapped in loops of friction; whose labour is accelerated and whose is erased; whose dignity is protected and whose is repeatedly traded away for efficiency (e.g. Eubanks, 2018; Nemani et al., 2023; Richardson, 2021). AI increasingly functions as an infrastructure of social ordering, distributing power in ways that are often opaque and unaccountable (Crawford & Paglen, 2021; Eubanks, 2018). As a result, questions of *justice*—not only accuracy or performance—sit at the core of contemporary algorithmic governance.

However, the global discourse on "AI fairness" has largely narrowed to statistical parity and compliance checklists (e.g. Lifshitz & McMaster, 2020). These tools have value, but they do not resolve the deeper political, historical, and structural dynamics through which harm emerges. Fairness metrics cannot recognise the mother denied rental housing by an opaque risk model, nor the migrant worker whose income is destabilised by a content moderation algorithm that misinterprets their dialect, nor the public servant whose job disappears because optimisation was prioritised over social value (e.g. Dastin, 2018; ILO, 2023). As Noble (2018) and Benjamin (2019) argue, algorithmic systems are never neutral: they reflect the social conditions, power relations, and institutional logics from which they emerge (Hoffmann, 2021; Shieh et al., 2025; Winner, 1980).

This chapter argues that the real problem is not that AI occasionally goes wrong, but that it often goes *right*: optimising for institutional priorities, economic logics, and governance structures that were never designed with everyone in mind. To do this, I introduce the Five Horsemen of the AI Apocalypse, a diagnostic framework through analysis of hundreds of real-world deployments. These five dynamics (development bias (Ofosu-Asare, 2024; Walter & Suina, 2019), training data bias (Crawford & Paglen, 2021), access inequality

 DOI: 10.1201/9781003626510-15

(Kaakandikar, 2025; Van Bussel, 2024), displacement risk (Kyriakidou et al., 2025), and feedback loop amplification (McIntosh et al., 2024; Papamichail et al., 2024)) reveal how injustice creates structural exclusion.

To illustrate the framework in practice, this chapter examines Estonia's AI-enabled public sector—often celebrated as the global exemplar of digital government (Paes, 2023; Robinson et al., 2021). Estonia's KrattAI ecosystem demonstrates both the promise of coordinated, national-scale AI adoption and the limitations of technocratic governance strategies (Robinson et al., 2021). Through the lens of the Five Horsemen, Estonia becomes a powerful case study for understanding how injustice can emerge not from malicious intent but from structural, institutional, and epistemic dynamics that are often hidden from view.

The chapter concludes with a set of actionable justice-centred questions designed for policymakers, technologists, and public sector leaders. These questions extend beyond compliance and ask what justice demands—who is heard, who is accountable, and what forms of repair are necessary to meaningfully address harm. Fairness alone cannot create just AI systems. But by surfacing the deeper mechanisms through which injustice manifests, and by grounding analysis in real-world deployments, we can move toward governance approaches that centre equity and structural responsibility.

Theoretical Framework

AI Governance, the False Dichotomy and the Third Way

Governance is often framed as a binary choice: regulate tightly and stifle innovation, or step back and risk harm (De Almeida et al., 2021). This chapter advances a "third way": adaptive governance. Drawing on responsive regulation (Braithwaite, 2011), this model is dynamic, participatory, and iterative. Rather than "set and forget" rules, adaptive governance requires embedding oversight capacities into systems themselves, ensuring ethical parameters update alongside model evolution (Reuel & Undheim, 2024). The third way rejects both extremes:

- Rigid command-and-control regulation that quickly becomes obsolete, and
- Laissez-faire technological acceleration without public accountability.

Instead, adaptive governance is:

- dynamic rather than static
- community-shaped rather than imposed

- multi-layered rather than procedural
- iterative rather than one-off
- rooted in continuous learning rather than "set and forget" frameworks

Scholars of participatory technology governance argue that communities must shape the systems that govern their lives (e.g. Costanza-Chock, 2020). Practical mechanisms include:

- Community advisory boards with real decision-making power
- Participatory budgeting for AI systems affecting public services
- Algorithmic juries or citizen panels (Van der Veer et al., 2021; Warne et al., 2021)
- Iterative co-design between developers and affected populations

Adaptive governance also requires embedding governance capacities into the systems themselves (Braithwaite, 2011). Research suggests that external audits and voluntary principles cannot keep pace with rapidly evolving AI (Brass & Sowell, 2021; OECD, 2023). Governance must therefore be continuous, computational, and reflexive:

- Models must monitor their own drift and bias propagation.
- Ethical parameters must be updated alongside system evolution.
- Oversight structures must scale with model complexity.
- Institutions must build capacity to interpret and challenge AI-driven decisions.

Without this embedded adaptivity, regulatory oversight will always fall behind exponential technological change (Reuel & Undheim, 2024).

Gender as Diagnostic Lens

Gender serves as a diagnostic instrument for this framework. When AI systems fail women, they expose deeper design flaws. Three structural mechanisms shape this exclusion: the pipeline problem (women comprise only 18% of CS graduates, National Science Board, 2024); the retention crisis (women exit tech at twice the rate of men, World Economic Forum, 2023a); and the authority gap (women's expertise is systematically undervalued, Terrell et al., 2017). These mechanisms create homogeneous teams that encode narrow worldviews.

Displacement risk compounds these harms. The International Labour Organisation finds women are 40% more likely to experience automation-driven job loss because AI disproportionately targets administrative and service roles (ILO, 2023). Early adoption patterns reinforce these disparities: women made up only 30% of early ChatGPT users (Liu & Wang, 2024), not due to technophobia but because the systems—culturally, linguistically, and functionally—aligned with male norms and behaviours (Nemani et al., 2023). In this way, gender becomes a litmus test for algorithmic justice. When AI works for women—particularly those facing intersectional marginalisation—it is far more likely to work for society as a whole.

The Five Horsemen Framework: A Unified Lens for Algorithmic Justice

The Five Horsemen deliberately echo the Four Horsemen of the Apocalypse: not to dramatise, but to signal that these forces travel together, escalate one another, and leave systemic harm in their wake. Each mechanism is a rider in its own right, yet their true power emerges through convergence.

First Horseman: Development Bias

Development bias emerges from a fundamental question: who gets to build the future? This question anchors all Five Horsemen, determining not only whose problems merit technological solutions but whose worldviews shape those solutions' parameters. When 78% of AI researchers are male and 94% are based in the Global North (Asiedu et al., 2024), the resulting systems inevitably reflect these developers' assumptions about normalcy, value, and progress. This is not merely about representation statistics; it is about whose problems get solved and whose futures are imagined as worth optimising.

Development bias is also geopolitical. In Australia, for example, reliance on Silicon Valley-developed AI models has created what many describe as digital colonialism (e.g. Asiedu et al., 2024). Breaking this dependency requires not only localised models but fundamentally different approaches to AI development. Again, in using Australia as an example, this would mean developing AI rooted in Australian—and particularly Indigenous Australian—ways of knowing (Barrowcliffe et al., 2025). Without sovereign AI capacity, nations sacrifice not just data security but cultural autonomy and the ability to imagine technological futures aligned with their values (Allen et al., 2024).

Second Horseman: Training Data Bias

Training data bias is the most documented and persistently challenging dimension of algorithmic injustice (e.g. Cooper et al., 2022). AI systems learn from data that inevitably reflect historical inequities—but the deeper question is whose histories are preserved and whose are erased (Crawford & Paglen, 2021). Large language models are trained on internet text that overwhelmingly represents dominant perspectives (Bender et al., 2021). Wikipedia, a primary training source, has only around 16% female contributors (Farič et al., 2024), significant gaps in Global South coverage, and documented reliability issues for marginalised subjects (Handler et al., 2021). Articles about women are more likely to foreground personal relationships than equivalent articles about men (Sun & Peng, 2021), while topics from the Global South average fewer citations and shorter entries than Western equivalents (Cohen et al., 2022; Meibauer et al., 2023). These asymmetries become part of the statistical substrate from which models learn what is "normal," "relevant," or "notable."

Beyond documented dataset bias lies a second layer: the feedback properties of model architectures (Taori & Hashimoto, 2023). Context compression into tokens can create entrenched semantic pathways; once associations like "nurse–female" are statistically reinforced across billions of parameters, they become computationally cheaper to maintain than to correct (Shen, 2025). Post-training safeguards, such as alignment and Reinforcement Learning from Human Feedback (RLHF), can introduce additional distortions (McIntosh et al., 2024; Shen, 2025). RLHF teaches models to produce outputs human raters judge as "helpful," but when raters carry unexamined biases, the system learns to confirm rather than challenge prejudice (McIntosh et al., 2024; Shen, 2025).

The proliferation of deepfake technology starkly illustrates the intersection of training data bias with malicious uses (Yadav et al., 2025). Sensity AI (2023) found that more than 90% of deepfake videos online are non-consensual pornography targeting women. This reflects both the composition of training data and the demographics and incentives of those building and deploying these tools. For women, the gendered dimension is severe: deepfake pornography undermines credibility, fuels harassment, and creates plausible deniability for authentic evidence of abuse (Yadav et al., 2025).

Third Horseman: Access Inequality

Access inequality extends beyond classical notions of the digital divide to encompass who feels that AI is "for them." In early 2023, approximately 70% of ChatGPT users were male (Chatterji et al., 2025), a gap not fully explained by differences in connectivity. This adoption pattern reveals how perception and experience shape technological futures: those who abstain from early use are effectively excluded from shaping how systems evolve (Chatterji et al., 2025; Kaakandikar, 2025; Kacperski et al., 2025; Van Bussel, 2024). The dynamics driving this inequality operate through at least four mechanisms; confidence gaps (Rahman et al., 2024; Woźniak-Jęchorek et al., 2023), time poverty due to unpaid care work (Hanna et al., 2023), the masculine coding of technology (Chatterji et al., 2025), and risk perception (ILO, 2023).

These are rational responses to material realities, not irrational technophobia. Women who hesitate to adopt AI have often endured the "prove it again" bias—needing to repeatedly demonstrate competence in spaces where men's expertise is assumed (Benson et al., 2024); the "maternal wall," where mothers are presumed less committed (Bourcet Nguyen, 2024); and attribution bias, where their technical contributions are credited to male colleagues (De Gioannis, 2023). Hesitation is often a form of informed protection, not resistance to progress. Communication failures compound these dynamics. Companies market AI as universally empowering while designing systems around implicitly male, Western, time-rich user personas (Schulenberg et al., 2023). Women's lower adoption rates are then misread as disinterest rather than evidence of systemic exclusion, justifying continued neglect.

Most perniciously, a 70% male early-adopter base means systems literally learn to serve men better. Interaction data, RLHF processes, and product decisions are shaped by predominantly male usage patterns (Chatterji et al., 2025). Over time, models optimise for the questions, communication styles, and contexts of those users, making AI feel increasingly attuned to their needs and less to others. The initial perception—that AI is "not for them"—becomes self-fulfilling as systems evolve to confirm that assessment.

Fourth Horseman: Displacement Risk

Unlike earlier automation waves that predominantly impacted manual labour, contemporary AI systems increasingly threaten a wide spectrum of knowledge-intensive, service-oriented, and relational roles—areas where women and marginalised communities remain over-represented (Kyriakidou et al., 2025). The virtual assistant (VA) economy in the Philippines exemplifies these dynamics. Employing hundreds of thousands of workers—most of them women—this sector provides flexible, home-based income that sustains families and communities (Veto et al., 2025). Yet generative AI now automates many of the tasks core to VA work, from content drafting to scheduling and client communication (George, 2023). Here, displacement is not only about income loss. It also undermines autonomy, erodes bargaining power, and reshapes global labour hierarchies (ILO, 2023). Work that has long been invisibly feminised and outsourced becomes even more precarious as automation removes the very tasks on which these livelihoods depend.

Fifth Horseman: Feedback Loop Amplification

The fifth horseman is the most insidious: cascading exclusion (Farnadi et al., 2024). It describes how AI systems learn from biased usage patterns: when early adopters are disproportionately from dominant groups, models optimise around their behaviours, expectations, and norms (Farnadi et al., 2024; McIntosh et al., 2024). This amplification is visible across multiple domain. Papamichail et al. (2024) show that career recommendation systems, trained largely on male interaction patterns, suggest engineering roles to men at far higher rates than to women with similar profiles, while funnelling women toward care work. Nemani et al. (2023) document how misgendering errors for transgender users persist or worsen over time as models reinforce binary gender associations. Koenecke et al. (2020) find that voice recognition systems perform significantly worse on African American Vernacular English than on Standard American English, with updates that often improve majority performance more than minority performance.

These are not isolated glitches; they are emergent properties of optimisation. Each frustrated interaction by marginalised users reduces engagement. Lower engagement leads to reduced representation in training and feedback data. Models become increasingly tuned to majority users, making the system feel even less usable or safe for those already excluded. Over time, this generates a spiral toward algorithmic erasure. The AI companion industry offers an extreme illustration. Studies of Replika communities and incel-adjacent spaces show how AI "girlfriends" are used to rehearse entitlement, dominance, and misogyny (Allen et al., 2024; Reynaud, 2024). When users receive emotionally responsive but unresisting digital partners, systems learn to reward patterns of control rather than mutual negotiation (Allen et al., 2024; Reynaud, 2024). These feedback loops not only reflect existing gender norms; they intensify them, reinforcing adversarial attitudes toward real women who assert boundaries (Allen et al., 2024; Reynaud, 2024).

The cruelty of feedback loop amplification lies in its invisibility to those who benefit. Men who experience steadily improving AI performance interpret it as neutral technological progress (Korinek et al., 2021). Women and marginalised users encounter increasing friction and interpret it as personal inadequacy (Korinek et al., 2021). Inequality becomes naturalised as "just how the system works."

Case Study: The Five Horsemen in Action

Estonia's KrattAI System through the Five Horsemen Framework

Estonia's e-Governance Model: Promise and Tension

Estonia is routinely celebrated as the global benchmark for digital government (Paes, 2023; Robinson et al., 2021). Since the early 2000s, the country has built a highly integrated digital infrastructure where citizens routinely access services online, authenticate with a national digital ID, and interact with the state with unprecedented efficiency (e-Estonia, 2024). This ecosystem laid the foundation for KrattAI, the national programme for deploying artificial intelligence across the public sector (Paes, 2023; Robinson et al., 2021).

Yet, while Estonia boasts high trust and administrative speed, the Five Horsemen framework reveals the limits of its technocratic model. These limits do not necessarily represent a failure of the Estonian state, but rather serve as a critical warning for global policymakers attempting to scale similar systems in contexts marked by deeper structural inequalities

Estonia Through the Lens of the Five Horsemen

First Horseman: Development Bias

KrattAI was developed by teams that, while technically sophisticated, mirrored Estonia's demographic profile: majority male, ethnically Estonian, and drawn largely from STEM and administrative fields (Robinson et al., 2021). Consequently, interfaces were designed around assumptions of high digital fluency and deep institutional trust. While these assumptions largely hold true within Estonia's unique social contract (Paes, 2023), they are not universal constants. When exported as a "model" for other nations, this approach risks replicating a governance playbook that succeeds due to specific social capital, not because the technology is inherently neutral.

Furthermore, civil society groups have noted that early consultation processes relied heavily on technical experts, with limited structured engagement from minority communities (Paes, 2023; Robinson et al., 2021). The result is a governance model optimised for efficiency rather than pluralistic representation. Estonia's experience reveals a key insight: high-functioning technocratic systems can effectively obscure whose voices were absent during design.

Second Horseman: Training Data Bias

Many KrattAI systems are trained on decades of administrative data—tax histories, social service records, and court archives (Paes, 2023). While extensive, these datasets codify the institutional biases and classification schemes of previous eras (Information System Authority [ISA], 2023). Two distinct dynamics emerge.

First, historical decisions become algorithmic ground truth. Administrative data often embed differential treatment of Russian-speaking minorities and rural communities—not always through overt discrimination, but through historical patterns of service utilisation and bureaucratic complexity (Paes, 2023; Robinson et al., 2021). Audits cited by Estonia's Information System Authority found that certain automated systems produced higher inspection trigger rates for Russian-speaking applicants and exhibited different error resolution patterns depending on the region (ISA, 2023; Randver, 2025).

Second, linguistic asymmetry affects model accuracy. As a low-resource language, Estonian has significantly less training data available than English. Consequently, models perform better for citizens fluent in English or standard Estonian than for those relying on Russian or colloquial dialects (Koppel et al., 2024). This results in higher false negatives and poorer translation quality for linguistic minorities, demonstrating that training data bias persists even in highly digitised states.

Third Horseman: Access Inequality

While Estonia advertises "99% online" services (Espinosa & Pino, 2025), approximately 15% of citizens, primarily elderly and rural populations, struggle with access (Elmedany et al., 2024). For these groups, digital-first governance often functions as governance through friction. The distinction is stark: when systems are optimised for the digitally fluent, those on the margins experience algorithmic governance not as empowerment, but as a new form of administrative exclusion.

Fourth Horseman: Displacement Risk

Automation in Estonia's public sector has reduced administrative workloads—a shift framed positively as efficiency. However, because Estonia's administrative and clerical workforce is highly feminised, these efficiency gains have distinct gendered implications (Pavlenkova et al., 2024). Internal analyses show that automation initiatives in ministries such as social affairs, justice, and taxation have disproportionately displaced roles historically held by women (Paes, 2023).

While some job losses have been offset by new positions—such as data stewards and cybersecurity specialists—these roles require skillsets that displaced workers rarely possess and cannot easily acquire (Pavlenkova et al., 2024). Estonia's experience illustrates a broader pattern: automation increases inequality when upskilling pathways do not match the pace of technological transformation.

Fifth Horseman: Feedback Loop Amplification

Perhaps most insidiously, Estonia's AI systems become more efficient when citizens interact frequently and digitally, creating a reinforcing cycle of privilege. Digitally confident users generate high-quality interaction logs, which improve the model, which in turn improves services for those users (ISA Estonia, 2023). Conversely, digitally hesitant users generate fewer logs, causing the model to perform worse for them (ISA Estonia, 2023), further reducing their uptake.

Over time, this creates algorithmic stratification within a single population. An ISA Estonia analysis (2023) of 500 automated decisions found that citizens using digital channels regularly received faster turnaround times and higher accuracy scores. Meanwhile, those using mixed pathways experienced more errors and longer delays (ISA Estonia, 2023). This is not intentional bias; it is feedback loop optimisation. Ultimately, the system stops serving the public as it exists and begins optimising solely for the subset of the population that is easiest to process.

What Estonia Teaches Us about Justice-Centred Governance

Estonia demonstrates what is possible when digital government is well-resourced and widely trusted (Paes, 2023; Robinson et al., 2021). However, through the Five Horsemen lens, it becomes a diagnostic mirror rather than just a success story. It reveals that efficiency is not a proxy for equity. Even in a high-trust society, digitisation can obscure structural disparities, and feedback loops can quietly magnify inequality.

Estonia's model highlights the critical need for diverse development teams, continuous algorithmic auditing, and the maintenance of high-quality non-digital pathways. Crucially, it underscores a missing layer: participatory governance (Vooglaid & Randma-Liiv, 2022). While Estonia excels at technocratic excellence, true algorithmic justice requires structured opportunities for marginalised communities to shape the design and priorities of the systems that govern them.

Concluding Reflections and Actionable Pathways for Justice-Centred AI

Reframing AI Justice: From Bias Mitigation to Structural Transformation

The analysis of the Five Horsemen challenges the false dichotomy that has long dominated AI discourse: the idea that societies must choose between innovation and regulation (De Almeida et al., 2021). Instead, we see that governance is the architecture through which innovation becomes sustainable. As the Estonia case demonstrates, even world-leading digital models can reproduce inequality in subtle, systemic ways (Paes, 2023; Robinson et al., 2021). Estonia is not an example of failure, but of the limits of excellence when efficiency is privileged over diversity. In a high-trust, homogeneous society, the exclusions created by the Five Horsemen may be statistically narrow. However, in more unequal contexts, these same mechanisms produce severe, compounding harms—deepening the very divides governance is meant to repair.

The central lesson is this: justice does not emerge from well-built systems; it emerges from systems built with and accountable to the communities they serve. This is the heart of the "third way" governance model. It is neither technocratic optimism nor regulatory pessimism, but a dynamic paradigm that embeds plurality, adaptability, and structural equity at every point of the AI lifecycle.

Critical Questions for Policymakers, Institutions, and Developers

If we intend to build systems that promote justice rather than deepen inequality, policymakers and developers must move beyond technical checklists and confront five structural questions:

1. Development Bias: *Who is at the table—and who is missing?* Who shaped the problem definition? Which epistemologies were excluded at inception? What would this system look like if co-designed with its most marginalised users?
2. Training Data Bias: *What institutional memories are embedded in the data?* Whose histories are preserved, and whose are erased? Does the data reflect the world as it is, or the structural inequities we are trying to change?
3. Access Inequality: *Who can use the system with dignity?* Does the design assume digital fluency? Are non-digital alternatives equal in quality, or does the system create a hierarchy of citizenship based on tech-savviness?
4. Displacement Risk: *Who bears the cost of automation?* Is displacement random, or does it target feminised and racialised labour? Are reskilling pathways realistic, or does the system merely externalise the cost of efficiency onto vulnerable workers?
5. Feedback Loop Amplification: *Who is the system learning from?* Whose engagement patterns are over-weighted? As the model evolves, does it become more inclusive, or does it optimise for the dominant user at the expense of the invisible?

Actionable Recommendations: Toward Adaptive, Justice-Aligned AI Systems

To operationalise these insights, governments and organisations must adopt an adaptive governance framework grounded in structural justice.

1. Mandate Diversity and Development Audits: Transform development bias from an invisible assumption into a visible governance indicator. Before deployment, teams should publish demographic data of developers and evidence of how affected communities shaped the problem definition.
2. Require Dataset Provenance and Historical Review: Do not just "clean" data; document its social origins. Institutions must map what social conditions a dataset reflects and what historical harms it may conceal.
3. Build High-Quality Parallel Pathways: Efficiency cannot come at the cost of access. To prevent digital exclusion, non-digital pathways

must offer equal service quality, ensuring that citizens are not coerced into digital systems they cannot navigate.

4. Deploy Intermediary Oversight Bodies: Justice requires shared authority. Governance bodies—such as citizens' juries or algorithmic advisory panels—should have veto power over systems that materially affect their populations.
5. Implement Continuous Impact Monitoring: Harm emerges over time. Governance must track performance by demographic group and usage pattern, recognising that feedback loops can drift toward exclusion even after a successful launch.
6. Redefine Digital Literacy as Empowerment: Move beyond instructional tutorials. True digital literacy empowers citizens not just to use systems, but to question, challenge, and reshape them.
7. Institutionalise the Five Horsemen as a Diagnostic Tool: Organisations should operationalise this framework as a standard internal evaluation applied across the lifecycle of AI design, deployment, and maintenance.

Conclusion

AI systems do not simply make predictions; they make worlds. They classify, sort, allocate, prioritise, and adjudicate—often invisibly, and at a scale no human institution can match (Gichoya et al., 2023). Throughout this chapter, I have argued that the central question for AI governance is therefore not how to eliminate bias, but how to design for justice.

To do this, we must abandon the view of technology as a neutral artefact. As Science and Technology Studies has long established, AI systems embody the norms, histories, and power structures of the societies that produce them (Jasanoff, 2004; Winner, 1980). Consequently, injustice is not a technical glitch or an unavoidable by-product of complexity. It is the predictable outcome of decisions about whose knowledge matters, whose values count, and whose experiences shape the system.

The "third way" model offers a path forward. It rejects the paralysis of the regulation-versus-innovation debate in favour of adaptive governance—a commitment to continuous recalibration, participatory design, and structural awareness. It demands mechanisms that can learn alongside the technologies they oversee, placing affected communities at the centre of both design and accountability.

Using gender as a diagnostic lens, I have shown how exclusion is not a peripheral diversity issue but a structural signal—a warning that the system as a whole is misaligned with principles of fairness. When AI systems fail women, linguistic minorities, or low-resource users, they expose underlying failures in development processes and institutional priorities. Gender reveals the system's seams.

The Five Horsemen Framework synthesises these patterns into a coherent diagnostic tool. Development bias, training data bias, access inequality, displacement risk, and feedback loop amplification are not isolated problems; they are interlocking mechanisms that can turn minor inequities into systemic harm. As the Estonia case study demonstrates, even world-leading digital governance models are not immune. High-performance systems can still marginalise communities if diversity, participation, and structural equity are not built into their foundations.

Yet the Estonia example also shows what is possible. A state *can* invest in coordinated digital infrastructure, transparent documentation, and public accountability. The challenge, and the opportunity, is to extend these strengths with an explicit commitment to justice: pluralistic participation, culturally grounded design, and continuous monitoring of how systems evolve. Across this analysis, one key insight emerges clearly: AI systems do not fail because of technical imperfections; they fail because they reflect the worlds we have built. Justice, therefore, is not a technical feature but a design choice.

As societies accelerate toward automated public services and AI-mediated relationships, we must confront a fundamental question: What kind of future do we want these systems to enact? A future optimised for efficiency alone will entrench existing hierarchies. A future built on participatory, adaptive, justice-centred governance can instead redistribute power, dignity, and opportunity. The future of AI—its risks, its possibilities, and its social meaning—will not be determined by technological inevitability but by the choices we make now. We end where the work begins: The Five Horsemen ride only as far as we allow them to. They are not immutable forces but design choices we can remake. May we be proud of the ones we choose.

References

Allen, D. E., Hubbard, S., Lim, W., Stanger, A., Wagman, S., Zalesne, K., & Omoakhalen, O. (2024) A roadmap for governing AI: Technology governance and power-sharing liberalism, *AI and Ethics*, 5, 3355–3377. https://doi.org/10.1007/s43681-024-00635-y

Asiedu, M. N., Dieng, A., Haykel, I., Rostamzadeh, N., Pfohl, S., Nagpal, C., Nagawa, M., Oppong, A., Koyejo, S., & Heller, K. (2024). The case for globalizing fairness: A mixed methods study on colonialism, AI, and health in Africa. *Proceedings of the 4th ACM Conference on Equity and Access in Algorithms, Mechanisms, and Optimization* (pp. 1–24). Association for Computing Machinery, https://doi.org/10.1145/3689904.3694708

Barrowcliffe, R., Hutchinson, B., Abdilla, A., Acres, L., Beetson, B., Bell, A., Benton, P., Bligh, B., Bowen, R., Burton, N., Carlson, B., Cawthorne, R., Cook, B., Farrell, A., Fay, D., Fejo, J., Fewster, J., Gray, N., Hackman, D.,. . . Wright, S. (2025). Envisioning Aboriginal and Torres Strait Islander AI futures communique: March 2025. *Journal of Global Indigeneity*, *9*(1), 1–8. https://doi.org/10.54760/001c.133656

Bender, E. M., Gebru, T., McMillan-Major, A., & Shmitchell, S. (2021). On the dangers of stochastic parrots: Can language models be too big? In *Proceedings of the 2021 ACM Conference on Fairness, Accountability, and Transparency* (pp. 610–623). Association for Computing Machinery. https://doi.org/10.1145/3442188.3445922

Benjamin, R. (2019). *Race after technology: Abolitionist tools for the new jim code.* Polity Press.

Benson, A., Li, D., & Shue, K. (2024). Potential and the gender promotion gap. *SSRN Electronic Journal.* https://doi.org/10.2139/ssrn.4747175

Bourcet Nguyen, A. (2024). Maternal wall or stairs: Motherhood journey in leadership. In: *Journeys of women leaders pushing boundaries in Asia and healthcare* (pp. 41–55). Springer Nature Singapore.

Braithwaite, J. (2011). The essence of responsive regulation. *UBC Law Review, 44,* 475–520.

Brass, I., & Sowell, J. H. (2021). Adaptive governance for the internet of things: Coping with emerging security risks. *Regulation & Governance, 15*(4), 1092–1110. https://doi.org/10.1111/rego.12343

Chatterji, A., Cunningham, T., Deming, D. J., Hitzig, Z., Ong, C., Shan, C. Y., & Wadman, K. (2025). *How people use ChatGPT* (NBER working paper no. w34255). National Bureau of Economic Research.

Cohen, A., Fernández-Diaz, J., & Meeks, A. (2022). Exploring the nature of authority over, and ownership of data generated by archaeological LiDAR projects in latin america. *Archaeologies, 18*(3), 558–584. https://doi.org/10.1007/s11759-022-09464-z

Cooper, A. F., Moss, E., Laufer, B., & Nissenbaum, H. (2022). Accountability in an algorithmic society: Relationality, responsibility, and robustness in machine learning. In *Proceedings of the 2022 ACM Conference on Fairness, Accountability, and Transparency* (pp. 864–876). https://doi.org/10.1145/3531146.3533150

Costanza-Chock, S. (2020). *Design justice: Community-led practices to build the worlds we need.* MIT Press.

Crawford, K., & Paglen, T. (2021). Excavating AI: The politics of images in machine learning training sets. *AI & Society, 36*(4), 1105–1116. https://doi.org/10.1007/s00146-021-01162-8

Dastin, J. (2018, October 10). Amazon scraps secret AI recruiting tool that showed bias against women. *Reuters.* Accessible at: https://www.reuters.com/article/world/insight-amazon-scraps-secret-ai-recruiting-tool-that-showed-bias-against-women-idUSKCN1MK0AG

De Almeida, P. G. R., Dos Santos, C. D., & Farias, J. S. (2021). Artificial intelligence regulation: A framework for governance. *Ethics and Information Technology, 23*(3), 505–525.

De Gioannis, E. (2023). On the association between gender-science stereotypes' endorsement and gender bias attribution. *Quality & Quantity, 58*(4), 3087–3106. https://doi.org/10.1007/s11135-023-01790-w

e-Estonia. (2024). *AI strategy factsheet.* Accessed at: https://e-estonia.com/wp-content/uploads/factsheet-ai-strategy.pdf

Elmedany, W., AL-Abbasi, L., & Hewahi, N. (2024). Secure intelligent agent for Bahrain's e-government call center. *Authorea Preprints*. Accessed at: https://doi.org/10.22541/au.171129478.87347496/v1

Espinosa, V. I., & Pino, A. (2025). E-government as a development strategy: The case of Estonia. *International Journal of Public Administration, 48*(2), 86–99.

Eubanks, V. (2018). *Automating inequality: How high-tech tools profile, police, and punish the poor.* St. Martin's Press.

Farič, N., Potts, H. W. W., & Heilman, J. M. (2024). Quality of male and female medical content on English-language wikipedia: Quantitative content analysis. *Journal of Medical Internet Research, 26,* e47562. https://doi.org/10.2196/47562

Farnadi, G., Havaei, M., & Rostamzadeh, N. (2024). Position: Cracking the code of cascading disparity towards marginalized communities. In *Proceedings of the 41st International Conference on Machine Learning* (Vol. 235, pp. 13072–13085). Proceedings of Machine Learning Research.

George, A. S. (2023). Future economic implications of artificial intelligence. *Partners Universal International Research Journal,* 2(3), 20–39.

Gichoya, J. W., Thomas, K., Celi, L. A., Safdar, N., Banerjee, I., Banja, J. D., Seyyed-Kalantari, L., Trivedi, H., & Purkayastha, S. (2023). AI pitfalls and what not to do: Mitigating bias in AI. *The British Journal of Radiology, 96*(1150), 20230023. https://doi.org/10.1259/bjr.20230023

Handler, S. J., Eckhardt, S. E., Takashima, Y., Jackson, A. M., Truong, C., & Yazdany, T. (2021). Readability and quality of wikipedia articles on pelvic floor disorders. *International Urogynecology Journal, 32*(12), 3249–3258.

Hanna, T., Meisel, C., Moyer, J., Azcona, G., Bhatt, A., & Valero, S. D. (2023). *Forecasting time spent in unpaid care and domestic work.* UN Women.

Hoffmann, A. L. (2021). Terms of inclusion: Data, discourse, violence. *New Media & Society, 23*(12), 3539–3556. https://doi.org/10.1177/1461444820958725

Information System Authority. (2023). Cyber security in Estonia 2023. Republic of Estonia Information System Authority.

International Labour Organization (2023). *World employment and social outlook: Trends 2023.* ILO.

Jasanoff, S. (2004). *States of knowledge: The co-production of science and social order.* Routledge.

Kaakandikar, R. (2025). Ethical and inclusive upskilling for the AI revolution. *SSRN.* https://doi.org/10.2139/ssrn.5169844

Kacperski, C., Ulloa, R., Bonnay, D., Kulshrestha, J., Selb, P., & Spitz, A. (2025). Characteristics of ChatGPT users from Germany: Implications for the digital divide from web tracking data. *PLOS ONE, 20*(1), e0309047. https://doi.org/10.1371/journal.pone.0309047

Ken Research (2025). *Global AI companion market, size, share, growth drivers, trends, opportunities & forecast 2025–2030.* Ken Research.

Koenecke, A., Nam, A., Lake, E., Nudell, J., Quartey, M., Mengesha, Z., Toups, C., Rickford, J. R., Jurafsky, D., & Goel, S. (2020). Racial disparities in automated speech recognition. *Proceedings of the National Academy of Sciences, 117*(14), 7684–7689. https://doi.org/10.1073/pnas.1915768117

Koppel, A., Selg, P., Radma-Liiv, T., Raju, M., Klasche, B., & Tõnurist, P. (2024). *Building capacity for evidence-informed policymaking in governance and public administration in a post-pandemic Europe: Final integrated country report – Estonia.* European Commission/Knowledge4Policy.

Korinek, A., Schindler, M., & Stiglitz, J. E. (2021). *Technological progress, artificial intelligence, and inclusive growth* (IMF working paper WP/2021/166). International Monetary Fund.

Kyriakidou, O., Goumas, B., Manteli, M., & Tasoula, E. (2025). AI and the future of work: Bridging divides for marginalised workers. In J. Vassilopoulou & O. Kyriakidou (Eds.), *AI and diversity in a datafied world of work: Will the future of work be inclusive?*(pp. 205–224). Emerald.

Lifshitz, L. R., & McMaster, C. (2020). Legal and ethics checklist for AI systems. *SciTech Lawyer, 17*(1), 28–34.

Liu, Y., & Wang, H. (2024). Who on earth is using generative AI? *World Bank Open Knowledge Repository.*

McIntosh, T. R., Susnjak, T., Liu, T., Watters, P., & Halgamuge, M. N. (2024). The inadequacy of reinforcement learning from human feedback—Radicalizing large language models via semantic vulnerabilities. *IEEE Transactions on Cognitive and Developmental Systems, 16*(4), 1561–1574.

Meibauer, G., Phull, K., Alejandro, A., & Ciflikli, G. (2023). Alternative metrics, traditional problems? Assessing gender dynamics in the altmetrics of political science. *European Political Science, 23*(2), 179–198. https://doi.org/10.1057/s41304-023-00431-y

National Science Board. (2024). *The state of U.S. science and engineering 2024.* National Science Foundation. https://ncses.nsf.gov/pubs/nsb20243/key-takeaways

Nemani, P., Vollala, S., & Subramanyam, R. (2023). Gender bias in transformer models: Challenges in language processing applications. *ACM Computing Surveys, 55*(8), 1–35.

Noble, S. U. (2018). *Algorithms of oppression: How search engines reinforce racism.* NYU Press.

OECD (2023). *Advancing accountability in AI.* OECD Publishing.

Ofosu-Asare, Y. (2024). Cognitive imperialism in artificial intelligence: Counteracting bias with indigenous epistemologies. *AI & Society, 40*(4), 3045–3061. https://doi.org/10.1007/s00146-024-02065-0

Paes, S. (2023). *From ethics to action: A study of human-centric AI implementation in public services, comparing the Estonian approach with approaches used in other countries* (Master's thesis, Tallinn University of Technology).

Papamichail, S., Karakosta, A., & Sklavou, K. (2024). The role of gender (m/f) in the workplace: The case of municipality of Athens, Greece. *International Journal of Gender Studies, 9*(4), 33–48. https://doi.org/10.47604/ijgs.3057

Pavlenkova, I., Alfieri, L., & Masso, J. (2024). Effects of automation on The gender pay gap: The case of Estonia. *Industrial and Corporate Change, 33*(3), 584–608.

Rahman, M. M., Babiker, A., & Ali, R. (2024). Motivation, concerns, and attitudes towards AI: Differences by gender, age, and culture. In *International Conference on Web Information Systems Engineering* (pp. 375–391). Springer.

Randver, L. (2025). Impact of personalized learning pathways based on Felder-Silverman learning styles on students' metacognitive regulation skills in Estonia. *Research and Advances in Education, 4*(3), 10–19. https://doi.org/10.56397/rae.2025.03.02

Reuel, A., & Undheim, T. A. (2024). Generative AI needs adaptive governance. *arXiv preprint* arXiv:2406.04554.

Reynaud, A. (2024). *A new wave of technology: Examining interactions between incels and AI girlfriends* [Bachelor's honours thesis, Mount Royal University]. Mount Royal University Open Access Repository. https://doi.org/10.60770/P44B-5Z56

Richardson, R. (2021). Racial segregation and the data-driven society: How our failure to reckon with root causes perpetuates separate and unequal realities. *Berkeley Technology Law Journal, 36*(3), 1051–1139.
Robinson, N., Hardy, A., & Ertan, A. (2021). Estonia: A curious and cautious approach to artificial intelligence and national security. In: *Routledge companion to artificial intelligence and national security policy.* Routledge.
Schulenberg, K., Hauptman, A. I., Schlesener, E. A., Watkins, H., & Freeman, G. (2023). "I felt like I wasn't really meant to be there": Understanding women's perceptions of gender in approaching AI design & development. In *Proceedings of the 56th Hawaii International Conference on System Sciences* (pp. 175–184). University of Hawai'i at Mānoa. https://doi.org/10.24251/HICSS.2023.022
Sensity AI (2023). *The state of deepfakes 2023: Realities, threats, and impact.* Sensity.
Shen, J. (2025). *Woman is to nurse as man is to… nurse too? Uncovering structural bias in GPT-2* (Master's thesis, Uppsala University).
Shieh, E., Vassel, F.-M., Sugimoto, C. R., & Monroe-White, T. (2025). Language models generate widespread intersectional biases in narratives of learning, labor, and love. In *Proceedings of the* 5th *ACM Conference on Equity and Access in Algorithms, Mechanisms, and Optimization.* Association for Computing Machinery. https://doi.org/10.1145/3757887.3767679
Sun, J., & Peng, N. (2021). Men are elected, women are married: Events gender bias on Wikipedia. In *Proceedings of the 59th Annual Meeting of the Association for Computational Linguistics and IJCNLP (Volume 2: Short Papers)* (pp. 350–360).
Taori, R., & Hashimoto, T. (2023). Data feedback loops: Model-driven amplification of dataset biases. In *Proceedings of the 40th International Conference on Machine Learning* (PMLR 202, pp. 33883–33920).
Tele-Law. (2023). *Overview of Tele-Law.* https://tele-law.in/overview-of-tele-law.html
Terrell, J., Kofink, A., Middleton, J., Rainear, C., Murphy-Hill, E., Parnin, C., & Stallings, J. (2017). Gender differences and bias in open source: Pull request acceptance of women versus men. *PeerJ Computer Science, 3,* e111. https://doi.org/10.7717/peerj-cs.111
The Guardian. (2025, February 4). DeepSeek banned from Australian government devices amid national security concerns. *The Guardian.*
Van Bussel, G.-J. (2024). The accessibility conundrum: The problematic phenomenon of information access and accessibility. *Papers on Information and Archival Studies III.*
Van der Veer, S. N., Riste, L., Cheraghi-Sohi, S., Phipps, D. L., Tully, M. P., Bozentko, K., Atwood, S., Hubbard, A., Wiper, C., Oswald, M., & Peek, N. (2021). Trading off accuracy and explainability in AI decision-making: Findings from two citizens' juries. *Journal of the American Medical Informatics Association, 28*(10), 2128–2138. https://doi.org/10.1093/jamia/ocab127
Veto, N. G. N., Cariño, J. S., Saldo, I. J. P., & Zamayla, G. M. C. (2025). Virtual Assistants' job satisfaction and productivity: A correlational study. *American Journal of Educational Research, 13*(2), 71–77.
Vooglaid, K. M., & Randma-Liiv, T. (2022). The Estonian citizens initiative portal: Drivers and barriers of institutionalized e-participation. *Engaging Citizens in Policy Making,* 104–119.
Walter, M., & Suina, M. (2019). Indigenous data sovereignty and data futures. *Journal of Indigenous Social Development, 8*(1), 1–12.
Warne, H., Dencik, L., & Hintz, A. (2021). *Advancing civic participation in algorithmic decision-making: A guidebook for the public sector.* Data Justice Lab.

Winner, L. (1980). Do artifacts have politics? *Daedalus, 109*(1), 121–136.
World Economic Forum (2023a). *Global gender gap report 2023.* World Economic Forum. https://www.weforum.org/publications/global-gender-gap-report-2023/digest/
Woźniak-Jęchorek, B., Rydzak, W., & Kuźmar, S. (2023). Decoding the interface: Exploring women's perspectives on integrating AI in professional work. *Human Technology, 19*(3), 325–351. https://doi.org/10.14254/1795-6889.2023.19-3.2
Yadav, G., Sadique, M. Z., Kumar, S., Sharma, R., Sharma, M., Sharma, R., & Rattan, T. (2025). Psychological trauma and legal challenges of deep fake technology. *Sciences of Conservation and Archaeology, 37*(1), 143–150.

Index

Note: Page numbers followed by f, and t indicate figures and tables, respectively.

For Product Safety Concerns and Information please contact our EU representative GPSR@taylorandfrancis.com
Taylor & Francis Verlag GmbH, Kaufingerstraße 24, 80331 München, Germany

www.ingramcontent.com/pod-product-compliance
Ingram Content Group UK Ltd.
Pitfield, Milton Keynes, MK11 3LW, UK
UKHW021957220926
475880UK00003B/104

* 9 7 8 1 0 4 1 0 4 0 3 3 0 *